SETTING THE STAGE

Setting the Stage

Transitional playwrights in Irish 1910–1950

PHILIP O'LEARY

CORK UNIVERSITY PRESS

First published in 2021 by
Cork University Press
Boole Library
University College Cork
CORK
T12 ND89
Ireland

Library of Congress Control Number: 2021932849
Distribution in the USA: Longleaf Services, Chapel Hill, NC, USA

British Library Cataloguing in Publication Data
A CIP record for this book is available from the British Library.

ISBN: 978-1-78205-458-0

Printed in Malta by Gutenberg
Print origination & design by Carrigboy Typesetting Services
www.carrigboy.co.uk

COVER IMAGE – Courtesy of shutterstock.com

www.corkuniversitypress.com

IN MEMORY OF

Alf Mac Lochlainn and Robert Tracy

Contents

Acknowledgements

This book could not have been written without the support and assistance of friends and colleagues. In particular I would like to thank Angela Bourke, Fiontán de Brún, Gearóid Denvir, Margaret Kelleher, the late Tomás Mac Anna, Nollaig Mac Congáil, Ríona Nic Congáil, Máirín Nic Eoin, Tomás Ó Cathasaigh, Brian Ó Conchubhair, Pádraig Ó Siadhail, Gearóid Ó Tuathaigh, Rob Savage and Alan Titley. I also benefited from the research and insights shared by speakers and attendees of the February 2016 Dublin conference on 'Drámaíocht na Gaeilge' organised by Brian Ó Conchobhair and myself and sponsored by the Irish Studies Program at Boston College. I am also grateful to those who attended the Harvard Celtic Colloquia in 2013, 2014, 2016 and 2018, and the California Celtic Colloquium at the University of California, Berkeley, in 2017. Like all researchers, I am deeply indebted to the librarians who preserve and make available the sources on which we depend. While it is impossible to thank them all, I would like to express my profound gratitude to Anne Kenny and the staff of the interlibrary loan office and to Kathleen Williams at the O'Neill Library at Boston College; to the staff in the reading room and the manuscript division at the National Library of Ireland; to those in the special collections division at the Hardiman Library at the National University of Ireland, Galway, especially archivist Kieran Hoare; and to the interlibrary loan staff at the Bergische Universität Wuppertal. Special thanks are, of course, due to Maria O'Donovan, Mike Collins, Aonghus Meaney and the readers at Cork University Press. As always, Joyce Flynn's support and incisive comments on theatre in general and Irish theatre in particular have been invaluable. No one who knows me will doubt that any errors or inanities are entirely my own.

Abbreviations

AA	*Ar Aghaidh*
AC	*Anglo-Celt*
BH	*Ballina Herald*
ACS	*An Claidheamh Soluis*
CC	*Clare Champion*
CE	*Cork Examiner*
CS	*The Connacht Sentinel*
CT	*The Connacht Tribune*
CWE	*Cork Weekly Examiner*
DD	*Dundalk Democrat*
DI	*Drogheda Independent*
DM	*The Dublin Magazine*
DO	*Dublin Opinion*
DP	*Derry People and Donegal News*
EH	*Evening Herald*
EM	*Evening Mail*
FJ	*Freeman's Journal*
FL	*Fáinne an Lae*
GR	*Garda Review*
IG	*Irisleabhar na Gaedhilge/ The Gaelic Journal*
II	*Irish Independent*
ILB	*Irish Library Bulletin*
IM	*Iodh Morainn*
IMN	*Irisleabhar Mhuighe Nuadhat*
IP	*The Irish Press*
IS	*The Irish Statesman*
IT	*The Irish Times*
K	*The Kerryman*
KWR	*Kerry Weekly Reporter*
LL	*Limerick Leader*
M	*Misneach*
MC	*Meath Chronicle*
ME	*The Munster Express*
MN	*The Mayo News*
MO	*Muimhneach Óg*
NG	*The Nenagh Guardian*
NYT	*The New York Times*
SSA	*Shannonside Annual*
SF	*Sinn Féin*
SI	*Sunday Independent*
WF	*Weekly Freeman*
WP	*Western People*

The *Ralph Royster Doyster* Stage and Beyond[1]

In 1903, Seán Ua Ceallaigh ('Sceilg'), the editor of *Banba*, published the one-act play *Muinntear Chillmhuire nó Bó i bPoll* (The People of Cill Mhuire or a Cow in a Hole) by Séamus Ó Dubhghaill ('Beirt Fhear') with the following bemused disclaimer:

> We will present the first volume of *Banba* to anyone who will tell us how a wave can be set in motion on the stage, how seven men can gather around a bog-hole, how the cow can be kept on the stage with water and mud flowing from her sides, how she can be driven from there to the byre, how, - how, - how, will the play be put on the stage, that is what we want to know (*Banba*, June 1903, pp. 201–4).[2]

It was a good question, and one with wider application, for while no other Gaelic playwright of whom I am aware ever listed a large farm animal among his dramatis personae, many of them had equally unrealistic expectations of what was possible in a play actually meant to be performed. For example, An tAthair Peadar Ua Laoghaire was one of the major literary figures of the Gaelic revival, but when he turned in his plays from the simple rural life depicted in his one-act comedy *Tadhg Saor* (Tadhg the Carpenter) to the grand subject of Irish history, he lost all sense of proportion. Thus, he packed eight scenes, all with different settings, and nine speaking parts, plus extras, into *Aodh Ó Néill*, his brief one-act historical play about the sixteenth-century Ulster chieftain Hugh O'Neill. Likewise, Pádraig Ó Séaghdha ('Conán Maol'), another literary pioneer in Irish, expected would-be producers of his own one-act *Aodh Ó Néill* to stage manage more than twenty characters through seven scenes involving six separate sets. It is, then, hardly surprising that one 'E.' could complain in his review of the one-act history play *Tá na Francaigh ar an Muir* (The French Are on the Sea) by Peadar Mac Fhionnlaoich ('Cú Uladh') that the playwright had fallen into 'the mistake so common in nearly all written plays in Irish' and that 'it is scarcely right to have five acts, entailing numerous changes of scene, in a play which can be read in a quarter of an hour' (*ACS*, 4 July 1903).

In 1909, the Oireachtas committee burdened with reading such plays for its drama competition felt compelled to set out guidelines for what it considered a play capable of being staged: 'No act should contain more than one scene. Competitors are requested to bear in mind that the number of speaking parts should be limited, as far as is consistent with the treatment of the subject. Simplicity of scenery and dress is recommended' (*ACS*, 2 October 1909).[3] More ambitious playwrights were loath to believe that such restrictions applied to them, so that the two anonymous authors of the historical play *Eoghan Ruadh Ua Néill, nó Ar Son Tíre agus Creidimh: Dráma stardha ag baint le cogadh 1641* (Eoghan Rua Ó Néill, or for Country and Faith: An historical drama dealing with the war in 1641) had a cast of twenty and the play ran for over five hours when it was produced at the seminary in Maynooth. Writing of the play in *Irisleabhar Mhuighe Nuadhad*, a presumably well-disposed critic saw 'the influence of that pre-eminent English author' (*rian an phríomh-ughdair ghallda soin*) everywhere in the play, and went on to state redundantly 'that the author of this play is no Shakespeare yet' (*ná fuil ughdar an dráma so 'n-a Shacspeare fós*) (*IMN*, 1906–7, p. 51).[4]

The reference to Shakespeare here is suggestive. A significant problem Gaelic playwrights had when trying to create plays for performance was that they knew very little about the theatre. Priests like An tAthair Peadar and An tAthair Pádraig Ó Duinnín (the lexicographer Patrick Dinneen) were among the very first Gaelic playwrights to have their work performed, but at that time and for decades after members of the Catholic clergy were not allowed to attend plays without a special dispensation and, needless to say, frivolous plays for popular audiences, not to mention plays with what were seen as controversial subjects or themes, would have been judged particularly objectionable. For the laity, physical distance was the problem. Unless a would-be playwright lived in or near Dublin, Cork, Belfast and perhaps Galway, or in exile in London or another British city, it is unlikely he (or she) would have had many opportunities to attend the theatre unless a travelling company, more often than not English, brought a show to a town near them. And naturally enough, a play in English would have been no help in Gaeltacht areas. Thus, what even the better educated and more enthusiastic Gaelic writers knew about theatre was of necessity based on what they had read, and for many that may well have been limited to the plays of Shakespeare and maybe a small handful of others. One 'Connla Caol' was aware of the consequences of this situation when he wrote in 1904: 'Some of our Irish writers in drama have wasted effort in trying to breathe new life into the Elizabethan conventions, which are as dead to-day as their founders' (*Inis Fáil*, December 1904, p. 6). With regard to Irish playwrights, there were probably Irish speakers, in the cities and large towns at least, who were aware of the Irish melodramas of Dion Boucicault like *The Colleen Bawn* or *The Shaughraun* or had even seen one of them.[5] However, with the possible exception of plays by Shakespeare, Boucicault, and a few others, fledgling Gaelic playwrights, unless they lived in or near a city and took an interest in theatre, would have faced terra incognita when they sat down to create a play.

Of course, given the cultural climate in the Gaelic movement at the turn of the twentieth century, more than a few such writers may well have seen an ignorance of English dramatic conventions as a source of pride or a prophylactic against corrupting influences on the native tradition. If, however, they had turned to that tradition itself for inspiration, they would have found nothing. There was no native tradition of theatre in Irish. Some Gaelic intellectuals did try to find indigenous models for a new Gaelic drama in the medieval dialogues between St Patrick and Oisín, the son of Fionn mac Cumhaill, works that *Fáinne an Lae* in 1899 called 'the nearest thing to stage dialogues which we possess' and 'the starting point' for a 'truly Irish National theatre' (*FL*, 23 September 1899). Such people must have taken heart when the 'St Patrick at Tara' scene in Irish was included in Father O'Growney's play *The Passing of Conall* at Aonach Thír-Chonaill in 1898. This scene, often called the first 'play' in Irish, was, however, to have little if any meaningful influence on the future development of Gaelic drama.[6]

Others in the Gaelic movement with an interest in theatre saw potential for a native Irish drama in the oft histrionic performance style of Gaelic storytellers (*seanchaithe*), whose repertoire might, by the way, have included modern versions of the Ossianic dialogues. Thus, the native speaker and University College Galway professor Tomás Ó Máille could write about listening to such performers:

> You would think that you were listening to the people speaking to each other and that you were watching them as he described them. You would think that you could see the clothes and the gear they had on. You would think that you could see the expression they had when they spoke to one another, whether it was friendly or hostile. In other countries they had another way. The story would first be composed, but instead of telling it all orally, every action in it would be presented or shown in front of the people who were present (*Stoc*, February–March 1918, p. 4).[7]

The question of the influence of native storytelling on Irish plays in both Irish and English deserves a book to itself; here we may simply note that while the *seanchaithe* may well have bequeathed a wealth of incident and a store of elegant, vivid, subtle and precise Irish to future playwrights in the language, they never themselves generated anything like an actual stage play.[8] As another Pádraig Ó Séaghdha ('Pádraig na Léime') acknowledged in 1909, 'It is a source of great regret for us that we lack native writing for the stage as a model for our task now' (*SF*, 23 October 1909).

These discussions of native sources for Gaelic drama did have one major, and not infrequently deleterious, effect on the development of theatre in Irish. On the positive side, there was a logical focus on the dramatic potential of rural, particularly Gaeltacht, life and its concerns, subject matter with which so many speakers of Irish were intimately familiar. As a result, we have a wealth of plays, especially comedies, with rural or Gaeltacht settings and simple plots based on local activities, customs or folklore. Indeed, the best plays from the early revival, and the ones with the most popular appeal, were the one-act plays of Douglas Hyde ('An Craoibhín Aoibhinn') that showed the generative possibilities of this kind of grassroots theatre. On the negative side, however, such a focus on rural life could and easily did become an obsession with some playwrights, particularly with regard to plays set in the Gaeltacht. Thus, in 1906 'An Rábaire' wrote:

> The fact remains that Irish drama, if it develops at all, will grow in its own way, naturally out of humble beginnings. It will not be generated in the incubators of artificial sgoláirí [scholars] in Dublin, nor in the hothouse of editorial leading articles. It must be popular if it is to do anything at all. It must appeal to the taste of the ordinary Irish-speaking Gael ... Any more ambitious efforts that have been made are only calculated to inspire regret (*IG*, June 1906, p. 145).

The major result of this kind of thinking was an outpouring of short and simple plays of rural and Gaeltacht life.[9] Thus, we have, among many others, An tAthair Peadar Ua Laoghaire's *Tadhg Saor* (1900), Hyde's *Casadh an tSúgáin* (The Twisting of the Rope) (1901), Séamus Ó Dubhghaill's *An Táilliúir Cleasach* (The Crafty Tailor) (1902), W.P. Ryan's *An Mí-Ádh Mór* (The Great Misfortune) (1903), Tomás Ó hAodha's *Seaghán na Sguab* (Seán of the Brushes) (1904), Pádraic Ó Conaire's *Bairbre Ruadh* (Red-Haired Bairbre) (1908), Seán Ó Muirthile's *Pósadh an Iascaire* (The Fisherman's Wedding) (1914), and so on. It was doubtless plays like these that led 'E.' to believe that 'perhaps we are still at the *Ralph Royster Doyster* or the *Gammer Gurton's Needle* stage' (*ACS*, 1 October 1904).

Most of the plays in Irish in the early years of the twentieth century were performed by branches of the Gaelic League, whose Craobh an Chéitinnigh (The Keating branch), for example, was particularly active in Dublin. Not surprisingly given the pragmatic nature of the league in its first decades, these performances were often seen primarily as propaganda vehicles or as teaching tools to assist language learners. The first real Gaelic theatre groups were not formed until 1913, when both Na hAisteoirí (The Actors) and Na Cluicheoirí (The Players) came on the scene. Of the two, Na hAisteoirí, the brainchild of Piaras Béaslaí, would leave the greater mark, providing many of the actors who were to re-emerge in 1921 after the virtual absence of any Gaelic theatre in the years between the Easter rising of 1916 and the end of the Irish war of independence in 1921. It was Gearóid Ó Lochlainn, who had spent fourteen years acting in Copenhagen before returning to Ireland that year, who organised the scattered remnants of Na hAisteoirí, and others, to form Aisteoirí Átha Cliath (The Dublin Actors). This group was inactive during the Irish civil war, but returned in

June 1923 to perform plays in Dublin's Gaiety theatre for the short drama festival that was called the Oireachtas that year. It was Ó Lochlainn's Aisteoirí (and through them Béaslaí's original company) that formed the nucleus of An Comhar Drámaíochta (The Drama Society), which began life as a theatrical management and promotion organisation and went on to become the most important force in Gaelic drama in Dublin until its absorption by the Abbey theatre in 1942. It was An Comhar that was responsible for almost every Dublin production to be discussed below, with Compántas Amharclainne na Gaeilge (The Irish-Language Theatre Company), founded in 1943, also producing a few plays and skits.

Meanwhile, in Galway, Irish speakers with an interest in theatre were making their own plans, in January 1928 sending a delegation to meet with the Free State's finance minister Ernest Blythe, a language and theatre enthusiast himself. With a subsidy from Blythe in hand, they were able to purchase and remodel the building that became and remains their own theatre in Galway, a luxury that An Comhar Drámaíochta was never to enjoy. Beginning on 27 August 1928, Galwegians were able to see plays in Irish on a regular basis. Thus, the Gaelic theatre movement now had groups performing full seasons of plays on both the east and west coasts of Ireland. Needless to say, Gaelic League branches and local theatre groups continued to rehearse and perform, most notably at the Gaelic League *feiseanna* (festivals) throughout the country.

The little rural plays mentioned above were particularly popular at these *feiseanna*, for they were easy to produce and appealed to what 'An Rábaire' called 'the taste of the Irish-speaking Gael'. Just as, if not more, important was the fact that they also had the potential to entertain Irish-learning Gaels, those whose command of the language might to varying degrees be less than adequate to follow what they were hearing on stage. This was another problem that went back to the earliest days of the theatre movement. Writing in 1900, Bernard Doyle, the editor of *Fáinne an Lae*, summed up his own situation with a nod to his dog:

> Most of those at the Gaelic play will be in the position of the retriever. We will be dying to understand what is going forward, and will be most anxious to impress our neighbours with the intelligent interest we are taking in the performance. Yet we will be able to do no more

than listen for some familiar word so that we may be able to wag our tails with effusion (*FL*, 17 March 1900).[10]

When the 'St Patrick at Tara' scene was performed in Derry the following month, readers of *Fáinne an Lae* were informed that 'the audience thoroughly enjoyed the piece, though it was presented in a vernacular foreign to probably most of them' (*FL*, 15 April 1900). After attending a performance of Father Dinneen's *An Tobar Draoidheachta* (The Magic Well) in Dunmanway, County Cork, in 1902, a local critic wrote that the play was 'generally enjoyed even by people who did not understand a word of Irish' (*MO*, June 1903, p. 5). In fact, when an audience did understand the dialogue, that fact merited comment. Thus, *An Claidheamh Soluis* reported of a 1902 production of Hyde's *Casadh an tSúgáin* in Ballaghaderreen, County Roscommon, that 'the best thing is that many who were present understood Irish' (*ACS*, 22 February 1902). If they were honest with themselves, few if any Gaelic revivalists would have found fault with Padraic Colum's sympathetic assessment of the situation in 1910: 'For a long time there will be, in the general audience for Irish plays, many who do not know the language, or know it imperfectly, many who, in Mark Twain's phrase, "average it up". A play depending on subtility [*sic*] of characterisation and refinement of nature could not be a success with such an audience' (*ACS*, 27 August 1910).

In this regard, however, the *Ralph Royster Doyster* stage was to drag on for decades, and those with an interest in theatre in Irish must have been both keenly disappointed and increasingly concerned when they could not find a solution to the problem. Over the years, references to the linguistic shortcomings of the audiences at Gaelic plays were common. For instance, in September 1923, Éamonn Mac Giolla Iasachta (Edward McLysaght) advised those acting in Irish that 'it would be better to speak too slowly rather than too quickly as long as we are relying on people who are learning the language – or, better, trying to bring them in and encourage them' (*Sguab*, September 1923, p. 227).[11] Having attended a student production of a play at Maynooth a decade later, Brian MacTréinfhir concluded that 'it is not easy to find suitable plays in Irish, and I do not believe that the audience understood too well the Irish in *Aiséirghe Dhonncha* [Pádraig Ó Siochfhradha's translation of Seamus MacManus' *The Resurrection of*

Dinny O'Dowd]. And what good is performing a play in a language that is not understood?' (*IMN*, 1932, p. 84). Ernest Blythe faced up to the problem forthrightly in 1939:

> Up to the present it may safely be said that no dramatist writing in Irish has ever had a good audience to judge his work, that is to say, an appreciative and critical audience which would neither abuse the play on principle nor excuse it on principle. The result is that the Gaelic playwright has had to work, as it were, in the dark without his natural stimulus and without feeling the stir of artistic emulation (*Leader*, 16 December 1939).

This was a problem with which the playwrights in this study were personally familiar and one that they knew was symptomatic of a larger challenge. In 1942, Piaras Béaslaí wrote:

> Now whatever the number of Irish-speakers may be in Dublin I doubt that there are really very many of them who can follow every word of every play in Irish spoken from the stage with the same ease with which an Abbey audience follows a play in English. There must be a certain strain, an effort of attention ... the language itself is a barrier to that perfect rapport between playwright, actors and audience which is necessary for complete success (*Leader*, 12 September 1942).

Of course, Béaslaí was well aware that having a command of Irish was not enough to guarantee that an audience member would understand and/or appreciate a play once (s)he had processed the dialogue. Having noted that 'the plays in Irish which have most popular appeal are simple farcical comedies of elementary humour, with conventional situations and themes', and that even at the Abbey the most popular plays in English were 'those of the lowest intellectual level', he wrote that if

> a play which contains fruitful ideas, food for thought, subtlety, can only be understood or appreciated by a minority of an English-speaking audience ... if the dramatist has to express these ideas in unfamiliar Irish, and add an extra handicap, an extra obstacle to the

> appreciation, he has no right to complain if his work lacks proper appreciation (*Leader*, 12 September 1942).

Séamus de Bhilmot, another of the playwrights to be discussed in this study, expressed similar ideas in a 1941 piece in which he wrote that 'a knowledge of Irish is not the same as an interest in drama in Irish. One should not expect an Irish speaker to go to the performance of a play any more than to any other Gaelic pastime.' And if they did, all too often 'they would not come as the result of an interest in drama as drama' (*ní de thoradh suime sa dráma a thiocfaidís*), 'but because the play was written in Irish' (*toisg gur sa Ghaedhilg a sgríobhadh an dráma*) (*IM*, 1941, p. 3).[12] In an interview with Kitty Clive the following year de Bhilmot developed these ideas. First, he addressed the question of the linguistic abilities present in a putative pool of 20,000 Irish-speakers and potential theatregoers in Dublin, but then went beyond a narrow focus on the basic ability to understand what was being said on stage, pointing out that 'the person with an acquired knowledge [of Irish], and with few opportunities of practice in Dublin, is trying to do two things at the same time – follow the story of the play and understand the language'. His conclusion was that 'a great soldier cannot arise in a community of cowards. A big writer cannot emanate from an audience that cannot follow him in all his vagaries, as a woman follows a man in an intricate dance – or steps away from him in terror or hate, or fear' (*Leader*, 9 May 1942).[13]

Unfortunately, as de Bhilmot and his fellow playwrights knew all too well, the vast majority of those putative 20,000 potential audience members, whatever their command of Irish, were turning away in apathy from Gaelic plays. The Gaelic theatre movement had been struggling since its inception to build any audience – a discerning one with excellent Irish was far too much to expect. Complaints about the failure of Irish speakers to attend Gaelic plays were a regular feature in reviews and articles on theatre throughout the 1920s and '30s. For example, in 1937, 'S. Ó M.' wrote: 'How many thousand Irish speakers are there in Dublin to-day? Yet what of the audience for Gaelic plays in the chief city of the Irish Nation? In the Peacock theatre of 100 seats it is not an unusual thing for the Gaelic players [An Comhar Drámaíochta] to play to 50, 40, 30, aye, and sometimes only 20 people' (*Leader*, 12 June 1937). Nor were things always better at Taibhdhearc na Gaillimhe in Galway, despite the proximity of the Conamara Gaeltacht and the presence in or near the city of University College Galway and the Irish army's *Céad Chath Gaelach* (First Irish-Speaking Battalion). Thus, in 1929, when the Taibhdhearc was less than a year old and still presumably a novelty in a small city not overly endowed with entertainment options, a critic for *The Connacht Sentinel* wrote: 'The Taibhdhearc last evening was far less than half full, and on Sunday evening the attendance was as bad.' Having stressed the low price of admission, 'the beauty of the settings', and acting 'of a kind rarely witnessed outside Dublin', he asked, 'What do the people want?' (*CS*, 23 April 1929).

Others at the time had less positive opinions about what 'acting of a kind rarely witnessed outside Dublin' might mean. Critics regularly found fault with the quality of performances in both the capital and the Taibhdhearc. First of all, a good number of those critics believed that the linguistic command of some of the actors was almost as limited as that of many of the audience members. In 1904, one 'Ardánach' wrote: 'It does great damage to the Gaelic drama to put people on stage who don't have any idea what the words they say mean. It is difficult to find suitable people everywhere, and most likely we will have to put up with what we have now until we get something better' (*IG*, April 1903, p. 272).[14] More than twenty years later, the problem still had not been solved, so that 'D. Ó D.' could complain in 1927 that 'there is nothing that more disgusts an audience than weak and broken Irish. If an actor undertakes to play a part he should have that part properly, and if he is not a native speaker, he should practise the sounds intensively' (*Leader*, 19 February 1927).[15] In 1938, An tAthair Pádraig Eric Mac Fhinn declared: 'The Irish must be spoken well, for there is nothing that more annoys an audience than to be trying to understand bad Irish, and it is truly difficult to understand it' (*AA*, December 1938, p. 2).[16] Writing in 1946, Máirtín Ó Direáin, who had had considerable experience acting at the Taibhdhearc, claimed that there were Irish speakers who avoided plays in the language altogether because of the bad Irish they had heard on stage, adding that while he thought this was just an excuse for many, 'I have been disgusted and twisting in my seat because a language as beautiful when it is spoken correctly was being destroyed and ruined on stage. No group with respect for their language should put up with it' (*Glór*, 13 July 1946).[17]

The redoubtable Séamus Ó Grianna ('Máire') believed that the bad Irish he heard from the actors of An Comhar Drámaíochta provided an irrefutable argument for insisting that all actors in plays in Irish should be native speakers, and that the Gaelic theatre movement itself should be based in the Gaeltacht and not in Dublin or Galway:

> The drama will have to come from the place where Irish is spoken naturally by the people. I will, of course, be told that the people of the Gaeltacht have no knowledge of that craft. I admit that. But however bad they are, they are as good as the crowd that has been in the Abbey Theatre for the past five years. In the first place they don't rely on Liverpool Irish (*FL*, November 1929, p. 1).[18]

The following month he was on the attack again, referring to An Comhar Drámaíochta as 'a flock of genuine yahoos ... stammering on stage and trying to convince us that they have the language of our ancestors' (*sgaifte de yahoos macánta ... a bheith ag snagarsaigh ar ardán agus ag iarraidh a chur i gcéill dúinn gur teanga ár sinnsear atá aca*) (*FL*, December 1929, p. 1).

Criticisms of the general amateurism of Gaelic actors, particularly in Dublin, were also common right into the 1950s. Of course, on one level such criticisms were unfair. These actors, virtually every single one of them, were amateurs, rehearsing in a second language after a day's work for what were always very short runs, sometimes just a single evening. Still, some of their shortcomings must have on occasion made for less than engaging nights in the theatre. Thus, one 'R. Ó P.' wrote of a performance by An Comhar Drámaíochta in 1930: 'Some of them [were] carrying themselves unnaturally, because their minds were focused entirely on the dialogue that they had not fully memorised, or that did not come fluently to them. A weak voice projection (but not on the part of the prompter behind!), awkward acting – a clear sign that the majority had not rehearsed the drama well' (*Poblacht*, 25 October 1930).[19] Frank O'Connor also stressed the actors' failure to learn their lines, writing that audiences had come to expect that 'actors should come on with only the haziest notions of their lines, stumble, stammer, and pick themselves up, allow the angel of silence to draw a long sigh from the audience between challenge and response' (*IS*, 22 February 1930). Indeed, O'Connor wrote of one performance by

An Comhar Drámaíochta that the cast 'acted as in a secondary school production of Shakespeare' and concluded: 'The great fault of these players at the moment is inadequate production. Only one or two of the company have any real conception of acting technique, and the plays are a succession of slight errors, false starts, awkward or repeated gestures and over-emphasis, while no attempt is ever made at securing a broad general effect' (*IS*, 18 January 1930). In 1937, Seán Ó Meadhra wrote snidely of An Comhar's production of *Deirdre an Bhróin*, a translation by Liam Ó Briain of Synge's *Deirdre of the Sorrows*: 'If most of these players are actors, then a tin whistle player outside a pub is a musician and, funny enough, both expect to get money from it' (*Ireland To-Day*, November 1937, p. 75).[20]

Particularly damning were the comments of Ernest Blythe, long a champion of Gaelic theatre and the man who as a government minister first provided funding for both An Comhar Drámaíochta and Taibhdhearc na Gaillimhe, as well as, and more famously, for the Abbey. In 1939, he wrote:

> In general dramatic performances in Irish are crude and clumsy and of a standard that would infallibly empty the theatre completely if lack of artistic quality were not partly neutralised by the draw of the language. As far as I can judge most of those associated with the staging of Irish plays have no higher ambition than to give a passable amateur performance (*Leader*, 16 December 1939).

Again, the problem persisted, with Máirtín Ó Direáin asking sarcastically in 1942, 'Why don't the Gaelic director and the actors write the play themselves in the first place, and not trouble the poor author at all?' He continued:

> For example, if you come to the performance, it is certain that you will not recognise your own play since we will have changed it so much … We will also put people on stage who do not have any acting talent, never did and never will, and who do not have an actor's voice, but all of that is, of course, according to the Gaelic custom, and drama in Irish is as it is (*Glór*, 28 February 1942).[21]

Gaelic actors may have been more enthusiastic about taking to the stage had they had more and better plays with which to hone their craft. Once again, the lack of engaging new scripts – indeed any new scripts – had bedevilled the Gaelic drama movement from the start. Translations of plays from foreign languages – including, of course, that most widely understood 'foreign' language, English – provided an obvious short-term solution. However, while more than a few in the movement, including Piaras Béaslaí and Gearóid Ó Lochlainn, espoused the idea and themselves did translations and/or adaptations, it was generally accepted that a native theatre movement could never rely on what 'An Ball Geal' in 1932 called 'insipid foreign dramas that never appealed to Irish sentiment' (*Leader*, 5 November 1932).[22] At any rate, very few translations were ever popular with Gaelic audiences. Nonetheless, with little else to put on stage, both An Comhar Drámaíochta and the Taibhdhearc included a significant number of them on their schedules throughout the 1920s and '30s and into the '40s.[23] For example, it was not until its fifth season in 1927–8 that An Comhar had more original plays on its schedule than it did translations.

It is, then, hardly surprising that complaints about the shortage of new original scripts in Irish were heard again and again. Writing in 1924, 'Gaedhilgeoir' stated: 'Another thing that is causing us problems is the scarcity of plays in Irish and the fact that of the few of them there are, there are still fewer suitable for performance, since the majority were written for another world altogether' (*CWE*, 10 May 1924). Twelve years later, Canon J. Vaughn, the president of St Flannan's College in Ennis, wrote: 'In regard to Irish plays ... it is true to say that they do not come up to the standard, either in conception, outlook or technique. There is a very restricted repertoire and those wishing to stage Irish plays are hampered by the narrow range from which the selection must be made' (*CC*, 26 December 1936).[24] Addressing the Sligo Feis in 1940, Séamus de Bhilmot, who, as we will see, did more than his share to address this problem, asked, 'Are we to have no new writers of Gaelic drama?' He then continued: 'If not, the movement will become moribund ... Dramatic companies complain that they have run through all the available Irish plays, and that they will have to go back again on one which they had performed in previous years' (*II*, 30 March 1940).

Writing the following year, Piaras Béaslaí expressed his own frustration with many of his colleagues in the Gaelic theatre movement:

> What they talk and write of under the title 'Gaelic Drama' is – production, acting, scenery, costumes, make-up, stages, and how far we are 'behind' the English-speaking stage in these respects. As for the plays – well that is a minor matter. All we want is a play in Irish. If we cannot get a new original one let us translate one. There are plenty in English (*Leader*, 19 July 1941).

In this regard. Galway was no better off than Dublin, as 'S. O'F.' (Sean O'Faolain) made clear in a piece on the Taibhdhearc company's 1941 visit to the capital. O'Faolain praised the actors, but was disappointed that the plays they had brought with them were all translations: 'The play's the thing, and for the lack of that the Galway Players cannot be blamed ... But if the writers will not, or cannot, write, the players may shut up shop. No artist – and these are real artists – could long be content to act as mere linguists, and it is not fair for them that they should be asked to go on doing so' (*Bell*, January 1941, p. 87).

The problem was compounded by the fact that those like O'Faolain, with an interest in the drama as well as in the language, knew that the desired plays had to be more than just new. For example, in 1937 'Oisín' faced hard truths: 'The people of this country are not that keen about the Irish language. They need plays that would be performed in any language at all and in any country at all, and it is now high time for us to make the like available in place of defective, meaningless, and senseless little plays. These things are doing nothing but damage to the language' (*DP*, 1 May 1937).[25] In 1944, the playwright Labhrás Mac Brádaigh also upped the stakes, blaming the Taibhdhearc's difficulties in drawing audiences in Galway on 'a lack of worthwhile original plays' (*easba bun-drámaí fiúntacha*), and writing of the potential Gaelic playgoer: 'He wants something, something to think about through the medium of Irish – something he has not already seen produced on stage in English. Until we have something of this kind available dramatic affairs in Irish will remain in the rut they are in at present' (*Glór*, 5 February 1944).[26]

One could hardly blame Mac Brádaigh had he given in to pessimism or accepted that English would have a monopoly on the Irish stage, but in fact he did neither, declaring in 1945 that better days might well lie ahead for the Gaelic theatre, and that 'this golden age will evolve from the hearts and minds of our playwrights if they set to work with loyalty to their ideals' (*Glór*, 1 December 1945).[27] As this brief survey of the challenges facing that theatre should have made clear, the playwrights discussed in this book – Piaras Béaslaí, Gearóid Ó Lochlainn, Leon Ó Broin, Séamus de Bhilmot and Walter Macken (Uaitéar Ó Maicín) – faced daunting prospects because they chose Irish as their literary medium, but choose it they did and, as we will see, by accepting Mac Brádaigh's challenge to provide 'worthwhile original plays' with 'something new, something to think about through the medium of Irish', and by 'working with loyalty to their ideals', they helped broaden the horizons and raise the ambitions of the more accomplished playwrights who would follow them in what was the closest thing to a 'golden age' that theatre in Irish has ever experienced.

Before turning to the work of our five playwrights, we should first address a few practical questions. First of all, actual dates rarely serve our attempts at periodisation. Béaslaí's first play, *Cormac na Coille*, was produced as early as 1906. It was, however, an apprentice effort. He didn't write any significant plays from the point of view of this study until the comedies he provided for de Bhilmot's theatre company Na hAisteoirí after its foundation in 1913. At the end of my timeline, de Bhilmot's final play was produced in 1957, but the one-act is very much a rehash of subject matter and themes he had worked with before. Because of references in the book to plays from the early revival, I have used 1910 as a reasonable starting point for this study with the endpoint in 1950, a year by which all of the plays by our authors had been produced except Séamus de Bhilmot's slight one-act *Caithfidh na Tancanna Dul Tríd* (The Tanks Must Go Through) produced in 1957.

Second, and more important, I have no doubt that people with a knowledge of Gaelic theatre may question my omission of a few writers from the discussion. My major criterion here was that a playwright should have written a number of plays that made a significant contribution to the development of a more mature and sophisticated drama in Irish. This standard meant that I excluded a few playwrights whose work would have been well worth discussing had there been more of it. Liam Ó Flaithearta (Liam O'Flaherty) only wrote one play in Irish, the powerful and controversial *Dorchadas* (Darkness), produced at the Abbey in 1926.[28] Micheál Mac Liammóir's *Diarmuid agus Gráinne* was the first play performed at Taibhdhearc na Gaillimhe in 1928, and is still regarded as one of the finest plays in the Irish language. Moreover, Mac Liammóir himself was, as producer, director, actor and designer in both Galway and Dublin, one of the most significant figures in the history of the Gaelic theatre. However, apart from *Diarmuid agus Gráinne*, the only play he wrote in Irish was the short comedy *Lúlú*, in which the rival that a family fears may have replaced them as the future heir of a wealthy old aunt turns out to be a dog.[29] *An t-Údar i nGleic* (The Author in a Quandary) (1943) by Labhrás Mac Brádaigh is a full-length play about an author's ambition to write a play dealing truthfully with Irish life, and his disillusion and bitterness when the work is attacked by a mob that finds it morally objectionable. What sets the play apart is Mac Brádaigh's willingness to experiment with metatheatricality and fantasy and his courage in taking on controversial subject matter, such as suicide, alcoholism, the philistinism of priests and the middle classes, and, above all, the mistreatment of unwed mothers and their babies – two decades before Máiréad Ní Ghráda's *An Triail* (The Trial) (1964). The play was favourably received in both Galway and Dublin,[30] but his only other dramatic work was the intriguing one-act play *Céad Feadha Síos* (A Hundred Fathoms Down) (1943), which was set on a German U-boat during the Second World War.[31]

On the other hand, Patrick Pearse wrote several short plays and pageants in Irish, of which the most important are *Íosagán* (Little Jesus) (1910) and *An Rí* (The King) (1912). While Pearse had a greater understanding of drama than any Gaelic playwright at the time with the exception of Piaras Béaslaí, the fact that his plays were written for his students at St Enda's for performance at the school greatly limited their influence, as did their settings, subject matter and themes – salvation outside of the traditional ceremonies of the Catholic Church in *Íosagán*, and medievalism and messianic self-sacrifice in *An Rí*.[32] One might think the plays of Pádraic Ó Conaire would have made an impression on later writers of Irish, but this does not seem to have been the case. Of course, his real gift was as a writer of fiction, particularly of short stories, and the superiority of his fiction is evident if we compare how he uses the same material in three short stories and in three of his six plays.[33]

Other readers may be more surprised by a writer I have included rather than any I excluded. Leon Ó Broin was a writer far better known for his biographical and historical work in Irish and English than for his plays, which, judging from *Just Like Yesterday: An autobiography*, he seems to have all but forgotten.[34] During the 1920s he was, however, an active member of An Comhar Drámaíochta, for whom he wrote and adapted several short plays. Indeed, one gets a clear notion of how important Ó Broin's contribution to the repertoire of An Comhar was when one realises that his plays made up a disproportionate percentage of the group's offerings in the fourteen years between 1926 and 1940. Ó Broin was also a thoughtful and perceptive writer on the challenges facing theatre in Irish in his time. While his plays are never staged today, the same could be said of the work of his contemporaries writing in Irish. Moreover, two of his plays, *An Mhallacht* (The Curse) (1927) and *An Oíche Úd i mBeithil* (That Night in Bethlehem) (1939), stand out and might still be of some interest today.

As will surely and properly be noticed, no female playwrights are discussed in this book. There were women among the earliest Gaelic playwrights – Máire Ní Chillín, Máire Ní Chinnéide, Searloit Ní Dhúnlaing, Máire Ní Shíthe. However, while women remained active in the theatre movement as actors, very few wrote plays in the years dealt with in this study. The most prominent were Máiréad Ní Ghráda in Dublin and Eibhlín Ní Bhaoighill at the Taibhdhearc. The former's long and productive career as a playwright began as early as 1930. Not only did she explore new techniques and themes in her plays and thus prepare the way for future innovators, she herself became one of the most accomplished playwrights in Irish and is as such discussed at length in *An Underground Theatre*. Also, it should be noted that some of the most important Gaelic playwrights at work now are women like Éilis Ní Dhuibhne, Celia de Fréine and Biddy Jenkinson.

Most of the published texts of these plays include a subtitle indicating the number of 'acts' (*gníomha*) or 'scenes' (*míreanna*) that make up the play. This can be misleading, as even some of the ones I call 'full-length' can be quite short, fifty to (rarely) a hundred small pages in length. Quotations from Irish are given in my own English in the text with the original Irish in the notes. As in previous books, I am uncomfortable with the term 'Gaelic', but have used it in phrases like 'Gaelic playwrights' and 'Gaelic drama' to avoid excessive reliance on circumlocutions like 'playwrights who wrote in Irish' or 'drama written in Irish'.

Finally, in a review of the published texts of plays by Seán Ó Tuama, Séamus Ó Néill, Críostóir Ó Floinn and Seán Ó Coistealbha in 1968, Séamus de Bhilmot wrote:

> A play in print and the same play under the lights and the magic of the theatre are two different things. There seems to be little connection – even a distant one – between the page covered with cold, dry words, and the stage version of the play, where the characters of the author's imagination are brought to life and the author's speech and philosophy are given greater scope and enriched by the voices, movements and gestures of the actors. In a way, the text is just the changeling that was or will be brimming with vigour and life on the stage. It is, therefore, clear that it is no easy task to assess the worth of a play in writing, whether in manuscript or in a printed book. The most highly educated reader could make a fool of himself … (*Feasta*, December 1968, pp. 31 and 33).[35]

I myself have seen none of these plays, but then, considering that the most recent of them had its premiere in 1957 and few of them have ever been revived in the past half-century or more, I doubt there are many still with us who have. So, knowing full well of the perils of those places angels fear to tread …

CHAPTER ONE

The Indispensable Man: Piaras Béaslaí (1881–1965)

In a 1931 letter to the editor of *The Leader*, Máire Ní Chróinín expressed concern for the future of An Comhar Drámaíochta, worrying that, among other problems, the company had become a one-man operation (*Leader*, 18 July 1931). The man in question was doubtless Piaras Béaslaí, and, allowing for a bit of hyperbole, Ní Chróinín was not altogether wrong about his role with An Comhar. Moreover, a similar criticism could have been expressed nearly two decades earlier about Na hAisteoirí, the company from which An Comhar Drámaíochta evolved. No other figure in Gaelic drama was as ubiquitous, versatile and effective as was Piaras Béaslaí from the time his first play, *Cormac na Coille* (Cormac of the Woods), was produced in 1907 until the time of Ní Chróinín's complaint a quarter century later.[1] Moreover, during much of the time he was most involved with theatre in Irish, he was also active in many of the most stirring events in the history of modern Ireland.

Born of Irish parents in Liverpool in 1881, Béaslaí took an early interest in all things Irish.[2] By 1896 he was studying the Irish language on his own from the pages of *Irisleabhar na Gaedhilge/The Gaelic Journal*, and in 1900 he joined a Liverpool branch of the Gaelic League, having already by this time attended that year's Oireachtas in Dublin. In 1901, his fellow branch members chose him to be their official representative at the league's annual *ard fheis* in Dublin. Convinced that it was only in Ireland that he could give adequate scope to his Irish interests, he moved to Dublin in 1905.

Once there, he immediately joined some of the cultural nationalist organisations that sprang up in Ireland in the last decade of the nineteenth century and the first decade of the twentieth. For example, he was soon a member of Craobh an Chéitinnigh (the Keating branch) of the Gaelic

League, one of the league's most active and controversial branches and one very much associated not only with the province of Munster and its dialect of Irish, but also eventually with physical-force nationalism. Two years later he was already a member of the league's Executive Committee (Coiste Gnó). Nor were his interests by any means exclusively linguistic and cultural. In 1907, he was, on the recommendation of Cathal Brugha, sworn into the Irish Republican Brotherhood, thus beginning his career as a militant separatist republican, a commitment that was to consume much, though by no means all, of his formidable energy until 1923.

He was, for example, active in the founding of the Irish Volunteers in 1913 – it was he who gave them their Irish-language name Óglaigh na hÉireann. When the Volunteers split over the parliamentarian John Redmond's attempt to gain control of the movement, Béaslaí predictably stayed with the militant wing. He was also a member of the so-called 'eite chlé' or 'left-wing' of the Gaelic League, which wanted the organisation to renounce its 'non-political' stance with regard to Irish independence. Indeed, it was he who drafted the amendment to the league constitution to that effect at the 1915 *ard fheis,* the acceptance of which led to the resignation of Douglas Hyde as league president. During Easter week 1916, Béaslaí was an officer fighting in the North King Street area, his involvement bringing him the first of his prison sentences. When the Volunteers re-organised after the release of prisoners who had served in the rising, Béaslaí became a close associate of Michael Collins, a friendship that would provide him with both inspiration and much material for his two-volume biography *Michael Collins and the Making of a New Ireland* (1926) and a later single-volume biography, *Michael Collins: Soldier and statesman* (1937). Elected a Sinn Féin member of the first Dáil Éireann, he was then chosen to translate into Irish both the Declaration of Independence and the Democratic Programme of the First Dáil to be read at its first sitting in January 1919. It was also Béaslaí who coined the term *saorstát* for 'republic', thus making possible the name 'Free State' for the new Irish state in 1922.[3]

During the war of independence, he served as editor of the Volunteer paper *An tÓglach,* as director of publicity for the Volunteers, and as press officer for Éamon de Valera. During the civil war he sided with the Free State, and it was he who moved acceptance of the Anglo-Irish treaty in the Dáil. He also travelled to the United States as a representative of the new government to explain its position on the treaty to influential Irish-Americans suspicious about the agreement. He eventually attained the rank of major-general in the army, acted as press censor for the government, and helped prepare the Irish-language version of the Free State's constitution.[4] As Pádraig Ó Siadhail underscores in his biography of Béaslaí, he was profoundly disillusioned by the civil war split, and with the conclusion of the third Dáil in 1923 he left politics for good.[5]

As has perhaps become obvious, Béaslaí was a great joiner of clubs and organisations whose ideals and goals he shared, and his commitment and energy often led to his being chosen for leadership positions in these groups. We have already noted his membership in the league's Keating branch, the IRB, the Irish Volunteers and Sinn Féin, but over the years he belonged to Cumann na hÉigse in both its original incarnation in the early twentieth century and its successor Cumann na hÉigse/Éigse Bhaile Átha Cliath in the 1940s; the literary group Cumann Oisín; the Irish Journalists' Association; the drama group Na hAisteoirí and its successor An Comhar Drámaíochta; the Catholic Commercial Club, of which he wrote a history; and the Association of the Old Dublin Brigade, the organisation with which he was most actively involved in the last decades of his life. When he felt there was need for an organisation not yet in existence, he was more than willing to take on the responsibility of helping create it, as was the case with Cumann Oisín and the Irish Journalists' Association, as well as the drama groups to be discussed below. Of particular significance for the Gaelic revival was the leading role he played in founding An Fáinne, a group of Irish speakers pledged to speak no English to each other, 'except when there will be a special need for it' (*acht amháin nuair a bheidh gádh fá leith leis*). He was chosen as the first president of An Fáinne, although, as with so many of his enthusiasms, his involvement with the organisation fell victim to his despondency about the civil war and its aftermath.

Frustrated by the many difficulties faced by writers of Irish, he also worked hard to promote interest in an organisation that would bring those writers together to discuss the issues affecting them. As early as 1915, in an article entitled 'Irish Writers and Their Troubles', he dealt with the challenges facing writers of Irish and stressed the central importance of literature in the revival. By 1920, fed up with what he called the 'spasmodic, haphazard, undirected' efforts to assist Gaelic writers, he urged the founding of an organisation for authors, arguing that such a group would 'improve the present wholly unsatisfactory state of affairs', remove 'a great many obstacles to the creation of a modern literature of importance and value', and promote 'serious, sober thinking and combined action on the part of writers of Irish' (*FJ*, 31 January 1920). When such an organisation came into existence as Cumann na Scríbhneoirí (The Writers' Association) at the 1920 Oireachtas, Béaslaí was on its provisional steering committee and was soon chosen president. Cumann na Scríbhneoirí was yet another initiative that did not survive the civil war, but when it was revived in 1939 Béaslaí was again at the forefront of those involved and served as the group's president in 1945–6.

Somehow, despite his need to earn a living as a journalist, his involvement in positions of responsibility in so many organisations, and, after 1919, the burden of living as a wanted man when not actually behind bars, Béaslaí managed to do an impressive amount of creative work in Irish spanning several genres. Soon after his arrival in Dublin he joined Cumann na hÉigse (The Poetry Association), a group of poets dedicated to the preservation and promotion of traditional Gaelic metrics and verse forms.[6] Two of his own poems were included in *Saothar Suadha a Dó* (The Work of the Masters, Number Two), an anthology published by the group in 1912, the same year Béaslaí was chosen to write and recite 'Óid an Oireachtais' (The Oireachtas Ode) at the annual Gaelic League cultural festival. Poetry was to remain a lifelong interest of his. In 1920, he published at his own expense *Bealtaine 1916 agus Dánta Eile* (May 1916 and Other Poems), a collection of his 'lays of captivity' (*laoithte braighdeanais*), poems he had written in prison. In 1933 appeared his two-volume scholarly study *Éigse Nua-Ghaedhilge: Tráchtas ar fhilíbh agus ar fhilidheacht na Gaedhilge ó 1600 go dtí 1850* (Poetry in Modern Irish: A treatise on the poets and poetry of the Irish-language from 1600 to 1850), based on lectures he had delivered at Coláiste na Mumhan in the early 1910s and that continued to see use in Irish secondary schools and universities into the 1960s. And when Cumann na hÉigse (also known as Éigse Bhaile Átha Cliath) was revived after a long hiatus in 1941, Béaslaí took a leading role, serving as 'Príomh-Éigeas' (Chief Poet) for its first year, writing 'Óid an Oireachtais' for that year, and, in a startling reversal from his own previously conservative if not reactionary attitude to poetry in Irish, championing the work of the young innovator Máirtín Ó Direáin.[7]

His novel *Astronár,* about a nationalist uprising in an imaginary European country, was serialised in the *Weekly Freeman* in 1921–2 and published in book form by An Gúm in 1928.[8] His short-story collection *Earc agus Áine agus Scéalta Eile* (Earc and Áine and Other Stories) did not appear until 1946, although his first story had been published as early as 1907 and all the others in the book were in print in the late 1910s and the 1920s, at the peak of his involvement in the struggle for Irish independence. In many ways, however, his most important contribution to Gaelic literature at this time, apart from his plays, was his literary criticism. Indeed, he was later to state with some justification, 'I think I was almost the first writer to attempt elaborate literary criticism in Irish.'[9] At any rate, in 1917, just before the war of independence, he took on the editorship of the Gaelic League's official organ *An Claidheamh Soluis,* which was soon to change its name to *Fáinne an Lae* and then *Misneach* in attempts to circumvent British censorship. It was in editorials and essays in this paper that he shared his ideas about literature in general and literature in Irish in particular, ideas that were considerably more sophisticated than those of the vast majority of his contemporaries in the Gaelic movement. Among these critical pieces were 'Sgríobhadh na Gaedhilge' (The Writing of Irish) (*FL,* 12 January 1918); 'Meastachán' (Assessment) (*FL,* 19 January 1918); 'Léirmheas' (Criticism) (*FL,* 9 February 1918) and '"Riaghalacha" agus Léirmheas Litríochta' ('Rules' and Literary Criticism) (*FL,* 17 August 1918). His ideas about literature drew an angry response from the formidable native speaker Séamus Ó Grianna ('Máire'), with whom he engaged in a sporadic but intense debate in the pages of the league organ between 1918 and 1921. In 1919 he rejected out of hand Ó Grianna's doctrine that writing in Irish, if it was to be authentic, must reflect 'Gaelic thought' (*smaoineamh Gaedhlach*) and 'the Gaelic mind' (*an aigne Gaedhlach*), asking 'How could any literature progress when the majority of its writers held such a view?' (*FL,* 31 May 1918).[10] In a January 1921 editorial entitled 'An Aigne Ghaedhlach: An bhfuil a leithéid ann?' (The Gaelic Mind: Is there such a thing?), he went so far as to ridicule this key tenet of Ó Grianna's nativist creed: 'But "the Gaelic mind" is the mystery beyond all mysteries. That mind is so mysterious, so difficult to understand, that only a few chosen people are able to comprehend it or to read it' (*M*, 8 January 1921).[11]

When Ó Grianna responded with his most reasoned contribution to the controversy, Béaslaí answered by stressing the importance of the issue in question and acknowledging the passionate sincerity of his opponent's views, while simultaneously dismissing his arguments:

> The question is, which of the two worlds now existing in Ireland is more important, which of them is stronger and more worthy of attention in the work of the language? There are two worlds in Ireland at present, the old world and the new world, the world of the Gaeltacht and the world to be found in the rest of Ireland ... The question is, then, whether we should save, if possible, and restore to the rest of the country the old world of the Gaeltacht and all that goes with it, or should we take the new world as it is and try to Gaelicise it?

However powerful his respect for the Gaeltacht,[12] Béaslaí was convinced that there could be but one answer to the question as it applied to literature: 'For better or worse, contemporary art is the only art in which contemporary people take interest' (*M*, 26 February 1921).[13] As we will see, Béaslaí put this principle into practice in his plays with some success.

Béaslaí also wrote in English on many of these same questions in the 1920s in the *Freeman's Journal* in essays like 'Books and Critics' (*FJ*, 21 February 1920); 'Gaels and Modern Culture' (*FJ*, 6 March, 1920); 'Self-Consciousness' (*FJ*, 10 April 1920); 'Ornamentalism' (*FJ*, 24 April 1920); and 'Purists and Pedants' (*FJ*, 22 May 1920). It was also to English that Béaslaí turned two decades later in the pages of *The Leader*,[14] joining in one of the most significant debates about Irish culture to take place in the 1940s, a debate to which Liam Ó Rinn, W.P. Ryan, Donn Piatt, Séamus Ó Néill and Stephen J. Brown, SJ also made thoughtful and provocative contributions. For example, in words that must have enraged Ó Grianna, Béaslaí wrote in 'The "Native Speaker" Humbug':

> In the present case a fundamental fallacy is the assumption that Irish speakers are divided into two classes – 'native speakers' and 'learners' ... Of course, there is no such clear-cut division. There are dozens of

> gradations and distinctions among both those who call themselves native speakers and those who do not. But there are no educated Irish-speakers in any way comparable to a 'native-speaker' of English or French (*Leader*, 31 May 1941).

Those were brave words for a learner of Irish who began his study of the language in Liverpool! And in a prophecy that could very well apply to himself, he stated of the kind of Gaelic critic he envisioned in the future that 'when he comes and tries to shine a light into the dark places of our minds, is he not more likely to be stoned than welcomed?' (*Leader*, 6 September 1941). Béaslaí was never to become the Messiah of Irish literary studies, but he was certainly one of the most articulate voices crying in the wilderness in the first fifty years of the revival.

There was, however, no literary genre to which he devoted more time and thought than he did to drama. Indeed, he himself, Gearóid Ó Lochlainn, Micheál Mac Liammóir and Walter Macken are probably the only Gaelic dramatists in the first fifty years of the revival whose interest in theatre predated their interest in the language. Pádraig Ó Siadhail tells us that he became fascinated with the theatre as a boy in Liverpool so that he could write in his diary in 1898, 'I have got (in this case, unintentionally) quite a dramatic critic and regular theatre goer.'[15] It was, then, only natural that he would become involved with theatre in Irish when he got the chance, acting in a Liverpool production of Peadar Mac Fhionnlaoich's one-act play *An Dochtúireacht Nuadh* (The New Doctoring) in 1903 and in Séamus Ó Beirne's one-act *An Dochtúir* (The Doctor) the following year. After moving to Dublin, he was active with the amateur group Na Saoirseantóirí, with whom he played a villainous landlord in a production of Tomás Ó hAodha's historical melodrama *Seabhac na Ceathramhan Caoile* (The Hawk of the Slender Thigh) at the 1906 Oireachtas, and, with his own Keating branch's theatre company, taking a lead role in Máire Ní Chinnéide's *An Dúthchas* (Heritage) at the 1908 Oireachtas. Moreover, his own first play *Cormac na Coille* was entered in the drama competitions of the 1906 Oireachtas, although much to his disappointment it failed to win a prize.

It was also the theatre that first brought Béaslaí to the attention of those outside the language movement when he was arrested for taking part in the disturbances that greeted the first production of Synge's *The Playboy of the Western World* at the Abbey theatre in January 1907. Indeed, he had the distinction of being singled out to the police by Yeats himself and earning Lady Gregory's scorn as 'Little Béaslaí'.[16] He was fined £2, but had no regrets about his protest, writing as 'Duine Áirithe' in the *Freeman's Journal* in reply to Yeats' call for 'freedom of the theatre': '"Freedom for plays", is it? Fine, oh tailor. I will have something to say about "freedom for plays" in Ireland before long. I have knowledge and experience with regard to the question. It's well I should when William himself taught me what freedom is. I understand the situation now since it happens I had to pay two pounds for the teaching. That's "freedom for plays" in Ireland for you!' (*FJ*, 1 February 1907).[17] Speaking at the discussion of 'Freedom of the Theatre' Yeats organised at the Abbey days later, Béaslaí remained unrepentant, stating that he hoped no one would forget Yeats' 'pose in the Police Courts' and adding, 'Its nature breaks out through the eyes of the cat. They had called in the claque of the garrison and police, and had rendered that place a place to which no Irishman could give the slightest support.'[18] Acting on that conviction, Béaslaí and his fellow members of the Keating branch cancelled the March 1907 performance of *Cormac na Coille* for which they had hired the Abbey.

Unlike many of his fellow protestors, Béaslaí had devoted a good deal of thought to the theatre, particularly to the prospects for theatre in Irish. In the same year he was arrested for his involvement in the *Playboy* riots, he wrote that a true national drama could never develop in English and declared: 'It has been made clear to me that it is high time for us to establish a theatre for ourselves ... It would be worthwhile for us to buy or build a home in Dublin for our original plays' (*FJ*, 12 April 1907).[19] As we will see, this was an idea to which he was to return again and again. Writing as 'Liúdaidhe Óg' the same year in an essay on 'Aistigheacht' (Acting) that won him a prize from *Irisleabhar na Gaedhilge*, Béaslaí offered would-be Gaelic dramatists some sound practical advice on how to write stage-worthy and effective plays, and urged them to read the work of the great dramatists from the Greeks onwards (*IG*, March 1907, pp. 289–92). And still in 1907 he was again stressing the need for a theatre dedicated to plays in Irish while also supporting Edward Martyn's proposal that groups of actors should be formed to tour the Gaeltacht areas with plays in Irish, another idea that continued to intrigue Béaslaí and that he was eventually able to try out, albeit only briefly and on a limited scale.

With time Béaslaí came to realise that regular performances by competent actors were more important than the acquisition of a building in which they could showcase their talents. A potential source of such actors was the drama group of Béaslaí's own Keating branch, one of the most active companies in the first decade of the twentieth century. It was the Keating branch that provided many of the actors for the Irish Literary Theatre's historic 1901 production of Douglas Hyde's *Casadh an tSúgáin* (The Twisting of the Rope) in Dublin's Gaiety theatre. They continued to appear on stage with some regularity in the following years, and by 1909 they had organised a dramatic class in the branch. Béaslaí was actively engaged in all of their theatrical activities after he moved to Dublin. For example, there can be no doubt that he was instrumental in the Keating actors' decision to perform his Liverpool friend Alphonsus Ó Labhradha's *An tSnaidhm* (The Knot) at the 1910 Oireachtas. Also during 1910, he took charge of the branch's drama class. After directing the Keating players' production of Seán Ua Ceallaigh's one-act play *Cú Roí* at the 1912 Oireachtas, he and other members of the group felt that it was time to take the next step and create a real Irish-language theatre company that, while still very much an amateur venture, could perform plays more regularly and with a greater degree of commitment and competence than was previously possible. In keeping with the general movement orthodoxy with regard to drama at the time and well into the 1940s, the initiative was at first framed in terms of its potential pedagogic and propaganda value, so that even Béaslaí himself could be reported as stating that 'the work of the company was the first practical attempt at what had been a favourite dream of many Gaels for years – the propagandist value of the performance by actors with the correct *blas* [accent] of plays in Irish simple in plot and treatment' (*II*, 21 July 1914).[20] As we have noted, it was from these tentative beginnings and under the leadership of Béaslaí that Na hAisteoirí evolved. His actual title with Na hAisteoirí was *teagascóir* (instructor),[21] but as Pádraig Ó Siadhail has pointed out, 'the job of the teacher was the same as the job of director-manager' (*b'ionann post an teagascóra is post mar léiritheoir-bhainisteoir*).[22] Béaslaí also took on the challenge of providing material for Na hAisteoirí, and his one-act *Beirt na Bodhaire Bréige,* an adaptation of Jules Moinaux's *Les deux sourds,* was one of the three short plays on the programme for the company's opening night on 12 April 1913.[23]

In the following years Na hAisteoirí, under Béaslaí's direction, were to have a significant inspirational and practical impact on the embryonic Gaelic drama movement in both Dublin and the provinces. Indeed, the success of their 1914 production of Béaslaí's *Cluiche Cártaí* (A Game of Cards), another adaptation, gave 'Pádraig na Léime' (Pádraig Ó Séaghdha) the confidence to pay a backhanded compliment to the Abbey, writing: 'However excellent are the English-language actors of the Abbey Theatre, it is not likely that they have boasting rights over Na hAisteoirí now' (*ACS,* 4 April 1914). Moreover, Na hAisteoirí were able to make a brief tour to Cork city and the Cork Gaeltacht on their way to an appearance at the 1914 Oireachtas in Killarney, County Kerry. However, as Béaslaí himself wrote of the company in a 1918 editorial in *Fáinne an Lae,* 'We were making good progress when Easter Week came and Na hAisteoirí were scattered, for there was not one man amongst them who did not have some connection with the work of that week' (*FL,* 5 October 1918). While it is intriguing to ponder what the company might otherwise have accomplished, there can, of course, be no answer to such a question. We can, however, be certain that it was the example of Na hAisteoirí – and to a lesser extent that of their rivals, Na Cluicheoirí – that paved the way for the next major venture in Gaelic theatre, a venture in which Béaslaí and many of his colleagues from Na hAisteoirí would be central.[24]

In an editorial note in 1921, the *Freeman's Journal* stated: 'When Piaras Béaslaí founded Na hAisteoirí some years ago to produce plays in the city and in the Gaeltacht, he had considerable success. It is a pity that there is no such group now. It would be much more successful than the old Aisteoirí.' Pointing out that many of the original actors were still available in Dublin, this writer continued that 'perhaps Piaras could lure them back into the group again if he put it together again. Will he try?' (*FJ,* 24 October 1921).[25] In autumn 1923, a group of people interested in Gaelic drama did come together at Gaelic League headquarters in Dublin to found An Comhar Drámaíochta, a company independent of the league despite their choice of meeting place. Predictably enough, it was Béaslaí who was chosen as the first president of An Comhar, a position he would hold for the next five years.[26] Almost all of the members of this new company had been involved with Na hAisteoirí, or its successor Aisteoirí Átha Cliath, a group brought together in 1921 by the professional actor Gearóid Ó Lochlainn from the alumni/alumnae of Na hAisteoirí. Just back in Ireland after several years performing in Copenhagen, Ó Lochlainn was, as we will see in the next chapter, to play a major role in the work of An Comhar Drámaíochta and in the development of Gaelic drama in general in the years to come.

Having hired the Abbey theatre for the occasion, An Comhar offered its first programme on 12 November 1923, with Béaslaí's *Fear an Sgéilín Grinn* (The Man with a Funny Story) one of three plays on the bill. As we will see, his plays were essential to An Comhar's success, if not its very survival, in the first decade of its existence. For example, An Comhar performed three of his plays in the inaugural 1923–4 season, two in each of the next three seasons, three in 1927–8, 1928–9, 1929–30, then two in 1930–1, none in 1931–2 and one in 1932–3. Moreover, when the company sponsored a lecture series in 1926 and '27, Béaslaí spoke four times, on 'Nódh-Dhrámaí na Gaoluinne' (New Plays in Irish), 'Samplaí Iasachta' (Foreign Examples), 'An Bealach Atá Romhainn' (The Road before Us) and 'Drámaí agus Aisteoirí Gaedhilge' (Irish-Language Plays and Actors).

In its first four seasons, An Comhar's productions were directed by Gearóid Ó Lochlainn, but in the 1927–8 season it was, by his own testimony, Béaslaí who served as director for all the plays. In the 1928–9 season, this work was divided among four directors – Béaslaí, Ó Lochlainn, Micheál Mac Liammóir and Pól Ó Fearghail – with Béaslaí directing two plays. In 1929–30, he was again president of An Comhar and responsible for all of the company's productions, including that of his own *An Danar* (The Dane) in London in July 1930, appropriately enough the last play he would direct for An Comhar.[27] Indeed, while he held the title of chairman of An Comhar's board in 1935–6 and his plays continued to be produced by the company, he was after 1930 no longer an active member of the group.[28]

As well as writing plays, Béaslaí continued to appear regularly on the Gaelic stage through the 1920s, first with the Keating players, then Na hAisteoirí, and finally with An Comhar Drámaíochta. For example, with the Keating players he took the lead role in his own *Cormac na Coille* in 1907. According to a critic in the *Freeman's Journal*, he gave 'a knightly portrayal of the part. His declaration of the heroic speeches in the first act being highly appreciated.' Moreover, this critic added that 'successful as he was in the sterner phases of the character, he was equally so in the tender passages. His telling of the old, old story was exquisite' (*FJ*, 6 August 1907). At the 1908 Oireachtas, he again took the lead, this time in Máire Ní Chinnéide's temperance melodrama *An Dúthchas,* while in 1912 he played a less important part in the Keating branch's production of Seán Ua Ceallaigh's *Cú Roí.* Despite all his other responsibilities with Na hAisteoirí, he stepped in to take the place of an actor who fell sick during the production of *Beart Nótaí* (A Bundle of Banknotes) by Máire Ní Shíthigh and Eilís Ní Mhurchadha, one of the group's inaugural offerings in April 1913. With An Comhar Drámaíochta, he appeared on stage in, among other plays, Liam Ó Rinn's *An Saoghal Eile* (The Other World), in which he played the lead role, and his own *Cúigeachas* (Provincialism) in 1925; in Risteárd Ó Foghludha's translation of François Coppée's *Le luthier de Cremonne* as *An Bheidhlín Buadha* (The Violin of Victory) in 1926, again playing the lead in his own translation of Oliver Goldsmith's *She Stoops to Conquer* as *Ísliú chun Buadha* in 1929 where he played Sir Charles Marlowe; and in 1931 in a minor role in his own original full-length tragedy *An Bhean Chródha* (The Brave Woman).

His gradual withdrawal from An Comhar Drámaíochta was in no way indicative of a total loss of interest in the future of theatre in Irish or its practitioners. In December 1936, he was among the founders as well as a board member of An Sgiath, a short-lived organisation whose purpose was 'to expedite and improve the provision of suitable dramas in Irish and to benefit the authors' (*soláthar drámaí oireamhnacha i nGaedhilge do bhrostú agus d'fheabhsú agus na h-ughdair a chur ar a leas*). As a professional writer who could not afford to be cavalier about royalties, Béaslaí was both concerned about what we would now call intellectual property rights and frustrated by the way he and his fellow playwrights were regularly cheated out of payments due by small amateur companies that produced their work without ever notifying them.[29] An Sgiath did not last long, nor did its successor Cumann na nDrámathóirí (The Dramatists' Association), a sub-committee formed by the newly revived Cumann na Scríbhneoirí in 1941, with Béaslaí a member from the start. This group also fell apart soon after An Comhar Drámaíochta, with which most of its members were involved, was absorbed into the Abbey in 1942.

Few figures in the first forty years of the Gaelic revival, apart from Gearóid Ó Lochlainn and Micheál Mac Liammóir, could even begin to match the range of Béaslaí's contributions to the theatre as playwright, director, actor and administrator. But, as we saw above, he was also a pragmatic student of the theatre who had a good deal to teach both his colleagues in the drama movement and the general public. He had already lectured on the subject to the London branch of the Gaelic League in 1901. Soon after moving to Ireland permanently he was calling for a dedicated building for theatre in Irish, and in his 1907 essay 'Aistigheacht' offering those with an interest in Gaelic drama advice on successful play production. He must, then, have been discouraged watching An Comhar Drámaíochta shuttle its productions from the Abbey theatre to the Peacock to the Gate to the Torch and then back again to the Peacock before the company – and its state subsidy – were finally taken over by the Abbey in 1942. He did not, however, lose hope that he would one day see a theatre in Dublin devoted mostly, if not exclusively, to the production of plays in Irish. In 1917, he suggested that a theatre for plays in Irish would be a fitting memorial for Thomas Ashe, the young Kerry republican who had recently died after being force-fed while on hunger strike: 'A "Gaelic Theatre" could, for example, be started and a school of drama and acting properly established, not just for Dublin but for the people of Ireland' (*ACS*, 27 October 1917).[30]

Writing in 1928 as president of An Comhar to Ernest Blythe in the latter's capacity as minister for finance, Béaslaí explained An Comhar's need for its own theatre, pointing out that as long as the company had to rely on rented space in the Abbey, it would be limited to seven performances a year, making survival, not to mention development and experimentation, impossible: 'It is our strong opinion that as long as we are confined to seven productions per year it is not possible for us to make a better attempt … that there will be no further growth or progress in the work.' He also stressed that would-be playwrights would soon lose heart when they realised that performance of their work would be limited to a single evening. He told Blythe that An Comhar believed that with its own theatre it could stage four to six performance of each play every month during the season.[31] Participating in a debate on Gaelic theatre in the pages of *The Star* the following year, Béaslaí developed this idea: 'Personally,

I have no hope of ever doing better as long as the present system is continued. But if we had a little theatre of our own – just a tiny hall, any old place, but our own – what interesting things we could do, what developments might we not hope to attain' (*Star*, 29 June 1929). As late as 1954, at a meeting of Cumann na Scríbhneoirí with his fellow playwright Máiréad Ní Ghráda in the chair, he is reported as saying that 'there can be no Gaelic theatre movement unless they had both a drama movement and an actual theatre. In the Comhar they had had the movement, but they had not got the theatre, and had to move from place to place' (*II*, 30 October 1954). Surprisingly, however, he seems to have taken no practical interest in the planning for An Damer, the theatre that was to revolutionise drama in Irish in the 1950s and '60s. Moreover, he was not involved with that theatre when it opened, and never had any of his plays produced there.

Of course, by that time – indeed long before – Béaslaí had become despondent about the future of theatre in Irish, doubtless, at least in part, due to the failure of his own plans for a Gaelic theatre in Dublin. Moreover, his pessimism extended to literature in Irish in general, so that in 1931 he claimed that he was ready to join the by no means exclusive club of those who threatened to give up writing in Irish: 'However, I reached the mood where I decided that it was only a waste of time to write in Irish, except for my own pleasure. I must write in English if I hoped to gain recognition or make money. Then even the Gaelic fools would begin to appreciate me.'[32] It should also be noted that Béaslaí never thought much of the only theatre in the country where Irish was the language of all the productions, that is Taibhdhearc na Gaillimhe. Perhaps it was An Taibhdhearc's apparent unwillingness to take an interest in his own plays, only one of which, the translation *Ísliú chun Buadha*, was ever staged there.[33] At any rate, commenting on the proposed takeover of An Comhar by the Abbey under Ernest Blythe, Béaslaí wrote in his diary in 1941: 'I do not think that the new scheme – the Abbey one – will succeed; but it may be worth trying, but what I dread – with Blythe in charge – is a repetition of the awful Galway Theatre with translations of English plays.'[34]

Béaslaí was always a pragmatic man of the theatre, and he viewed this question of translation as one of considerable significance. From the beginning of the revival there were two primary schools of thought about the wisdom of translating plays into Irish, a problem made particularly acute since the Gaelic Irish had no tradition of drama. One group regarded translation as a significant danger to the very ethos of the Gaelic movement in that it would provide inappropriate alien models for would-be Gaelic playwrights and possibly even thwart the development of a dramatic movement in harmony with the native tradition. The other group saw translation as, in the short term at least, the only possible source of an adequate supply of stage-worthy and entertaining plays for which there was such an immediate need. Béaslaí was, with reservations, in the second camp. Thus, in 1924 he wrote of translation in general, advocating 'a favourite scheme of mine for the advancement of the Irish language – the supplying by the joint effort of a body of the best scholars and literary men, assisted by "native speakers" of the Gaeltacht, of versions in a standardised form of Irish of the great classics of the world', a scheme he pronounced 'essential to the salvation of the Irish language' (*FJ*, 5 May 1924). As is obvious from his comments about 'the awful Galway Theatre with translations of English plays', the translation of plays for performance was for him a trickier question. When in 1929 he responded to Liam Ó Briain's idea that 'translation of really good live foreign drama for years to come rather than producing poor original stuff' was 'the best way to obtain good native drama', he declared flatly: 'Perhaps he is right, but that is not "the development of Drama in Irish"' (*Star*, 29 June 1929).[35] Three years later, at a lecture by Micheál Mac Liammóir at which Liam Ó Briain and Gearóid Ó Lochlainn also spoke, Béaslaí was reported as saying that 'real drama in the Gaelic language was sadly lacking. He was not satisfied with translations from English and other languages' (*IT*, 5 April 1932).[36]

Béaslaí was, of course, himself a translator, one of his first publications being his Irish version of Adelbert von Chamisso's novel *Peter Schlemihls wundersame Geschichte* as *Eachtra Pheadair Schlemihl*, serialised in the *Freeman's Journal* in 1908 and published in book form the following year. And this was by no means his only contribution in this area. In the genre of drama alone, he translated four plays for the radio, as well as a scene from Sheridan's *The Rivals* (*CE*, 24 July 1958). The four full-length plays were Aristophanes' *The Archanians* as *Na Gualdóirí* (*IP*, 11 October 1950)[37] and three German plays: one by Rudolf Benedix translated as *Ceanndánacht* (Stubbornness),[38] one by Ernst Wiechert as *An tOllamh Dearmadach* (The Absent-minded Professor) and one by Louis Angely as

Fear na Foidhne (The Patient Man), the first broadcast in March 1959, the second in December 1960 and the third in April 1961.

By far the most important of his dramatic translations was *Ísliú chun Buadha*, his version of Goldsmith's *She Stoops to Conquer*, which was first performed by An Comhar Drámaíochta in the Peacock in December 1919, with Béaslaí both directing and acting, and Ernest Blythe and his wife in the audience.[39] As we will see, Béaslaí's preface to the published text of the play shows that he had given a good deal of thought to how this play could be most effectively brought into Irish. In a piece on 'The Art of Translation' six years earlier, he had set out his philosophy of translation: 'It should not, one could wish, be necessary to point out that the best translation of a work of genius is that in which the time, spirit, style, details and general effect of the original are most faithfully reproduced – in which approximately the same impression is made upon the reader as is made on him who reads the original' (*FJ*, 6 October 1923). In his preface to *Ísliú chun Buadha* – and virtually no other Gaelic translator at the time ever felt the need for such a preface no matter what liberties (s)he took with the original – Béaslaí identifies the challenges he faced if he wanted to give playgoers hearing the play in Irish an experience similar to the one many of them may have already had when they attended the play in English:

> What I wanted was that the Irish-language audience would understand every sentence and every point in the play, that the significance of the play would affect them properly, and also that the arrangement of the sounds and the flow of speech would suit actors on the stage – something many writers who have excellent Irish forget because of a lack of experience with acting.

Pointing out with regard to the Goldsmith play 'that some of the speech is pompous and unnatural and some of it so outdated that today's listeners would not catch the full meaning' (*go bhfuil cuid den chaint mór-chúiseach, mí-nádúrtha, agus cuid eile dhi chó sean-aimseardha sin ná béarfadh éisteoirí an lae indiu a lán-bhrigh leo*), Béaslaí explained how he had come to terms with this problem and in particular how he had dealt with linguistic registers important in the eighteenth-century world of the play but largely absent in modern Irish.[40]

Despite all the work he put into this translation, it had a mixed reception when produced. In *The Irish Statesman*, 'F. O'C.' (Frank O'Connor), a frequently vitriolic critic of the work of An Comhar Drámaíochta, praised both the translation and the production (*IS*, 7 December 1929). Writing in *The Leader*, 'D. Ó D.', having noted that there were only forty-eight people in the opening-night audience, suggested that the script be cut (*Leader*, 30 November 1929).[41] Béaslaí must have been particularly frustrated by the anonymous review in the *Irish Independent* in which the critic failed to recognise what the translator had tried to do and even chided him for discouraging original work by bringing a 'foreign' play into Irish: 'But is something like this appropriate for the Gaelic world? Piaras did his work well, but it is difficult to give a play of the sort the shape and form of the Gaelic world. But it is likely we will have to have that kind of thing until we have enough plays in Irish' (*II*, 2 December 1929).[42] And indeed, he must have found enraging the anonymous comments in *The Star*: 'If this is the kind of respect they [An Comhar] have for the public, it is little wonder that the Irish speakers turn to foreign entertainment or that there are empty seats in the Theatre of the Gaels [The Peacock]' (*Star*, 7 December 1929).[43]

The focus on audience that we see in his translator's preface to *Ísliú chun Buadha* runs throughout Béaslaí's thinking about Gaelic theatre. He was, for example, painfully aware how unpredictable and usually small audiences were for plays in Irish. Thus, in 1929, he declared:

> It is, however, necessary to remind our critics that neither playwrights nor players can make a successful dramatic movement without a sympathetic public. The audiences are as necessary an ingredient to the success of a dramatic production as players, producers or scenery. It is hardly too much to say that upon the support accorded by the public to this new experiment of An Comhar [an increase in the number of productions] depends the future of Gaelic drama in Dublin (*Star*, 5 October 1929).

He was, however, well aware that even if such audiences suddenly materialised, they were apt to be relatively unsophisticated – there in support of the language as much as from love of the drama – and that their command of that language would range from mastery to minimal, with most somewhere in the middle. Drawing on his own experience with his ambitious tragedies *An Danar* and *An Bhean Chródha* in 1928 and '29, he conceded that, in the short term at least, Gaelic playwrights and theatre companies would have to work with the audiences they had and accept the consequences of that compromise with reality. Addressing the Oireachtas in a lecture on Gaelic drama in 1942, Béaslaí urged his listeners to face facts:

> It is my opinion that we should give the Irish-language public what they want. What they want is fun, simple language, and thoughts a child could understand. Very well – give those things to them. We want a public – and if it is necessary to lure that public to us with simple humorous plays, as you would lure a child with sweets, in God's name let us do it.[44]

The following year he offered a more dispassionate view of the situation in a piece entitled 'Plays and Listeners' in *The Leader*. He began by setting out the harsh realities:

> Now whatever the number of Irish-speakers may be in Dublin I doubt if there are really very many of them who can follow every word of a play in Irish as spoken from the stage with the same ease with which an Abbey audience follows a play in English. There must be a certain strain, an effort of attention. Even in the case of 'native speakers' a difference of dialect can be confusing and so can defective pronunciation by an actor – a thing, I am afraid, not unknown on the Gaelic stage. This is true even in the case of simple colloquial Irish.

This state of affairs was especially problematic for the kind of ambitious and gifted playwrights that the movement hoped to attract: 'But if the dramatist wants to contribute to the drama of ideas, or deal with modern life or modern problems, or the great ultimate realities, he must use words and phrases which are not familiar to either native speakers or learners.' As a result, 'the listener is kept anxiously alert, trying to follow and interpret, and the strain may tire him into inattention'. If only 'a minority of English-speaking audiences' could follow a play containing 'fruitful ideas, food for thought, subtlety', even that minority was more than one could expect in a Gaelic audience. Béaslaí then went on to insist that it was altogether unfair 'to blame Gaelic audiences, actors, producers or playwrights for deficiencies which are inevitable under the circumstances'. One obvious consequence was that 'it is not surprising that the plays in Irish which have most popular appeal are simple farcical comedies of elementary humour, with conventional situations and themes'. Nevertheless, 'if a Gaelic audience prefers simple plays it is not necessarily a sign of its low intelligence. Probably – nay, almost surely – the mental capacity of those who have learned Irish, at all events, is greater than that of the English-speaking low-brow who never studies anything – except, perhaps, racing form' (*Leader*, 12 September 1942).

As is clear from his own dramatic work – all but three of his plays are 'simple farcical comedies of elementary humour, with conventional situations and themes' – Béaslaí usually accepted that he could not expect to deal successfully in Irish with all the complexities of modern life. He was, however, more than willing to face the challenge of giving his plays modern urban or town settings and characters. This decision represented a surprising shift in his thinking about the appropriate subject matter for a modern literature in Irish. In a 1907 piece in the *Freeman's Journal*, he discussed the deleterious effects of life in Dublin on the language of urban Irish speakers and then continued:

> But that is not the worst of it. If the Irish speakers of Dublin had the finest Irish, that would not matter. English is the language of the life of this city. The literature of the city will not be composed in a language that is not involved with the ordinary life of the city. No literature will grow out of the flagstones of Dublin until the people of Dublin have Irish as their usual language (*FJ*, 16 December 1907).[45]

The following year he challenged two of the literary heavyweights of the Gaelic movement at the time, reiterating 'that no Irish-language literature will grow from the stones of Dublin for a long while. I'm afraid few people understand that. Eoghan Mac Néill does not understand it. "Colm Ó Conaire" [Patrick Pearse] does not understand it' (*FJ*, 25 January 1908).[46]

Actually, there were probably far more in the movement who agreed with him than disagreed, but coming to terms with the improbability of an authentic literature in Irish developing in the city must have been painful for a man as urban and urbane as was Béaslaí. Perhaps predictably, as he wrestled with this problem his ideas evolved, so that in 1920 in an article entitled 'Standard of Revolt'[47] in which he was sharply critical of 'Athairpeadarachas' (Father Peterism), he declared:

> I felt what was wrong at the time without being able to perceive the whole truth. I felt that the expression in Irish of their thoughts and passions by men in whose lives Irish was not a living reality could only result in an artificial, unnatural product. I did not then realise that it was possible to make the Irish language a living reality in our lives even in the Galldacht; and when we were accustomed to accept Irish as the medium for the expression of all our thoughts and feelings – however alien to the Gaelic mind – the product may be ungraceful and clumsy, but it will not be unnatural nor artificial (*WF*, 11 September 1920).

Moreover, as he wrote the same year, 'I have always been a believer of [*sic*] the essentiality of the Gaeltacht and its atmosphere to Irish literature, but I realise that this dramatic movement must originate in big cities' (*FJ*, 20 March 1920). While his own first play was a historical drama, as would be his two finest plays, all of Béaslaí's other dramatic works dealt with the lives of everyday middle-class Irish people living in or near Dublin or a provincial Irish town.

We may now turn to those stage plays in Irish, omitting discussion of his radio play *Ar Thóir Mhíchíl Uí Choileáin* (In Pursuit of Michael Collins);[48] his unpublished play in English, 'Philoctetes';[49] or his unfinished film script, also in English, about Robert Emmet.[50] His first play to be produced, *Cormac na Coille,* had its origin in 'Philaster', a play in English he had begun to write as a teenager in Liverpool, as he later recalled in one of his notebooks: 'But in the case of Philaster I had the plot clearly planned and though I had discarded it, I recast it for Cormac which became a new play with just hints of Philaster.'[51] Béaslaí and his colleagues in the Keating players were aware that this new play would be a challenge for Gaelic playgoers accustomed to simpler fare, and went out of their way to prepare potential audience members for this new experience: 'Gaels who go there need not expect so much to receive a lesson, as to witness the representation of stirring events, a romance of a period of political confusion, love and hatred, of patriotism and opportunism' (*FJ*, 4 May 1907).

The play had its first production, for one performance only, by the Keating players at a branch concert in Dublin's Rotunda on 6 May 1907. It was directed by Cathal Mac Garbhaigh, the comic songwriter and owner of the shop-cum-Gaelic gathering place An Stad, and featured Béaslaí in the lead role. Reviews of the production were mixed. The critic for the *Freeman's Journal* called it 'an event of unusual interest', adding that 'the large Concert Hall was filled with a sympathetic and most appreciative audience and at the outset it may be said that the reception of the piece was highly flattering both to author and artistes'. He also wrote that 'the play is constructed with perfect consistency, and, for a first effort, shows altogether a striking grasp of stage techniques. The action runs smoothly, the characters are outlined with rare strength.' Moreover, 'there is no flagging of interest, there is a sufficiency of suspense from act to act, and the finale comes as a complete satisfaction', while 'the dialogue is fluent and pithy, and is gracefully musical to the ear'. Impressed by Béaslaí's 'honest earnestness and sincerity', this critic felt the young playwright 'has every reason to be pleased with his unmistakable success' (*FJ*, 7 May 1907).[52] Writing of the play in *An Claidheamh Soluis*, 'Seán' was far less impressed. While he called it 'the most interesting League event of the week in Baile Átha Cliath' and 'most important to the language movement', he also noted 'the obscurity of its plots' and continued: 'The reason for this obscurity is partly the nature of the subject. Mr. Béaslaí chose a period of political confusion, and by introducing characters of secondary literary importance he worried his audience by giving them more than enough to do to understand the motive of his personages.' Yet, despite what he regarded as the predictably amateurish quality of the staging and acting of the play at this point in the literary revival, as well as a lack of 'dignity' in the presentation of historical characters, he did add charitably that 'to mention these few points is not to say that the play and the performance had not many good points' (*ACS*, 18 May 1907).

When the Keating players revived the play for the 1907 Oireachtas, the anonymous reviewer for the *Freeman's Journal* noted that 'the vast proportions of the Round Room of the Rotunda failed last night to accommodate all those who were desirous to attend the entertainment', and stated that the play's reception at the Oireachtas 'utterly eclipsed' the 'great success' of the production three months earlier. While most of this review was just plot summary, the critic did praise the play's 'manifold merits', writing: 'Quick and vivid in action, breathing throughout of the tender passion, instinct with martial order and perfervid patriotism, it irresistibly captivates eye, ear and mind.' Indeed, he went so far as to pronounce *Cormac na Coille* 'the first production of the Irish Literary and Dramatic Revival' (*FJ*, 6 August 1907). Patrick Pearse was considerably more restrained and tactful in his comments on the play in *An Claidheamh Soluis*:

> As a play it is in the same category as 'Seabhac na Ceathramhan Caoile' – a courageous attempt at a 'sentimental' romantic drama of the type beloved by Mr. Martin Harvey. It takes great acting backed up with ample stage resources, to make such things 'go'. The players on Tuesday worked hard, notably Piaras himself, who more than deserved the friendly and encouraging reception accorded him by the audience (*ACS*, 10 August 1907).

Cormac na Coille is by no means a challenging play. There are two major strands running through it: the 'perfervid patriotism' of the protagonist and his problematic romance with the daughter of his most prominent Irish enemy. Set near Blarney, County Cork, in 1600 with the various Irish chieftains expecting the imminent arrival of Aodh Ó Néill and Aodh Ruadh Ó Domhnaill from the north, the play deals with the decision of Coramac Vác Cártha Ryach to rebel against the authority of the newly minted earl of Muskerry Dônal Vác Cártha and his young ally, Donacha Mac Heig Mác Cártha (known as Donacha na Ngoul, i.e. Donnchadh na nGall, Donnchadh of the Foreigners). Cian Ó Donchú makes clear what the real Gaels think of those who speak English and ape English ways: 'You never saw any spectacle like the hankering we have of late for the nobility of the Foreigners. There is a well-spoken babbler from Cork of the Ships now – Donnchadh of the Foreigners is his name – and he is a great man for spouting English at us.'[53] Coramac has no use for men of this kind, heaping scorn on the earl and Donacha: 'His tricks, his crafty counsels, his deceits and his crookedness! His boasting and his arrogance when he thinks he can get away with it. And that flatterer beside him listening to us and smirking! May I be forever tormented with sorrow if I let him have his way any longer.'[54]

Coramac's plan to rebel against Dônal is complicated by his love for the earl's daughter Úna, who is being courted with her father's approval by Donacha and who urges Coramac not to fight against the earl. The poet Brian's daughter Mór also loves Coramac and tries to warn him against Úna, since her principal loyalty will be to her father. When fighting breaks out, Coramac and Úna find themselves trapped in a dilemma from which there seems to be no escape. At one point, Coramac is ready to abandon the fight for love of Úna, but then remembers that abandoning the Gaelic cause will bring him lasting shame. Realising what his sacrifice for her will mean for the glory of his name, she agrees to let him join the battle. The earl is killed in the fighting, but Donacha returns to tell Úna he saw Coramac fall wounded and believes he is dead. Thereupon, Coramac enters, pale and weak but very much alive. Donacha accepts his defeat at Coramac's hands and departs with surprising dignity, saying that they might well meet again. One of Coramac's men then informs Úna that Coramac suffered his wounds while attempting unsuccessfully to shield her father in the climactic battle. The play ends with her expressing her love for him.

Obviously, there is a great deal of action in this play, but all of it is predictable enough. Equally predictable is what the critic for the *Freeman's Journal* called 'the perfervid patriotism' that pervades the play, a quality with which its audiences were doubtless in full sympathy. Nor could playgoers ever have been in much suspense about who would win the fair Úna at the final curtain. In effect, *Cormac na Coille* is pretty much stock melodrama, the kind of thing for which Béaslaí had little use when it was presented in English. The play was only revived that one time, and when Béaslaí tried in the 1940s to get An Gúm to republish it, presumably in a more reader-friendly standard Irish orthography than was the original, he was turned down – to his disappointment but probably not all that much to his surprise.

Béaslaí did take some pride in *Cormac na Coille*, for example paying for its publication out of his own pocket. Yet, despite the positive response of some contemporary critics, he understood that his ambition exceeded his artistry at this stage of his career and that, moreover, he had asked too much of his audience.[55] We have already seen how in 1942 he stressed that 'the plays in Irish which have most popular appeal are simple farcical comedies of elementary humour, with conventional situations and themes' (*Leader*, 12 September 1942), and after *Cormac na Coille* he would devote much of his talent and energy as a playwright to trying to create an audience for Gaelic drama with such 'simple farcical comedies'. It was certainly plays of that kind that he provided for both Na hAisteoirí and An Comhar Drámaíochta in the years to come, only briefly returning to full-length tragedies in 1928 and '29.

His first attempt at such a short and simple comic play was *Beirt na Bodhaire Bréige* (The Two Fake Deaf People) that, with *Beart Nótaí* (A Bundle of [Bank]Notes) by Máire Ní Shíthigh and Eilís Ní Mhurchadha, made up the programme for the inaugural appearance of Na hAisteoirí in April 1913. The play was an adaptation – actually more of a translation – of the French farce *Les deux sourds* by Jules Moinaux. Béaslaí provided the play with an Irish setting, made his characters Irish rather than French, and Hibernicised other details, so that Moinaux's *garde champêtre* becomes a *garda síochána*, francs become pounds, and for some reason the butler of the original becomes a maid. Otherwise, he followed the text of the play closely, changing just what it made sense to change for the sake of consistency or effect. Thus, in the original when the intruder is asked to give his name, he stutters, '*Monsieur, voici ce que …*' only to have the butler interrupt and say, '*Il s'appelle Voiciski … c'est un Polonais*.' In Béaslaí's play, the intruder replies, 'It does not matter what my name is, but …' (*Is cuma cad is ainm dom, ach …*), and the maid takes this to mean his name is 'Cumagad', prompting the policeman to comment: 'He is most likely an Englishman. They always have ugly and strange names.'[56]

The plot of the play is simple enough. A widowed father who is deaf refuses to let his daughter marry any man who does not share his condition. A hunter in pursuit of a rabbit bursts into the house and is arrested. To get out of his fix he pretends to be deaf, winning the immediate approval of the father. Soon, the daughter and the intruder pretending to be deaf find themselves attracted to each other. Meanwhile, the father is miraculously cured of his deafness and now no longer wants a deaf son-in-law. He and the man have dinner together, each assuming the other cannot hear the insults they exchange. Of course, all ends well, with the father blessing the young couple's engagement.

After his disappointment with the failure of *Cormac na Coille* to win recognition at the 1907 Oireachtas, Béaslaí must have been surprised when *Beirt na Bodhaire Bréige* took second prize in the competition for translated plays at the 1913 festival (*ACS*, 16 August 1913).[57] Moreover, the play stayed in the repertoire for decades. Among subsequent productions were those by Na hAisteoirí at the 1914 Oireachtas in Killarney, County Kerry; by the students of Dublin's Coláiste Mhuire in 1935 (*IP*, 26 February 1935)[58] and again in 1936, this time in the Peacock under the auspices of An Comhar Drámaíochta (*SI*, 15 November 1936); by Cavan Vocational School Group at the Cavan Drama Festival in 1953 (*II*, 22 March 1953); by the actors of the Gaelic League's Tralee branch at the Kerry Drama Festival in 1960 (*K*, 23 April 1960); and by the actors of the London branch of the league at the 1964 Oireachtas, where the production won the *Sunday Press* Trophy for best one-act play (*IP*, 4 May 1964).

Béaslaí obviously learned a useful lesson by translating *Les deux sourds*, that is that a single comic concept was all that was needed for a successful one-act play. That lesson would stand him in good stead for the rest of his career as a playwright, and he applied it at once in his next effort, *Fear an Sgéilín Grinn* (The Man with the Funny Story), which was first performed by Na hAisteoirí in the Gaelic League Hall in Dublin in January 1914, with, in all probability, Béaslaí as director.[59] Reviewing the play in the *Freeman's Journal*, an anonymous critic wrote: 'This is another play of a most successful character coming from the pen of the already famous and popular Irish composer Mr. Piaras Béaslaí. From all points of view it is an eminently successful piece, full of rich humour and altogether deserving of the appreciation it received on its first appearance' (*FJ*, 26 January 1914). When the play was published by An Comhar in 1925, the anonymous reviewer for the *Cork Examiner* praised it, but was quite clear about what kind of play it was meant to be: 'The present play is one that will have a vogue. It is easy to stage; the dialogue is bright, and the language easily understood, even by learners ... We hope our young societies will place this little comedy on their repertory. It is a feast of laughter from beginning to end' (*CE*, 26 May 1925). While this critic did not get his or her wish that the play become a staple of the Gaelic repertoire, *Fear an Sgéilín Grinn* was revived from time to time in the 1910s, '20s and '30s. The most important of those revivals were those by Na hAisteoirí at the 1914 Oireachtas in Killarney (*II*, 21 July 1914); by An Comhar Drámaíochta, with Gearóid Ó Lochlainn directing, at the Abbey in 1923 and 1925 (*FJ*, 13 November 1923 and 12 December 1923; *II*, 17 February 1925); by the Bandon, County Cork, branch of the Gaelic League in 1926 (*SS*, 17 April 1926); and, with Seán Ó Conchubhair directing, by Dublin's Thomas Davis branch of the league under the auspices of An Comhar in the Abbey in 1937 (*IT*, 13 January 1937).

As in *Beirt na Bodhaire Bréige*, Béaslaí wrings all the humour he can out of a single joke in *Fear an Sgéilín Grinn*. Liam has heard and is eager to share a funny story about the marriage of the diminutive Partholán Mac Cárthaigh to a very tall young woman. However, every time he tries to tell it he is interrupted – his listener has to hurry off, or asks too many questions, or is simply uninterested. One of those with whom he tries to share the tale turns out to be the father of the very tall young woman. Realising his mistake, Liam stops in mid-story, but the other man has grasped that the joke was to be at the expense of his daughter and leaves in a huff. We soon learn that Liam is famous for never finishing a story, and two of his friends bet on whether he will manage to tell this one all the way through. When Liam is telling them the tale, the one who bet against his finishing constantly attempts to break his train of thought, while the other man tries to keep Liam focused. The two gamblers are soon brawling, and in the confusion, Liam forgets how the story ends. Thereupon, the tall woman's father returns with Partholán Mac Cárthaigh, and the two set upon the hapless Liam as the play ends.

Béaslaí's next play, *Cluiche Cártaí* (A Game of Cards), won first prize for a dramatic adaptation at the 1913 Oireachtas and was first performed by Na hAisteoirí at the Gaelic League Hall in Dublin in March 1914, most likely with Béaslaí directing. This time he based his work on the eighteenth-century Irish playwright Arthur Murphy's *Three Weeks After Marriage*, first performed in 1764 as *What We Must All Come To*. Obviously sensitive about any suspicion that he had plagiarised Murphy's play,

Béaslaí in a 1914 letter to *An Claidheamh Soluis* acknowledged Murphy as the inspiration for *Cluiche Cártaí*, but then asserted: 'It is virtually a new play. There are different characters in the two plays. They do not have the same plot or the same scenes. The only resemblance between them is that a newly married couple have an argument about a game of cards in the two plays' (*ACS*, 11 April 1914).[60] He was still concerned enough about this question to return to it in virtually identical terms fifteen years later in his brief 'Rémh-Rádh' (Preface) to *An Sgaothaire agus Cúig Drámaí Eile*, a collection that included *Cluiche Cártaí*: 'I got the basic idea from a play in English written by Arthur Murphy in the year 1764 – "What We Must All Come To, or Three Weeks After Marriage", but I made a new play out of it. My play has a new plot and new characters. The only resemblance between the two plays is that there is a newly married couple fighting about a game of cards in each of them.'[61]

He was being less than fully forthcoming here. Both plays have eight characters; Béaslaí has simply Hibernicised his, turning Sir Charles Rackett into Muircheartach Ó Clúmháin, Mr Woodley into Partholán Mac Colm, Mr Drugget into Raidhrí Mac Curnáin, etc. He also moves the play from eighteenth-century England to his own twentieth-century Ireland, and changes the card game from whist to forty-five. In Murphy's work, the new husband storms out at the end, possibly ending the marriage, while in Béaslaí's version, he remains on stage, sulking but apparently unwilling to leave his wife. On the whole, however, we still have the same comic plot involving an argument between a newlywed couple about the proper strategy in a game of cards, a pointless argument that convinces Rackett / Ó Clúmháin to give his daughter to the man she loves, a man who has no interest in cards. Béaslaí often simply provides a close adaptation of speeches in the play, as he does, for example, when Sir Charles complains about having his strategy criticised. Murphy writes:

> Never was anything like her behaviour. I can pick out the very cards I had in my hand, and then 'tis as plain as the sun. – There – there – now – there – no – damn it – no – there it was – now let me see – They had four by honours and we play'd the odd trick ... Confusion! – This preposterous woman has put it all out of my head.[62]

Béaslaí's version of this speech reads: 'It would outrage anyone! I can find again every card that was in play. There they are. That's how it was – no – like that – but my mistake! – Yes, I have them now. That's how it was. They were at twenty-five and we were only at fifteen. … I'm getting confused. That confounded woman mixed me up.'[63] Béaslaí did, however, deviate from his original in one significant way, a deviation that, as Pádraig Ó Siadhail notes, is anything but an improvement: 'Whereas biting satire and painful life experience are interwoven throughout Murphy's farce, in Béaslaí's play we just have light comedy. Whereas in the English-language farce the treatment of the false values of the aristocratic class and the toadying of the middle class to those same false values are central, there is no social commentary of any kind in Béaslaí's *Cluiche Cártaí*, which gives the central place to the vapid romance of the young couple.'[64]

In the lead-up to the play's first performance by Na hAisteoirí in 1914, an anonymous writer in the *Freeman's Journal*, having noted that there was 'considerable interest' in *Cluiche Cártaí* and that its source was Murphy's *Three Weeks After Marriage*, continued: 'Piaras Béaslaí has subjected the work to considerable alteration, with a view to rendering it suitable for the Irish-speaking people of to-day, but all the essential humour of the original has been retained' (*FJ*, 20 March 1914). But neither critics nor playgoers seem to have been much troubled about the play's originality. For example, the anonymous critic for the *Irish Independent* called *Cluiche Cártaí* 'a new play', adding: 'The plot is well worked out and abounds in amusing scenes and situations while the dialogue is crisp and brilliant. "Cluiche Cártaí" is a valuable addition to the all too small stock of Gaelic drama' (*II*, 23 March 1914). The play was also welcomed warmly, with no mention of its being an adaptation, when Na hAisteoirí brought it to the 1914 Oireachtas in Killarney, where the reviewer for the *Kerry Weekly Reporter* wrote that *Cluiche Cártaí* 'proved an immense success being greeted with almost continuous laughter and applause' (*KWR*, 1 August 1914). Reviewing a 1924 production of the play by An Comhar Drámaíochta in the Abbey, 'Connla' seemed entirely unaware that the play was an adaptation, writing: 'It's a pity that Piaras Béaslaí does not give us more plays like this – without a doubt or a joke he has a talent for creative work. It's a kind of 'Taming of the Shrew', but if so, there is Gaelic humour and fun in it – humour that has a particular relation to Ireland and to Gaels' (*FJ*, 12 February 1924).[65]

The play remained in the Gaelic repertoire throughout the 1920s and '30s. Indeed, in a review of An Comhar's 1925 production directed by Gearóid Ó Lochlainn, 'Oscar' declared: 'It's not long until we will know the characters in this play as well as we used to know those in the "Eloquent Dempsey"' (*FL*, 14 November 1925).[66] In addition to this 1925 revival, other performances of *Cluiche Cártaí* include those by Na hAisteoirí in Bandon, Macroom and Inchigeela, County Cork, in July 1914 on their way to the Oireachtas in Killarney; by the Keating players in the Rotunda in 1920 (*FJ*, 4 August 1920); by the students of a summer school in Bray, County Wicklow, in 1921 (*FJ*, 28 July 1921); by An Comhar in the Abbey in 1924, with Ó Lochlainn directing (*IS*, 23 February 1924); by An Comhar, directed by Béaslaí in the Peacock in 1930 (*IT*, 13 January 1930);[67] by the Keating players in the AOH Hall in Dublin in 1934 (*SI*, 13 May 1934); by An Comhar, with Cathal Ó Ceallaigh directing, in the Peacock the same year (*IP*, 20 November 1934); and by Limerick's An Comhar Drámaíochta in that city in 1935 (*LL*, 26 October 1935). Thereafter, the play seems to have silently slipped from the repertoire.

Béaslaí's next play, *An Sgaothaire* (The Braggart), won first prize for 'a long play suitable for the people of the Gaeltacht' (*dráma fada oiriúnach do mhuintir na Gaeltachta*) at the 1914 Oireachtas[68] and had its first performance by Na hAisteoirí at the Foresters' Hall in Dublin in May 1915, with Béaslaí in all likelihood directing. While the Oireachtas prize might suggest that *An Sgaothaire* was an entirely original play, it was actually another adaptation. In his preface to *An Sgaothaire agus Cúig Drámaí Eile* (1929), Béaslaí wrote that he had gotten 'the basic idea' (*an bun smaoineamh*) from a play by David Garrick that was itself based on *Le menteur* by Pierre Corneille, pointing out that as Garrick had made 'almost a new play' (*dráma nua, beagnach*) of Corneille's work, he himself had done the same with Garrick's. However, Pádraig Ó Siadhail has shown that Béaslaí was mistaken here, that Garrick never wrote such a play, and that Béaslaí's actual source was *The Lyar* (1762), Samuel Foote's adaptation of *Le menteur*.[69] He took considerably more liberties with his source here than he had in his previous adaptations. As was his usual practice, he

Hibernicised both settings and characters, but in *An Sgaothaire* he also provided several explicit references to Irish life. Thus, when his protagonist needs an excuse in case his father sees him in Killarney rather than at his studies in University College Cork, his plan is to claim he has come to Kerry with a professor to work on his Irish. In Foote's play, the protagonist's friend pretends to be a French nobleman and there is no real explanation for why the young braggart left Oxford. Among the main character's boasts in *An Sgaothaire* is that he served as an adviser to the Spanish army and took part in the Easter rising. Foote has his self-proclaimed hero boast that he fought at Québec in the seven years' war and that 'Cherokees, Catabaws, with all the Aws and Ees of the continent, have felt the force of my arms'.[70] On the whole, however, Béaslaí seems not to have been up to the challenge presented by his original, an original that was perhaps a poor choice in the first place. It is, for example, difficult to imagine what the Gaeltacht audience for whom the Oireachtas adjudicators deemed the play appropriate would have thought had Béaslaí's Éibhlís Pléimionn, a clever and mischievous enough young woman, but ultimately one of impeccable Gaelic respectability, resembled more closely the character on which she was based, Foote's devious Miss Grantam, with her ability to toy with the affections of several suitors simultaneously. Indeed, Béaslaí revises his original throughout, eliminating all references to the social complexities of eighteenth-century London and Foote's satiric take on them, while reducing the English playwright's often cynical wit to something considerably more genial, a kind of humour that would neither challenge nor offend the least sophisticated playgoer. Of course, these changes enabled him to create in *An Sgaothaire* just the sort of simple, humorous, linguistically accessible play that he felt was appropriate for the audiences Na hAisteoirí hoped to attract at that time.

In Béaslaí's play, the *sgaothaire* Brian and his friend Conall arrive in Killarney, where Brian has come to rest from the university studies to which he devotes very little of his time anyway. Conall neatly sums up his friend's greatest failing: 'You have polished speech and a quick mind, and you have an excellent sense of humour ... But the world would not satisfy you if you could not tell amazing stories to widen the eyes of the listeners.'[71] We soon see him in action with Éíbhlís and Méidhbhín, as he claims to have won fame as a war-hero, dancing champion and poet, though when he recites one of his compositions, Éibhlís immediately recognises it as a poem by Eoghan Ruadh Ó Súilleabháin. Brian is unfazed: 'Look at that now. Eoghan Ruadh and myself had the same thoughts. That sort of thing happens sometimes.'[72] Not surprisingly, the young women see through him, although Éibhlís remains interested in him.

When his father comes to Killarney and announces that he has found him a wife, Brian at once responds that he already has one in Cork, a sickly woman unable to leave that city to meet his father. Exasperated by all his lies, his father, Éibhlís and another of Éíbhlís' suitors decide to turn the tables on him, and at the end of the play he is confronted by both of the young women with whom he has flirted as well as another claiming to be his wife. When an exasperated Conall finally refuses to help him avoid the consequences of his boasting, there is nothing left for him to do but rush off stage to the laughter of the other characters.

Both critics and audiences seem to have accepted *An Sgaothaire* on its own humble terms. Writing of a production of the play by the Keating branch in 1920, the reviewer for the *Freeman's Journal* called it 'perhaps the best of Mr. Béaslaí's short plays' and reported that it 'kept the large audience in roars of laughter from start to finish' (*FJ*, 5 August 1920). In his review of a 1926 production by An Comhar Drámaíochta in the Abbey, an anonymous critic for *The Irish Times* mistakenly called *An Sgaothaire* 'an original three-act comedy' and wrote that it 'gave great delight last night' (*IT*, 2 November 1926). The play does not, however, seem to have been as popular as Béaslaí's other comedies during this period, at least if we judge from the number of revivals. Apart from the 1920 production by the Keating players and those by An Comhar in the Abbey in 1925 and '26, the only other productions of *An Sgaothaire* I have found were by the Waterford Gaelic Players in 1931 (*CE*, 5 May 1931) and by the students of Coláiste Íde in Dingle at a one-act play festival in Beaufort, County Kerry, in 1979 (*K*, 30 November 1979). Radio Éireann also broadcast it in October 1945 (*BH*, 29 September 1945).

Fear na Milliún Púnt (The Millionaire) was an original work that won first prize for a one-act play at the 1915 Oireachtas[73] and had its initial performance by Na hAisteoirí in the Abbey in November 1915. Once again, Béaslaí was probably the director. In an otherwise rather odd review, the critic for *An Claidheamh Soluis* wrote, quite correctly: 'Piaras

Béaslaí is learning the dramatist's craft.' However, he then went on to state, 'This little play is a droll bit of fun', but 'there is no danger in the play, and that lessens the comedy. The greater the danger, the greater the comedy' (*ACS*, 13 November 1915).[74] The play never seems to have attracted much attention from reviewers. Thus, when the Keating players performed it under the auspices of An Comhar in the Abbey in 1937, the critic for *The Irish Press* simply stated: 'As for the first piece "Fear na Milliún Púnt", I don't have much to say. It wasn't half as good as the second piece' [Gearóid's Ó Lochlainn's *Na Gadaithe*] (*IP*, 10 February 1937).[75]

The comic premise on which this entire play is based is that Liam Ó Súilleabháin, an American millionaire born in Clonakilty, County Cork, is rumoured to be in the vicinity of Inchigeela, County Cork, and the local people are eager to make his acquaintance. They are not, however, motivated solely or even mostly by traditional hospitality. A servant doubtless speaks for all or most of them when she declares: 'If Liam Ó Súilleabháin happens to come this way it would be well for us to keep an eye out. If he settles down in Inchigeela, I promise you that we will have a great time with the million pounds. What good is it for a person to be a Yank with a million pounds if he doesn't scatter the money extravagantly.'[76] A pair of students from Coláiste na Mumhan are in Inchigeela, where one of them hopes to meet his girlfriend. When they notice the servant eavesdropping, they pretend to be wealthy American tourists, and, predictably enough, are at once assumed to be the visiting millionaire and his friend.[77] Moreover, when one of the students is heard proposing to his sweetheart, the people of the town are delighted that a millionaire plans to make an Inchigeela woman his wife, with one of them seeing an excellent opportunity for gain: 'Wouldn't it be right for us to have a celebration. He will scatter the money – to drink his health!'[78] The locals cannot be convinced that he is not the millionaire, the confusion is never resolved, and the play ends with the people of Inchigeela cheering loudly for the 'American' and his Inchigeela spouse.

Fear na Milliún Púnt is a trivial play even by the standard of Béaslaí's comedies, but its simple plot and easy humour gave it some appeal for contemporary theatre groups and audiences. Thus, Na hAisteoirí revived it immediately in the Rotunda in December 1915, only a month after its premiere (*FJ*, 21 December 1915). Other productions include those by the Cork branch of the Gaelic League in Cork City Hall for the 1919 Oireachtas (*FJ*, 5 August 1919); by An Comhar Drámaíochta in the Abbey, with Gearóid Ó Lochlainn directing, in February 1927 (*II*, 8 February 1927); by students from the School of Domestic Economy in Kilmacud, Dublin, in March 1930 (*II*, 31 March 1930); by the Gaelic drama group at University College Galway, at Feis Chonnacht in May 1931 (*II*, 16 May 1931); and, directed by Diarmuid Ó hAlmhain, by the Keating players, under the auspices of An Comhar, in the Peacock in February 1937 (*IP*, 20 February 1937).

Deeply involved in the Easter rising, the war of independence and the civil war, Béaslaí did not have another play ready for production until March 1927, when An Comhar Drámaíochta staged his one-act *Cúigeachas* (Provincialism), directed by Gearóid Ó Lochlainn in the Abbey. This play has never received its due from critics and scholars, who in general have seen it as 'an amusing squib', as did 'E.C.' in his review of the first production for *The Irish Statesman* (*IS*, 16 April 1927), or have regarded it as merely a short work to fill out a programme, as did the writer of a brief piece announcing the following year that An Comhar would include it on the bill with Micheál Ó Siochfhradha's three-act historical tragedy *An Ball Dubh* (The Black Spot) (*IT*, 3 March 1928). Most recently, Pádraig Ó Siadhail has written in *An Béaslaíoch*: 'It is difficult to see *Cúigeachas* as a step forward in Béaslaí's writing.' With regard to dramatic technique, Ó Siadhail is entirely correct. *Cúigeachas* is another of Béaslaí's simple comedies in which he works out the farcical consequences of a single concept. But, as Ó Siadhail himself points out: 'Unlike in the early comedies, Béaslaí had a message to drive home and he had to proclaim it straight out – "I prefer any sort of Irish to English. It's not (Donegal) Irish or (Connacht) Irish or (Munster) Irish that is the enemy – but English."'[79]

The plot of the play could not be more straightforward. Domhnall Ó Gríofa, a merchant in Tralee, County Kerry, is a bigoted partisan of all things Munster, and especially of Munster Irish. He carries this obsession to the point of refusing to accept any suitor for his daughter who is not of Munster birth. As a result, her would-be fiancé, who was born in Connacht, must pretend to be from County Clare, and he extravagantly imitates the Munster dialect when he speaks with her father. Predictably, Ó Gríofa finds at the end of the play that the young man was born on the wrong side of the border between County Clare in Munster and County Galway in Connacht – as was he himself. Despite the play's light-hearted approach to the subject, provincial, particularly linguistic, chauvinism was a real problem in the Gaelic revival from the beginning until well into the 1940s and even beyond. Séamus Ó Grianna ('Máire'), Béaslaí's native-speaking adversary from the Donegal Gaeltacht, would even go so far as to say that Munster Irish and Donegal Irish were not a single language and that speakers of the southern dialect were trying to kill the Irish language (*FL*, 21 February 1925; *Ultach*, February 1925, p. 1). *Cúigeachas* was, then, Béaslaí's comic intervention in a major cultural debate, and we should acknowledge that it took some nerve for a learner of the language from Liverpool to take as his theme, even in a modest farce, the serious consequences of linguistic chauvinism for a language facing the threat of a medium as powerful as English.

Cúigeachas deserves to be better known, but as is true of Béaslaí's plays in general, with the demise of An Comhar Drámaíochta as an independent body, it dropped out of the Gaelic repertoire. Among revivals in the decade and a half after its first production were those by An Comhar at the Abbey in 1928 (*II*, 5 March 1928); by the students of Dublin's Coláiste Mhuire at the Schools Drama Festival in 1935 (*IP*, 9 April 1935); by the Waterford Dramatic Class at a concert in the city's Gaelic League Hall in 1939, a concert broadcast over Radio Éireann (*II*, 5 June 1939); and by a company of actors from Enniskillen, County Fermanagh, at the All-Irish Drama Festival in Dungannon, County Tyrone, in 1959 (*FH*, 7 March 1959).[80] The play had a longer life on the airwaves than it did on stage. Other Radio Éireann broadcasts of *Cúigeachas* were in October 1954 (*CE*, 6 October 1954); February 1959 (*IP*, 3 February 1959); September 1969 (*AC*, 26 September 1969); and December 1976 (*II*, 18 December 1976).

Béaslaí again used contemporary or near contemporary issues – in this case the hunt for wanted IRA men in the streets of Dublin during the war of independence – to give an edge to an otherwise harmless comedy in *An Fear as Buenos Aires* (The Man from Buenos Aires), first performed by An Comhar Drámaíochta in the Abbey in January 1928, with Gearóid Ó Lochlainn directing. By now, a pattern seems to have established itself with regard to Béaslaí's one-act comedies. Audiences liked them, while critics largely ignored them, perhaps feeling that each one was, in the words of 'T. Ó R.' in his review of the first production of *An Fear as Buenos Aires*, just 'a new and clever comedy along familiar lines' (*IS*, 14 January 1928). Actually, however, the play is an odd one given that Béaslaí knew from personal experience that life on the run was no laughing matter. Moreover, while the play was set during the war of independence, by 1927 an audience might identify the IRA man with the diehard republicans whose continued opposition to the Irish Free State Béaslaí deplored. Nevertheless, if audiences managed to ignore such contemporary resonances – and in all likelihood they probably did – they could have found this comedy enjoyable escapist entertainment. A gunman, Flann Ó Rónáin, escapes detectives by entering the house of Pilib Móinvial, a rich businessman who is expecting a visitor from Argentina whom he has never met. A sympathetic maid explains the situation to Ó Rónáin and suggests he assume the identity of the visitor, Santiago Ó Briain. Having done so, he finds himself in a fix when he meets the owner of the house, since he neither speaks Spanish nor has any idea what business affairs he has supposedly come to Ireland to discuss. Checking the window and seeing the detectives still searching for him, he is forced to stall for time, pretending to be sick and introducing irrelevant topics into his conversation with Móinvial, to Móinvial's great annoyance. Eventually, informed by the maid that the detectives have left, he is about to depart when the real Santiago Ó Briain arrives. Enraged, the Argentinian attempts to attack him, at which point Flann, claiming Santiago is a mortal enemy from Argentina he has mentioned to Móinvial, runs out of the house, supposedly to fetch the police.

An Fear as Buenos Aires is an entirely competent little comedy, but again, like Béaslaí's other one-act plays for An Comhar Drámaíochta, it was not destined to retain its original appeal, and there were only rare revivals, even in the 1920s and '30s. Among those productions were those by An Comhar, directed by Micheál Mac Liammóir, in the Gate theatre in May 1931; by students of Dublin's Scoil Bhríde in the drama competitions of the 1932 Oireachtas in Dublin (*IT*, 3 November 1932); by students at Maynooth in 1943 (*IMN*, 1946, p. 86); and by students from Carnmore at Féile Scoildrámaíocht na Gaillimhe in 1965 (*CT*, 5 March 1965). The play was also broadcast over Radio Éireann in February 1955 (*IP*, 16 February 1955).

Perhaps fed up with writing formulaic comedies to little serious acclaim, or maybe hopeful that An Comhar Drámaíochta had finally created an audience capable of appreciating more sophisticated fare, Béaslaí in 1928 returned after two decades to the kind of ambition that had inspired *Cormac na Coille*. At any rate, only four weeks after *An Fear as Buenos Aires* had its premiere, An Comhar presented a very different kind of play by Béaslaí in the Abbey,[81] a play that won the gold medal in the Irish-language drama competition at the 1928 Aonach Tailteann. In anticipation of the opening of this play, a writer in *The Irish Times* informed would-be audience members that *An Danar* would be 'a striking departure from the usual type of drama with which Gaelic playgoers are familiar', and that while 'Piaras Béaslaí has been hitherto chiefly known as a writer of light comedies', the focus in his new play would be 'rather psychological than historical, being concerned with the clash of conflicting temperaments, creeds and philosophies of life in a semi-barbaric age' (*IT*, 4 February 1928). The anonymous critic for the *Irish Independent* began his review by stating that 'players and playwright were on trial last night', for *An Danar* was not 'one of those clever humorous short plays on which [Béaslaí's] reputation as the foremost Gaelic dramatist has been built up'. Obviously, this writer was impressed with what Béaslaí had accomplished: '"An Danar" has in it all the essentials of great drama: the clash of ideas, the development of dramatic situation, and, above all, beautiful poetic rhythmic language to which it was a delight to listen.' In particular, he felt that 'Piaras Béaslaí makes these figures of Danish Dublin in the tenth century interpret the emotions and feelings of people of our own day' (*II*, 7 February 1928).[82] Complimenting Béaslaí for keeping the battle scenes off-stage, 'T. Ó R.' declared: 'In the midst of all this clash of war, the quiet tone of the actual scenes was very effective and restraining. This, with the help of a touch of cynical humour and general good craftsmanship, navigated the shoals of philosophical discussions' (*IS*, 11 February 1928). Reviewing a 1933 revival of the play for *The Irish Press*, 'C. Ua D.' (Cearbhall Ua Dálaigh) wrote: 'Back and forth go the people of the drama: every one as he pleases, so that we can see clearly that they are individuals, every one of them. It is their dialogue that most revealed their qualities to us, and that, of course, left the play short of action from time to time. But despite all that it was fine, polished, poetic dialogue that was not reluctant to discuss the hard questions of philosophy in detail' (*IP*, 2 May 1933).[83]

In his brief 'Réamh-Rádh' to *An Danar* in the text of the play published by An Gúm in 1929, Béaslaí tells us that the 'original idea' (*bun-smaoineamh*) for the play came to him when he was incarcerated in Lewes Prison in 1917, but that he did not finally write *An Danar* until 1927. Moreover, the play did not first come to him in Irish but rather in English, as a work to be called 'The Dragon'. The outline of this work had existed as early as the summer of 1924, when he wrote:

> Well, what is the idea? It is that Amlaf cannot rest in peace and comfort. He seeks glory and beauty in his life & fails. Where he might have had happiness he brings only misery & death, yet he dies proclaiming he was right, that the only life worth having is a strife [*sic*] for the prize of your life. In a sense it is Browning's idea seen from opposite [*sic*] angle:
>
> Let a man contend to the uttermost
> For his Life's fixed prize, be it what you will.[84]

But while he originally envisioned *An Danar* as a play of ideas, an ambition noted by the critics cited above, he obscured his initial intention for the play when he wrote in his 'Réamh-Rádh': 'It is not, however, history or the telling of old stories that concerned me most. I just wanted a world, a time, and a place that would be suitable for the story of Olaf and Inga.'[85] *An Danar* is not, however, in any meaningful way a love story about Olaf and Inga – indeed the devout Christian and would-be nun Inga has absolutely no romantic interest in Olaf, while for him she exists as an ideal rather than a flesh and blood woman. Instead, Béaslaí's real interest was in the abstractions the two embody. As the play opens, Olaf has just returned to his native Danish Dublin after a turbulent but ultimately unsatisfying life as a warrior. He is accompanied on a visit to the house of his old friend Thorolf by a young admirer, the poet Harald. Life has been good to Thorolf – played in the first production of the play by Gearóid Ó Lochlainn – now that the Vikings have firmly established themselves in Irish society as traders and merchants, intermarrying with the Irish and adopting Christianity. As he tells his sister Sigrid, who longs for more excitement in her life, Thorolf, like most of the Danes in Dublin, believes that it is 'the heroes who do all the harm in this world' (*na gaisgidhigh a dheineann an díobháil ar fad ar an saoghal so*), for they are 'people who cause themselves trouble and heartscald when they have the chance to be happy' (*daoine a dheineann buairt agus sgóladh croidhe dóibh féin, agus breith acu a bheith sona*).[86] In his first conversation with Olaf, Thorolf develops this idea:

> Everyone must achieve his own share of happiness and peace in his own way. As for me, I find it the high point of comfort and satisfaction to spend my life here as a hostel keeper, providing accommodation to warriors and poets, to sailors and travellers from countries overseas. I enjoy sitting here, listening to the poems and stories.[87]

While his lifestyle infuriates Sigrid, who dismisses it as 'weak, lazy comfort' (*sóghchur leamh, leisgeamhail*), it simply baffles Olaf, who declares that 'there is something in me that would not allow me to take my ease'.[88]

Béaslaí uses their attitudes to the sea to take the measure of his characters. Olaf loves the sea: 'As for peace, there is no peace on the sea. That is a special quality it has. It is never still or corrupted as is the world ashore.'[89] Not surprisingly, Thorolf is a landsman who likes to be near but not on the ocean: 'There are many people who love the sea. Look at me, who would never go out onto the open sea, but I must build my dwelling by the sea. I find the sound of the waves near me is like music.'[90] The young Harald is afraid of the sea: 'I have no affection for the sea … The earth is my mother. But the hungry shriek of the sea terrifies me. It is an enemy to the human race – we can't control it – it has neither pity nor compassion for us.'[91]

Olaf soon meets the king's daughter, the otherworldly Inga, for whom the sea is the magnificent masterpiece of 'the King of the Elements' (*Rí na nDúl*). Inga speaks to Olaf about 'people … who seem to hear a voice calling to them – a voice that does not let them sit in peace but is eternally urging them on after a deeper, more intense joy, finer than is to be found in this life'.[92] Bewitched by her passion but altogether ignorant of its Christian source, Olaf declares: 'That is a beautiful and wonderful message you have, Daughter of the King. It's many a mystery you understand.'[93] Still, he always responds to her as a symbol rather than as a woman, and even then mistakes her for an incarnation of his philosophy rather than her own. As the first act ends, Inga wants to convert him to Christianity; Olaf wants to make himself into a man worthy to replace Christ in her life.

When the second act opens, a year has passed, during which time Olaf has become a very powerful man as head of the king's troops. Needless to say, these developments trouble those who want no part of the ancient Viking code by which Olaf lives. As Hjalmar, one of the people thus troubled, states: 'We had a quiet and decent life until he came into our midst. We had our own ways to manage our affairs, but life has changed now.'[94] Hjalmar is, however, convinced that Olaf will ultimately fail to win over the people, particularly 'the most important people' (*na daoine is mó tábhacht*): 'They have no liking for turmoil or for these new efforts. They want a quiet, satisfied life. They have no trust in Olaf. They feel that he is a reckless and violent man who will lead them into disaster.'[95] Of course, that kind of man is unlikely to care much about the opinions of others, above all those of people for whom he has only contempt. Olaf is now a man with a mission, to awaken to their true destiny people he sees as 'lazy, sluggish, cowardly' (*leisgeamhail, támáilte, meata*), people who have rejected their own heritage to accept the culture of the Irish.[96] And he owes his new sense of purpose and overweening confidence to Inga:

> What was I when I met her in Thorolf's house but an insignificant man, ignored by everyone, without support, without wealth, without a direction or a goal in life, sick of myself. Here I am now the strongest and most powerful and commanding man in Dublin … Inga caused that; it is she who put the courage and the spirit in me.[97]

Yet, when Harald asks Olaf whether he has spoken with her since their first meeting, Olaf replies: 'I have not. I avoided her. I prefer to wait until I am able to speak with her forthrightly.'[98] He shares with Harald his glorious vision of the future he will create for the people of Dublin – whether those people themselves want that kind of future or not. When Harald questions whether this vision can be realised, Olaf responds: 'A person can get anything if only he believes he can. It is a matter of belief.'[99] Again, Inga tries to convert him to Christianity, telling him, 'There is a way to raise yourself so that you will be the equal of any Christian alive … I can show you an activity higher and more noble than anything you yourself planned.'[100] But by this point he is blind to any vision but his own: 'You're right. You are my guide on the way to glory. The look in your eyes and the few words you spoke to me last year made a great chieftain out of a poor, bitter wanderer.'[101] As the second act ends, Olaf is amazed to find he has been defeated by 'the fools and the cowards' (*na hamadáin agus na meatacháin*).

The third act of the play, set a fortnight later, begins with Thorolf praising the benefits of peace that enable him 'to live in a fine place with decent friends and beautiful things around me' (*maireachtaint i n-áit bhreágh agus cáirde cneasta agus nithe áille timcheall orm*), able 'to sit by a fire and shorten the day with songs and stories' (*suidhe cois teineadh agus an lá a ghiorrú le ceolta is sgeulta*).[102] To Sigrid's fervent defence of 'the life of Olaf, a vital, vigorous, active life' (*saoghal Olaf, saoghal beódha, bíodhgach, gníomhach*), Thorolf replies bluntly: 'It is the likes of Olaf and their aspirations and their foolish dreaming that cause life's trouble and hardship. Whether they succeed or fail, nothing comes of their great activity but slaughter and destruction, devastation and poverty.'[103] Significantly, among the disasters he accuses Olaf and his ilk of causing is 'civil war' (*cogadh bráthar*). Into this domestic scene between Thorolf and his sister bursts the hunted Olaf, still clinging to his now thoroughly discredited fanaticism:

> A person is better for having some belief that will overcome the fear of death. I made a strong attempt to achieve for myself the highest power, the finest beauty, the greatest good. It is the business of everyone to put some goal before himself and to do his utmost to achieve it. I did not succeed, but that does not matter. The benefit is not in the victory but in the fight.[104]

The triumph of failure with a vengeance! It is no wonder that Olaf cannot even understand Thorolf's argument: 'Moderation is the best virtue for a person – to be satisfied with the good he can achieve.'[105]

Olaf's desperate plan is now to seize and carry off Inga, a plan thwarted by the arrival of the king's soldiers and the arrest of Olaf and Harald, who has fallen entirely under Olaf's influence. Once more Olaf expresses his devotion to Inga, and once more he is incapable of understanding her plea that he pray for forgiveness, instead telling her: 'The part of me that will not die will reach you. My soul is yours. I don't regret anything. We are not separated from each other forever.'[106] As Olaf is led away for execution, Harald declares his pride in joining him on the scaffold: 'A person is better for having something or someone he thinks it worthwhile to die for.'[107] After these high heroics, the responses of the victors are anticlimactic at best. Thorolf repeats his condemnation of the extremists – saints and warriors – who bring misery to the world, while Inga, in the final speech in the play, conventionally seeks God's mercy for the souls of Olaf and Harald. In a sly touch that echoes that play of Synge's he had protested twenty years earlier, Béaslaí has Hjalmar channel Shawn Keogh in his smug triumph: 'It is a good thing that we are done with that mad plotter. We will have the old quiet life from now on, as it used to be before Olaf interfered with us.'[108]

In his discussion of *An Danar* in *An Béaslaíoch*, Pádraig Ó Siadhail calls the play 'an interesting and ambitious work' (*saothar spéisiúil uaillmhianach*) before providing a list of some of its serious flaws and contradictions. In particular, he calls attention to the fact that Inga never really comes alive, no small problem if Béaslaí wants us to read the play primarily as a love story with her as the heroine. Ó Siadhail also, however, suggests a far more interesting way of interpreting the play. He points out that a scene at the beginning of Act III involving Sigrid, Thorolf, Olaf and Harald could be seen as 'the story of the Split and the Civil War in a nutshell' (*gearrinsint ar an Scoilt agus an Cogadh Cathartha*). Ó Siadhail suggests that Sigrid could represent the female members of the Dáil, women like Mary MacSwiney, who opposed the Anglo-Irish treaty; Thorolf, those in favour of the treaty; Olaf, the diehard republicans; Harald, 'the young men deceived by the likes of de Valera (*na fir óga a bhí meallta ag leithéid de Valera*);[109] with Inga representing 'the prize of the Republic' (*duais na Poblachta*). Although Inga seems more a 'sky woman' (*spéirbhean*) for Olaf, his own version of Caitlín Ní Uallacháin, there is much to be said for Ó Siadhail's reading, especially when one remembers that among the evils Thorolf says men like Olaf bring on the world is 'civil war' (*cogadh bráthar*). Moreover, the civil war split haunts the whole play in its depiction of the struggle between all-or-nothing extremists and those willing to accept the realities with which they are faced.[110] Interesting here, of course, is that Béaslaí, a committed supporter of the treaty, gives many of the most stirring lines to Olaf, the kind of man incapable of the compromises Béaslaí himself made. In addition, one could argue that Olaf is no more a mad extremist than are Cormac na Coille and Astronár, the protagonists of Béaslaí's first play and his only novel respectively. It is, however, clear from notes he made in 1927 that he had given a great deal of thought to this question and concluded that while each of these men is 'a rough, warlike, fiery man dissatisfied with things and striving for his aims through war & revolution', and each 'deceives himself, cherishes illusions', there is one great difference: 'The Dane is a mature man while Cormac & Astronár are boys.'[111] In effect, Béaslaí seems to be saying that Olaf should have known better, as should de Valera and those who brought civil war on the country. Thorolf is the voice of both Béaslaí and reason, but he was too honest a playwright and had agonised too much over these questions not to know that calls to heroism in the face of reason can be profoundly powerful – he had answered such calls himself – but that in the end, unless tempered by mature reflection, they can only bring destruction and the deep disillusionment he saw, and experienced, in post-civil war Ireland.

An Danar is Béaslaí's best play and one of the finest plays written in Irish from the start of the revival until the 1940s. Moreover, it had enough appeal for contemporary audiences to be revived by An Comhar *Drámaíochta* in the Abbey in February 1929, just a year after its premiere (*II*, 5 February 1929) and again, with Mac Liammóir directing, at the Gate in May 1933 (*II*, 2 May 1933). We also know that writing the play brought Béaslaí great – and rare – satisfaction, as he noted in his diary: 'The best part of my life was the thirties [i.e. his thirties, between 1911 and 1921]. The close of the thirties was the end of my happiness … Only at one period since did I attain happiness and peace of mind – in the spring and summer of 1927 – the time when I wrote *An Danar*.'[112] It was doubtless his sense of achievement and the relative success of the play that gave him the confidence and energy to immediately write another full-length historical drama for production by An Comhar.

Although *An Bhean Chródha* (The Brave Woman) had its first performance in the Abbey in April 1929, with Pól Ó Fearghail directing,[113] the play had, according to Béaslaí's 'Réamh-Rádh' to the published text, been 'alive in my mind for many years' (*ar marthain im aigne le mórán bliadhanta*). Indeed, he tells us that the play had its origin in a story he had read as a boy about the fighting between Covenanters and Royalists in seventeenth-century Scotland, and that 'that thought took a hold of me and stuck with me over the long years. The play grew and matured in my mind. Máiréad and Domhnall and the Colonel appeared to me and gradually revealed to me their traits and qualities. I have known them for so long that it is hard for me to believe that it is I myself who created them.'[114] Béaslaí also refers in the preface to the story of the eighteenth-century Irish rebel and rapparee Domhnall Ó Caoimh and his treacherous lover Máiréad Ní Cheallaigh, acknowledging that it must have left 'a mark on my mind' (*rian ar m'aigne*) despite the fact that Ní Cheallaigh's greed has nothing in common with the motives of his own Máiréad de Barra.

Critics were less taken with this play than they had been with *An Danar*. Writing in *The Irish Statesman*, Seán Beaumont declared:

> The dialogue is moulded with care and skill, but the play is overloaded with it. While the author shows evidence of a certain faculty for projecting himself into that past of which poets have sung so often, his methods for attaining conflict of passion are all well-worn, and, on the whole – to judge him severely – it may be said that he has added but little to his reputation (*IS*, 13 April 1929).

'D. Mac C.' was blunter in his review in *The Nation*: 'The play is nowhere near as good as "An Danar"' (*Nation*, 13 April 1929).[115] In *The Star*, 'Scrúdóir' was scathing, writing that the play's

> long prose passages ... bored the audience on Wednesday night to such an extent that they forgot to call 'Ughdar!' (Author) on the drop of the final curtain. The opening act was much too slow and explanatory, and even in the remaining acts there was a surfeit of verbosity which at times was not very coherent or intelligible (*Star*, 13 April 1929).

On the other hand, reviewing the 1931 revival at the Gate, the anonymous critic for *The Irish Times* pointed out that while 'Mr. Béaslaí deals with his story in a rather conventional manner reminiscent of the middle nineteenth century … he does succeed, after the first act, in making his story interesting and getting life into his characters'. As a result, 'he gets near enough to great drama to be counted amongst playwrights who have mastered the technique of the stage, and that itself is an achievement' (*IT*, 27 January 1931). More enthusiastic was the anonymous critic who, in a review of the 1943 revival at the Abbey, declared of the play that 'its place amongst the best original pieces that have been done on the stage in Irish is secure' (*IT*, 1 February 1943).

Béaslaí himself considered *An Bhean Chródha* a play of ideas, writing in his 'Réamh-Rádh' to the published text:

> The basic cause of this tragedy is the desires that do not achieve their natural satisfaction, the desires that a person himself won't understand, that lure him onto the path of destruction. It relates to the 'subconscious' … Perhaps there is nothing in this whole play but a distorted vision. Perhaps Máiréad – and Domhnall – were a bit out of their minds.[116]

For Cearbhall Ua Dálaigh, who reviewed the 1931 revival for *An Phoblacht*, the ideas overwhelmed the drama in the play. Having acknowledged that Béaslaí was a writer 'given to ideas' (*tugtha dos na smaointe*), Ua Dálaigh wrote that those ideas would have been better dealt with 'in a philosophical treatise about them as Kant would discuss the like, not to mention Thomas Aquinas' (*i dtráchtas feallsamhnachta féibh mar do phléidhfeadh Kant a leithéid nó Tomás d'Aquin, dá luadhfainn é*). For Ua Dálaigh the play was full of 'great stretches of talk with no action' (*sraitheanna móra cainnte gan puinn gníomha*), a fault he found forgivable in a playwright like Shaw, but not in Béaslaí. *An Bhean Chródha* ultimately left Ua Dálaigh 'unsatisfied and uneasy' (*gan a bheith sásta socair*), feeling that only 'the odd clever person who spent his life with the difficult problems of philosophy' (*an corrdhuine cliste do chaith a shaoghal le cruadh fhadhbaibh na feallsamhnachta*) could appreciate and enjoy the play (*Poblacht*, 31 January 1931). Actually, while there are significant thematic similarities between *An Danar* and *An Bhean Chródha*, in *An Danar* Béaslaí, despite his own view of the play as a love story, largely sacrifices everything even resembling romance to the development of his major psychological and political themes, whereas in

An Bhean Chródha the love plot in the end takes precedence, leaving the larger philosophical concerns of the play inadequately resolved.

The eponymous protagonist of *An Bhean Chródha* is Máiréad de Barra, the daughter of a Catholic Irish father and a rebellious Ascendancy Protestant mother. As the play opens, she is staying in the home of Colonel Hungarford near Bandon, County Cork. Máiréad is, in the words of Colonel Hungarford's wife Rós, 'a wild, restless girl' (*cailín fiadhan, mhí-shuaimhneach*) with 'some strange strain in her – most likely the heritage of the Anglo-Irish' (*stradhain ait éigin innti – dúchas an Ghaill-Ghaedhil is dócha*).[117] Having been raised by a strict Protestant aunt in Cork city, Máiréad feels life has always passed her by, and she is, as she tells her friend Agata, eager for new adventures: 'Since I left my aunt's house I am mad to make the most of the little time of freedom. I am tired of looking out the window. O Agata, I think my whole life has been nothing but – looking out the window.'[118] Early in the play, Máiréad presents herself as a woman of action, eager to follow the example of the biblical Judith, who deceived and decapitated Holofernes, the great enemy of her people. To the timid Agata, she declares: 'Wouldn't it be worth risking death to do a great noble deed like that?'[119] And her reading of the Judith story could be seen as unabashedly feminist:

> The meaning I take from it is that – that the marvellous world God created and this drab, cowardly world controlled by men are not the same – that there are great deeds and marvels on the other side of the border wall that customs and rules have put around us – that it is possible to go over that wall – to do an extraordinary, glorious deed – a deed that would fill the heart with joy and terror –[120]

Soon that desire to perform 'a wonderful, glorious deed' (*gníomh éachtach, glórmhar*) awakens her interest in Domhnall Ó Mathghamhna, who had killed her step-brother in a fight in self-defence and who is now 'living on the bare mountains like a wild animal and the soldiers hunting him' (*na chomhnuidhe ar na cnocaibh loma mar a bheadh beithidheach allta, agus na saighdiúirí dá fhiadhach*).[121] For the rest of the play she will struggle to reconcile her attraction for the rapparee with her belief that it is her duty to stand by her own people and to avenge her step-brother.

At this point in the play, we get to meet some of those who are hunting Domhnall and are quickly made aware of the deep class and cultural divisions within the Protestant population in Cork. In many ways, the most interesting character in the play is Colonel Hungarford, an interest most likely heightened for the original audience by the fact that the role was played by the gifted Gearóid Ó Lochlainn. Béaslaí's stage directions, the most detailed in any of his published plays, make clear that the colonel is not an ignorant anti-Catholic bigot, but rather a mordant, cynical realist:

> He was in the English court (of the second Charles) for a long time and he spent a while in the court of 'le Grand Monarque'. He has a sceptical mind, with no strong opinions about religion or politics, with no trust in zeal or fervour, but he is patient and tolerant of the opinions of other people. He scorns the narrow-mindedness and the intolerance of the people he deals with, though he lets on to be of one mind with them, but it is obvious that he doesn't care whether they believe that or not. He satisfies his disposition by mocking them – mockery that they do not underestand.[122]

Unlike the virulently anti-Gaelic and anti-Catholic upstart militiamen with whom he has to deal, Hungarford feels a deep identification with Ireland as his own native land: 'It is true that I know this district. I was born and raised in it, and my offspring are firmly rooted in the soil of the country. I spent years abroad, and the Gaels have no affection for me because I sided with their enemies – with God's cause, I mean to say – but I understand them better than any foreign captain, or any butcher from London ...'[123] Moreover, this understanding has led him to respect Ó Mathghamhna, whom he describes as 'a man of noble blood, who got an education in France and a good upbringing' (*fear go bhfuil braon uasal ann, do fuair oideachas san bhFrainnc agus oileamhaint mhaith*) and who could have had 'a career and fame in the French Army if he had shown there half the courage or half the cleverness he uses when he is evading us' (*réim is clú i nArm na Frainnce dá gcuireadh sé i bhfeidhm annsan leath an mhisnigh nó leath an ghliocais a chleachtann sé agus é ag teicheadh uainn-ne*).[124]

Yet, while he feels that it would be a shame for a man like Ó Mathghamhna to be captured by the likes of his own Protestant militiamen, Hungarford is determined that he be taken: 'I pity him. I would like to catch him, but I have no enmity towards him. There is nobility in him – and a corresponding courage – but the poor man is out of his mind. He is making things very hard for us. He must be captured.'[125] In a conversation with Máiréad, Hungarford sounds much like Thorolf in *An Danar*: 'I do not want to persecute my fellow human beings for the love of God. I only take life as it is, and yield to the truth. I just want my own wellbeing without harm to anyone else, in this unfortunate turmoil in Ireland between mad, superstitious tribes.'[126] But unlike Thorolf, Hungarford must actively protect his colonial prerogatives and maintain the peace he claims to desire. A self-serving realpolitik guides his actions throughout the play. Thus, his understanding of 'this unfortunate turmoil in Ireland' is brutally unsentimental:

> On this side are Bateman and Beastún and others like them – and on the other side are Quick-Tempered Tadhg and Mad Diarmuid. I had to take one side or the other – and I took the side that looked like it meant business. Tadhg and Diarmuid have been crushed. There is peace in the country again. Everyone is better off to leave things like that, and not to incite any more conflict.[127]

In his mind, failure to see the logic of his choice is not merely misguided; it is mad, and that is why Ó Mathghamhna must be eliminated.

Yet, when we meet Ó Mathghamhna we soon see that he is also very much a realist. It is just that his is a different reality. Like Hungarford, he feels a rooted love for his native place, though in his case the roots go far deeper than do those of Hungarford. Like Hungarford, he is also a complex and troubled man. Once again, Béaslaí's stage directions are revealing: 'He represses the pride, the anger and the passion that are in his heart. He rarely gives them free rein, but sometimes a fit of madness suddenly comes over him. A hard man to understand, for he does not understand his own mind, nor does he reveal what of it he does understand.'[128] In a scene with a priest and poet that parallels that between Hungarford and the Protestant militiamen, Ó Mathghamhna shows a subtle understanding of his own situation and that of his people and their culture. The poet is obsessed with the aristocratic past in which poets enjoyed high status and generous patronage, and he has nothing but contempt for 'the churls – the inferior people' (*na bodaigh – na daorchlanna*).[129] The priest's main concern is predictably the Catholic Church, and he therefore sees Hungarford in purely sectarian terms as 'the heretic, the atheist, the destroyer, the plunderer of the Church' (*an t-eiriceach, an t-ainchreidmheach, an léirsgriosadóir, creachadóir na hEaglaise*).[130] Ó Mathghamhna, like Hungarford, has come to terms with the world as it is, fully aware what that means for his own place in it:

> More than anything else, what I would like best would be to expel the fat, ugly Foreigners from the land of my ancestors with the clash of swords. But I know I cannot do that. All I can do is to act in opposition to them – and I do so. I am always tormenting and plundering them, and then to pass the time I play the flute or I discuss poetry with the priest, or – I make small talk with the women.[131]

In effect, he is a dilettante, painfully aware of what the realities of eighteenth-century Ireland have done to his earlier dreams: 'I once thought I would be a great chieftain in the war between the Gaels and the Foreigners, slaughtering and destroying the louts – winning victory and a military career abroad, over in France or Spain …' None of these things have ever happened or ever will: 'As for me, my life has been a failure. I have done some fighting against the Foreigners, but it was just a struggle without significance. I never won any victory or fame. I went abroad as a student, but I didn't stay with it. I composed some poetry that was just mediocre.'[132]

In a way, Máiréad plays the role of Olaf by challenging the disillusioned certainties in the lives of Hungarford and Ó Mathghamhna. At the thematic heart of the play are her conversations with the two men. She tries to explain to Hungarford her quest for something to believe in, but his initial response is typically cynical:

> Faith and loyalty? Without a doubt, my dear – and faith is a very useful, a very beneficial thing – and loyalty is a very convenient thing – loyalty to some king or even a republic[133] – some cause. If it weren't for faith and loyalty the world would be in turmoil; neither control nor order could be established. If there weren't any religion, it would be necessary to create one.[134]

By this point, Máiréad has decided that the great deed of her life will be to do what she sees as her duty by betraying Ó Mathghamhna. She will be Delilah, not Judith. When she tells Hungarford that Ó Mathghamhna has visited her in the colonel's own home, he is stunned by her audacity. And when he learns that she has invited him there again, he quickly agrees to her plan to trap the rebel. Forever beyond his comprehension, however, are the motives behind her fearlessness in carrying out the plan and her death by suicide when, realising the magnitude of what she has done, her love for Ó Mathghamhna, and the justice of his disgust for her treachery, she runs against his sword as his enemies move to seize him. As she dies, he forgives her and expresses his love for her. Meanwhile Hungarford and his men rush in to arrest the now passive and mourning rebel. Hungarford, not yet knowing Máiréad is dead, once more gives expression to his world-weariness and his disappointment with Ó Mathghamhna's lack of heroic resistance: 'That is a great pity! I expected great deeds from him.'[135] Despite all she has told him, he apparently never expected great deeds from Máiréad.

Of course, Ó Mathghamhna understands her no better than does Hungarford. On his first visit to her in the colonel's house he declares: 'You looked in my eyes and challenged me. The spark that was in your breast stirred up the spark in me.'[136] In effect, she gives him a new sense of purpose that cuts through his disillusionment with his life as a committed but ineffectual patriot: 'I feel it is in me to do better deeds, that it is in my nature to achieve a finer, more glorious life for myself. The flame is still in my breast.' And he needs her with him to share this more fulfilling and meaningful life: 'I believe that you are the princess that appeared to me through the visions of my youth, the skywoman who surpassed all for beauty, for dignity, for bravery.'[137] At this point she still thinks that she and Ó Mathghamhna share the same vision: 'What is the meaning of the unsatisfied desires that torment us? Why do we not enjoy the safe, quiet, ordinary life we know? What drives us to change it? I fear that there is no basis for it but distorted visions and that nothing will come of it but – sorrow, bitter torment and death.'[138] She is, of course, right, but while Ó Mathghamhna should understand that, he can still declare: 'Let us stick to our own vision. Let us follow our heritage, ignoring the counsel of the old. Let us go our own road, even if death be on the other side of the wall.'[139] And of course, she takes him at his word with tragic consequences. Béaslaí's new insight in this play is that life rarely makes it easy for us to find that road or to comprehend what our heritage is or what our visions demand, that tragedy results when our own blindness makes it impossible for us to keep our ideals and our obsessions apart. Máiréad is well aware of how little she knows of her own deepest thoughts: 'We do not understand too clearly the true origin of our deeds. We do the deed and then we create an excuse to explain it to ourselves.'[140] Ó Mathghamhna shares this awareness: 'No one understands the true basic cause of his deeds. He can mention causes – but they are just the skin his reason puts on the matter. Instinct is stronger than reason.'[141] Yet, such an abstract awareness is totally inadequate in face of the psychological and emotional complexities with which life confronts them.

One question Béaslaí leaves unanswered in this play is whether heroism is only possible for people willing to follow their own inexplicable impulses wherever they think they lead, even at the expense of those around them content to live without such passionate ideals or ambitions. Is Thorolf ultimately right that it is the visionaries who bring destruction on both others and themselves? At the end of *An Bhean Chródha*, Máiréad has betrayed the man she loves and taken her own life, while Ó Mathghamhna has been betrayed by the woman he loves and taken off to his execution. Like Thorolf, Hungarford is alive and victorious, although for once his smug self-confidence has been rocked to its core.

Philosophically and thematically, *An Bhean Chródha* is an advance beyond *An Danar*, as Béaslaí deals with the complexities of human ambition and obsession with greater insight and subtlety. As a play, however, it is considerably less satisfying than *An Danar* as for the most part Béaslaí fails to integrate his psychological analyses into the action of the play, instead relying on rather artificial intellectual discussions to make his points and thus lecturing at the members of the audience rather than letting them experience the play on their own terms. Yet, if *An Bhean Chródha* was a mixed success at best, it was also, unlike most of the plays in Irish at the time, a serious play for adults willing to think about important issues of contemporary and timeless relevance.[142]

After having two ambitious full-length tragedies produced by An Comhar Drámaíochta in a little over a year, Béaslaí began to move away from playwriting. Moreover, his last two plays in Irish were the same kind of simple and harmless comedies he had written for Na hAisteoirí two decades earlier.[143] He must have been hurt by the lukewarm critical reception afforded *An Bhean Chródha*, and despite its comparative success, even the production of *An Danar* may have caused him some concern. For example, in addition to the usual worries about the linguistic competence and literary sophistication of Gaelic audiences, there was also the question of whether An Comhar itself was ready to take on challenging full-length plays, particularly tragedies. The critic for the *Irish Independent* wrote tactfully:

> If plays of the type of 'An Danar', which depend so much for their proper interpretation on complete mastery of the lines, are to form a regular part of the repertory of An Comhar Drámaíochta, the problem of complete rehearsal and frequent production will have to be considered. Last night's performance shows that the time for considering it has arrived (*II*, 7 February 1928).

Blunter was 'Scrúdóir', who declared: 'Depending as it does on the dignity of the prose style, this play was mutilated in Monday night's production.' Worse, perhaps, apart from Gearóid Ó Lochlainn and Máire Ní Shíothcháin, the actors put a 'constant strain on the resources of the prompter' (*Star*, 9 February 1929). Evidently, the situation had not improved for *An Bhean Chródha*. In his review for *The Nation*, 'D. Mac C.' wrote: 'The author has written fine dialogue through much of the play, but what good is that when the Aisteoirí cannot deliver the dialogue.'[144] And in this production, it was one of the lead actors, Pól Ó Fearghail, playing the part of Domhnall Ó Mathghamhna, who was said to be 'prone excessively to depend on natural gifts and to neglect his primary duty, which is to master his lines' (*Nation*, 13 April 1929). Neither *An Danar* nor *An Bhean Chródha* was ever popular. After early revivals by An Comhar in 1929 and 1933, the latter directed by Mac Liammóir at the Gate, *An Danar* was largely forgotten. It was also Mac Liammóir who directed a revival of *An Bhean Chródha* at the Gate in 1931, while Seán McCavett directed the play for the Limerick Gaelic Dramatic Society in that city in 1937 (*CE*, 29 November 1937),[145] and in 1943 Frank Dermody, using many of An Comhar's actors now performing at the Abbey, directed a production of the play there (*IT*, 1 February 1943).

Looking back in 1941 on what he called his 'plays in which there was poetry and philosophy' (*drámaí go raibh filidheacht agus feallsamhnacht ionnta*), Béaslaí stated that those plays had been successful, but 'I felt that the Irish-language public preferred simple speech, ordinary conversational speech (I'd almost say common speech), to literary speech or imaginative speech'. Nor could he have been optimistic when he declared: 'Today's Irish-language public does not like complicated speech, and they don't like depth or unconventional ideas.'[146] There is certainly neither 'complicated speech' nor 'depth or unconventional ideas' in his final plays in Irish. Béaslaí had ceased to be actively involved with An Comhar Drámaíochta by the time the company produced his *An Fear Fógraidheachta* (The Advertising Man), directed by Gearóid Ó Lochlainn, in the Peacock in October 1934. While the play was awarded An Comhar's Craobh Óir (Golden Branch) for an original play in the 1934–5 season (*IP*, 7 May 1935), reviews in the three major Dublin daily newspapers were perfunctory, with the critic for *The Irish Times* best illustrating the general consensus: 'Piaras Béaslaoi [*sic*] has written another farce which amuses both by its dialogue and its situations' (*IT*, 16 October 1934).[147]

In his 'Fógra don Léiritheoir' (Notice to the Director) in the text of the play published by An Gúm in 1938, Béaslaí stated: 'This comic play is a farce and it must be performed accordingly, quickly, actively.'[148] Even played rapidly, the play must have dragged a bit, for once again Béaslaí takes a single comic concept and rings changes to it, but this time over three acts instead of one.[149] Cathaoir, an eager young advertising man, arrives in a Munster town to visit his uncle Domhnall, a chemist whose shop is suffering from competition from more modern shops new to the town. Although the young man offers his professional services to revive the business, this sub-plot is never developed. Instead, Cathaoir decides that he will 'sell' his uncle as a marriage partner to Rós, a local widow with whom the uncle is in love. There is, however, a problem, for the uncle has a rival in the local butcher, Seán. Still, Cathaoir feels up to the task, for, as he says, 'there is a good deal of trickery and wizardry involved in the business of advertising'.[150] Drawing on these tricks of the trade, he decides he will attempt 'the kind of thing the Yanks call a "Stunt"' (*an sadhas ruda go dtugaid na Púncánaigh 'Stunt' air*).[151] He actually attempts three such 'stunts', the most elaborate involving a tired and toothless old circus lion from whom he plans to have his uncle rescue Rós. Unfortunately, in all three cases Seán manages to turn the tables, either anticipating the 'stunt' or in some other way making himself look like the hero. Even when he is exposed as a plagiarist who has passed off a poem written and published by another as his own, he twists the situation around by telling Rós that it was he, compelled by modesty to use a pseudonym, who was the author of that published poem. At last, Cathaoir arranges to stage a fake armed robbery and while Seán cowers in terror, Domhnall saves the day. Even worse for Seán, a letter he has accidentally dropped is found by Rós' young cousin Úna and it is learned that Seán is deep in debt and desperately wants to get his hands on Rós' dowry. Thus, as the play ends, Seán is shown to be a coward and a fraud, and Domhnall is engaged to Rós.

Béaslaí's last play in Irish was *Blúire Páipéir* (A Bit of Paper), first produced by An Comhar Drámaíochta in the Peacock during the 1936 Oireachtas with Cyril Cusack directing. It must have been a source of ironic amusement for Béaslaí that there were some more impressed by this forgettable little farce than they had been by what he regarded as his two masterpieces. Thus, writing of the first production of *Blúire Páipéir* in *Ar Aghaidh*, an anonymous critic (probably An tAthair P. Eric Mac Fhinn) proclaimed: 'Piaras Béaslaí is the Irish-speaker – possibly the only Irish-speaker – who knows the dramatist's craft. He is able to put the pieces together in a clever and artistic manner so that he will have an interesting and stageable play' (*AA*, November 1936, p. 3).[152] More astute was 'L. Ó R.' (possibly Béaslaí's friend Liam Ó Rinn), who in a review of the play as published by An Gúm two years later wrote: '"Blúire Páipéir" is a three-act comedy. Love affairs, complications and intrigues, a resolution, everyone happy in the end … It is as good as any drama of this kind that Piaras Béaslaí has written. Very suitable for Irish-language actors. An excellent plot' (*II*, 1 February 1938).[153]

That plot deals with the attempt by a brother to arrange a marriage between his sister and a friend of his who is in love with her. The sister is, however, in love with a man claiming to be a writer who has lived in Dublin, London and Paris, and is always taking notes for a new novel or play. He has no interest at all in her and therefore agrees to act as an intermediary for the man who loves her. Needless to say, his intervention only makes things worse. He ends up convincing her that he is the one who loves her and that he is proposing to her, a 'proposal' she accepts. Meanwhile, her brother, knowing that she is more in love with the idea of marrying a writer than she is with the writer himself, finds out the man is a fraud. Able to steal a page from the man's notebook without his noticing, he drops this 'bit of paper' where his sister is sure to find it. When she reads the writer's negative description of a character with her name, she is immediately cured of her infatuation and all ends well.

Thus ended Piaras Béaslaí's thirty-year career as a playwright in Irish. As we have seen, his interest in Gaelic theatre continued through his involvement in An Sgiath and in Cumann na nDrámathóirí, but he would no longer be a force in the movement. Moreover, when we consider that from 1929 until 1934 – that is, after the production of his two major tragedies in Irish – he was working on a full-length play in English that he titled 'Philoctetes (A Greek Tragi-Comedy)', it seems clear that he had decided that anything of any significance he would write for the stage would have to be in English.[154] Of course, that dream was never realised. English was also – although here for purely practical reasons – the language in which he wrote the script for what he hoped would become a Hollywood movie about Robert Emmet, a script that was never optioned, much less shot.[155]

Béaslaí's reputation as a dramatist must, then, rest on his work in Irish. His comedies may now seem trifles of little literary significance, but in his time, they regularly won prizes at the Oireachtas and were essential contributions to the tiny repertoire of plays in Irish. Whatever their faults, these comedies were entertaining and competently constructed plays that audiences of all levels of ability in Irish could enjoy and that small amateur companies could produce without undue expense or difficulty. Moreover, their urban and town settings and middle-class characters showed that Irish could – with a certain willing suspension of disbelief – deal credibly with a way of life far removed from that of the Gaeltacht. Of his three tragedies, we can safely dismiss *Cormac na Coille* as an apprentice effort, most interesting for its author's sheer ambition and grasp of stage technique at a time when other playwrights were packing their short plays with multiple scenes and set changes and impracticably large casts.[156] Béaslaí's later tragedies, *An Danar* and *An Bhean Chródha*, show the same ambition, but with a markedly superior command of his craft. As noted above, *An Danar* is one of the two or three finest plays in Irish from the first fifty years of the revival, while *An Bhean Chródha*, while less artistically successful, is also a play that deals with serious and challenging ideas in a way that thinking adults could appreciate. We can get some idea of how highly Béaslaí was regarded by his contemporaries from the comments of Shán Ó Cuív in *Prós na hAoise Seo* (Twentieth-century Prose) (1934), one of the first books of literary criticism in Irish. Writing just after the productions of Béaslaí's two mature tragedies, Ó Cuív stated: 'If I were asked who, apart from An tAthair Peadar Ua Laoghaire, is the most important author working in Irish, I would say without any doubt that it is Piaras Béaslaí.' He praised Béaslaí for his comedies, 'plays that have never since been surpassed however much has been done since the new movement began some years ago' (*drámaí nár sáruíodh riamh ó shoin dá mhéid atá déanta ó thosnuigh an iarracht nua roinnt bhlianta ó shoin*). And of *An Danar* and *An Bhean Chródha*, he stated: 'There is nothing better than those two to be found either.'[157]

Nor should we forget that Béaslaí's contributions to Gaelic theatre were not limited to playwriting alone. Indeed, in retrospect what makes him so important in the history of theatre in Irish is the full range of his contributions. He lectured and wrote on theatre history and practical stagecraft; he directed dozens of productions for Na hAisteoirí and An Comhar Drámaíochta– he was a central figure in the creation and development of both groups – and he acted regularly in roles large and small. It is a matter of real regret that his antipathy for Taibhdhearc na Gaillimhe kept him from ever working with the Galway company.[158] Even more unfortunate is that he seems never to have taken an active interest in the Damer theatre in Dublin, a theatre that might have benefited from his vast experience with all aspects of Gaelic drama and from his abilities as actor and director. In a flight of hyperbole, 'A. Ó L.' wrote in his review of the published text of *Blúire Páipéir* in 1938: 'We can compare what he has done for drama in Irish with what Lady Gregory has done for drama in English' (*GR*, March 1938, p. 453).[159] To be sure, Béaslaí lacked Lady Gregory's real theatrical genius, but for more than three decades he did share her tireless commitment to Irish theatre, and in that commitment, each was in his or her own way indispensable.

CHAPTER TWO

Pragmatic Idealist: Gearóid Ó Lochlainn (1884–1970)

Readers of *An Claidheamh Soluis* may well have been startled when in 1912 an informed insider reported in Irish on developments in Scandinavian theatre and the Danish film industry.[1] Many of them must also have been surprised to learn that this Copenhagen insider was one of their own, a young man they had seen performing in both Irish and English in Dublin just a few years earlier. Gearóid Ó Lochlainn was born in Liverpool of Irish parents and raised in Tullamore, County Offaly. It was there he joined the Gaelic League, and, according to Muiris Ó Droighneáin, learned Irish 'as a youth from a native speaker' (*le linn a óige ó chainteoir dúchais*).[2] After moving to Dublin, he was present in April 1902 in St Theresa's Hall in Clarendon Street for the Fay Brothers' production of Yeats' *Kathleen Ni Houlihan* with Maud Gonne in the title role, as well as for the Abbey theatre's first production of Synge's *The Playboy of the Western World* in February 1907.[3] He studied speech with Frank Fay and became a member of Dudley Digges' National Players, a breakaway company formed by Digges, Máire Quinn and Maud Gonne after they left Yeats' Irish National Theatre Society over the question of nationalism in the theatre. Among the productions he appeared in with this company was *An Talamh*, Tadhg Ó Donnchadha's translation into Irish of Padraic Colum's *The Land*. He also performed with various Gaelic League theatre groups and in most of the plays staged at the Oireachtas from 1904 to 1907.

In 1907, he went to Denmark to develop his stagecraft. While there he studied languages, philosophy and psychology at the University of Copenhagen, and worked for a while in silent films while he perfected his spoken Danish – he apparently had a slight Norwegian accent[4] – after which he returned to the stage to perform in the most prestigious theatres in Copenhagen.[5] It is, however, worth noting that despite his immersion in the cultural life of Copenhagen, he remained a committed Irish nationalist. Indeed, he recalls in one of the autobiographical pieces he published in *Feasta* in 1968 that, before he left Ireland, he had been asked by Arthur Griffith to take part in 'an initiative that the National Council of Sinn Féin was developing to set up a consular service in countries overseas' (*beartas a bhí á chur i gcionn ag Comhairle Náisiúnta Shinn Féin chun seirbhís chonsalach a chur ar bun sna tíortha thar lear*) (*Feasta*, August 1968, p. 6). In their entry on Ó Lochlainn in *Beathaisnéis a Trí* (Biography Three), Diarmuid Breathnach and Máire Ní Mhurchú state that Ó Lochlainn apparently did 'diplomatic work throughout Europe' (*obair thaidhleoireachta ar fud na hEorpa*).[6] This would, however, seem to overstate by a good deal what he was actually up to in this regard. When Griffith asked for his help in 1907, Sinn Féin was a small group on the margin of a national movement dominated by John Redmond's Irish Parliamentary Party in Westminster, and the idea of an Irish diplomatic service could have been little more than a dream. Ó Lochlainn makes clear in his serialised memoirs that while he may have considered himself 'as what you might call an underground representative in the service of Ireland' (*im thoscaire faoi thalamh, mar déarfá, i seirbhís na hÉireann*), his assignment was limited to Denmark and altogether mundane: 'By getting to know journalists I would be able to broadcast the truth about the national movement of Sinn Féin, as the English papers had for a while been spreading false reports about it in an attempt to deceive the foreigners.'[7] He also recalls that Griffith had instructed him to write 'from time to time when there would be anything to tell that I thought would be interesting to the Executive Council' (*ó am go ham nuair a bheadh éinní le hinsint a cheapfainn a bheadh suimiúil don Ard-Chomhairle*) (*Feasta*, May 1962, p. 5). Griffith himself, however, does not seem to have kept up his end of the correspondence very well, for in another instalment of his memoirs Ó Lochlainn writes that he and his colleague in Denmark, Seán Ó Duinn, often went considerable periods of time without hearing anything from him at all (*Feasta*, September 1968, p. 19).[8] Despite his apparent failure as an amateur diplomat, the British authorities were well aware of his republican loyalties. He had followed his father's example and been a member of the Irish Republican Brotherhood since the age of eighteen, and he subscribed to both *An Claidheamh Soluis* and *Sinn Féin*.

As a result, the British authorities did not allow him to return to Ireland until October 1921, three months after the truce that ended the fighting in the war of independence.

Those who had watched his early performances at the Oireachtas could hardly have expected that he would return to Ireland as an experienced professional man of the theatre as well as a visionary with very down-to-earth ideas about how to realise those visions.[9] Almost immediately on his arrival home he became, as he would remain, one of Dublin's busiest performers in both Irish and English. Among the roles he played in English at the Abbey alone – and the following list is just a sampling – were Hjalmar Ekdal in Ibsen's *The Wild Duck* (1932), the title role in Shakespeare's *Macbeth* (1934), Conchobar in Synge's *Deirdre of the Sorrows* (1935), the Sergeant in Lady Gregory's *The Rising of the Moon* (1946) and the Philosopher in Brecht's *Galileo* (1965). At the Gate theatre, of which he was a co-founder and on whose original board of directors he sat, he appeared in, among other plays, Ibsen's *Peer Gynt* (1928), Eugene O'Neill's *The Hairy Ape* (1928), Denis Johnston's *The Old Lady Says 'No!'* (1929), Karel Čapek's *R. U. R.* (1931) and Dmitry Merezhkovsky's *Czar Paul* (1931). At the Pike theatre, he co-directed and appeared in the first production of Brendan Behan's *The Quare Fellow* in 1954, in the same author's *The Big House* and in Sartre's *No Exit* in 1958, and in the highly controversial production of Tennessee Williams' *The Rose Tattoo* in 1957, a role that almost cost him his job in the civil service.[10] In the Gaiety theatre, he performed in Cyril Cusack's production of Shaw's *The Doctor's Dilemma* in 1947, and in Sean O'Faolain's only play, *She Had To Do Something*, the same year.

If anything, he was even more active, though doubtless less well-paid, on the Irish-language stage. Again, the following lists of plays in which he featured are by no means comprehensive. With An Comhar Drámaíochta he acted in Hyde's *An Tincéir agus an tSidheog* (The Tinker and the Fairy); in translations of Lady Gregory's *Spreading the News*, Synge's *In the Shadow of the Glen*, and Molière's *Le médecin malgré lui* (all in 1924); in Liam O'Flaherty's only play, *An Dorchadas* (Darkness) (1926); in Piaras Béaslaí's *An Danar* (The Dane) and in Leon Ó Broin's *An Clósgríobhaí* (The Typist) (both in 1929); in *Aiséirghe*, a translation of Daniel Corkery's *Resurrection* and of Molière's *Le bourgeois gentilhomme* (both in 1930);

in translations of Molière's *Les fourberies de Scapin* and Shaw's *Arms and the Man* (both in 1931); in a translation of Molière's *L'avare* (1934); in a translation of Lennox Robinson's *The Whiteheaded Boy* (1935); in Micheál Ó Siochfhradha's *Aon-Mhac Aoife Alban* (The Only Son of Aoife of Scotland), in which he played Cú Chulainn (1937); in Séamus de Bhilmot's *'San Am Soin* (In That Time) (1938); in Séamus Ó Néill's *Buaidh an Ultaigh* (The Triumph of the Ulsterman), in which he played Fionn mac Cumhaill (1939); in de Bhilmot's *Grádh níos Mó* (Greater Love) (1940) and *Déamar agus a Bhean* (Damer and His Wife) (1941); and in Gearóid Ó Sléibhín's *An Crann Caorthainn* (The Rowan Tree) (1941). With the Abbey, he acted in Béaslaí's *An Bhean Cródha* (The Brave Woman) (1943); in Peadar Ó hAnnracháin's *Stiana* (1944); and in the Gaelic *geamaireachtaí* or pantomimes *Muireann agus an Prionnsa* (Muireann and the Prince) (1945), *An tUbhall Óir* (The Golden Apple) (1945), *Fernandó agus an Dragan* (Fernando and the Dragon) (1946), *Réalt Dhiarmada* (Diarmaid's star), in which he again played Fionn mac Cumhaill (1948), and *Brian agus an Claidheamh Soluis* (Brian and the Sword of Light) (1948). He also performed in Irish at the Taibhdhearc, the Damer, where he created the role of Monsúr in Brendan Behan's *An Giall* (The Hostage),[11] and with Aisteoirí Ghaoth Dobhair.

This is an impressive record, made more so by the fact that Ó Lochlainn was not just a busy and versatile actor; he was also, to judge by the near unanimous verdict of contemporary critics, quite a good one. A few examples should serve to make the case here. In 1928, 'J. W. G.' pronounced him 'excellent' in the Gate's production of Eugene O'Neill's *The Hairy Ape* (*II*, 28 October 1928). Referring to him the following year as 'that very fine actor', the same critic wrote that 'Mr. Gearóid Ó Lochlainn made Mr. Gall a splendidly impressive figure' in Karel Čapek's robot play *R. U. R.* in the Gate (*II*, 1 May 1929). When he played the part of the ballad singer in Padraic Colum's *The Betrayal*, 'M. M.' praised Ó Lochlainn and the actress Dorothy Casey for taking 'much of the stiffness out of the play' and thus accounting 'largely for its success' (*II*, 27 March 1932). Of his role in O'Faolain's *She Had To Do Something* in the Gaiety 'T. M.' (Tony Molloy) stated: 'Gearóid Ó Lochlainn played the Canon with gentle understanding. The author lavished most care in creating this character. Gearóid missed none of this' (*IP*, 16 June 1947).

Given the, to put it kindly, inconsistent quality of acting in Irish at the time, critics of his work in that language both enjoyed and appreciated his professionalism. As 'Connla' pointed out in his or her review of An Comhar's production of Douglas Hyde's *An Tincéir agus an tSidheog*, in which Ó Lochlainn played one of the title roles: 'Gearóid is a good actor' and clearly '"at home" on the stage' (*Aisteoir maith ... 'sa bhaile' ar an stage* [*sic*]) (*FJ*, 7 April 1924). Writing of his performance with An Comhar in the title role in a translation of Molière's *Les fourberies de Scapin*, 'C. Ua D.' (Cearbhall Ua Dálaigh) commented on the lengthy ovation Ó Lochlainn received at the end of the play, a tribute he felt was well deserved, for 'He carried off every action and all of the antics as if he had been Scapin his whole life. It is no lie to say that it has been a long time since acting like this has been seen on any stage' (*II*, 17 October 1931).[12] An anonymous reviewer of An Comhar's 1932 production of Micheál Mac Liammóir's farcical *Lúlú* in the Gate wrote that 'Gearóid Ó Lochlainn excelled himself as the gouty and testy father, especially in the fall that brought down the curtain on the most genuinely comic play in An Comhar's repertory' (*IT*, 13 December 1932). The anonymous critic of his performance as Fionn mac Cumhaill in Séamus Ó Néill's *Buaidh an Ultaigh* in the Peacock similarly felt that he 'gave an interpretation which left nothing to be desired' (*IT*, 8 December 1939). And there was more praise along the same lines.

It is particularly noteworthy that Ó Lochlainn was able to find so many important parts in Irish-language plays at a time when many in the movement were complaining of the state of Gaelic theatre in general and particularly about the sporadic and disorganised way in which Gaelic plays were produced, often in shifting and entirely inadequate venues. Ó Lochlainn certainly shared this frustration, but he was far too pragmatic not to try to find, indeed create, a solution. To put it simply, if no one was producing the kind of plays he felt were needed, he would. As we have seen, Dublin's An Comhar Drámaíochta had its ultimate origin in Na hAisteoirí, the group founded by Piaras Béaslaí in 1912 while Ó Lochlainn was in Copenhagen. This company had, however, disbanded because so many of its members were, like Béaslaí himself, involved in the Easter rising and subsequent war of independence. As a result, there was for a while no major Gaelic theatre group in the capital, and it was Ó Lochlainn who filled this void after his return to Ireland in 1921 by gathering together many of the former members of Na hAisteoirí into a new group called Aisteoirí Átha Cliath. It was this company that was the immediate predecessor of An Comhar Drámaíochta with Ó Lochlainn as one of the co-founders. As the previous chapter made clear, Béaslaí played a major role in An Comhar in its early years, but every bit as important was the experienced, ambitious and multi-talented Ó Lochlainn.

The existence of An Comhar was the kind of opportunity Ó Lochlainn would not allow to pass, and he threw himself into all aspects of the group's work, taking such a prominent role that already by 1926 a critic for *The Dublin Magazine* could refer quite accurately to the group as 'Gearóid Ó Lochlainn's brilliant troupe of Gaelic actors' (*DM*, December 1924, p. 287).[13] Over the years, he served on and chaired An Comhar's board of directors, acted in and/or directed many of its shows (almost all of them between 1923 and 1929), and provided it with six original plays and eight translations or adaptations. He was, moreover, An Comhar's vigilant, but always fair-minded, champion and defender. For example, in July 1929 he pointed out that An Comhar's project was very much a work in progress, with what success it had had to date threatened by its failure to find a real home for its productions: 'The launching of the Comhar in 1923 was an ambitious attempt to advance Gaelic drama from the phase of sporadic performances in small halls to that of regular and efficient productions in a properly equipped theatre – in other words, to found a permanent Gaelic stage' (*Star*, 13 July 1929). When the group's commitment to the language was attacked by Pádraig Ó hUigínn, who stated that English was their working language, Ó Lochlainn replied that anyone familiar with An Comhar knew that Irish was 'the usual language of the actors and the members of the committee' (*gnáth-theanga na n-aisteoirí agus baill an choiste*) and adding that he had never heard more than 'a very small amount of English' (*fíor-bheagán den Bhéarla*) in all his time with the group (*Glór*, 28 March 1942). Ó Lochlainn was also among those who opposed the Abbey's ultimately successful plan to absorb An Comhar into the National Theatre Company. Looking back in 1951 on what he saw as little more than a ploy to take control of An Comhar's meagre state subsidy, he wrote:

> The Abbey had no use for An Comhar of course; it was the subsidy An Comhar was getting that they had a use for – for the sake of drama in Irish, needless to say ... The Abbey's audience had no interest in drama in Irish, and it is a waste of time to be putting plays in Irish on the bill with plays in English in an attempt to force them on them (*Comhar,* May 1951, p. 21).[14]

Given that some of his own best roles were in English-language plays on the Abbey stage, it took some courage for Ó Lochlainn to question so publicly the theatre's policy concerning plays in Irish.

The lack of an adequate and predictable audience long troubled Ó Lochlainn. For example, in a 1926 lecture on the Danish theatre sponsored by An Comhar, he is reported to have said: 'Our young dramatists have not an audience to listen to them. There are not enough Irish-speaking people in Dublin to keep a theatre going and to go touring the Gaedhealtacht is not financially feasible' (*Leader,* 10 July 1926). It was doubtless in part to address this pressing problem that in 1944 he joined with playwrights Séamus de Bhilmot and Micheál Ó Siochfhradha and actor Tadhg Ó Scannaill to found Compántas Amharclainne na Gaeilge, the company that brought variety entertainment in Irish to the Dublin stage, in the process drawing some of the largest and most enthusiastic audiences ever seen at Gaelic productions.[15] The so-called *Sea-Seóanna* performed regularly by An Compántas from 1945 into the 1950s were up-to-date bilingual entertainments and thus anathema to some purists and champions of a narrowly defined *Gaelachas* (Gaelicism). But the cosmopolitan and polyglot Ó Lochlainn had no such concerns. For example, in a 1945 piece in *Éire* he acknowledged that in order to make a living, actors committed to the Irish language would also have to take roles in English (*Éire,* 1945, p. 83). And in another piece the same year, he argued that bilingual productions were actually a logical evolutionary step towards a fully Gaelic stage (*Indiu,* April 1945, p. 2). As was true of his work with An Comhar, his involvement with An Compántas was multi-faceted, so that in addition to founding and helping run the company, he regularly acted in its shows over the years. To round out this discussion of his seminal role in the development of Gaelic theatre in Dublin, it should be noted that he was also involved in 1954 in the planning stages of a 'Gaelic Theatre Club in Dublin', an initiative that came to fruition in the Damer theatre, in which were seen from 1955 to '76 some of the finest productions ever done in Irish.[16]

Ó Lochlainn's ready acceptance of Ireland's bilingualism is also evident from his long and distinguished involvement in English-language theatre. Ó Lochlainn did accept the orthodox view that 'normal truly Gaelic theatres' would provide 'a protective barrier against the tide of Anglicisation', but, unlike many of his colleagues in the Gaelic theatre movement, his interest was as much, if not more, in the theatre than in the language. Furthermore, in addition to acting in English he was also a leading figure in the development of the English-language theatre in Ireland. In 1928 he joined Micheál Mac Liammóir, Hilton Edwards and Madame Bannard-Cogley to found the Gate theatre, which introduced Dublin audiences to exciting new plays from continental Europe and America. Moreover, he felt it was while performing at the Gate from November 1930 to February 1934 that An Comhar Drámaíochta did its best work.[17] In 1953 he was one of what the *Irish Independent* called 'The Big Five' who started the Pike theatre that brought the plays of Beckett, Sartre, Ionesco and Tennessee Williams to Ireland.[18]

Of course, like so many in the Gaelic theatre movement, he was involved with amateur and school groups throughout the country. The most notable of such companies with which he worked, and the one with which he worked most extensively, was Aisteoirí Ghaoth Dobhair in the Donegal Gaeltacht. As early as 1942, Séamus Ó Néill could write of the group (which he called 'An Comhar Drámaidheachta Ghaoth Dobhair') that they were 'as good an amateur group as you would find anywhere, and far better than most', adding: 'It is only just to add that much of their skill is due to the brilliant coaching of Gearóid Ó Lochlainn' (*IP*, 27 August 1942). Ó Néill's comment was prompted by his enjoyment of a performance by Aisteoirí Ghaoth Dobhair of *An Murlán Práis*, Eoghan Mac Giolla Bhrighde's translation of Matthew Boulton's *The Brass Doorknob*, with Ó Lochlainn playing the male lead. Ó Lochlainn's association with the Gweedore players was to last more than two decades. In 1953, in his capacity as inspector of Gaelic drama for the Department of Education, he began what became a regular course in theatre in the Donegal Gaeltacht.[19] The first course was held in Ros Guill, and when in 1955 it was hosted in

Na Doirí Beaga, the home of Aisteoirí Ghaoth Dobhair, Ó Lochlainn 'had the assistance of the Aisteoirí for demonstration purposes'. This course also featured another production of *An Murlán Práis,* with Ó Lochlainn reprising his star turn (*DP,* 6 August 1955). Lest it be thought he limited his appearances with the Aisteoirí to productions of this one play, we should note that as early as 1940 a reporter for the *Derry People* discussed Ó Lochlainn's enthusiasm for the group's work and stated that 'the well-known Dublin actor and Government adviser on drama' had taken part in 'several of their productions' (*DP,* 27 July 1940).[20]

This reporter also noted that Ó Lochlainn had first seen Aisteoirí Ghaoth Dobhair at 'one of the Provincial Festivals' (*DP,* 27 July 1940). Ó Lochlainn certainly attended many such *feiseanna,* both in his official capacity as a drama inspector for the schools and as an adjudicator for drama competitions. Among such contests that he judged, often more than once, were events in Dublin, including Feis Átha Cliath (*IP,* 26 February 1937; *IP,* 2 May 1939; *IP,* 10 December 1940; *IP,* 7 September 1941; *II,* 10 June 1954); Galway, including the Galway Drama Festival sponsored by Cumann Drámaidheachta na Scol (*IP,* 11 February 1938; *IP,* 26 March 1949); Letterkenny (*DP,* 1 June 1934; 6 November 1936), and Gaoth Dobhair (*DP,* 25 September 1959). To share his own hands-on experience of the theatre with students, he also published a step-by step essay entitled 'Conus Dráma Scoile d'Ullmhú' (How to Prepare a School Play) in *Láimh-leabhar Drámaíochta* (A Drama Handbook), edited by Proinnsias E. Ó Súilleabháin and published in 1938 or 1939.[21] In addition, he was an occasional lecturer on theatre topics,[22] a critic and essayist,[23] a visiting director, a member of a special committee of Cumann na Scríbhneoirí formed to promote drama in Irish,[24] a vice-president of Irish Actors' Equity,[25] a visiting director,[26] and an occasional singer of Danish songs on Radio Éireann.[27]

One might well imagine that Ó Lochlainn was primarily a hard worker at best, a rather frantic dilettante at worst, but such an impression would be altogether mistaken. Like many of his colleagues in the theatre movement, he dealt with the seemingly overwhelming challenges besetting the Gaelic theatre by confronting them, in the process sacrificing time and energy that could have been spent thinking and writing. Clearly, he felt he had no choice but to take on boring and doubtless often frustrating work motivated by the simple realisation that it had to be done and that no one else was likely to do it. Yet, even given his hectic schedule as actor, organiser and activist, he still managed to think insightfully and provocatively about the problems to be overcome if theatre in Irish was to survive, much less thrive. One of those problems was ideological. In 1924, he engaged in a debate with Máighréad Ní Annagáin in the pages of *The Leader*. Ní Annagáin began by attacking what she called 'triangle plays' like *In the Shadow of the Glen* by Synge, whom she called 'foreign in name, in training, in outlook, and in race … a fungus-like excrescence on the country, making his literary reputation by depicting any diseased spot he could find in the moral life of the Irish people' (*Leader*, 25 October 1924). Ó Lochlainn, who, as we have seen, had reservations about Synge, nevertheless came to his defence, stating that Synge had 'actually added to our reputation as a race with literary gifts'. He then turned his attention to what he saw as the subtext for Ní Annagáin's attack on Synge: 'National self-conceit can be carried too far, and puritanism is not morality' (*Leader*, 8 November 1924). Unabashed, in a piece the following week entitled 'Triangle Plays: The Gaelic view', Ní Annagáin widened the scope of her argument while simultaneously making it ad hominem with her reference to the theatre group with which Ó Lochlainn was so centrally involved:

> By the way, I see in the 'Sunday Independent' that the Government has endowed the Comhar Drámaidheachta to the extent of £500. It is to be hoped that steps will be taken to ensure that none of this money shall be expended on poisonous programs … The language of the Catholic Gael must not be used to propagate anti-Christian doctrines or pagan notions of morality; and it is up to us Irish-speaking Catholics to see that it is not (*Leader*, 15 November 1924).

By now, Ó Lochlainn had had enough, responding that he did not intend 'to waste any more time correcting this lady's misconceptions and rebutting her sophistries'. At which point he declared:

> I will only say in conclusion that as a Gaedheal I dispute the assertion conveyed in the title of her last article that she represents the mind of Gaelic Ireland. She may represent the narrow views of a section

> of Gaelic Ireland – a small section, I hope – but judging from what she has written on this subject of plays, there is also a strong tinge of intolerant puritanism in her mentality which is not at all Gaelic (*Leader*, 29 November 1924).

After this, he may well have been glad to return to more practical questions of the kind he addressed in a 1926 lecture to members of An Comhar Drámaíochta on the lessons to be learned from the Danish stage. Among the issues he raised was a problem the Danes did not have, 'namely, that our young dramatists have not an audience to listen to them' (*Leader*, 10 July 1926). He was aware that the makings of such an audience might exist in the Gaeltacht, but stressed that its cultivation and development would require imaginative effort, and intimated that in all likelihood the cities and towns would remain the battlegrounds for the survival of Gaelic theatre:

> Our most native dramatists live in An Ghaedhealtacht, but they don't know much about stage technique. If a committee of An Comhar could make it its business to teach as well as it could … that technique, something might come of it. Indeed, if the dry bones, so to say, of dramas were sent from Dublin to known writers in An Ghaedhealtacht, they might come back clothed with flesh and blood, the Irish origin of which there would be no mistaking or disputing (*Leader*, 10 July 1926).

Of course, nowhere was his belief in the potential of the Gaeltacht for the theatre movement more evident than in his ongoing enthusiasm for and involvement with the work of Aisteoirí Ghaoth Dobhair.

It is doubtless this awareness of the limitations the lack of audiences imposed on Gaelic playwrights and producers that explains Ó Lochlainn's ready acceptance of the kind of bilingualism practised by his own Compántas Amharclainne na Gaeilge. In a piece on 'An Amharclann agus an Ghaedhilg' (The Theatre and the Irish Language) published in the annual journal *Éire* the year after An Compántas was founded, he once more affirmed his pragmatic acceptance of the way things really were by arguing that while the ultimate goal was obviously to see a full-time professional company of Irish-language actors, 'in the meantime if it is possible to provide a company of full-time actors for the plays in Irish by allowing them to take part in plays in English as well, that is the most practical way to give the work a proper foundation'.[28] Moreover, he felt that such a compromise might well enable theatre in Irish to spread beyond Dublin, Galway and the Gaeltacht to places like Cork, Limerick, Waterford, Sligo and Kilkenny, for 'wouldn't full-time permanent theatres that could produce plays in the two languages be better than theatres in which all the craftsmanship would be on the English-language side with the drama in Irish relying on the efforts of amateur actors who have no chance to perfect their work' (*Éire*, 1945, pp. 83–4).[29]

His hopes for the eventual creation of a full-time professional company playing in Irish notwithstanding, Ó Lochlainn knew that the Gaelic stage would be the all but exclusive preserve of amateurs, often very raw ones, for years if not decades to come. To help such neophytes, and to give already dubious audiences some reason to attend their performances, he called for more competent directors to put the actors through their paces. Convinced that 'the quality of the work depends mostly on the directors in the case of drama in Irish' (*ar na léiritheoirí is mó a bhíonn fiúntas na hoibre ag brath i gcás dhrámaíocht na Gaeilge*), he suggested that 'if all companies in the country that perform plays in Irish co-operated, I would not say but that some plan could be created to set up a course for directors once or twice during the year. Something like that would help greatly to raise the standard of the work' (*Comhar*, November 1951, p. 18).[30]

He also insisted that 'the standard of the work' could be raised if Gaelic plays were staged in more suitable venues that would enable regular rehearsals and proper performance schedules, rather than being staged in what in 1940 he called 'unsuitable places to which to resort and unattractive places in which to play' (*IT*, 15 November 1940). This was no new concern for him, as he had written in 1929 with his experiences with An Comhar Drámaíochta in mind: 'Playing one night in the month means no less work of preparation than playing for an entire week, and one night a month on the boards is of very little use in training actors who are learning their business' (*Star*, 13 July 1929). In 1943, he indulged in a little flight of fancy, writing: 'The fact of the matter is that that standard [i.e. 'the high standard that was our aim when An Comhar was founded'] will not be reached until there is a permanent Irish-language theatre in which there will be a company of trained actors with nothing at all to do except act' (*Éire*, 1943, p. 30).[31] A statement like this makes painfully clear how great was the compromise he was willing to make in his embrace of bilingualism as an unavoidable surrender to hard realities. By 1951, he had, however, begun to run out of patience: 'An Irish language theatre in the capital of the country. That was the chief goal of An Comhar Drámaíochta. It now seems that we are further from it than ever, and if something is not done within a few more years I fear that it will be too late' (*Comhar*, May 1951, p. 23).[32]

We are back on the more solid ground Ó Lochlainn typically favoured when we examine his thinking about the kinds of plays that were needed in Irish. As we have seen, the chance of getting good – or even playable – scripts in the language was an ongoing concern from the very beginning of the literary revival, and that problem had only become more pressing with the founding of An Comhar Drámaíochta and Taibhdhearc na Gaillimhe, as well as the proliferation of other amateur Gaelic groups around the country. With his wide knowledge of the Irish, English and European dramatic repertoire, Ó Lochlainn knew that translation could provide a steady supply of such worthwhile scripts – and in a hurry. Unlike those who saw translation as a threat to the ineffable *Gaelachas* that they believed to be no less – perhaps even a good deal more – important than the language itself, he had no difficulty about bringing new ideas, forms and methods onto the Gaelic stage. Thus, in a 1929 piece entitled 'Drámaí Iasachta/An Fiú Aistriúcháin a Dhéanamh?' (Foreign Plays/Is it Worth Doing Translations?), he wrote: 'The person who is so lacking in self-confidence that he feels he must remain in ignorance of the thoughts and opinions of his fellow human beings lest they influence him too strongly is to be pitied. It is also absurd not to take an interest in the cleverness of your neighbour and to learn something from him, if possible.'[33] And while he believed that it was only right 'to help the Gaelic dramatists and give precedence to their work if it is any good at all' (*cuidiú lesna drámathóirí Gaodhalacha agus tús áite a thabhairt dá gcuid saothair má bhíonn aon mhaitheas i n-éan chor ann*), he argued that there was little such original work available, 'and therefore we will still be dependent on a good deal of translation for a long while' (*agus d'á bhrí sin beifear i dturtaoibh le roinnt mhaith aistriúchán go ceann i bhfad fós*). Indeed, he added that even if there were to be 'an abundance of original plays in Irish available it would still be right to leave some space on the programme for translations of worthwhile plays from other countries' (*flúirse bun-drámaí Gaedhilge le fáil ba cheart slí éigean d'fhágaint ar an chlár i gcomhnuí d'aistriúcháin ar dhrámaí fiúntacha ó thíorthaibh eile*), for 'that is an acknowledgement that we have some interest in the intellectual work and the artistic cleverness of our fellow nations – something that would, perhaps, be of benefit to us' (*Star*, 20 July 1929).[34]

In 1943, he again stressed the shortage of stage-worthy new plays in Irish, adding rather mischievously 'and I hear that it is none too easy to find a good original play even in English in this country' (*agus cloistear dom nach ró-fhuirist fiú bundráma maith Béarla d'fhághail sa tír seo*). His solution had not changed: 'And until there are enough original plays being written in Irish, we might as well produce translations of good plays' (*Éire*, 1943, p. 30).[35] Two years later, he offered his colleagues a challenging vision of a dedicated Irish-language theatre in Dublin 'in which not only original Gaelic plays will be artistically produced, but the best dramatic work of other countries as well. In a word, a theatre in which the Irish language is a mirror that will give us a look at every aspect of human nature' (*ina léireófar go h-ealadhanta, ní h-amháin bun-drámaí Gaedhealacha, ach scoth saothar drámaidheachta na dtíortha eile chomh maith. I n-aon bhriathar amháin, amharclann inarbh'í an Ghaedhilg scathán a thabharfaidh radharc dúinn ar an uile ghné den nádúr daonna*) (*Éire*, 1945, p. 82).

As we saw in the previous chapter, the whole question of translation had long been a subject of fierce debate in Gaelic circles. Most of the controversy focused on An Gúm's policy of bringing into Irish a large number of foreign works of fiction, the vast majority originally in English. But the same objection could be, and was, levelled against An Gúm's publication of translated plays, almost all of them from England or by Irish writers of English. Having embraced the idea of putting foreign plays into Irish, the polyglot Ó Lochlainn was in a position to do something about this problem. And he did. His translations of plays from languages other than English were *An Cheist Chinneamhnach* ('Die Frage an das Schicksal', the first act of the seven-act play *Anatol*) by the controversial Austrian playwright Arthur Schnitzler, produced by An Comhar Drámaíochta at the Abbey in 1924; *Heirciléas* (*Verdems Hercules*) by the Danish writer Adolf Reche, produced by An Comhar in the Abbey in 1925;[36] and *Námhaid don Phobal* (*En Folkefiende*, i.e. Ibsen's *The Enemy of the People*), produced by An Comhar in the Peacock in 1939.[37] All of these plays were translated from the original languages, not from available English translations as was often the case with translations into Irish from languages other than English. Not that Ó Lochlainn avoided translation from English, for he also created versions of Henry Meyer's *The End of the Book* as *Deire an Leabhar*, produced by An Comhar in the Abbey in 1926; of Lord Dunsany's *The Jest of Hahalaba* as *Greann Háthalába*, produced by An Comhar in the Gate in 1931; of T.H. Stafford's *The Fisherman's Wife* as *Bean an Iasgaire*, produced by An Comhar in the Peacock in 1934; and of *Old Mag* by 'Kenneth Reddin' (Kenneth Sarr) as *Sean-Mhaighréad*, produced by An Comhar in the Peacock in 1938. In addition, he translated various scenes from Shakespeare for performance on stage and on the radio. The trial scene from *The Merchant of Venice* was staged at the Taibhdhearc in 1949, with Ó Lochlainn himself playing Shylock with what a reviewer for *The Connacht Tribune* called 'an awful inhuman coldness' (*CT*, 27 May 1949). This scene, with himself again as Shylock but this time with Siobhán McKenna as Portia, was broadcast over Radio Éireann in September 1954 (*IP*, 3 and 15 September 1954), and his version of 'dhá radharc as *Hamlet*' (two scenes from *Hamlet*) was heard on the station in March 1960 (*IP*, 15 March 1960). A collection of his translations from Shakespeare was published by An Gúm in 1966 as *Radhairc as Drámaí Shakespeare* (Scenes from the Plays of Shakespeare), of which the critic Andrew Maxwell wrote: 'In many ways it is a remarkable piece of translation, preserving to a great extent, and sometimes even embellishing, the better-known portions of these plays' (*IP*, 30 July 1966). In collaboration with Muiris Ó Catháin, Ó Lochlainn also turned 'The Croppy Boy', the well-known song of the '98 rising, into a very short musical play, *An Craipí Óg*, first staged by An Comhar in the Peacock in 1935.[38]

Of course, however positive Ó Lochlainn was about the place of translation in the evolving Gaelic dramatic repertoire, like all of his colleagues in the movement he felt that it could only be a stopgap measure until playwrights began to produce a significant corpus of good plays in Irish. And he insisted that all kinds of original plays were needed. Thus, writing in 1923 as 'An Lochlannach', he stated: 'Without a doubt there should be room and scope for the comic play also in any Gaelic theatre, but it is not healthy for a nation to be dependent solely on comedy for intellectual sustenance' (*II*, 10 April 1923). Reviewing Walter Macken's original comedy *An Fear ón Spidéal* (The Man from Spiddal) on its publication in 1952, he again called for a mix of genres in the repertoire: 'And it is likely that none of us wants the tragic mask, the brooding mask, on the drama always; we like the other one, the comic mask, now and again' (*Feasta*, July 1952, p. 20).[39]

Ó Lochlainn's ambition was never to be a playwright, a point he made explicit in a 1951 letter to *Comhar*: 'I did not take up acting to learn how to write plays; I took it up because that is what I wanted to do and what was natural for me. I never set out to be a playwright, but after a few years I felt I wanted to write a play and I did. It succeeded fairly well, and I wrote another one from time to time after that.' He was not, however, under any illusions about the quality of his writing for the stage: 'I had no foolish belief that I was an excellent dramatist, for in order to write an excellent play special intellectual talents are needed, talents the ordinary run of playwrights do not have' (*Comhar*, May 1951, p. 22).[40] Thus, it is hardly surprising that one sometimes gets the impression that, like many others in the Gaelic drama movement, he wrote more to fill a need than from any deep creative inspiration.[41] What may be surprising in this context is that his plays were among the best of their time. We will now focus on those original plays that were published, referring in passing to works produced but not put into print, and leaving aside his translations, as well as *The Glamour of the Green Isle*, an unpublished radio play in English broadcast over Radio Éireann in August 1937 (*IP*, 1 September 1937).

Had his first been his only play, silence would be the kindest response to his ambitions as a playwright. The one-act *Bean an Mhilliúnaí* (The Millionaire's Wife), first performed by Aisteoirí Átha Cliath in July 1923 in the Gaiety theatre during that year's much diminished Oireachtas, is a dreadful play.[42] 'Marbhán' (Seán Ó Ciarghusa) was actually too kind in the few sentences with which he dismissed it in his review of the production: 'I don't know whether there was too much "Teaching" in it and too much of the influence of the Abbey on it, but, at any rate, I did not like it' (*Leader*, 4 August 1923).[43] Whatever that comment about the Abbey was intended to convey, those involved with that theatre had every right to be insulted for being in any way linked to *Bean an Mhilliúnaí*. The play is an inert and preachy melodrama in which Ó Lochlainn himself played the role of the millionaire whose ruthless and unethical business practices have ruined an imaginative young entrepreneur, who now plans to murder him in revenge. The millionaire, Proinnsias Ó hArtagáin, contemptuously rejects all progressive theories that would in any way restrict his cut-throat methods, social Darwinism being the code by which he lives and thrives:

> Business is war … and cleverness and money are the weapons used in that war. The person who does not understand how to make use of those two instruments is struck down without pity or mercy. It would be just as well for the person who would allow charity or pity to divert him from advancing his business to give up the game altogether![44]

The climax of the play comes when his young victim sneaks into his house to kill him, only to spare his life because of the wife's sympathy for him and her rejection, to Ó hArtagáin's face, of his worldview and business ethics: 'When this man told me a while ago that you were a man without heart, without conscience, an unscrupulous, greedy man, I did not believe him, but – Alas, I fear that I never really knew you until tonight.'[45] Apparently moved by her reproaches and her compassion for the young man, Ó hArtagáin implausibly sees the error of his ways and offers his would-be killer a just, even generous, business proposition that will enable him to remain solvent and keep his company in operation.

Along with all its other problems, the play obviously raises more questions than it even tries to answer. Is Ó Lochlainn here condemning the capitalist system itself or, as seems more likely, merely its worst excesses? And where does one draw the line? Was the play meant as a lesson for those who would form the financial elite in the newly independent Irish Free State? Are we to see Ó hArtagáin's repentance and generosity as signs of genuine reformation or only as a ploy to placate his naive and squeamish wife? His condescending final speech in response to her apology for confronting him so directly is suggestive here: 'Of course I have nothing to forgive you for, dear. Between ourselves, you understand, I wouldn't say but you were more or less right!'[46] The play was never revived, although, as we will see, Ó Lochlainn returned to the general theme in a far more sophisticated and engaging manner in his award-winning one-act play *Ag an Ladhrán* in 1941.

Ó Lochlainn's next play, *Cótaí Móra* (Overcoats), was first performed by An Comhar Drámaíochta in the Peacock in February 1930. It has never been published, and the Playography Ireland website says that there is 'no synopsis currently available'. It was, however, described in a brief notice in the *Sunday Independent* as 'a jovial, rollicking, farcical comedy of student life in Dublin, full of droll dialogue and droller situations, in which the Aisteoirí get full scope for their talent for comic acting' (*SI*, 16 February 1930). Reviewing the production for the *Evening Herald*, an anonymous critic wrote that the play 'afforded a good contrast' to the tragic play with which it was paired (a translation of T.C. Murray's *Birthright*) and was 'a most amusing play, perfect in technique, and full of rollicking situations' (*EH*, 18 February 1930). The anonymous reviewer for *An Phoblacht* was probably more on target when he stated, 'As for "Cótaí Móra", I expected a better effort from the author. It is altogether too short and too thin. If Gearóid Ó Lochlainn thought it was worth writing, it wasn't worth his putting it on stage. It's a pity he did' (*Poblacht*, 22 February 1930).[47] 'D. Ó D.' was no kinder: 'I wonder what An Comhar thinks about little plays like this one, but in my opinion, they should have more respect for the Gaels of this city, who have a chance to see plays in English. After all they are people who understand what drama is and also what humour is' (*Leader*, 22 February 1930).[48]

Fortunately, these daunting reviews did not discourage Ó Lochlainn, for he kept writing, and his next play, the three-act detective comedy *Na Gaduithe* (The Thieves), became one of the most popular Gaelic plays of the time. First performed at the Gate in February 1933 by An Comhar under the direction of Micheál Mac Liammóir, it was revived in March 1936 in the Torch theatre, with Cyril Cusack as director, by the actors of the league's Keating branch under the auspices of An Comhar in the Peacock in February 1937, and at the Abbey in 1940 for that year's Oireachtas. In December 1935, it had become the first of Ó Lochlainn's plays produced at Taibhdhearc na Gaillimhe (*CT*, 11 November 1935). Aisteoirí Ghaoth Dobhair put the play on in August of 1940 (*DP*, 6 September 1940), and the following March it was performed by the students at Maynooth (*IMN*, 1946, p. 86). In 1949, actors from the Letterkenny, County Donegal, branch of the Gaelic League produced the play in Letterkenny, Gaoth Dobhair and Fál Carrach (*Ultach*, May 1949, p. 2). The radio audience got to hear *Na Gaduithe* on Radio Éireann in February 1937 (*IP*, 11 February 1937) and again in February 1939 (*IP*, 10 February 1939).

This time reviews were unanimously positive. Writing of the premiere, 'C. Ua D.' (Cearbhall Ua Dálaigh) declared: 'It can be said that the audience really enjoyed this play ... A detective play is something new in Irish and we can congratulate Gearóid Ó Lochlainn on his accomplishment' (*IP*, 7 February 1933).[49] On the occasion of its 1936 revival, an anonymous critic called the play 'an excellent detective play by Gearóid Ó Lochlainn' (*sár-dhráma bleachtaireachta le Gearóid Ó Lochlainn*), adding: 'I recommend it to every Gael, teachers and students, young or old' (*IP*, 27 March 1936).[50] A brief anonymous note on the 1937 production stated that 'The Keating Players continue to draw large audiences to the Peacock theatre. Their production of Gearóid Ó Lochlainn's "Na Gaduithe" is one of the best performances in Irish seen for a number of years' (*IP*, 13 February 1937). Particularly impressed was the critic for the *Derry People*, who, after seeing the play in Gweedore in 1940, called it 'a three-act play which has earned the highest praise in the capital and elsewhere' and writing: 'In a class by itself, out of the run of the usual line of Gaelic plays, "Na Gaduithe" gripped the attention of the large audience from the first, and through humorous side-plot and striking dialogue progressed to a climax as unexpected as it was brilliant' (*DP*, 6 September 1940).

Na Gaduithe is much more a comedy of errors than a true detective drama. The scene is set in a country hotel where one of the workers, a voracious reader of detective stories, becomes suspicious of two guests when he learns of a bank robbery in the area. These guests are a pair of young Dublin men about town whose suspicious behaviour is in part due to the fact that they are also conducting their own amateur investigation of this robbery. At the same time, they are falling in love with the two daughters of the hotelier, whom they take to be servants in the hotel. Among the other guests at the hotel are an ostensibly wealthy businessman somewhat along the lines of the industrialist in *Bean an Mhilliúnaí*, and a wealthy and apparently rather ditzy spinster who appears to be infatuated with him. A comic courtship scene between the two reveals that the businessman is far more interested in her money than in herself, and that she seems incapable of resisting his dubious charms. When another robbery occurs, this one at the hotel itself, the plot thickens, and we soon learn that the 'businessman' is 'The Gunman Mac Craith' (*An Gunnaire Mac Craith*), a thief in cahoots with another hotel guest pretending to be a German professor collecting Irish folklore as a cover for casing the countryside. To compound the farcical confusion – and the fun – the apparently flighty spinster turns out to be a hard-nosed, quick-witted, and gun-wielding detective. All, of course, ends well, with the Dubliners getting an undeserved reward for exposing the thieves and also winning the two young women. After they announce that they will invest their reward money in the hotel, the play ends with their successful marriage proposals and a feast.

The most interesting thing about the play is the way Ó Lochlainn manipulates various stereotypes and the resultant audience expectations. Thus, the 'businessman' clearly bases his 'authoritative behaviour typically found in important businessmen' (*iompar ughdarásach fé mar a bhíonn de ghnáth fé dhaoine móra gnótha*) on his own – and our – preconceptions about how a crass, bombastic financial tycoon would behave.[51] The 'spinster' adroitly plays on – and entirely shatters – contemporary society's low expectations concerning the intelligence and life skills of an unmarried woman of a certain age. Blocking the criminals' escape, she says with 'a threatening glint in her eyes and an edge on her voice like that on the point of a sword' (*spréacharnach bhagarthach ina súilibh, agus faobhar ar a glór mar a bheadh rinn claidhimh ann*): 'Throw away those guns, I say, and raise your hands! I'll have you dead or alive! I'll count to three and on three I'll riddle you with bullets! One! Two! –'[52]

Preconceptions about class are satirised in the scene where the young Dubliners initially assume the hotel owner's daughters are servants, a misunderstanding the sly young women briefly allow to stand for their own amusement. The fan of detective fiction is also blinded by his conviction that his reading has given him a fool-proof understanding of how criminals look and act, and his suspicions are ridiculously wrong-headed. Given his audience, Ó Lochlainn has particular fun with Von Hincilbaum, the 'German professor', who speaks German almost as badly as he seems to speak Irish: 'Yes, Yes; Deutschland über alles – nicht wahr?

But there is no need for you German to speak with me. I have the good Irish – das heiszt, ziemlich – cuibhseach maith? Verstehen sie?'[53] He is eventually unmasked as Cathal Dalatún, a fluent Irish speaker with, oddly, 'a bit of the nasal quality of the American in his voice' (*beagán de shrónaighil an Phonncáin ina ghlór*).[54] At any rate, its intentionally less-than-probable plot twists, outrageous characters, bits of slapstick, and frequent use of music must have made *Na Gaduithe* an entertaining relief from the usual fare Gaelic audiences were too often compelled to endure. With a little judicious updating, it might still have entertainment value today.

In his 1966 book *Ealaín na hAmharclainne* (The Art of the Theatre), Ó Lochlainn wrote of Sean O'Casey's *The Plough and the Stars* (1926): 'In this play O'Casey gave a true and realistic picture of the life and thoughts of the ordinary people, the inhabitants of the tenements in his time. He had a profound understanding of them, and his heart was always with them.'[55] Ó Lochlainn did not, of course, have any such experience of life in the Dublin slums, but in his next play, the one-act *An t-Éirighe Amach* (The Rising), he boldly stepped onto O'Casey's home turf.[56]

An t-Éirighe Amach was first produced by An Comhar Drámaíochta in the Peacock in March 1937, with Ó Lochlainn in the principal role of Pádraig de Clár. At least one critic was impressed by the play. Writing in *The Irish Press*, 'Sinéad' declared: 'Gearóid Ó Lochlainn, with the aid of a very fine cast, has shown what can be done through drama for this lethargic city of ours.' For this critic, the play was a 'fast-moving drama' with 'some of the best dialogue we have had so far in this type of drama', and 'the small audience was held enthralled by the theme of "An t-Éirighe Amach"' (*IP*, 31 March 1937).[57]

Actually, the theme is one of the few things Ó Lochlainn did not lift from O'Casey, whose influence is everywhere in this short play. For example, like O'Casey, Ó Lochlainn uses his characters to embody a range of perspectives on the rising. Thus, among those characters we get a long-suffering mother worried about her son, another woman critical of those who started the revolt, a neighbour who is pessimistic about the success of the rising, a comic drunk who boasts of his patriotism and claims he can't wait to join the battle but never does, and the protagonist's son, who loses his nerve in the fighting and flees home for shelter. The woman distrustful of the rebels says to the mother of Liam de Clár, who is out fighting: 'God help those poor boys and God forgive those who drove them into this war – it's on their knees they should be tonight seeking His pardon for the evil deed they have done and for bringing this slaughter and terror down on top of us.'[58] Set against all of this pessimism and blame is the steadfast patriotism of Liam's father Pádraig de Clár, an old Fenian anguished that poor health and age keep him from joining the rebels as have his son and an old comrade from Fenian times. He sees the rising as something to be proud of, regardless of the outcome: 'And even if it does not succeed. It is not a source of sorrow or shame for Ireland, but the opposite altogether … I am an old man now … But nevertheless, I should be down there on the street among those fine and faithful lads with my gun in my hand like everyone else.'[59] He does, however, feel that his son has redeemed the family honour by going out to fight: 'My heart is glad that a son of mine is amongst the loyal, brave men who had the courage to challenge the English in spite of the traitors and the cowards who would sell Ireland to her enemies.'[60]

When he realises that his son has become one of those traitors and cowards, deserting his fellow rebels with no intention of returning, his first response is anger and shame: 'Is that how it is? You are the first person of our stock who failed when the time and the chance came to strike a blow for this unfortunate country.'[61] But then the young man tells him of the horrors he has seen – horrors that recall the death of Lieutenant Langon in O'Casey's play: 'Two were killed beside me … One of them got a couple of bullets through the throat. He fell, choking on the blood. He was writhing on the floor like an animal, vomiting blood for ten minutes before he died.'[62] Having come to understand the depth of his son's terror, de Clár forgives him and tries to restore some of the young man's dignity by telling him he should stay home to protect his mother and sisters. He then rushes out, firing at a squad of British soldiers before they gun him down in the street. Unlike O'Casey, Ó Lochlainn was no pacifist. Indeed, he believed that what Patrick Pearse did in 1916 was perhaps 'the greatest deed any one man ever accomplished in the history of Ireland since the English came over' (*an éacht ba mhó, b'fhéidir, dá'r dhein aon fhear amháin riamh a chur chun críche i stair na hÉireann ó tháinig na Gaill anall*) (*Comhar*, December 1943, p. 7). As a result, he ends his play with the orthodox homage to heroic death for Ireland, a thematic ending that, according to 'Sinéad', the opening night audience found enthralling, but that could instead be seen as merely facile, as all other attitudes towards the rising are forgotten in the awe inspired by de Clár's patriotic sacrifice. As the now abashed pessimistic neighbour puts it: 'I think that poor Pádraig got the death he would have preferred. The light of paradise to his soul and to the soul of every loyal man like him.'[63] An audience today might find his son's obvious post-traumatic stress reaction more interesting than his father's act of traditional bravery.

Ó Lochlainn stayed with recent history in his next play, the ambitious full-length *Na Fearachoin* ('*Fearachoin Groidhe ná Claoidhfeadh Céadta*') (The Dogs of War {'Strong Dogs of War Hundreds Would Not Defeat'}), set in west Kerry during the war of independence. The play had its premiere by An Comhar Drámaíochta in the Peacock in January 1938, with Ó Lochlainn playing the role of the English major, and the poet Máirtín Ó Direáin playing the leader of an IRA flying column. In a brief review, the anonymous critic for the *Irish Independent* wrote: 'The plot of the play is put together artistically and the production and the dialogue that were seen and heard were effective' (*II*, 26 January 1938).[64] Forgetting or ignoring Béaslaí's exploration of some of the same issues in *An Bhean Chródha* nearly nine years earlier, 'T. Ó M.' praised Ó Lochlainn for breaking important new ground by having the members of a Big House family as his protagonists and by focusing on their dilemma in having to decide between identities and loyalties.[65] 'T. Ó M.' did, however, feel that Ó Lochlainn had allowed his fascination with the characters' ideas and beliefs in the play to overshadow his interest in them as people: 'When he was creating his characters, he was too concerned with revealing opinions in order to explain the period to bother much showing those characters' fundamental qualities. That left the characters more symbolic than substantial' (*IP*, 26 January 1938).[66] Of course, this same criticism would not be altogether out of place in a discussion of Lennox Robinson's classic 1926 play *The Big House* – a play that surely influenced Ó Lochlainn. Both are plays about identity and allegiance – descent and consent – issues of considerable significance in an emergent state trying to define its attitude towards a minority of potentially questionable loyalty while that minority simultaneously wrestles with the dilemma of its own identity and allegiance in radically altered political circumstances.

In *Na Fearachoin*, Réamonn Calbhail, the son of a Big House family in west Kerry, is urged to spy on the local IRA by Major Blaic, his former commander in the First World War British army who is now commanding a company of the Black and Tans. Réamonn respects the major, whose heroism in the war earned him the Victoria Cross, but he is appalled by how little the major knows or cares about Ireland and its people. And when Blaic suggests that he spy for the British as a loyal Englishman would have spied on the Germans during the war, Réamonn points out that despite his ancestry he is not in fact English, but rather Irish: 'Yes, do you understand, Major, there's a little difference in this case. The Sinn Féiners are not Germans but Irishmen – and we are Irish also, although we are not of one mind with them concerning what is best for this country.'[67] At this point, Réamonn sees some form of Irish independence as inevitable, but he continues to believe 'that it is best for us to remain inside of the Empire' (*gurab é ár leas fanamhaint taobh istigh den Impireacht*).[68] At the same time, he realises that the majority of the Irish people would never trust anyone of his background and thus 'it is best for us to be neutral in this war'.[69] Réamonn's father, disgusted by the violence of both the IRA and the Black and Tans, whom he calls 'that crowd of barbaric villains let loose on us in this country' (*an sluagh san de ropairí barbardha a scaoileadh isteach 'sa tír chughainn*), is thinking of taking his family out of Ireland altogether, but even he finds himself incapable of maintaining his former staunchly unionist politics: 'Ah, if the Irish people had followed poor John Redmond it would be a different story.'[70] Réamonn's sister Maighréad is in an even more painful predicament as she tries to reconcile her family traditions with her love for Donnchadh Mac Craith, the local IRA leader. Donnchadh comes to see her to end their relationship, telling her his love of country must take precedence until the war is won, but she angrily rejects 'this mad patriotism that I think is nothing but hatred' (*an tírghrádh buile seo, ná fuil ann dar liom-sa ach fuath*). His response makes clear the apparently unbridgeable divide between them: 'You, the Anglo-Irish, although you have been rooted in Ireland for centuries, you do not have the least understanding of the country in which you live. You are still like a foreign tribe among us and have little respect for everything Gaelic.' Yet, he still sees some hope for her and her people: 'Still and all, you're not English but Irish.'[71] As the play progresses and the indiscriminate violence of the Black and Tans accelerates, Réamonn, his father and his sister all find themselves seeing and even accepting the logic of the republican position. Indeed, the ex-soldier Réamonn is beaten by the Black and Tans for refusing to sing 'God Save the King'.

Their hands are forced when the wounded Mac Craith is brought to their house, and they assert their new allegiance by sheltering him from the searching Tans. Shortly thereafter, the major is captured by Mac Craith's column, and when the Black and Tans torture an IRA prisoner, the major is executed. This is, of course, an episode already familiar in Irish literature from Frank O'Connor's 1931 story 'Guests of the Nation', from Micheál Ó Siochfhradha's 1931 one-act play *Deire an Chuntais* (The End of the Account), and from Ernie O'Malley's 1936 book *On Another Man's Wound*, where O'Malley tells of how he himself had shot a British officer in similar circumstances.[72] Here, the entire scene is handled with considerable restraint and sensitivity, all involved, including the British officer, behaving with courage, dignity and a deep sense of duty. The IRA men are profoundly troubled by what they know they must do, but ultimately accept the justice of their commander's decision, as does, apparently, the condemned man himself, his courage winning the admiration of his executioners.[73] As the play ends, Réamonn joins the IRA column, a decision his father reluctantly accepts before leaving for Scotland with his daughter. The family's changed sense of their own Irishness is now secure, and we are left with the impression that father and daughter will return home to Kerry after the war, she to marry the rebel Mac Craith and merge her identity with that of the native Irish.

Many if not most of the ideas in this play had been anticipated in a more focused and nuanced manner in Robinson's *The Big House*, and they have been developed since by writers like Molly Keane, Jennifer Johnston, John Banville, and even Tom Murphy, who have kept the Big House sub-genre alive far longer than anyone could have realistically expected. Still, Ó Lochlainn does link the Irish struggle with a global fight for justice, if not explicitly with a rejection of colonialism. Thus, Mac Craith rejects Maighréad's view of the IRA's campaign as rooted in tribal hatred by declaring: 'We don't know what the end of the story will be for the human race. Perhaps we will always be fumbling ahead of us like poor, foolish, blind creatures. But the day there are not men who will stand and fight against evil and injustice, the human race is damned for good.'[74] *Na Fearachoin* might still interest audiences in modern multicultural Ireland, but even if it did not, its ambition and willingness to present in a serious way characters and beliefs often seen merely as sources of pity or parody by Irish nationalists and language activists make it deserving of inclusion on any list of significant plays in Irish from the first fifty years of the literary revival.

Ó Lochlainn's next play, the one-act *Lá na Paráide* (The Day of the Parade), was first produced by An Comhar Drámaíochta in the Gate in December 1940 with the author in one of the lead roles, and was then taken by the group to An Taibhdhearc in the summer of the following year. The play has never been published, but we are told in an anonymous review in *Ar Aghaidh* (probably by An tAthair Eric Mac Fhinn) that it was 'in a way a "sketch"' (*léireog*) set in a public park in Dublin with the first characters we see 'ordinary people of the city' (*gnáthlucht cathrach*). The main characters are an IRA veteran dying of his old war wounds, and his friend, a street musician (*AA*, January 1941, p. 4). Another anonymous critic present on the first night of the play wrote that '"Lá na Paráide" is a tragedy, and the author, Gearóid Ó Lochlainn, paints a picture of an ex-IRA man who has lost everything in the fight for freedom'. The reviewer added: 'While the individual characters were well-drawn, the incidents were somewhat too circumstantial' (*IP*, 11 December 1940). Commenting on the upcoming production in Galway the following year, another critic seems to have agreed, stating somewhat cryptically that 'though the theme is tragic and there is too much bearing on co-incidence, there are many amusing lines' (*IP*, 17 February 1941).[75]

Ó Lochlainn took a real step forward with his next play, the one-act *Ag an Ladhrán* (At the Junction), which had its premiere in the Abbey during the 1941 Oireachtas with Frank Dermody directing. It also won first prize in that year's Oireachtas competition for one-act plays, with one of the judges, Micheál Mac Liammóir, calling it 'a beautiful piece of work' (*IP*, 8 September 1941). It was broadcast over Radio Éireann in February 1959 and again in November 1965. The opening-night critics seem to have been underwhelmed, or perhaps simply baffled, by the play. Writing in *The Irish Press*, 'A. Ó M.' (Antoine Ó Maolaoidh, i.e. Tony Molloy) simply noted that Ó Lochlainn's play was on the same bill as Gearóid

Ó Sléibhín's *An Crann Caorthainn* (The Rowan Tree), the winner of the 1941 Oireachtas prize for a full-length play, on which he then focused his review (*IP*, 27 October 1941). The critic for the *Irish Independent* missed the point of *Ag an Ladhrán* entirely, writing that it dealt with 'a very worn-out subject' (*ughdar súgh-spíonta go maith*) and 'were it not for the pistol there wouldn't be much action in the play' (*marach an gunna póca ní mórán gnímh a bheadh 'san drama*) (*II*, 27 October 1941). Indeed, when the play was published in 1948, Tomás de Bhaldraithe, the critic for the *Irish Library Bulletin*, seems never to have heard of it, writing of *Ag an Ladhrán* and Séamus Ó hAodha's *Glaodh an Chuirliúin* (The Curlew's Call): 'We don't know that either of these plays was ever performed on any stage' (*ILB*, November–December 1948, p. 195).[76]

Seeing the text in print seems, however, to have given some critics a better chance to understand what Ó Lochlainn was up to. Thus, reviewing An Gúm's publication of the play, Brian Ó Mórdha noted its potential and the challenges it presented: 'It is an effective play, but a play that only trained actors could do justice to. There is not much movement at all in it, and the actors would have to convey all the meaning of the play with their voices – something amateurs could not do' (*Ultach*, June 1948, p. 7).[77]

Even more perceptive was 'M. Ó D.' (Máirtín Ó Direáin), who stressed in his review of the published text that *Ag an Ladhrán* was very different from the usual Gaelic dramatic fare: 'There is a war of another type in the second play – a war between the man who prospered in the world and his conscience, his youth or the Doppelgänger. Let everyone make his own judgment. The author effectively shows the extraordinary tension of this play by using words and phrases sparingly. It is bare and taut as is fitting for this kind of play' (*Feasta*, May 1948, p. 14).[78]

In this, his finest play, Ó Lochlainn drew on his wide experience of contemporary European theatre gained both during his time in Copenhagen and from all the work he had done at the Gate theatre with Micheál Mac Liammóir, Hilton Edwards and Denis Johnston, in whose expressionist classic *The Old Lady Says 'No!'* he had, it will be recalled, acted. *Ag an Ladhrán* makes deft use of expressionist techniques to create an ominous, eerie and paradoxically atemporal setting in which to explore the theme of conscience he had treated so clumsily in his 1924 melodrama *Bean an Mhilliúnaí*. There are only three characters in the play:

Pilib Mac Eoin, 'a middle-aged man ... dressed fashionably, arrogant and imperious' (*duine meadhon-aosta ... é gléasta go galánta, é mustarach agus máighistreamhail*); 'An Fear Eile' (The Other Man), who bears a curious resemblance to Mac Eoin despite his being thin and pale; and an oddly unsettling stationmaster who speaks 'in a monotonous, deliberate voice, like a person without much interest in anything' (*de ghuth aontonach, righin agus é ar nós duine ná beadh mórán suime aige i n-aon rud*). The three are alone at night in a small rural train station. The stationmaster sets the tone for the play right from the start in his flat, emotionless voice: 'They come and go. Everyone with his own story. Everyone with his own secrets in his heart. And do you know what else runs through my mind? For some of them it's the last train – if they only knew it.'[79] Pilib recognises the Other Man, saying that he had once foolishly listened to him and taken his advice, but that since he had stopped doing so he had become rich and powerful – always, however, like the rich man in *Bean an Mhilliúnaí*, staying scrupulously within the letter of the law as he sees it: 'I played the game according to the rules. Every man for himself.'[80]

Nevertheless, the Other Man relentlessly strips away Pilib's pretensions, exposing him as a religious hypocrite, a slumlord and a parasitic war profiteer. Again, like the rich man in *Bean an Mhilliúnaí*, Pilib has callously ruined the lives of others, driving one of his victims to suicide in a prison cell. The Other Man tells Pilib he has now come to offer him a last chance to repent and gain peace of mind: 'Listen to me, Pilib. We are at the junction, at the place where the ways to travel separate from each other. Let me make this journey with you. It could be the final journey.'[81] When the Other Man goes on to tell Pilib that he knows the depths of his self-loathing and despair – 'he unknown to the world being gnawed deep inside by the dregs and the corruption in his heart' (*é dá chreimeadh ina lár istigh i ngan fhios do'n tsaoghal ag an moirt agus an morg atá ina chroidhe*) – Pilib acknowledges he has had bouts of depression, but claims he has overcome them. He draws a pistol, but the Other Man continues his inexorable analysis, pointing out that Pilib has no one at all who cares for him, not even his family. Driven to rage, Pilib becomes what the Other Man calls 'a beast in the shape of a man. An ugly, disgusting beast' (*beithidheach i gcrot fir. Beithidheach gránda, déisteanach*) and pulls the trigger. Meanwhile, a train has arrived, and Pilib backs slowly away from the corpse and out the door with his victim's dying words echoing in his ears: 'The final journey! I pity you. I truly pity you!'[82] The only person left on stage is the stationmaster, who, we realise, has never showed any sign that he noticed anyone in the station except Pilib, and who does not now see the Other Man's body. He can only mutter to himself in 'the same monotonous lifeless voice' (*an glór aontonach marbhánta céadna*): 'That gentleman had a strange appearance. As if something was troubling him.'[83]

In his previously quoted review of the published version of *Ag an Ladhrán*, Brian Ó Mórdha wrote that despite the challenging nature of the play, 'it would be worth it for a clever director with two good actors in his company to give it a try' (*Ultach*, June 1948, p. 7).[84] At least two directors did give it a try. After its initial production at the 1941 Oireachtas, the play was performed by a company from Virginia, County Cavan, at Feis Átha Cliath in 1969 (*II*, 5 March 1969) and by actors from Ballingeary, County Cork, at the 1975 Oireachtas (*II*, 25 April 1975). It is still well worth reviving. And wouldn't Rod Serling have made good use of a script like this for *The Twilight Zone*?

Ó Lochlainn returned to comedy for his final play.[85] *An Balbhán Bréige* (The Fake Mute) was first produced at Taibhdhearc na Gaillimhe in May 1950, with Ó Lochlainn both directing and playing the role of Uncle Dáithí, and had its Dublin premiere by the actors of the Keating branch of the Gaelic League the following May, with a young Niall Tóibín in the lead role. It was broadcast over Radio Éireann in March 1955 (*II*, 15 March 1955). Writing of the Galway production, the critic for *The Connacht Tribune* called *An Balbhán Bréige* 'a very fine comedy' and pronounced Ó Lochlainn 'the outstanding actor on the stage' (*CT*, 20 May 1950). Equally vague about the play was 'R. S.', who in his brief review of its Dublin production on the same bill with two other one-acters simply said that Ó Lochlainn's 'farce' provided 'suitable comic relief' and was 'the best entertainment on the night's programme' (*II*, 12 May 1951).

What is most interesting about *An Balbhán Bréige* is its setting, one altogether new in Gaelic drama. The play takes place during the Irish 'Emergency' of the Second World War, and follows the misadventures of a group of sophisticated young Dublin bohemians. The protagonist, Domhnall Ó Loingsigh, is a painter,[86] one of his friends a singer, and his love interest Máirín a liberated young woman who seems almost as interested in the arts as she is in the artist. The young women in this play smoke; the young lovers kiss passionately; the singer offers songs in Italian and French as well as in Irish; the friends joke about George Bernard Shaw, Sherlock Holmes and Charlie Chan, read the new Gaelic literary periodical *An Iris* (an actual journal of the time), enjoy American cigarettes as well as fine wine and champagne, and discuss contemporary topics like the number of British people coming to wartime Dublin to enjoy freedom from food rationing.

The protagonist wants to marry his fiancée but cannot for financial reasons. His one hope here is his wealthy uncle Dáithí, who lives in England and has been sending him money to help him raise an orphaned boy who can neither hear nor speak. Unfortunately, the boy has died, but Domhnall, reluctant to turn off the cash spigot, has never notified his uncle of this fact. Dáithí is now planning to visit Dublin, so Domhnall, in desperate need of an appropriately silent object of charity, gives in to what he calls a friend's 'profiteering' in order to get him to take on the role.[87] Needless to say, much of the comedy revolves around the friend's ever more frantic and implausible attempts to convince Dáithí that he is indeed hearing and speech impaired. For example, entirely ignorant of sign language, the friend is nonplussed when he realises that Dáithí intends to converse with him through signs, and he begins 'working the fingers frantically, imitating Dáithí' (*ag oibriú na méar go mear ag déanamh aithrise ar Dháithí*). When the flabbergasted Dáithí demands to know what all these odd gesticulations are supposed to mean, Domhnall answers that his friend was born in County Donegal and therefore signs in Ulster Irish 'according to the sounds you know. There are as well very difficult sounds in that dialect. And to make things worse, they make the sounds in the new spelling.'[88] Thereupon, to Dáithí's apparent satisfaction, Domhnall and his friend engage in a spirited conversation in signed 'Ulster Irish'. Of course, eventually the whole scheme comes tumbling down, but the play still ends happily with the thoroughly amused Dáithí making Domhnall the manager of an art gallery he has just bought near Stephen's Green, a position that will enable him to marry Máirín and enjoy a lifestyle both cultured and comfortable.[89] There is much in *An Balbhán Bréige* that is genuinely funny, but obvious and legitimate concerns about jokes at the expense of the hearing and speech challenged would make it difficult to stage successfully today.

Gearóid Ó Lochlainn continued to act in plays in Irish until near the end of his life in 1970. Why, then, did he write no plays in Irish after 1950? There is no single obvious answer to this question. A simple and credible enough explanation would be that his busy schedule as an actor in two languages and, to a lesser extent, his apparent interest in autobiographical writing left him little time for playwriting. But we also know that by 1951 he was becoming increasingly concerned about the state of Gaelic drama. After attending the plays at that year's Oireachtas, he wrote: 'One who would go to the Oireachtas Drama Festival expecting a high standard – I don't mean a professional standard, but let us say the standard that is reached in amateur drama in English – would be disappointed.' Still, he never lapsed into pessimism, much less defeatism, writing of these same plays: 'To be sure, most of the work was flawed, some of it very flawed, but even so, here and there one saw enough understanding and cleverness to take the edge off the disappointment with the rest' (*Comhar*, November 1951, p. 11).[90] On the other hand, his mood could hardly have been improved when he learned of the burning of the Abbey theatre that same year, as he undoubtedly would have recognised that disaster as potentially another major setback for Gaelic drama, even if he could not have foreseen precisely what problems the Abbey's temporary new home in the much larger Queen's theatre would create for plays in Irish over the next decade and a half.

The challenges he saw in 1951 were nothing new to him, and his approach towards them had always been to seek or create the necessary solutions. Nor did that approach ever change, as is evident from his involvement in 1953 with what would become the Damer theatre and from his ongoing work with Aisteoirí Ghaoth Dobhair, not to mention his usual work as a drama adjudicator at *feiseanna*. As early as 1935, in a report on his appointment as the Department of Education's organiser/inspector for Gaelic drama, a correspondent for *The Irish Press* wrote: 'Few men have had as wide experience of the theatre and few have played as big a part in the creation of a Gaelic stage' (*IP*, 14 September 1935). The year before *An*

Balbhán Bréige had its premiere, the theatre critic for *The Irish Press,* Tony Molloy, wrote of Ó Lochlainn that 'he never ceased to keep an eye on the possibility of Gaelic drama' and that 'Gearóid now looks at the theatre with knowledge and maturity, but the youthful enthusiasm is still there' (*IP,* 16 May 1949). Throughout his career, Ó Lochlainn always combined that enthusiasm with a pragmatism that identified and tried to overcome obstacles. If one argues – as we have here – that his plays were sometimes stopgap solutions to the contemporary shortage of worthwhile scripts, one must still concede that four of his eight plays may be considered worthy of inclusion in any Gaelic dramatic canon, and that two of those might still, with some sensitive adaptation and direction, entertain audiences today. That statement can only be made of the work of a tiny handful of playwrights from the first half of the past century. In *Ealaín na hAmharclainne,* Ó Lochlainn expressed his respect for the melodramatists Dion Boucicault and J.W. Whitbread as 'men of the theatre who knew the tricks of the trade inside and out' (*fir amharclainne a raibh seifteanna na ceird go paiteanta acu*).[91] He also was one of that irrepressible tribe.

CHAPTER THREE

Accidental Playwright: Leon Ó Broin (1902–90)

When he was writing his 1985 autobiography *Just Like Yesterday*, Leon Ó Broin seems to have mostly forgotten that he had been a prolific playwright in Irish a half-century earlier. At any rate, he only mentions three of his plays, just one of them by name. Moreover, he calls that one, *An Boisgín Ceoil* (The Magic Melodeon), a ballet, although to judge from the published text, if it was in any sense a ballet it must surely have been the chattiest one ever composed.[1] Nor does he have much to say in his autobiography about his involvement with An Comhar Drámaíochta from the 1920s right through to the 1960s. Indeed, he mentions An Comhar just once, using the English translation of the group's name, the Gaelic Drama League. Perhaps this downplaying of his role in the Gaelic literary revival should not, however, be all that surprising, as over the course of his long and distinguished life he accomplished more than enough to fill another full volume of autobiography.[2]

Born in Dublin in 1902, he began studying Irish in a class run by Sinn Féin, and later joined the Gaelic League's Ard-Chraobh, eventually becoming a teacher of Irish there as well as the branch secretary. He continued to study Irish in the Gaeltacht, first at the Connacht Summer School of Irish in Spiddal, County Galway, and then at Coláiste Chonnacht in Tourmakeady, County Mayo. In addition, he studied at the Gaelic League's Leinster College of Irish and attended a class taught by Alf Sommerfelt at the School of Irish Learning in Dublin, where he came to know the scholars Osborn Bergin, Myles Dillon and Gerard Murphy.[3]

As did so many others at the time, he combined a keen interest in Irish with a broader involvement in nationalist politics, a logical development given the Parnellite loyalties in his home, loyalties that led his father into Sinn Féin and, it seems likely, into action during Easter week 1916.[4]

Moreover, one of his brothers brought rifles back to Dublin after the Howth gun-running in 1914, an uncle deserted the British army in 1916 and became an intelligence officer for Michael Collins, and Ó Broin himself, along with his father and another uncle, was briefly imprisoned by crown forces as members of Sinn Féin after Bloody Sunday in 1920. When the Anglo-Irish treaty was signed in 1921, Ó Broin took the pro-treaty side and eventually served, in what he himself called 'an utterly surprising development', as an officer in the Free State army. Recalling his army days in *Just Like Yesterday*, he wrote: 'I had no military experience whatever, of course, nor was I now given any training. Indeed, I doubt if I could have done anything to defend myself if attacked ...'[5]

Even before the signing of the treaty, he had begun what would be a lifetime career in the civil service, with his first post being in the underground government of the outlawed Dáil Éireann. After the treaty and the civil war, and despite being called to the bar in 1924, he decided he liked life in the civil service and held successive posts over the years in the Land Commission, the customs and excise service, the Department of Education, and in the Department of Finance, where he rose to the rank of private secretary to the minister. The respect in which he was held within government circles earned him appointment in 1940 as commissioner for Galway and Mayo, one of eight such regional commissioners in the country responsible for keeping the peace, maintaining essential services, and managing supplies in the event of an enemy invasion of Ireland, a possibility that seemed very real at the time. Recalling the day that he and his fellow commissioners received their orders from Taoiseach Éamon de Valera, Ó Broin wrote in *Just Like Yesterday*: 'We knew already that if an invasion occurred we would have the father and the mother of a job on our hands. As we paused for a moment outside the Cabinet room, someone raised a laugh by saying that in all the uncertainty one thing was certain; we the Regional Commissioners were going to be shot.'[6]

From Finance he went to the Department of Posts and Telegraphs, where he played a major role in the development of Irish radio and television. Writing of the evolution of Radio Éireann along the lines of the BBC, Maurice Gorham, the director of Radio Éireann in the 1950s, stated that it was Ó Broin who was 'largely responsible for the setting up of the semi-independent regime and for the move towards full independence that was always kept in view'.[7] On a more cultural level, it was also Ó Broin who took the lead in creating the Radio Éireann Symphony Orchestra – and in making the ringing of the Angelus bell a daily feature of Irish broadcasting.[8] When the question of Irish television was being debated in the late 1950s, Ó Broin was again an influential voice, not least because of his awareness of what the new medium could mean for the Irish language. Thus, in a 1959 communication to Taoiseach Éamon de Valera, he wrote: 'If ... the whole or bulk of the Irish television programmes are to be operated by a commercial group, Irish or foreign, with financial profits as its primary objective, the revival movement might be regarded as dead.'[9] On the other hand, as a realist with long experience of how government worked, he knew that the idea that television should become primarily a means of language revival was a non-starter. As had been true in his approach to radio, Ó Broin, in another memorandum to the government, proposed that 'television be controlled and operated by a public service body'.[10] In the end, in what he called 'an extraordinary *volte face*', his ideas carried the day with the new taoiseach, Seán Lemass, meaning that Irish television, whatever its challenges and failings over the years, escaped the clutches of those who wanted either a state-controlled or a largely profit-driven service.[11]

Given his professional and family responsibilities, one might think that he had plenty enough to keep him occupied, yet he somehow managed to engage in an impressive range of other activities. He was, for example, a founder member of An Cumann le Béaloideas Éireann (the Irish Folklore Society) in 1927, and continued to serve as a government appointee on its board after it became the Irish Folklore Commission.[12] He was also present at the foundation of Cumann na Scríbhneoirí Gaeilge, and was actively involved for years with An Club Leabhar (The Book Club), which distributed selected titles in Irish to its members.[13] 'A devout man and a staunch Catholic' (*fear cráifeach agus Caitliceach stóinseach*) in the words of Máire Ní Mhurchú and Diarmaid Breathnach,[14] he took a leading role in several faith-based organisations. Thus, for ten years he edited *Maria Legiones*, the journal of the Legion of Mary, a group founded by his friend Frank Duff, whose biography he wrote and whom he felt worthy of canonisation by the church. Among other Catholic organisations to which he belonged were two ecumenical groups, the Pillar of Fire Society and the Mercier Society, the former to bring together Catholics and Jews, the latter Catholics and Protestants. Both of these groups aroused the suspicion of Archbishop John Charles McQuaid and as a result were predictably short-lived.[15]

Apart from his duties in these and other organisations, Ó Broin regularly lectured on a wide range of topics to a wide range of audiences, both in person and via the radio. A sampling of his public lectures would include talks to Cumann na nGaedheal on 'Éire Ghaedhealach' (A Gaelic Ireland) in 1924 (*FJ*, 7 February 1924); to the Pan-Celtic Congress in Wales on Gaelic drama in 1927 (*II*, 28 July 1927); to Cumann Gaedhealach na Stát-Sheirbhíse (the Civil Service Gaelic Society) on 'An Cúigeadh Aois' (The Fifth Century) in 1936 (*II*, 12 March 1936); to the Congress of the Irish Association of Catholic University Students on 'The Catholic Graduate in Public Life' in 1952 (*IP*, 5 July 1952); to the Merriman Summer School on Daniel O'Connell in 1972 (*IP*, 29 July 1972); to an audience at the Abbey theatre on 'Cúlra Réabhlóideach W.B. Yeats' (The Revolutionary Background of W.B. Yeats) in 1973 (*IP*, 12 May 1973); to an audience at the Technical College in Granard, County Longford, on Michael Collins and Kitty Kiernan in 1983 (*Longford Leader*, 3 February 1983); to the Merriman Winter School on Liam Ó Rinn in 1986 (*IP*, 3 February 1986).[16] Listeners to Radio Éireann could have heard him speak on, among other topics, 'Leabhra Spioradálta' (Spiritual Books) (*CE*, 19 August 1935); 'Ath-Armáil' (Re-Armament) (*CE*, 11 June 1937); 'Neithe is Cuimhin Liom (Things I Remember) (*IP*, 27 August 1941); learning Irish (*NG*, 21 February 1942); Parnell (*II*, 9 July 1952); the Easter rising (*IP*, 8 January 1966; *IP*, 19 March 1966; *II*, 9 June 1980; *IP*, 2 November 1985); the Irish in the First World War (*IP*, 2 January 1977); Louise Gavan Duffy (*IP*, 12 April 1986); and, fairly regularly, on new books in Irish (*IP*, 5 August 1935; *CE*, 19 August 1935; *IP*, 12 February 1938; *IP*, 18 April 1938; *IP*, 29 June 1939; *IP*, 5 July 1940; *IP*, 4 February 1941; and *IP*, 3 August 1942).

Needless to say, given all of his commitments in so many different directions, writing would always be a part-time activity for Ó Broin, until his retirement from the civil service. In *Just Like Yesterday*, he tells us that he began writing in Irish first, in 1918, a decision he saw in retrospect as 'a ridiculous thing to do; and yet in the atmosphere of that time, I could do nothing else'.[17] His first published piece appeared in *The Connacht Tribune*, and by 1919, he writes, 'I was doing articles for the Gaelic League weekly, though saying nothing of consequence in any of them.'[18] In 1920, he was judged 'best writer of Irish at the Dublin Feis', an award about which he would comment dryly half a lifetime later: 'The competition may not have been severe.'[19] Of his early literary efforts, he wrote in the autobiography that 'what I was really doing was giving myself practice in a language I was still learning'.[20] Apparently, within two years he felt he had had enough practice, for that was when his first collection of short stories, the self-published *Árus na nGábhadh agus Sgéalta Eile* (The House of the Dangers and Other Stories), appeared. Looking back six decades later he recalled that he gathered the stories into a book. It was not a success. With 3,000 unsold copies at the printer's and himself in debt for his literary ambitions, he read in the paper one morning a story 'to lift my heart'. His printer's business had gone up in flames. Hoping to receive compensation from the printer's insurance, he was shocked to learn that one of the workers had managed 'at considerable risk to himself' to save his books from the burning building. Ó Broin took the news philosophically: 'With my tongue in my cheek I commended the man's gallantry!'[21] Undeterred by the drama surrounding the failure of his first literary effort, he would go on to write three more collections of better stories: *Béal na hUaighe agus Sgéalta Eile* (The Mouth of the Grave and Other Stories) (1927), *Ag Stracadh leis an Saol agus Scéalta Eile* (Struggling with Adversity and Other Stories) (1929) and *An Rún agus Scéalta Eile* (The Secret and Other Stories) (1932). He himself seems to have come to see these works as of no great significance – the only one he mentions in *Just Like Yesterday* is *Árus na nGábhadh* – but leaving aside the best stories of writers like Pádraic Ó Conaire, Séamus Ó Grianna ('Máire'), Seosamh Mac Grianna, Liam Ó Rinn, Pádraig Ó Siochfhradha ('An Seabhac') and Seosamh Ó Torna ('Seán Sabháiste'),[22] his short stories were as good as, if not better than, most being written in Irish at the time.

Furthermore, unlike the majority of Gaelic fiction with settings in either a real or an idealised Gaeltacht then being written by both native speakers of Irish and learners of the language, his stories had settings with which urban readers of Irish could identify. Nor did Ó Broin offer any apology for writing about what he knew best, telling Muiris Ó Droighneáin: 'Most of my literary work deals with the life of Dublin ... Why wouldn't it? I understand the people of the city and I do not understand the people of the Gaeltacht any more than the people of English-speaking Ireland do. I believe, however, that the city has a story to tell to the rural areas and it might as well be told in Irish.'[23] His success in this regard and his contribution to the development of the short story in Irish are neatly and fairly summed up by Aisling Ní Dhonnchadha in her pioneering study *An Gearrscéal sa Ghaeilge 1898–1940*:

> The variety of the subject matter, the originality of the invention, the allusiveness of the commentary – these are the principal qualities of Ó Broin's work. His work in and experience with theatre benefited his craftsmanship in the short stories. He understood the limits of his own ability as a short-story writer so that he never attempted to produce deep, great and substantial literature. And that said, it is certain that his work was a source of courage and hearty inspiration.[24]

As we will see below, this assessment also holds true of the plays in Irish he was writing at the same time he was working on these stories.

Ó Broin's interest in literature and his responsibilities as a high-ranking civil servant came together neatly in 1925 when he, along with Seoirse Mac Niocaill and Micheál Breathnach, was given what he later called 'the outline of a scheme of publications involving the Department of Education and Stationery Office jointly, and asked to put it into effect. The result of their efforts came to be known as An Gúm'.[25] Ó Broin would serve on its first editorial board along with major figures in the language revival like Douglas Hyde, Tadhg Ó Donnchadha ('Torna'), Piaras Béaslaí, Pádraig Ó Siochfhradha ('An Seabhac') and Colm Ó Murchadha (*II*, 9 February 1929).

With the publication of *Parnell: Beathaisnéis* (Parnell: A biography) in 1937, Ó Broin's own writing took a new turn into biography and history, the two genres to which he would devote the rest of his literary life. Despite poor sales, *Parnell* was well received by the critics. Thus, noting quite correctly that it was 'the first full-length original political biography in Irish' – indeed the first serious and significant full-length biography of any kind in Irish – an anonymous critic for *The Irish Press* declared that 'its appearance is accordingly in the nature of an historical occasion' (*IP*, 28

April 1937). Ernest Blythe, Ó Broin's erstwhile boss, declared: 'It is cause for joy and a source of courage that such a book in Irish is available. The author has done research and study so that he understands the ins and outs of the story better than anyone who has given an account of Parnell's life in English, and that is clear in his book from start to finish.'[26] Despite a few reservations, Sean O'Faolain praised Ó Broin for 'his excellent Gaelic Life' and wrote: 'It is marvellous value for five shillings. It deserves to be widely read.' He was particularly impressed by Ó Broin's treatment of Parnell's love affair with Katharine O'Shea, writing that 'it is one of the greatest stories in the world, and … Leon Ó Broin has told it well' (*IP*, 20 May 1937). Frank O'Connor wrote to Ó Broin to congratulate him on the book, stating, in Ó Broin's summary of the letter in *Just Like Yesterday*, that 'my *Parnell* was as good as any biography in English which was saying a lot because Parnell attracts writers and competition was keen … It was well to be able to praise a book in Irish as though it were in English and without making reservations to cover the non-existent standard of writing in Irish.' Ó Broin was pleased that O'Connor felt 'it was great relief to read in Irish a book that was first and foremost a book'.[27]

That statement could be made about all of Ó Broin's later biographical and historical works in Irish. The next of these to appear, *Miss Cruickshank agus Coirp Eile* (Miss Cruickshank and Other Corpses), is a fascinating case study in historical detective work as Ó Broin tells us of all the fruitful leads and frustrating dead-ends he encountered in his attempt to identify the famous mummies in the vaults of St Michan's church in Dublin. The book was a Club Leabhar selection in 1951 and remains as fascinating today as it was then, when, in the words of Philip Rooney, it 'very deftly roused the curiosity of a wide circle of readers' (*IP*, 16 June 1952).[28] *Miss Cruickshank* was followed in 1955 by *Emmet,* which won Duais an Chraoibhín as the outstanding book published in Irish that year.[29] Then came *Comhcheilg sa Chaisleáin* (Conspiracy in the Castle) (1963), *Na Sasanaigh agus Éirí Amach na Cásca: Scéal Nathan* (The English and the Easter Rising: Nathan's story) (1967), and *An Maidíneach: Staraí na nÉireannach Aontaithe* (Madden: The Historian of the United Irishmen), another Club Leabhar selection (1971).[30]

He also produced English-language versions, at times revised and/or expanded, of some of his Irish titles. Thus, we have *The Unfortunate*

Mr Emmet (1958) and *Dublin Castle and the Easter Rising: The story of Sir Matthew Nathan* (1960). In the 1960s he had also begun to write historical works in English as well as in Irish, and after 1971 in English only, eventually producing *Charles Gavan Duffy: Patriot and statesman* (1967), *The Chief Secretary: Augustine Birrell in Ireland* (1969), *Fenian Fever: An Anglo-Irish dilemma* (1971), *The Prime Informer: A suppressed scandal* (1971), *Revolutionary Underground: The story of the Irish Republican Brotherhood 1858–1924* (1976), *Michael Collins* (1980), *Frank Duff* (1982), *No Man's Man: A biographical memoir of Joseph Brennan* (1982) and *Protestant Nationalists in Revolutionary Ireland: The Stopford connection* (1985). In addition, he edited *In Great Haste: The letters of Michael Collins and Kitty Kiernan* (1983).

Ó Broin's move from Irish to English for his historical and biographical work was obviously disappointing to many in the Irish-language community. It was not, however, the result of a sudden change in thinking or commitment on his part. As early as 1937 he had been frustrated over the failure of *Parnell* to reach a larger audience, a fact that he notes in *Just Like Yesterday*, writing that he 'derived little satisfaction from the publication' for despite having had a second printing it sold poorly and 'after many years there were still copies available of the second printing, and a good number of those that had been sold went as prizes at *feiseanna*, which meant, I fear, that they were unlikely to have been read at all'.[31] He obviously felt the situation had improved little after the passage of a half-century, so that he could in 1984 tell listeners to Radio Éireann 'that he had given up writing in Irish because his books were not being read' (*go raibh sé éirithe as scríobh i nGaeilge mar nach raibh a leabhair á léamh*) (*IT*, 25 June 1984).

Frustration of that kind does not explain his decision to stop writing plays in Irish in the early 1940s after devoting so much of his limited time to the Gaelic theatre in the previous two decades. In all probability, the explanation is even simpler. As noted above, Aisling Ní Dhonnchadha has pointed out his awareness of his limitations as a creative writer with regard to his short stories, and those limitations are no less clear when one looks at his plays. Moreover, it is difficult to say how important drama really was to Ó Broin. As we have seen, he says very little about his involvement in theatre in *Just Like Yesterday*, so that we are reliant on other primary sources to trace his origins as a playwright. We first hear of him as an actor, playing the important role of An Búrcach in Pádraic Ó Conaire's *Na Gaiscidhigh* (The Heroes) when it was produced by the Gaelic League's Ard-Chraobh in Dublin's Rotunda at the 1920 Oireachtas (*FJ*, 5 August 1920). Given the significance of this role, he must have had at least a fair amount of previous experience on stage to be trusted with it, although one does get the impression that in many of these early Gaelic productions the willingness to act was more important than the ability to do so.[32] In 1923, he was one of the founding members of An Comhar Drámaíochta,[33] and by 1925 he was the group's secretary and *de facto* public relations officer (*IT*, 21 November 1925). He was at least partly thinking in that capacity when, in a Yeatsian gesture, he called in the police when he heard rumours that there would be a riot at An Comhar's performance of Liam O'Flaherty's play *An Dorchadas* at the Abbey. He recalled in his autobiography that

> we were told that some university students intended to prevent the play being done at all … I went to General Murphy, the Deputy Commissioner of the Garda whom I had got to know in the army, and he filled the house and wings with plain-clothes men on the night. There was no disturbance whatsoever, however, which I rather regretted, for there is nothing like a row to publicise a play.[34]

Even when he turned almost exclusively to the writing of history, he retained his interest in An Comhar Drámaíochta. Although he does not seem to have been actively involved in the 1937 re-organisation of An Comhar as an umbrella group sponsoring productions by other companies, he took a keen interest in 1942 when An Comhar, and its £600 annual subsidy from the state, were brought under the control of the National Theatre Society (i.e. the Abbey), leaving the Gaelic group little more than a nominal existence. At that time, he agreed to serve as a representative of the minister for education on An Comhar's six-person board of directors, a board of which he would become chair in 1946. Among other members of that first board were Ernest Blythe, who in truth made all the important decisions, the Gaelic writer Roibeárd Ó Faracháin, also from the Abbey's board, Seán Ó hÉigeartaigh, Diarmuid Ó hÁinlighe and Proinsias Mac Síthigh (*IP*, 22 August 1942). In 1963, with the Abbey company still playing in the Queen's theatre, he was one of the Abbey's representatives who welcomed President Éamon de Valera and his wife, the former Gaelic actress Sinéad Ní Fhlannagáin, to a performance of *An Claíomh Solais*, the Abbey's 1962–3 holiday *geamaireacht* or pantomime (*IP*, 5 January 1963). By this time, however, he already felt that the vestigial Comhar Drámaíochta had outlived, maybe long outlived, its usefulness. At a meeting of An Comhar's board in 1960, with the new Abbey theatre in the planning stages, Ó Broin is reported as saying 'that he thought it would be proper when the new building was ready that an end be put to An Comhar Drámaíochta and that the statutory obligation to provide for drama in Irish be put on the Abbey'.[35] His motion was adopted, thus ending the noble experiment that was An Comhar Drámaíochta, although the group's grant was not turned over to the Abbey until 1967.

Ó Broin had long hoped that the Abbey would play a role in the development of quality drama in Irish. Speaking at a meeting of the Trinity College Gaelic Society in 1935, he is reported to have stressed the value of Gaelic drama, pointed out the role radio could play in its evolution, and declared that 'the Abbey and Gate should co-operate in developing the drama' (*II*, 5 November 1935). By 1966, however, that hope was pretty much gone. In the constraining circumstances of a ceremony to celebrate the opening of the new Abbey, he made no mention at all of drama in Irish. Moreover, given the occasion, one might well find his praise of the Abbey curiously lukewarm: 'Mr. Leon Ó Broin … said the Abbey, it was true, had its great days but relatively few great plays. But the Abbey was designed to foster the drama, not to be a commercial theatre in the strict sense of the word, and that meant that the audiences often saw plays of mediocre merit.' Still, he added that 'the teamwork of today was as consistently good as ever, while production was better than ever, and the new playwrights, when they came, would … be well served' (*IP*, 21 July 1966). Theatre in Irish would not be, however, and Ó Broin must have felt some betrayal when he realised that the Abbey had never actually signed any contract accepting what he had in 1950 called the theatre's 'statutory obligation to provide for drama in Irish', and that its board obviously felt, as Tomás Mac Anna reported being told by the Abbey's chairman in 1993, 'that they had no legal obligation to produce plays in Irish' (*nach raibh dualgas de réir dlí orthu drámaí Gaeilge a léiriú*).[36]

All of this was, of course, well in the future when Ó Broin was most directly and regularly involved with An Comhar in the 1920s and '30s. Nor was his engagement with Gaelic drama limited to his work with that group. Like so many of his colleagues in the Irish-language theatre movement, whether playwrights, directors or actors, he was willing to serve on occasion as an adjudicator at various drama competitions and festivals. Thus, we find him acting in this capacity at Feis Maitiú in Cork in 1930 (*CE*, 28 April 1930); at the Marian Arts Guild of Dramatic Art in Dublin in 1934 and 1935 (*IP*, 12 November 1934; 6 May 1935); at the St Vincent de Paul Society's Myra Feis in Dublin in 1937 (*IP*, 9 March 1937); and at Feis Átha Cliath in 1938 (*IP*, 28 March 1938).[37] In 1935 he was an adjudicator in a competition for verse-speaking sponsored by the Marian Arts Guild in Dublin, where he commented that verse-speaking was 'a very important adjunct to dramatic art competitions' (*IP*, 14 May 1935). At Feis Maitiú in Dublin the same year he judged the entries in a competition for musical plays, but was reported as saying that 'he was in a quandary with regard to the dramas presented because none of them were musical plays, though each of them had songs which were not knit into the plays in the way desired' (*IP*, 13 May 1935).[38] His experience in 1935 did not discourage him from returning to Feis Maitiú the following year to adjudicate a competition for an Irish operetta. This time, there was only a single entrant, but he thought it a good one, stating that 'the performance could not be praised too highly. The whole production was delightful' (*IP*, 21 April 1936).[39] It should perhaps be noted here that unlike some of his colleagues who travelled around the country to attend drama competitions and festivals, Ó Broin, apart from his trip to Cork in 1930, seems to have limited his activity in this regard to Dublin, in all probability because of his administrative duties in the capital. On the other hand – and this is a point worth pondering – theatre does not seem to have been something he was ever inclined to go very far to see. In an extraordinary note in passing in *Just Like Yesterday*, he tells of travelling in an official capacity with Ernest Blythe to see Micheál Mac Liammóir's translation of Shaw's *Arms and the Man* at Taibhdhearc na Gaillimhe in 1931, and then states matter-of-factly: 'The Shaw play was the only Taibhdhearc play I ever saw; I did not even see an adaptation of a French farce of my own they put on.'[40]

This lack of interest in the extraordinary experiment that was taking place in the Taibhdhearc in the 1930s might well be a sign that if Ó Broin's interest in Gaelic theatre was briefly intense, it was not at all deep. We should, then, look at how he thought about theatre in Irish before turning to the plays he himself wrote for that theatre. First of all, it is clear that he had little if any interest in theories of drama; his concern was with more immediate issues involved in the creation of an Irish-language theatre. Among those issues was a question that was far more ideological than practical, one that stirred up powerful emotions in the language movement: would a truly national Irish drama have to be in Irish, or was there a legitimate place in the national culture for drama written by Irish people in English? For a majority at the time, the idea of any authentic expression of Irish culture in any language but Irish was anathema, but Ó Broin would ultimately take a more nuanced approach to the question. In a piece on 'An Dráma Náisiúnta' (The National Drama) in 1926, he argued that 'national drama' was a misleading term because no art form was ever 'national' in the sense that it was bound up 'tightly with the mind of the nation' (*go dlúth le haigne an náisiúin*) or evolved 'from the work of the people' (*ó shaothar an tsluaigh*).

Instead, he insisted that it was 'a small group of people who are serious about art' (*sgata beag daoine atá dáiríri i dtaoibh na h-ealadhan*) who produced that art. A handful of such artists – even a single individual – could, however, 'give to those who will come after them a goal and a way of working' (*ceann scribe agus módh oibre a thabhairt dóibh seo a thiocfas ina ndiaidh*), setting them on the path to a true 'national' drama, for there was 'in every human creature some share, small or big, of the heritage that is rooted in the country in which he was born, in which he suffered the pains of life, and of which he is always thinking' (*i ngach créatur daonna a bheag nó a mhór de dhúthchas atá préamhaithe sa tír inar rugadh é, inar fhulaing sé pianta na beatha agus ar a mbíonn sé i gcomhnuí ag cuimhneamh*).[41] Dismissing the claims of the Abbey to be the real 'national theatre', Ó Broin at this stage in his thinking felt the future was with the Gael: 'What is in store for drama in Irish? Growth! It will grow as surely as the child grows, and nothing is needed for the growth except for a person or two or a small group of people. Time is a good storyteller' (*II*, 31 May 1926).[42]

Apparently time's tidings were not as encouraging as he had hoped they would be, for when he returned to the topic in 1929 in an essay entitled 'An bhFuil Drámaíocht Náisiúnta Againn?' (Do We Have a National Drama?), he focused largely on drama in English: 'The person who knew nothing about us, if he were to read the majority of the stories written about Ireland for the past seven or eight years, if he were to go to see a good share of the plays that were produced during that time, what would he say about us?'[43] What they would have seen, he asserted, was that 'we are stupid, blind people ... people from whom you could not get the truth, people who killed and plundered for their own good, but pretended that they did those deeds for the good of their country' (*daoine dúra dalla sinn ... daoine nach bhféadfá an fhírinne a bhaint asta, daoine do mharbhaigh is do chreach ar mhaithe leo féin, ach gur leigeadar go léir orra gur ar mhaithe le n-a dtír a rinneadar na bearta sin*). For outsiders reliant on the books and plays being produced by Irish writers, it would be hard to escape the conclusion 'that the Irish were just hypocrites, poor mouthers and liars' (*nach raibh ins na Gaedhil ach lucht fuar-chrábhaidh, lucht an bhéil bhoicht agus lucht éithigh*). Determined to rectify these misperceptions, for which he felt playwrights bore a particular responsibility, he argued that Irish writers had been too quick to focus on post-civil war disillusionment, and had forgotten the heroic years of the independence struggle. Notable here is that he did not regard this failure as limited to Irish playwrights working in English. All contemporary 'Irish writers' (*sgríobhnóirí Gaedhealacha*) – a title that, unlike most of his colleagues in the language movement, he did use here to refer to all Irish writers, whatever their linguistic medium – were afflicted with 'gloom' (*gruaim*) and 'sorrow' (*dólás*) that prevented them from seeing and depicting the country honestly and accurately: 'The mark of those traits is strong in the plays of the Abbey and in plays in the Irish language ... It is the duty of our writers to have a knowledge of nature; that in Ireland and every other country nature is just laughter and crying mixed together' (*IR*, November 1929, pp. 864–5).[44]

Issues more specifically relevant to theatre in Irish were, needless to say, also of concern to him at this time. Since the very start of the Gaelic drama movement, many had stressed the great potential educational value of theatre as an aid in teaching correct, fluent and colloquial Irish. Indeed, more than a few seem to have believed that the principal reason to write plays was pedagogical, and that the literary quality of those plays was, for the foreseeable future at least, largely irrelevant.[45] Ó Broin was certainly aware that staging and attending plays in Irish could improve the Irish of all involved. For instance, in a talk at the Rathmines library in 1930, he is reported to have stressed 'how it is possible to use the plays for educational purposes' (*cionnas is féidir na drámaí a oibriú mar ghléas oideachais*) (*II*, 5 April 1930). Addressing the Trinity College Gaelic Society five years later, he spoke of 'the value of Gaelic drama and the radio in reviving the language' (*II*, 5 November 1935). In school plays, at least, he felt that 'the chief aim in drama was good diction, well-pronounced Irish, and clear speaking', but he also added that 'at the same time the dialogue must be rational and so must the acting' (*IP*, 13 May 1935).

In a major essay on 'Contemporary Gaelic Literature and Some of Its Paradoxes' that provoked a lively discussion in the pages of *The Capuchin Annual* when it appeared in that journal in 1935, Ó Broin wrote of the government's encouragement of Gaelic drama in the schools: 'Incidentally, the teaching of dramatics will improve the diction of our educated speakers who, the native and the non-native alike, speak Irish barbarously in most cases. The way, for instance, in which it is spoken on the radio is enough to drive people who are sympathetic into violent opposition to the revival of such a language.' While he conceded that 'bad phonetics' was forgivable for learners, he joked that 'educated speakers who grind out their words on the radio should be made amenable by law as public nuisances' (*CA*, 1935, p. 132). Doubtless he had a similar opinion about bad Irish on stage, although at times he must have had to keep it to himself in the company of some of his colleagues in An Comhar Drámaíochta.

Of course, he knew well that while the appearance of actors with good Irish would make Gaelic drama a more effective pedagogical tool for language learners and a less penitential experience for fluent audience members, theatre in Irish would still have a long way to go before its cultural influence was as significant as it should be in a modern, Gaelicising Ireland. With this challenge in mind, in 1928 he lectured to the Gaelic League's Ard-Chraobh on 'New Subjects for Dramatic Treatment' (*II*, 14 February 1928).

Needless to say, new subjects would require new plays, or at least new Irish-language versions of older ones, and for that reason Ó Broin found himself once again involved in the debate over the role of translation in the Gaelic theatre. He had no theoretical or ideological reservations about translation *per se*, recognising that if the language was not only to survive but also to evolve in the kind of modern, increasingly urbanised world it had never had to confront, it would have to draw on all the resources available to it, no matter whence they came.[46] Indeed, he was a translator himself, producing, for example, Irish versions of four novels from English: *An Fuadach* (Robert Louis Stevenson's *Kidnapped*) (1931), *Triúr Fear i mBád* (Jerome K. Jerome's *Three Men in a Boat*) (1932), *Cogadh na Reann* (H.G. Wells' *The War of the Worlds*) (1934), and *An t-Oileán Draoidheachta* (Ernest A. Jelf's *Jill's Magic Island*) (1939).[47] These translations were all well done and would have provided engaging reading matter in Irish while also developing readers' familiarity with and command of the national language.

There was, of course, a pressing need for new playscripts for Gaelic actors to perform. In a 1926 piece on 'Dráma ar an Tuaith/Comhairle do Ghaedhilgeóirí' (Plays in the Country/Advice for Irish Speakers), Ó Broin declared: 'This cannot be said too often: plays, plays, and more plays is the best and most appropriate battle cry for someone today. It is plays, both translations and original plays, that are needed.'[48] Indeed, he urged all capable of even trying to write a play to do so, with the following significant caveat: 'I would, however, advise them not to compose original plays until they have translated or read carefully and studiously a good number of foreign plays.'[49] Acknowledging that this was an opinion unlikely to be shared by 'many of my friends' (*a lán dem chairde*), he wrote: 'The new dramatic movement will progress more quickly if a numerous band of trained playwrights are helping us. It is of no use to have people with no knowledge of the rules of the stage or the principles of composition and dialogue writing plays.'[50]

It is, then, hardly surprising that Ó Broin was pleased by what An Gúm was accomplishing in this regard, writing in 1935: 'What is particularly startling is the number of plays of all sorts on all sorts of subjects … The achievements in the theatre are really remarkable, more particularly when it is recalled that there were no plays in Irish before Dr. Hyde's "Twisting of the Rope" …' (*CA*, 1935, p. 131). Of course, most of the plays published by An Gúm were translations, a situation Ó Broin could, for a while, accept on purely pragmatic grounds. The next question to be faced involved the kind of plays that should be brought into Irish. Ó Broin recommended 'clever comic plays that will not be too long; preferably one-act plays' (*drámaí cliste grinn nach mbeidh ró-fhada; cluichí-aon-ghníomh is fearr*). Plays from English already likely to have been seen in Ireland were to be avoided, if possible, in favour of 'good foreign plays' (*drámaí maithe iasachta*). But with regard to a writer 'without an exact knowledge of one of those languages' (*gan eolas cruinn ar cheann de na teangthacha sin*), he was willing to see him 'turn to English and give up anything else' (*iompódh ar an mBéarla agus droim láimhe do thabhairt ar aoinní eile*), for 'he will have a big wide field to plough there' (*beidh páirc mhór leathan le treabhadh annsin aige*) (*FL*, December 1926, p. 4).

In June 1929, the weekly paper *The Star* published a lengthy editorial entitled 'Drama in the Saorstát' critical of An Comhar Drámaíochta, and suggested that the group exercise more care in the choice of translated plays to perform. A debate followed in the pages of the paper, with one contributor to the controversy, Seoirse Ó Broin (no relation to Leon), declaring: 'Translation, however excellent, is just a second-hand thing.' For Seoirse Ó Broin, the guiding principle was: 'Your own effort, however bad, is better than imitating the work of someone over there, however good it might be' (*Star*, 13 July 1929).[51] Leon Ó Broin's response to this letter, written in what he knew would be a more widely read English, appeared in the paper the following week, a response in which he moved quickly beyond the question of translation to a careful assessment of the state of An Comhar Drámaíochta and of Gaelic theatre in general. Much of his analysis of the problems facing An Comhar rehashes the standard list of difficulties with which the group was grappling: the need for a dedicated Irish-language theatre, for an adequate subsidy from the state, for larger and more reliable audiences, for more frequent and longer runs of plays, for more sophisticated and helpful drama criticism. It was not, however, these self-evident problems that engaged his attention here. Rather, he was determined to set out what was at stake should An Comhar not be revitalised and what could – must – be done to restore the group's original vision and sense of purpose. Many must have found startling his discussion of why An Comhar had not evolved more successfully: 'The intimate alliance between the Comhar Drámaíochta and the Language

Movement, while adding to the strength of the latter, has robbed the Gaelic Theatre of much-needed vitality.' He argued that for many in the language movement theatre in Irish was just 'the Gaels' "night out" … a rainbow which was displayed in the firmament seven times a year'. While such Gaels might well enjoy such special occasions, these brief and infrequent performances were largely responsible for the 'hit-and-run-away nature' of theatre in Irish, 'its very freakishness' leaving it 'a kind of intellectual-cum-linguistic side-show which, by its very nature, could never be expected to fall into line with art movements elsewhere or to progress very substantially beyond the stage it had reached'. To begin the reversal of this downward spiral, Ó Broin urged those with a real interest in theatre in Irish to take an all but unthinkable step:

> And above all, there must be an immediate divorce between the people who believe in the drama for the drama's sake and the people who are interested in the drama because it is Gaelic drama or because the Irish language is the medium of expression used. The first fruit of this divorce will be a vote of confidence in the language. Dramatists and actors alike will accept the inevitable meaning of the theatre, that the language medium is alive and kicking, that it is possible to perform miracles with that language and that in time these miracles will happen (*Star*, 20 July 1929).[52]

One of those anticipated miracles would be the creation of worthwhile original plays by Irish-language playwrights, including Leon Ó Broin. If his work as playwright was largely forgotten over time – even by himself – he achieved considerable recognition, in Gaelic circles at least, during the years he was most active in the theatre in the 1920s and '30s. Thus, when in 1930 he visited Cork to adjudicate the drama competitions at Feis Maitiú, the *Cork Examiner* said of him:

> He has written three Irish plays and has translated others into Irish that have been produced by the splendid Irish players of Dublin. He represents the young Irishman of the future who will go out to draw all the culture of the world literature to the service of Irish as our own Irish tongue. He stands in with the small but growing body of

> Gaelic speakers whose minds have stored in them all that is of value in English and Irish, while they have their eyes also on the continent, like the Gaels of history (*CE*, 28 April 1930).[53]

He had certainly taken his own advice about studying and translating a 'good number of foreign plays', producing Irish versions of six foreign plays, one of which was a full-length work, and five of which were from English, the other from French. Neither these translations nor his 1942 radio play *Sláinte an Bhradáin* (Excellent Health) fall within the scope of this study.[54] Still, it is worth mentioning that when he translated Tristan Bernard's one-act *L'anglais tel qu'on le parle* (1899) into Irish as *Labhartar Béarla Anseo* (English Is Spoken Here) – first performed by An Comhar Drámaíochta at the Abbey in October 1926 – he shifted the setting from Paris to Dublin and the languages in comic conflict from French and English to Irish and English. Needless to say, it is a quite different play when the dynamic is not between two widely spoken world languages, but rather between an imperial language and that of the culture its speakers had colonised. In the original the humour arises from the fact that a monoglot Englishman in Paris is unable to communicate with the locals, and that the 'interpreter' provided for him can't speak English – or indeed anything but French. Transposing this situation to his Irish setting, Ó Broin presents a fantasy scenario in which Ireland is entirely Irish-speaking, with even most of the population of Dublin, including those in the hospitality business, unable to speak English. However far-fetched, this premise allows Ó Broin to sidestep one of the great bugbears that has always bedevilled the Gaelic stage – the idea that there are characters in a play who speak Irish, even Dublin Irish (*Gaedhilg Bhaile Átha Cliath*), who would never do so in real life. Bernard was no Molière and Ó Broin no Shaw, but the play was a well-translated and amusing addition to the Gaelic repertoire in the mid-1920s. His other translations were *Ní Mar Síltear Bítear* (Eliot Crawshay-Williams' *E. and O.E.*); *Ruaidhrí Réamhráite* (*Rory Aforesaid* by 'John Brandane' [John McIntyre]); *An Fear ar an gCasán* (Alfred Sutro's *The Man on the Kerb*); *Lapa an Ápa* (W.W. Jacobs' *The Monkey's Paw*); and the full-length *Clann na Gealaighe* (Martin Flavin's *Children of the Moon*).

His major contributions were, of course, the original plays, of which there was such a pressing need at the time. He wrote eight of these, seven one-acters and one full-length play, between 1927 and 1945: *Rogha an Dá Dhíogh* (A Choice Between Two Evils), *An Mhallacht* (The Curse), *Siamsa Gaedheal* (A Gaelic Entertainment), *An Scríbhinn ar an mBalla* (The Writing on the Wall), *An Clósgríobhaí* (The Typist), *An Oíche úd i mBeithil* (That Night in Bethlehem), *Slán le Muirisg* (Farewell to Murrisk) and *An Boisgín Ceoil* (The Magic Melodeon). The predominance of one-act plays here was, of course, largely the result of the state of Gaelic theatre when they were written. Ó Broin himself was to write in 1935 that 'while nowadays much exploited by Irish and by some writers with considerable success, I think the short-story and the one-act play the least suited of all literary forms to our particular genius' (*CA*, 1935, p. 127). Yet, these were the very genres to which he devoted his literary efforts, well aware that it was stories the various journals publishing Irish were looking for, and it was short plays that theatre groups like An Comhar found most useful, plays that part-time actors could learn fairly easily and that would not tax the attention span of playgoers, some perhaps wrestling with a language they did not know well. Moreover, one-act plays could be more easily kept in the active repertoire and revived quite flexibly in combination with other short plays to fill out an evening's programme with considerably less trouble than would be involved in mounting a full-length production.

One gets a clearer notion of how important was Ó Broin's contribution to the repertoire of An Comhar when one realises that of the twenty plays the group produced at the Abbey during the 1926–7 season, five were the work, either original or translated, of Ó Broin (*Labhartar Béarla Anseo* was done twice that season). Of the fourteen plays the following season, three were his, and he also had plays performed in the 1928–9, 1929–30, 1931–2, 1934–5, 1935–6 (two plays), 1937–8 and 1939–40 (two plays) seasons. And while his plays have not enjoyed an enduring popularity, neither have those of any other playwrights who began writing in the 1920s and '30s with the exception of those of Máiréad Ní Ghráda. In their own time, however, they furnished reliable entertainment that suited both the talents available to An Comhar and the tastes of the admittedly small audiences the company drew to its productions.

Rogha an Dá Dhíogh, the first of his original plays to be staged and his only full-length work, was produced by An Comhar Drámaíochta in the Abbey in March 1927 with Gearóid Ó Lochlainn directing. As we have already seen in our discussion of the plays of Piaras Béaslaí and Ó Lochlainn, reviews of the early performances of An Comhar were often short and superficial, telling us next to nothing about the plays themselves. In the case of *Rogha an Dá Dhíogh*, the most interesting thing about the production according to 'D. Ó D.' was that one of the actors still needed his script in hand to deliver his lines (*Leader*, 26 March 1927).[55] 'D. Ó D.' himself might not have minded having a script to keep track of the chaotic plot. Nuala Ní Shúilleabháin is a young woman who finds herself in the unenviable condition referred to in the play's title. The daughter of a bank manager in a country town in the early years of the Free State, she learns that both of her parents have chosen potential husbands for her, and she has no use for either one of them. Her father's choice is Conán Ó Mathghamhna, a bank clerk currently basking in the glory of having foiled an attempted robbery at her father's bank and looking forward to a reward and an immediate promotion. Her mother's favourite is Gearóid Ó Casaide, the sub-editor of a newspaper who sees himself – and is seen by Nuala's mother – as a poet. Despite being badgered by her parents, Nuala is not without support, as Bríd, the family's maid, keeps her up to date with their machinations, a service for which she loses her job, although she remains in the house throughout the play. The next character we meet is the detective Cathal de Fréinne, who has come to inquire about the attempted bank robbery and who seems to have some previous connection with Nuala. After some fairly predictable complications, we find out that de Fréinne has been in love with Nuala for several years, sending her letters to which she has never replied.

At this point, Ó Broin introduces a surprising twist into the play as we learn that the reason Nuala has never answered his letters is that de Fréinne, in the uniform of a Black and Tan, had taken part in a raid on her family's home during the war of independence. He seems, however, to have been that rarest of all figures in Gaelic literature – a Tan with a heart of gold. As Nuala tells her maid, 'It was Cathal de Fréinne … who saved us from the Black and Tans. That was the person who knocked down that big ugly giant who was trying to kiss me … He was not like the rest of them. There was a noble streak in him somehow.'[56] Still, she realises that for her father, the neighbours and the vast majority of the Irish people, the only good Tan might not have to be dead, but he certainly could not be an in-law in a good nationalist family. Perhaps predictably, de Fréinne turns out not to have been a Tan at all, but rather one of Michael Collins' intelligence officers assigned to infiltrate the enemy and rewarded after the war with a post in the new Garda Síochána. As he puts it, 'I went into the Black and Tans, do you understand, not for love for England or hatred for Ireland, but because I had to do so for the sake of the Volunteers.'[57] After another bout of farce that leads to the capture of an inept burglar, Conán Ó Mathghamhna is exposed as the villain of the piece, having arranged for an accomplice to 'rob' the bank as a 'stunt' that would enable him to act the hero. All ends well, with de Fréinne and Nuala splitting the reward for capturing the 'robber' and Nuala planning to join him as his spouse on a farm he has recently purchased.[58]

Were *Rogha an Dá Dhiogh* (much) funnier, an audience might forgive its disjointed and improbable plot, or were the plot more engaging, that audience might overlook the hackneyed comic bits. As it is, the play is eminently forgettable and seems to have been forgotten almost immediately. At any rate, I have found no record of a revival. Yet, before we write it off, we may note three points of interest about it. First of all, when it was produced by An Comhar in 1927, there weren't many plays in Irish with settings with which an urban Irish speaker could identify and it could thus have been a welcome addition to the regular fare of rural Gaeltacht dramas. Second, by even suggesting the possible humanity of a Black and Tan – even if it turns out that the human being was not a Tan after all – the play breaks away from the all too often justified stereotype of British soldiers, particularly Black and Tans and Auxiliaries, as conscienceless monsters. And third, the play's comic treatment of the parents' botched attempt at matchmaking may have given relief to Gaelic audiences weary of reading about or seeing stage depictions of Gaeltacht marriage negotiations of the kind now best known from Blasket Island autobiographies like Tomás Ó Criomhthain's *An tOileánach* (The Islandman) (1929) or Peig Sayers' *Peig .i. A Scéal Féin* (Peig, i.e. Her Own Story) (1936).

Just eight months later in November 1927, An Comhar performed *An Mhallacht*, his only tragedy, at the Abbey, with Gearóid Ó Lochlainn again directing. Of particular interest is its civil war setting. According to 'D. Ó D.' in his review for *The Leader*, 'The author found his setting in Warsaw in Poland, and according to him the story concerned the uprising of the leader Pylowski [*recte* Piludski] in the year 1925 [*recte* 1926].'[59] 'D. Ó D.' was, however, well aware of what Ó Broin was up to in his attempt to deal by proxy with tragic events just a few years in the past and still raw in Irish memory and so avoid exacerbating wounds on both sides of the civil war split. 'D. Ó D.' wrote: 'Perhaps Leon was right, but the story could have been told far better if the setting had been left here in Ireland during the Civil War.' Apparently, at least according to 'D. Ó D.', the audience, far from being disturbed by this play about civil war, failed to see its relevance to their own history and politics: 'People would take more interest in it if it were brought closer to home … The play did not really grip the audience as Leon intended' (*Leader*, 26 November 1927).

For once, a playwright may actually have heeded a critic's advice, for when *An Mhallacht* was published by An Gúm in 1931, the play was set in Dublin during the civil war. One can understand both Ó Broin's initial attempt to distance the play a bit from the Irish civil war he had himself experienced as an officer in the Free State army, and the nerve it took for him to confront in any way at all a topic on which almost all Gaelic authors chose to remain silent, doubtless from motives similar to those of Ó Broin's fellow playwright and civil servant Micheál Breathnach, who wrote in his autobiography *Cuimhne an tSeanpháiste*: 'I do not intend to discuss the harm the Civil War did nor the evil consequences it left behind. I would rather draw a big black curtain down on that period and put it out of my memory altogether if I could.'[60] Ó Broin's own verdict on the conflict was succinct; it was 'a war in which uncontrollable forces were being released to do unjustifiable deeds'.[61]

Unfortunately, Ó Broin's achievement did not do justice to his ambition in *An Mhallacht*. Instead, he fell back on a variant of the oldest trope in writing on civil wars, the notion of brother fighting brother, although in his play it is brother-in-law who kills brother-in-law. More original was his use of what may be termed the 'guests of the nation' scenario famous from Frank O'Connor's 1931 story of that title and from Ernie O'Malley's account of his personal involvement in a similar episode in *On Another Man's Wound* (1936).[62] The play is set in 'a comfortable-looking sitting room' (*seomra suidhe go bhfuil rian na compóirde air*), where, over tea, Colm Ó Duibhir and his wife Eibhlín are telling Máiréad, who is married to Eibhlín's brother Séamas, about their recent honeymoon in Paris. All three are cheerful young people in their thirties able to joke about scantily clad dancers in a Paris nightspot and Colm's encounter with a flirtatious woman, who was either 'a friendly tall young woman' (*slibire lághach óg*), as Colm remembers her, or 'a very ugly hag' (*cailleach úr-ghránna*), according to Eibhlín. Absent from the gathering is Séamas, 'who threw away ... his fine job to go off into the Free State Army – fighting, if you please'.[63] Worse, as Máiréad informs Colm and Eibhlín, Séamas would have been home 'except that he was afraid that you, Colm, would be on the other side and there would be no welcome for him' (*ach ab é gurbh eagal leis go mbeifeá-sa, a Chuilm, ar an taoibh eile agus nach mbéadh aon fháilte roimhe*). Colm remains silent, but Eibhlín reassures Máiréad: 'Well! Well! Colm is not with any one group rather than another' (*Mhuise! Mhuise! Níl Colm i dtaoibh le haon dream seachas a chéile*). She is, however, nowhere near as confident as her words here would suggest, for she has had suspicions that Colm has joined the anti-treaty republicans, suspicions she finally shares with Máiréad: 'Last night when we were here talking about this conflict among ourselves, between the defenders of the Free State and the Republicans, I thought that I saw that old shadow on his face – that shadow that used to be on him in the time of the fighting as if the courage of his mind was trying to overcome the weakness of his body.' This time it is Máiréad who reassures Eibhlín, telling her that Séamas has declared that this conflict is just 'a fight of hornless cows' (*troid na mbó maol*) and adding: 'A fight between friends does not last.'[64]

Eibhlín's deepest fears have, however, been awakened, and she expresses an opinion of Irish patriotism that many in the original audience must have found shocking: 'The old, passionate love I had for Ireland has gone from my heart altogether. Now I just have a steadfast love for Colm. That old instinct that is in all women told me that Ireland was trying to cut my feet out from under me as the Hag of Beare used to do with the scythemen – if what the old people say is true – tripping me up against my will and snatching Colm as she often did already with other men.'[65] For Eibhlín, Ireland is now 'more powerful ... than the Hag of Beare and more treacherous' (*cumhachtaighe ... ná an Chailleach Bhéara agus cealgaighe*), and she wonders: 'Why is Ireland so voracious, so impatient that she must swallow up the best men, that she cannot let this generation escape.'[66] Indeed, she has come to believe that there is a curse on both

Colm and Séamas because, in the previously mentioned 'guests of the nation' scenario, they executed two British captives in reprisal for the execution of an IRA prisoner. Looking back on that incident, Eibhlín recalls: 'We were laughing and boasting about the damage done to the English army ... We forgot that the wives of those two, their mothers and children were mourning for them, cursing a thousandfold the people who snatched them from them forever. That curse is still on us. The curse of the men's blood and the curse of the women's lament.'[67] The curse plays itself out when a republican sniper shoots a Free State soldier from the roof of Séamas and Máiréad's building and a squad of soldiers under Séamas' command arrives, tracks down the sniper, and kills him. It should come as no surprise that the dead republican is Séamas and his killer Colm, who returns to the flat 'as white as a ghost ... a trace of blood on his face' (*chomh bán le taidhbhse ... rian fola ar a cheannaightheacha*). Distraught, he states that he hadn't recognised Séamas in the dark, that both had fired, and that only after his opponent fell did he realise he had shot 'the loyalest and kindest friend I ever had ... May God forgive me for it' (*an cara ba dhílse agus ba chaoine dá raibh riamh agam ... Go maithidh Dia dhom é*). The play ends with Eibhlín unable to speak, 'her hands stretched out before her imploringly' (*a dhá láimh sínte amach roimpi go himpidheach*); Máiréad standing at the door, 'a marble statue' (*na híomhágh marmair*); and Séamas on one knee, 'his head down in his palms, weeping softly' (*a cheann anuas ar a bhosa, ag gol go bog*).[68]

The working out of the tragedy is without doubt too obvious, but in its own time this play had the potential to force audiences to face uncomfortable truths about what their acceptance of, if not active support, for violence had done to them and their country since the beginning of the war of independence in 1919, and especially during the civil war in 1922–3. Moreover, Ó Broin neatly juxtaposes the superficial normalcy of the lives of these two couples, their comfort and cosmopolitanism, with an atavistic nationalism they have internalised and that so easily breaks through their civilised facade. While *An Mhallacht* is far too melodramatic to appeal to modern audiences, in its own time and place it was a forthright and even daring contribution to a debate about the unthinking glorification of violence and its future role in the evolution of Irish democracy, a debate that the Irish people very much needed to have.

The one-act comedy *Siamsa Gaedheal* (A Gaelic Entertainment) had its premiere by An Comhar at the Abbey just five months later in April 1928. It was one of three one-acters that evening, all directed by Ó Lochlainn. It is, to say the least, a lightweight effort about which the only thing one anonymous critic could think to write was that it was a 'lovemaking comedy' and thus 'in interesting contrast to the other two plays' (*II*, 3 April 1928).[69] Once again the setting may be the most original element in the play, which takes place not in a rural garda barracks where the pursuit of *poitín* distillers would offer comic possibilities, but rather in garda headquarters in Dublin. The protagonist is a superintendent who, it turns out, has been unable to make his own 'choice between two evils' (*rogha an dá dhíogh*) and thus finds himself engaged to two women and in danger of legal action from both. Discussing his dilemma with his solicitor, he explains how having already proposed to one of the women, he goes to 'a Gaelic entertainment' (*siamsa Gaedheal*), where he finds himself alone, feeling 'that I was the only old person there' (*gur mise an t-aon seanduine amháin dá raibh san áit*). Worse, 'the utter shame would not let me bring a woman out to dance' (*ní leigfeadh an dearg-náire dhom bean do thabhairt amach ag rinnce*). Approached by 'a fine, beautiful, well-dressed young woman' (*ainnir bhreágh álainn deigh-ghléasta*), he soon finds himself dancing with her and 'within a quarter of an hour we were out on the stairs in the darkness courting each other – I don't know now which of us was worse. Within a half-hour I had kissed her many times.'[70] Before the night is over, he has asked her to be his wife. The reference to *siamsa Gaedheal* is a nice touch here, as Ó Broin is no doubt poking fun at how writers of Irish dealing with urban life regularly tried to sidestep the issue of linguistic verisimilitude by setting their works in a Gaelic ghetto of sorts, a Gaelic League branch, a *céilí*, or An Stad, the well-known Dublin hangout for Irish speakers, for example.

The solicitor claims he can handle the situation if the superintendent provides him with a good sum of cash with which to buy off one of the women. Unfortunately, he first attempts to bribe the woman in whom the superintendent is actually most interested. When she faints at learning what her fiancé has done, he rushes in to revive her and to try to explain himself. It is, of course, just at this point that the other woman arrives in his office, leaving him struggling to somehow mollify both of them. The play ends with the two women striking him, one with an umbrella, while he literally throws money at them and his sergeant blows his whistle to summon reinforcements. Done right, the play might once have been amusing, but in its treatment of women as enemies of male autonomy and its general silliness (as opposed to wit), it could have little lasting appeal. Nevertheless, it was revived at Taibhdhearc na Gaillimhe in February 1937 and, as performed by the Cork Gaelic Society (Comhar Drámaíochta Chorcaighe), broadcast over Radio Éireann in May 1936 (*CE,* 20 May 1936).

His next play, *An Clósgríobhaí* (The Typist), was first performed by An Comhar at the Abbey in February 1929, again less than a year since his previous play. Pronounced 'a bright little comedy' by one of the opening-night critics (*II,* 5 February 1929), it is indeed his best humorous play. When it was announced that the play was to be revived by An Comhar in November 1934 on a bill with Piaras Béaslaí's *Cluiche Cártaí,* a correspondent for *The Irish Press* stated: 'These two plays were produced by An Comhar a few years ago, but there are many Irish-speakers in the city who never saw them and the people who did see them enjoyed them so much at that time that they will come again' (*IP,* 17 November 1934).[71]

Apparently, those who did go to the plays were rewarded, whether they were seeing them for the first or the second time. According to a brief unsigned review in the *Irish Independent,* 'the people who saw them last night were fully satisfied with them' (*II,* 20 November 1934).[72] When the play was staged at the beginning of the Second World War by the Limerick Gaelic Dramatic Society (Comhar Drámaíochta Luimnighe), on a bill with *Na Lóisdéirí* (The Lodgers), Aindrias Ó Cuinn's translation of Fand O'Grady's *Apartments,* a correspondent in the *Limerick Leader* urged his readers to attend the production, for 'both plays are amusing and interesting and are certain to provide the comic relief which is necessary for all of us in these days of worry and strain' (*LL,* 14 October 1939). Particularly effusive was Séamus Ó Néill, who in a review of the play as broadcast over Radio Éireann in 1936 wrote: 'The author has a good understanding of drama. It is clever how he makes use of the telephone instead of boring us with a long "soliloquy". He has his craftsmanship "up to date" in that regard. It is a great pity that we don't have an abundance of plays of this kind in good Irish' (*Ultach,* November 1936, p. 5).[73] Given the success the play enjoyed and the fact that it is a Gaelic comedy that is actually funny, one would have expected it to remain in the repertoire, but it seems instead to have been largely forgotten after the early 1940s.

An Clósgríobhaí, like Ó Broin's other comedies, is pretty much based on a single comic premise to which he gives a few humorous twists. Here, we have an attractive and stylish young woman who, on the pretence of helping a newcomer arriving in the city to take up a new job, manages to steal her letter of introduction to her new employers and then impersonates her to get the position in her stead. The employers, a pompous uncle and his feckless nephew – who according to Ernest Blythe's review of the published text were father and son in the original stage production – have just begun their difficult-to-characterise business, their sole accomplishments so far the rental of an office and the purchase of office furniture and a typewriter. Both father/uncle and son/nephew (the latter played by Ó Broin himself in the original production) are smitten with the new typist. Indeed, their attraction blinds them to the point that they accept her as a naive country girl just out of school despite her fashionable clothes and the make-up she at one point tries frantically to rub off her face, and pretend not to notice her obvious unfamiliarity with the workings of a typewriter. Although the older man initially claims he only wants to hire 'a girl who was raised in the country … a girl who will work' (*cailín a tóigeadh ar an tuaith … cailín a dhéanfas obair*) and not 'one of those girls you would see in the movies … a flapper' (*duine de na cailíní úd a chífeá ar na pictiúirí reatha … flapper*), he soon joins the younger man in trying to court his employee and ends up chasing her around the office and boorishly trying to kiss her. This problematic treatment of what is clearly sexual harassment in the workplace is rendered minimally less offensive by how farcically it is played and by the fact that the young woman is more than able for either of the men or both together. At any rate, she dupes both of them into 'lending' her money and then absconds with their cash box while the older man frantically chases the younger around the furniture. As the play ends, the two realise that they have been thoroughly outsmarted and decide to shut down their entire enterprise – before either the audience or they themselves have figured out what that enterprise was actually supposed to do in the first place. At this point, to their surprise the real jobseeker arrives, leaving the pair speechless. With a few revisions to update the situation and to defuse the offensive behaviour of the two men with regard to their 'typist', this play might still work as an entertaining curtain-raiser for a modern audience.[74]

The one-act play *An Sgríbhinn ar an mBalla* (The Writing on the Wall) was published by An Gúm in *An Mhallacht agus Trí Drámaí Eile* in 1931, but seems never to have been produced. It is very much in the mould of *Rogha an Dá Dhíogh* and *Siamsa Gaedheal. An Sgríbhinn ar an mBalla* is set in a town in County Galway in 1918. Áine Ní Bhriain's husband Tomás Mac Fhlannchadha has joined the British army and been missing in action for two years, and she is now being courted by Seán Mac Maolagáin, a pompous and overbearing county councillor. Máire Ní Mhaoileoin, Áine's servant, has no time for Mac Maolagáin, sure that he is more interested in the pub Áine owns than in the woman herself: 'He is just a flatterer. I think that he hopes to make a match with you, but it's not for your own sake he would marry you if you were willing to make a match with him, but for the sake of the pub.'[75] Indeed, it is obvious that Máire has far more respect for Tomás than does his wife, as she warns Áine not to marry Mac Maolagáin: 'Watch out for him, mistress, for compared to the man you had he is a real devil.'[76] Máire is, not surprisingly, enraged when Áine is willing to hang a framed picture of Mac Maolagáin in place of the one of Tomás on the sitting-room wall. After a few comic delays, Mac Maolagáin's portrait is finally on display, but another suitor, Michilín Mac Giolla Bhríde, identified as 'a cadger' (*geocach*) and clearly an alcoholic, arrives on the scene. Mac Maolagáin need only point to his picture on the wall to put Michilín in his place: 'I admit that it is very hard for you, but you should know that you had no chance when Seán Mac Maolagáin, County Councillor, was seeking her.'[77]

All seems to be going according to plan for Mac Maolagáin when Tomás Mac Fhlannchadha suddenly enters 'mad drunk' (*ar dearg-mheisge*) and singing, with 'khaki clothes on, and a kit-bag under his arm' (*éadach caicí air agus kit-bag faoi n-a asgaill*). To the amazement of all, he boasts that he is 'back in the old place, safe and sound, despite the whole world' (*ar ais san tsean-áit, slán folláin, i n-ainneoin an tsaoil go léir*). When his dumbfounded wife asks if he is indeed her husband, he responds that he has been in prisons and hospitals but now 'Here I am back to you, on my own dungheap and so thirsty that I could drink Ireland's Loch

Corrib if I had a slender beak.'[78] When he first sees Mac Maolagáin, he is magnanimous, though he doesn't miss the chance to remind that follower of John Redmond that he didn't take his leader's advice and prove the Irish worthy of home rule by joining the British army in the trenches of the Great War: 'And you never went to war after all, Seán. But, of course, to each his own, and death in Ireland. You are probably a Sinn Féiner by now. Here, where's your hand at any rate. Shake hands with me.'[79] When he asks Máire whether Áine has been faithful in his absence, she answers bluntly: 'She has been faithful to you so far, but she wouldn't be faithful to you much longer if you hadn't come home in good time.'[80] Furthermore, she points out that Mac Maolagáin's picture has replaced his on the wall. Learning of their marriage plans, Tomás confronts his wife and Mac Maolagáin, prompting excuses from Áine and evasions from the county councillor. Tomás' solution to the problem is simple: 'Let's make a deal. Let's fight. Let the one who is alive after the fight have the woman and the pub. His picture will be on the wall.'[81] Of course, Mac Maolagáin wants no part of the proposed duel: 'I don't want … I don't want the woman. I don't have any love for her … I don't … I don't.' He then runs off 'at full speed' (*i mbarr na bhfásgaí*) as Tomás fires a warning shot after him.[82] The play ends with Áine taking down the offending picture and then waiting on Tomás and Máire as they drink together in the pub, for 'pity the person who would be a teetotaller with a pub nearby'.[83]

By 1931, Ó Broin's interest in writing plays was waning, although as we have seen he retained his connection with An Comhar Drámaíochta for another three decades. His next play, *An Oíche úd i mBeithil* (That Night in Bethlehem), was not performed until December 1939, when An Comhar produced it in the Peacock theatre with Seán Ó Conchubhair directing.[84] The play offers Ó Broin's perspective on the nativity account in the Gospel of Luke, and quite an interesting perspective it is. Given the playwright's devout and orthodox Catholicism, one would not expect him to tamper in any way with the essential elements of the narrative in Luke 2:1–20, and he does not. Instead, he focuses on the effect of Christ's birth on the lives of several people in Bethlehem, most notably a Roman captain and his commanding officer. The most striking thing about the play is how directly Ó Broin confronts the issue of imperialism/colonialism. Obviously, his interest in this subject was rooted in the Irish experience of British imperialism, but he was no doubt also troubled by the rise and aggression of the Nazi Third Reich with the Second World War starting just months before his play opened. Early in the play, the young Roman captain and his commander debate the ethics of colonialism. The commander offers a timeworn defence of imperial intervention in the affairs of others: 'What would this land of Judea do if we were not here on behalf of Rome to keep them from each other's throats?'[85] However, the captain finds this argument altogether unconvincing:

> It would not be any worse than it is at present. We know of no way to establish peace except to take away a person's freedom when he reveals his dissatisfaction with something, with hunger, for example, or heavy taxes, or with an attempt to smother in his heart the love he has for his own gods. It's not only the armies I am blaming; there are other means besides armies and State police to do away with a person's freedom ... Why is Rome trying to dominate the whole world?[86]

For the captain, the end of colonialism will lead to the full expression of the suppressed culture of the colonised: 'I would prefer that people be happier, that they would have a way to spend their lives with no regard for armies and Empires, for power and for wealth. If they were like that they could develop the good qualities of their hearts and minds. There would be a place for beauty and for truth.'[87] Moreover, he is well aware of the corrosive effect imperialism has on the imperialists themselves:

> And look at Rome ... Is there anything in the world duller than Rome? It has utterly defeated the nations of the world. You would think to look at it on the surface that there is nothing that would defeat it, but we who were raised in the city of Rome itself know that the city is not what it claims to be. That the foundation stones are crumbling and rotting with the passing days under the Empire and the fine structure must fall apart sooner or later.[88]

His commander is at this point more interested in the realpolitik of the situation, pointing out that however peaceful Judea may look, 'the people are dissatisfied and in a mood to make trouble' (*tá mí-shásamh agus fonn miosgais ar na daoine*), that a rising is just a matter of time, and 'when it breaks out … we will have plenty to do to suppress them. The last time it happened … I was not here … but I heard that it was necessary to hang 3,000 of them as an example to the rest'.[89]

After a brief discussion about the Messiah with their innkeeper, the man who later can find no room for Joseph and Mary, the two Romans ponder what the appearance of such a figure would mean for imperial policy. When the commander states that he has heard the Messiah will be 'a Prince of Peace' (*Prionnsa Síochána*), and thus nothing for the Romans to fear, the captain agrees: 'I have always known that that is exactly the kind of person that is trampled on. The State that we are defending here in Judea, it has no pity for those who are humble and gentle at heart.'[90] There then follows a scene with the innkeeper and his wife, who has visited the manger and believes the child is indeed the Messiah. At this point, Ó Broin takes the play in a quite different direction. The stage directions read: 'The light of the lamps gradually diminishes until the entire stage is in darkness. A short pause … A mysterious, unearthly music begins playing and, by degrees, the spotlight settles on the face of the Arch-Angel Gabriel, who is standing at the exact centre of the stage.'[91] We are now at the manger, where we hear a chorus singing and see three shepherds come to worship the Christ child. Into this scene come the two soldiers, who are clearly disappointed with what they find. As the commander says, 'If the Child is the Messiah, why is there not some sign for us all to see clearly here that he is. It is just an ordinary couple and an ordinary child.'[92] To be on the safe side, however, he takes the opportunity to offer Joseph some ominous advice: 'Go back [to Nazareth] as quickly as you can. Keep on working as usual and don't allow anyone to change your situation. It is peace that Rome wants, and for its sake she does not mind nailing the odd person to a cross now and again. It would be a great pity if something of that sort happened to any of you.'[93] After his commander leaves, the captain remains and converses with the Archangel Gabriel, who tells him to believe in the Messiah, 'for it is here only that you will find your heart's desire, the one you were seeking. The God of Peace who was born in a human body to save the world'. At this point, the captain is, however, still unable to make the necessary leap of faith: 'I believe and I don't believe. O

God of Glory help my disbelief.'[94] In the presence of Mary, he asks Gabriel: 'Will I get from her the life that does not wither away and the hope that even Caesar himself cannot suppress?' (*An bhfuighead uaithi an bheatha nach meathann agus an dóchas nach féidir do Chaesar féin a chlaoi?*). With Gabriel assisting him, the captain kneels before Mary, and 'Mary lifts the child and blesses the Captain with him.'[95]

The play now reverts to its previous setting at the inn: 'The chorus begins and the lights gradually go out until it is entirely dark. The mysterious, unearthly music is heard again.'[96] We are obviously meant to take the entire scene at the manger as a dream or vision experienced by the captain, although there seems to be no reason why, given the very nature of the nativity play genre, that the miraculous should be eschewed, particularly since the scene could so easily have been incorporated into the 'real' world of the play. Either way, what he has gone through has an immediate effect on the captain, an effect intensified when he sees the star of Bethlehem moving in the sky, a sight that also astonishes his commander. When they notice people streaming out of their houses to search for the Messiah, they feel compelled to join them. The commander asks his subordinate: 'Isn't this what you have been hoping for many a day?'[97] Moreover, he adds, 'I feel that I myself want … to see this child.' If that slight hesitation indicates the commander is still uncertain of what he will find when he goes to the manger, there is no mistaking his eagerness and his hope: 'We will go there together. Come on. Quickly!'[98]

An Oíche úd i mBeithil is Ó Broin's finest play. It presents the gospel story in the respectful and devout manner one would expect in a traditional nativity play while simultaneously giving the traditional themes of peace and goodwill a striking new relevance for both its own time and the future. This is a play that could be staged today without any changes at all, and the fact that it was so quickly and entirely forgotten by those involved with Gaelic theatre is both a mystery and a missed opportunity.

Ó Broin's next play, *Slán le Muirisg* (Farewell to Murrisk), seems not to have had a stage production, although it was published by An Gúm in 1944 and broadcast over Radio Éireann in October 1953 (*MN*, 17 October 1953). Taking its title from an eighteenth-century poem by An tAthair Uilliam de Búrca, it is a historical play dealing with a partly fictionalised episode from the life of the legendary Father Myles Prendergast (An tAthair

Maoilre Piondargás) of Murrisk Abbey, County Mayo, who sided with the rebels in 1798, the 'Year of the French'.[99] The play opens with An tAthair Piondargás and his nephews in a Castlebar jail awaiting execution. They are being guarded by a sympathetic jailer, an elderly man who is aware that his former neighbours hate him as a traitor for his service with the enemy. An tAthair Piondargás recalls the spirit of hope animating the people when the rising in Mayo began: 'The lads from all the little townlands were stirring out that morning that we gathered at the foot of the Rick. They thought the day of the Irish had come. I myself thought so.'[100] But even imprisoned and condemned, he refuses to give up hope of escape, replying to his nephews' acceptance of their fate: 'Neither of you has been hanged yet, and if our own people outside do what they promised, none of us will be hanged.'[101] He has arranged to have a key smuggled in that will enable them to open the main door of the jail. Aware that the escape may not go as planned, he has also hidden away an iron stake for use as a weapon, stating, 'If the key comes, the escape will be easy. If it doesn't, we will have to try violence.'[102]

Even after the key arrives concealed in a salmon sent for their dinner, An tAthair Piondargás believes the weapon will be needed, and he tells his nephews to make their escape 'while I am settling accounts with the soldier' (*fhad's bhéas mise ag socrú cunntais leis an saighdiúir*). When one nephew is scandalised by the idea of a priest killing a man and states 'It is the priest's work to save souls and not to damn them', An Athair Piondárgas tells him to stop his 'sermonising' (*seanmhóinteacht*), but then agrees that they should draw lots to see who will carry the stake.[103] It is the priest who writes out the names and puts them in a hat, and we later discover that he has put his own name on all three pieces of paper, guaranteeing that any act of violence that needs to be committed will be his responsibility. The three realise they will have to bring the jailer with them, for they know full well he will be blamed and punished severely when they are missed. Almost immediately, their plans go awry and they are fired on but still manage to get away, largely because An tAthair Piondargás kills one of the guards, a man who, we learn, had a wife and four children.[104] The one man who does not succeed in getting away is their jailer, who lacks the strength to keep up with the others. Captured, he understands that he will soon be hanged, but, in a neat echo of the ending of Lady Gregory's play *The*

Gaol Gate (1906), he takes pride in the fact that his old neighbours will now celebrate him as a hero. Ó Broin also shows the possible influence of Yeats' *On Baile's Strand* (1904) by ending his play in effective anticlimax by having the jail guards, like the Blind Man in Yeats' play, indifferent to the heroic sacrifice of others in the play and thinking of nothing but their bellies as they eat the salmon the prisoners left behind.

While *Slán le Muirisg* is a slight enough play, it is at least as good as the majority of historical plays in Irish from this time and before. Moreover, its treatment of political violence is genuinely interesting. As we have already seen in *An Mhallacht*, Ó Broin was not at all comfortable with the usual moral arguments used to justify the use of violence to advance political causes. The fact that in *Slán le Muirisg* it is a priest who not only accepts but actively engages in violence raises the ethical stakes. Furthermore, Ó Broin goes out of his way to humanise the man the priest kills by mentioning his wife and children. A simplistic reading of this episode would be that an tAthair Piondargás is a straightforward patriotic hero who feels that the killing of an enemy is entirely justified in wartime. A more likely interpretation, given Ó Broin's devout Catholicism and interest in questions of personal and political morality, is that An tAthair Piondargás consciously takes on this terrible responsibility rather than have his nephews commit a sin that might damn their souls.

As we saw above, in *Just Like Yesterday* Ó Broin remembered his final play *An Boisgín Ceoil* (the only one of his plays he mentions by title in the autobiography) as a ballet based on a folktale in Peadar Ó Direáin's *Sgéalta na nOileán* (1929), with a score by Arthur Duff.[105] While there were ballets based on Gaelic themes by the time he wrote the play, when *An Boisgín Ceoil* was published by An Gúm in 1945 it was subtitled 'a fantasy' (*saoilneas*), and referred to by its author as 'a little one-act play' (*dráimín aon-mhíre*). Moreover, it had been broadcast as 'a magical play' (*dráma draoidheachta*) on Radio Éireann in December 1942 (*IP*, 23 December 1942). Although in the published text Ó Broin writes that the play was intended for 'young people, but there's a chance that people not too young would also enjoy performing it or seeing it' (*daoine óga, ach tá seans ann go mbainfeadh daoine nach bhfuil ró-óg sult as freisin ghá léiriú nó ghá fheiceáil*), I have found no record of a stage production. That Ó Broin expected that the play would be performed is evident from 'a special note' (*nóta speisialta*) he provided with the *dramatis personae*: 'It is recommended to any group that will perform this little play to let themselves go and to be as extravagant as they wish with regard to the staging and acting.' He also indicated that 'any lively music at all' (*ceol tapaidh ar bith*) would work with the mad dancing in the play as long as it was played as rapidly as possible, and suggested Strauss' *Perpetuum Mobile* as a good choice.[106]

There isn't much to *An Boisgín Ceoil*, as Ó Broin simply dramatises the folktale. His protagonist is Páidín, 'a wandering labourer with a childlike appearance' (*geocach d'fhear oibre go bhfuil cuma leanbach air*). We first see him dealing with his employer, a farmer for whom he has slaved for two years at a wage of a penny a year and who now tries, unsuccessfully, to cheat him of even that meagre compensation. Pay in hand, Páidín next meets an old woman and, on learning of how hungry she and her large family are, he gives her his tuppence. Like sovereignty in medieval Irish literature, she gives him her blessing and then turns into a lovely young woman, 'the beautiful queen of the fairies dressed in magnificent clothes' (*bainríoghain áluinn na sídheoga agus í gléasta faoi éadaigh taidhseacha*). At first he is terrified, afraid she might turn him into a goat, but she calms him, returns his tuppence, and bestows on him two things he has always wanted: 'a gun that would bring a bird down without causing it pain or tearing its beautiful little body with the grains of shot' (*gunna a thiubhradh éan anuas gan pian a chur air nó gan a chorp beag áluinn a stróiceadh leis an ngráinne*), and the ability to make music that would let him forget 'hardship and calamity, however painful' (*anró is anachain dá ghéire iad*).[107] She provides the gun with the titular magical melodeon, which has the power to make people dance until its music stops, however long that might be. The next person he meets is the archetypal Droch-Dhuine (Evil Person) of folklore, who promises Páidín £300 if he will bring down a bird he wants. Bird in hand, the Droch-Dhuine refuses to pay, whereupon Páidín uses the magical melodeon to set him dancing frantically until he begs for the music to be stopped and promises to pay up. Of course, he then tries again to cheat Páidín of the now twice-promised money and brings in a justice and two policemen, who seem more than willing to believe him over the less respectable-looking Páidín. Needless to say, the judge rules against the hapless Páidín and even sentences him to death. Another bit of music from the melodeon quickly resolves the problem, and An Droch-Dhuine is compelled to pay him 300 guineas. This time, however, Páidín is cleverer than his opponent, for after getting his money he keeps playing the music, and the play ends with Páidín vanishing in the distance, the music gradually fading, and the four dancers collapsing in a heap.

With *An Boisgín Ceoil,* Leon Ó Broin's career as a playwright came to an end, although, as we have seen, he was until 1966 still involved with An Comhar Drámaíochta, which by then had existed for a quarter of a century as little more than a fiction of the bureaucratic imagination. During the 1920s and '30s, however, the group had been at the forefront of the Gaelic theatre movement, and Ó Broin was among its most active members as an actor, board member, secretary, and, of course, for several years a prolific and successful playwright and translator of plays. Still, despite some evidence that he was genuinely interested in theatre – one thinks, for example, of his writings on the subject in the 1920s and '30s – it is hard to escape the conclusion that, like some others who took part in the Gaelic theatre movement at that time, he was drawn to the stage by his interest in language revival rather than by any love of drama itself. It is certainly difficult to believe that anyone truly passionate about theatre could allow it to fade so completely from his life as did Ó Broin from the 1940s on, his only remaining connection with theatre being his service on the board of An Comhar Drámaíochta, the sort of administrative task he could probably have handled in his sleep. Moreover, he never got involved in a theatre movement in English, despite the existence of the Abbey as a force in the national cultural revival. In the final analysis, it is probably fair to say that Leon Ó Broin was an accidental playwright, called forth by a concatenation of circumstances without which he would never have written for the stage. Still, those circumstances did concatenate, and he did produce a series of plays, including original ones, for An Comhar Drámaíochta, plays that at the time met a real need for something fresh to convince audiences that they could be entertained by stage fare in Irish. With so many other accomplishments to relish, Ó Broin himself may have come to dismiss the significance of his relatively brief career as a playwright, but those with an interest in the development of Gaelic drama at a key period in its history should not repeat his mistake.

CHAPTER FOUR

Questions of Conscience: Séamus de Bhilmot (1902–77)

Writing in *The Kerryman* in 1945, Piaras Béaslaí spoke of Séamus de Bhilmot as 'an outstanding writer of original plays in Irish' and continued that 'his plays are anything but conventional, being characterised by originality, variety, and a stimulating play of ideas' (*K*, 11 December 1945). Seven years earlier, Ernest Blythe had also praised de Bhilmot's ability as a playwright, but was more specific about the source of his originality. A correspondent wrote in the *Irish Independent* that Blythe had recently stated that 'Some years ago a dramatist with what he believed would be a remarkable future had started writing for the Galway Theatre. This was Mr. Seumas Wilmot ... Mr. Wilmot's first play, "Barabbas" [*sic*] and another play of his which he (the speaker) had not seen, a powerful pacifist play dealing with the war of the future, had been highly praised' (*II*, 20 August 1938). Béaslaí and Blythe were, in fact, right about de Bhilmot's importance for theatre in Irish both at that time and – potentially – in the future. That that potential influence has never come to fruition is, of course, hardly de Bhilmot's fault, nor is the fact that he is, in all probability, the least well-known of the playwrights in this book, even among those with an interest in Gaelic drama.

This ignorance of the man and his work for theatre in Irish is particularly unfortunate given that he is in many ways the Gaelic playwright from that period contemporary audiences might find most relevant to the world in which they live. He was, as we will see, by far the most politically engaged of the playwrights considered here, indeed of all the playwrights of his time period and many of those who have written since. In this regard, he obviously thought of himself as among playwrights of whom he wrote in 1968: 'Those authors are not concerned with the plot alone. They use it to illustrate their own outlook and their own philosophy to make us think about things that were, perhaps, not troubling us' (*Feasta,* December 1968, p. 33).[1] Dramatists like Béaslaí in *An Danar* and *An Bhean Chródha,* or Ó Lochlainn in *An t-Éirighe Amach* and *Na Fearachoin,* had, like many other Gaelic playwrights, short-story writers and novelists of the 1920s, '30s and '40s, dealt with the big issues that had transformed Irish political life in the early twentieth century: revolt, revolution, national identity. But apart from Ó Lochlainn's generic depiction of greedy and conscienceless capitalists in *Bean an Mhilliúnai* and *Ag an Ladhrán,* and, as we will see, Walter Macken's more subtle engagement with unfair business practices and the threat of occupational obsolescence in *Oighreacht na Mara,* no other playwright in Irish had much at all to say about the extraordinary real-life challenges facing Ireland and the world in the catastrophic 1930s and '40s. Moreover, de Bhilmot wrote of these issues with a consistently pacifist emphasis on the need for an informed ethical response on the part of the individual human being, whether leader or civilian. The need for such a response was made more insistent by his awareness that his contemporaries worldwide were living in an ever more amoral world in which they were threatened with being overwhelmed by new and frightening forces far more powerful and impersonal than anyone had ever experienced before from either the global or local perspective. From this point of view, he was a truly transitional figure, setting an example of literary engagement with contemporary political issues that his more gifted successors have developed with greater imagination and craft but certainly no more honesty and passion than de Bhilmot showed when he began this tradition eighty years ago.

If not a Renaissance man in the grand sense, de Bhilmot was certainly a highly accomplished and significant figure in the Gaelic renaissance and in Irish life for a full half-century. Born in 1902 in Listowel, County Kerry, the 'Lislawn' of his literary work, he was educated there in St Michael's College and then at University College Cork, where he took a degree in commerce. According to his son, the actor and theatre manager Ronan Wilmot, he had 'superb Irish' (*Gaeilge den scoth*), which he had learned in Listowel 'in the national movement there at the beginning of the 20th century' (*sa ghluaiseacht náisiúnta a bhí ann ag tús na 20ú haoise*).[2] Doubtless Wilmot is referring in part here to the classes of the Gaelic League, an organisation of which his father otherwise seems never to have been a particularly active member, but one whose flaws and foibles he was nonetheless able to skewer in his 1947 parable of the language movement *Mise Méara* (I Am Méara), an English-language adaptation of which, with some significant changes, he published in 1972 as *And So Began …*[3] After leaving UCC, he returned to Listowel to teach at St Michael's for five years and then went on to Dublin, where he was on the faculty of the Jesuit Belvedere College for three years, later taught at Rathmines Vocational School, and took an arts degree and a higher diploma in education from University College Dublin.

These experiences as a teacher at his *alma mater* and as a Kerry exile in Dublin would figure largely in his quasi-autobiographical 1947 novel *The Splendid Pretence*.[4] Leaving the teaching profession, he spent time as chief educational officer of the County Wexford Vocational Education Committee (in which role he opened Ireland's first rural vocational school in 1932). He then served several years as town clerk of Galway,[5] before being named chief clerk and then, in 1952, registrar of the National University of Ireland, a post he was to hold until 1972, with University College Dublin awarding him an honorary doctorate in 1953.[6] Moreover, while not at all strongly identified with the Gaelic League, he often served as an adjudicator at Gaelic League *feiseanna*. For example, he was a judge at Enniscorthy's Feis Charman in 1936; at Feis Shligigh (The Sligo Feis) in 1939, 1955, 1957, 1964, 1967 and 1972, and was involved with Dublin's Feis Maitiú (Father Matthew Feis) in 1951, 1952 and 1959. He was also an adjudicator in the drama competitions at the national Oireachtas in 1941, 1942 and 1956 and opened the Schools Drama Festival in 1965. In addition, in 1967 he published *Eochair na Sráide* (The Front Door Key), a collection of short stories that included 'Grá Triúir' (The Love of Three People), which won the Oireachtas prize for a short story in 1966.

When he died in 1977, his former student, the novelist and playwright Bryan MacMahon, offered an appropriate tribute in his obituary, writing that 'Seamus Wilmot was a man whose splendid and versatile spread of talents, endowments and endearing personal characteristics make it no easy task for anyone to do justice to his memory in fleeting words' (*K*, 4 February 1977).[7] In a piece on de Bhilmot in the *Irish Independent* in 1971, Kevin Faller agreed, stating:

> Seamus Wilmot is a prime example of a man, constantly besieged by time, who has managed to keep his powder dry. At various times a teacher, a C.E.O., a town clerk, registrar of the National University of Ireland, and chairman of the Abbey Theatre's board of directors, he has never allowed himself to be diverted from his chief interest, the making of literature (*II*, 19 February 1971).

While it is impossible to see how what must at times have been a hectic schedule could ever have allowed de Bhilmot to consider 'the making of literature' his 'chief interest', it is equally impossible not to be impressed by how many contributions he made to the making of Irish literature, and in particular Irish theatre, at points in his life.[8] Few if any Irish writers ever held important positions with so many major Irish theatres as did de Bhilmot. While teaching at Belvedere he served for three years as secretary of An Comhar Drámaíochta. Moreover, in addition to his administrative duties with An Comhar, he contributed plays for the group to stage. After moving to Galway, he became a member and later chairman of the board of directors at Taibhdhearc na Gaillimhe, to which he again contributed original plays.[9] Back in Dublin in the early 1940s, he was a founder member and from 1944 to 1956 vice-chairman of Compántas Amharclainne na Gaeilge, best known as the theatre group whose *Sea-Seóanna* brought topical variety entertainment in Irish to large and enthusiastic audiences in Dublin and, on tour, in Galway, Belfast, Cork, Carlow and Wexford. Indeed, Terence Ward, the theatre correspondent of *The Irish Press*, wrote in 1944 on the occasion of *Geamaí na Nodlag*, the group's first experiment in this form, that de Bhilmot was 'mainly responsible' for this 'new venture' for Gaelic drama, stating that 'it was when he applied the Taibhdhearc lessons of variety in Irish, through the [*sic*] Compántas Amharclainne na Gaeilge, that the theatre in Irish began to be noticed' (*IP*, 19 December 1944).[10] Among the playlets that made up various *Sea-Seóanna* were some by de Bhilmot himself.[11] It was doubtless this proven record of achievement as both playwright and administrator that caused the Irish government in 1956 to appoint de Bhilmot as one of its two representatives on the board of the Abbey theatre – the other being Ernest Blythe. He later became a shareholder in the Abbey[12] as well as chairman of the board. It was, by the way, de Bhilmot who formally welcomed President Éamon de Valera to the dedication ceremony for the new Abbey theatre in July 1966.[13]

While this position at the national theatre might seem the logical pinnacle of what was after all a part-time career in the theatre, he still had more to do for the Irish stage, serving as an original board member and later as an active supporter and innovative chairman of Tralee's Siamsa Tíre, Ireland's National Folk Theatre. Nor should it be forgotten that he was the guiding spirit in the creation of Listowel Writers' Week in 1971, also serving as president of its organising committee and a judge of its regular drama competitions until his death.[14]

It could perhaps be thought that as a teacher at the prestigious Jesuit Belvedere College in Dublin, as town clerk in Galway, and as registrar of the National University, de Bhilmot might well have been named to these various boards in a primarily decorative capacity. Any such suspicion would, however, be utterly mistaken. Theatre was a lifelong interest for de Bhilmot, one he took very seriously. Not only did he, as we have seen, contribute stage-worthy plays to An Comhar Drámaíochta, Taibhdhearc na Gaillimhe, the Abbey and Compántas Amharclainne na Gaeilge, but he also devoted a good deal of thought to the stage, and especially to the many and imposing challenges facing drama in Irish. That he felt there was much to be gained by overcoming those challenges is clear from his 1936 comments to an interviewer concerning what the interviewer called 'the Taibhdhearc movement'. Drawing on his own experience with the Galway theatre, de Bhilmot stated: 'The advantages of such a movement, from the viewpoint of Gaelic culture, are many. The Gaeltacht scholars who attend the University College usually take part as actors in the theatre's activities. Afterwards, as teachers, they are in a position to go through the country and play a big part in raising the standard of the Gaelic drama movement.' He continued: 'The Taibhdhearc is the most developed aspect of the Gaelic movement, and is the most interesting experiment for the language revival.' He then gave his reason for this rather striking claim, a reason that also explains the importance and appeal of his own best work for the theatre – the Taibhdhearc 'takes the language for granted' (*II*, 16 October 1936). Still, as a director of the theatre, he was well aware of the problems with which it continued to wrestle, stating in 1941 that 'if a permanent theatre were part of the solution of the anomalous position of the Drama, then the Gaelic drama in Galway, where there is a good cheap permanent Theatre, should be getting better support than it is' (*Leader*, 9 May 1942).

If he expressed doubts about the Taibhdhearc, it was not because he felt that the Abbey was or could be any more successful than its Galway counterpart. He was particularly concerned about the Abbey's absorption of An Comhar Drámaíochta. By this time, he himself had become an Abbey playwright when his one-act *Baintighearna an Ghorta* (Our Lady of the Famine) shared with Séamus Ó hAodha's *Donnchadh Ruadh* first prize in an Abbey competition for original drama in Irish and also became the first play performed under the theatre's new scheme to regularly include Gaelic work in its programme. But his own success in the Abbey play competition and on the Abbey stage had not convinced de Bhilmot that the Abbey could be trusted to deal justly with theatre in Irish once it had taken over An Comhar Drámaíochta, a company that, whatever its failings, had provided audiences in Dublin with regular productions of plays in Irish, many of them original, and three of them his own, for two decades. In May 1942, one 'Gaelic Playgoer' declared that (s)he trusted the current board of the Abbey and added that the incorporation of An Comhar was necessary, for 'notwithstanding all the efforts An Comhar has put into the work, the position is obviously worse now than it ever was, and there seems no prospect of improvement' (*Leader*, 16 May 1942). Responding the following week, de Bhilmot first conceded that 'Gaelic Playgoer' had given 'a fair presentation of the position – except for the connotations'. But he then went on to point out that there was already a connection between the Abbey and An Comhar, the value of which he himself did not see, and concluded: 'The direct influence on the theatre of a language other than Irish is not, I think sincerely, for the ultimate advantage of Drama or Dramatists in the Irish language' (*Leader*, 23 May 1942). Indeed, in a 1944 symposium on 'The Irish Theatre' sponsored by the Graduates' Literary and Dramatic Society in Dublin, he is reported to have said that 'he objected to Irish plays in the Abbey' because 'the Abbey had developed a technique which would be imposed on Irish plays' (*IT*, 17 November 1944).[15]

De Bhilmot seems never to have found a satisfactory resolution to his own doubts concerning the Abbey's role in the development of theatre in Irish. Thus, shortly after the new Abbey and Peacock theatres opened and at a time when he himself was on the Abbey board, he stated in a lecture on 'The Gaelic Theatre' that 'the whole future of Gaelic drama must now be considered in the light of the opening of the Peacock. It was there, ready and able to give the best to Gaelic drama, and it was controlled by people who were favourably disposed towards its advancement.' But, he added, 'the Peacock was a problem for the Abbey Theatre directors. It was difficult to assess its role in the Gaelic drama movement at the moment.' In fact, he suggested that it might be that the Gaelic theatre should be built up outside Dublin, in Galway or Gweedore, and other areas where Irish was more freely spoken than in Dublin and asked 'If the Abbey Theatre got a subsidy to enable it to produce plays in English in a professional manner consistent with its stature as the national theatre, why should a proportionate grant not be given to a Gaelic theatre situated in the natural surroundings and drawing on actors and from people who were expert in the use of their language' (*II*, 9 October 1967). One can only wonder what his fellow Abbey directors made of this suggestion.

De Bhilmot did not, however, limit his thinking about the theatre to institutional questions. For example, while in a 1941 piece on 'Amharclann na nGaedheal' (The Theatre of the Gaels) he again stressed the need for the Irish-language drama movement to have a theatre of its own, he acknowledged that mere possession of an appropriate building would not clear away all the difficulties that movement faced. Among the thornier of such difficulties he addressed – and one directly relevant to himself – was the fact that 'there is some truth in what was said by the person who said that the dramatic movement in Irish was a little bit artificial because the majority of the people involved with the drama are not native speakers of Irish' (*IM*, 1941, p. 7).[16] Moreover, in an interview with Kitty Clive the following year, he reminded readers – if they ever needed such a reminder – that adequate mastery of the language was also a problem for those who attended plays in Irish. Doubtless speaking from his own experiences in both Dublin and Galway, he focused on the difficulty a Gaelic dramatist faced when he tried 'to visualise the average playgoer', and stressed the 'different standards of Irish' to be found among potential audience members: 'One class will understand the language of the play fully, but will probably not know the niceties of the Theatre, the younger person will understand the niceties, and may not grasp the language of the play.'

Diplomatically conceding that 'a Gaelic audience is a most intelligent audience', he continued:

> As you say, there are twenty thousand Irish speakers in Dublin. What are they composed of? Old Gaelic Leaguers or native speakers, young people all with different standards of Irish and grades of sophistication. A cross section of the audience of twenty thousand would include Irish speakers who do not know the theatre in the way, for example, you know it as a pulsating live thing, and young people who are not old enough to possess that sophistication which is required for the appreciation of the Theatre (*Leader*, 9 May 1942).

He underscored that 'the person with an acquired knowledge [of Irish], and with few opportunities of practice in Dublin, is trying to do two things at the same time – follow the story of the play and understand the language'.

De Bhilmot was convinced that 'we have the dramatists, who in my opinion are equal to those writing in English, and some of them better. They can produce the material.' But he was at the same time concerned that 'many of them have laid aside the pen in the last four or five years'. And the reason was clear to him: 'But then a dramatist does not write except for an audience.' He developed this idea with strikingly disparate images: 'A great soldier cannot arise in a community of cowards. A big writer cannot emanate from an audience that cannot follow him in all his vagaries, as a woman follows a man in an intricate dance – or steps away from him in terror or hate, or fear' (*Leader*, 9 May 1942). Referring again to the estimate of 20,000 Irish speakers in Dublin, he pondered why so few were playgoers and offered several 'important reasons' (*fáthanna tábhachtacha*): 'First of all, knowledge of Irish is not the same as an interest in drama in Irish. One should not expect an Irish speaker to go to the performance of a drama any more than to any other Gaelic pastime.' Conjuring up the image of the Irish speaker who felt the obligation to attend all Gaelic functions – 'even be a member of the Gaelic Golf Club – to help the cause of the Irish language' (*fiú amháin bheith 'na bhall den Gholf-Chumann Gaedhealach – chun cabhruighthe le cúis na Gaedhilge*),[17] he insisted that if such people attended a play, 'they would not come as the result of an interest in drama as drama' (*ní de thoradh suime sa dráma mar dhráma a thiocfaidís*), but 'because the play was written in Irish' (*toisg gur sa Ghaedhilge a sgríobhadh an dráma*) (*IM*, 1941, p. 7). Indeed, unlike many if not most of his colleagues in the Gaelic drama movement, he was willing to absolve those who did not attend plays because of a lack of interest in the theatre in any language. Thus, an article about a symposium on Gaelic drama at the 1941 Oireachtas reported that in his response to Béaslaí's criticism of 'the Irish-speaking public' for not going to plays in the language, de Bhilmot stated that he 'did not agree with criticising the Irish speaking public because many might have less interest in music or golf or something else' (*IP*, 28 October 1941).

But he also worried about those who did attend plays 'because of an interest in drama'. In particular, he lamented the paltry repertoire of new plays offered to them. Here he was very much in the contemporary mainstream of thought about Gaelic drama, as writers, critics and producers like Piaras Béaslaí, Labhrás Mac Brádaigh and Ernest Blythe bemoaned the excessive reliance on translations and the lack of worthwhile original scripts in Irish. Addressing the 1940 annual conference of the Library Association of Ireland, de Bhilmot stated that 'the greatest complaint had by groups that were trying to produce plays at *feiseanna* was that they could not find any new plays and had to fall back again and again on plays they had produced again and again and that they were therefore less interested in the work' (*SI*, 26 May 1940).[18] He was also concerned that Gaelic playgoers with a real interest in theatre received so little guidance from critics (*Comhar*, September 1942, p. 8).

Of course, de Bhilmot's greatest contribution to the Gaelic stage was not as a theorist, theatre manager or activist, but rather as one of the small body of playwrights who were trying to provide audiences with entertaining and provocative new dramatic fare. Our discussion here will be limited to his stage plays, omitting unpublished radio scripts for Radio Éireann[19] or the unpublished playlets and skits he wrote for the bilingual variety shows staged by Compántas Amharclainne na Gaeilge.[20]

The first of de Bhilmot's plays to be produced was the one-act *Múchadh an tSolais* (The Extinguishing of the Light), which was directed by Piaras Béaslaí for An Comhar Drámaíochta at the Abbey theatre in November 1928. It was revived by An Comhar in a production directed by Cyril Cusack in the Torch theatre in December 1935 (*IT*, 13 December 1935); by the Cork Dramatic Society at the Kerry Drama Festival in Killarney in June 1947 (*K*, 31 May 1947); by the Gaelic League's Craobh na gCúig gCúigí at the 1949 Dublin Feis (*II*, 25 March 1949); and by a local group in Carraroe, County Galway, in January 1951. It was broadcast over Radio Éireann in July 1948 (*CE*, 30 July 1948). There were few reviews of these productions, none of them at all informative. Of the premiere in 1928, 'Guaire' had next to nothing to say about the play itself but did note with satisfaction that the audience was the largest he ever remembered seeing for a performance by An Comhar (*Leader*, 17 November 1928). For the critic from *The Irish Times*, those involved in the 1935 production 'were not successful in bringing out the full force of this drama of an ex-clerical student's temporary loss of faith …' (*IT*, 13 December 1935). On the other hand, the anonymous critic for the *Irish Independent* wrote that 'the audience enjoyed the production greatly. It would be worth it for every Gael in the city to see these plays' (*II*, 13 December 1935).[21]

Set on the Kerry coast, the play deals with a mentally unbalanced former seminarian's loss of faith and his rage at the passivity of his poor fisherman father in face of an economic and political system that has enabled the local gombeen man to become wealthy at his neighbours' expense: 'Look at the way this world is. There is no great mind directing it. If there were, poor people would not be wrestling with death on the sea and rich people fat and lazy by the fire – and God looking down on them all – but there is no God …'[22] On an appropriately dark and stormy night, he sets out to attack the gombeen man but is unable to get at him in his ostentatious home, where he is hosting a party and has all his electric lights on. Frustrated, the spoiled priest cuts the man's electric supply, thereby causing the deaths of several fishermen who were guiding themselves to shore by the bright light from the house. This focus on the moral consequences of an individual's actions would be a central theme throughout de Bhilmot's plays. The play ends with the young man expressing his remorse and coming to the bitter realisation that the God whose existence he had earlier denied was watching over the men whom his own misguided actions had killed: 'O God! … O God! You were there … You were protecting them. It is I who drowned them … out of blindness … by extinguishing the light.'[23] Unfortunately, this conventional and pious conclusion takes some of the sting out of the young man's earlier denunciations of the unjust *status quo*. And, of course, his return to faith may well provide him with a way to live with, if not escape, his guilt.

The next of de Bhilmot's plays to be produced also involved ethical issues and lighthouses. *Casadh an Rotha* (The Turning of the Wheel) has never been published, and does not seem to have survived. It is, however, possible to get some sense of what was apparently a quite ambitious work from contemporary reviews, in particular that by Frank O'Connor for the *Irish Statesman* and from de Bhilmot's response to that review. *Casadh an Rotha* had its premiere by An Comhar Drámaíochta at the Abbey theatre in October 1929 under the direction of Piaras Béaslaí, who also took the part of St Brendan the Navigator in a cast of nine actors playing twelve roles.[24] The play begins with a prologue in which Brendan speaks of America, after which the first act moves to the Battle of Kinsale, which is discussed by several characters but not actually depicted on stage. A man whom de Bhilmot describes as 'an Anglo-Irish adventurer' deserts the Irish side, running away from the battle.[25] The rest of the play deals with the fortunes of that man's American descendants, who have become lighthouse keepers across the Atlantic. As the curtain falls on the twentieth-century setting of an island off the American coast, a heroic young Irish airman making a trans-Atlantic crossing – from Kinsale of all places – runs into trouble and ditches his plane near the island on which the deserter's descendants live. One of those descendants, in whose 'heaving breast', as O'Connor writes, 'the black and insuppressible blood of the informer breaks out', attacks the airman. The latter, 'who is also well-versed in Irish history' and 'recognises the hated name', kills his attacker in self-defence and thus avenges an act of cowardice and treachery committed three centuries earlier.[26] Obviously, O'Connor hated the play, writing that 'when a puzzled member of the audience asked me what was the moral of the play', he answered that he did not know and 'could barely guess at a meaning. Perhaps it hadn't got a moral, like so much else of modern art. Perhaps it hadn't even got a meaning' (*IS*, 26 October 1929).

Not surprisingly, de Bhilmot was having none of it, writing to the *Statesman* to express his disappointment that the journal would send 'such an incompetent man as "F. O'C." to criticise Gaelic plays'. In particular he attacked O'Connor not only because he 'did not even understand the content of the much-abused play', but also because in calling much of the performance of the play 'inaudible', he may have been trying to 'cover an ignorance of the language of the play which he set out to criticise' (*IS*, 9 November 1929). The gloves were now off, and O'Connor responded that he came down so hard on 'Mr. Wilmot's little play' because he felt that 'sometime or another the attack on Gaelic infantilism had to begin'. For O'Connor,

> the issue between Mr. Wilmot and me is not the question of how much Irish I know, but of how much he knows about the construction of a play. In my opinion he knows nothing. It is no defence that many other Gaelic dramatists know no more. God tempers the wind to the shorn lamb, but it would be a bad critic who maintained that because other Gaelic writers know nothing Mr. Wilmot was a writer of average ability. Mr. Brinsley McNamara is; so is Mr. T.C. Murray, but Mr. Wilmot is not within miles of being as good as either.

He was, however, just warming up before going on to dismiss the play in terms that de Bhilmot must have found particularly galling:

> Plays like this would be impossible to produce before an English-speaking audience, and what concerns all of us who value the Irish language is to prevent a generation growing up which will finally label Irish as synonymous with ignorance and English with culture. Another five years of this sort of thing and Irish will be dead for ever.

Asserting the need for 'the fiercest criticism of everything second-rate, that will tolerate nothing but the best in literature and drama and art', he concluded by stating that it was 'a disgrace that thousands of pounds of public money should be wasted on the literary efforts of Mr. Wilmot of this kind' when Ireland had so many pressing cultural deficiencies (*IS*, 16 November 1929).

Perhaps overwhelmed by the vehemence and scope of O'Connor's attack, de Bhilmot's response two weeks later was entirely unconvincing:

> I entirely agree with 'F. O'C.' regarding 'the fiercest criticism of everything second-rate', but let us not forget that we must first catch the hare before we can have the soup. He says that plays like *Casadh an Rotha* would be impossible before an English-speaking audience. What connection has an English-speaking audience with a Gaelic play, or is the standard of such an audience an immutable standard? The obvious suggestion is that the audiences of Gaelic plays are simply 'the lesser breeds outside the law'.

More interesting is the insight he offered into the theme of the play, where he stated of the Battle of Kinsale that

> the real significance of the defeat was that we lost a chance of winning part of the New World for ourselves, and that, as a result of the defeat, we degenerated into a mere island; and, in the second act, that on account of the East to West flight starting from Ireland and an Irishman taking part in it, we won back *in a spiritual manner* some of the power and influence in the world which would have been ours if we had won the Battle of Kinsale (*IS*, 30 November 1929).[27]

In the final salvo in this war of letters, O'Connor ridiculed de Bhilmot's interpretation of the play, writing: 'Deprived of [*sic*] that defeat of aristocracy and artists, language and culture, to us its real significance at the moment is that Mr. Wilmot is writing bad plays, and that I am the only person who tells him so' (*IS*, 7 December 1929). I have dealt with this controversy at length for several reasons. First of all, it is one of the few times that Gaelic critics and writers engaged in such an extended and on occasion substantial discussion of a play as a work of literature. Second, while in the absence of a text it is impossible to judge how effectively de Bhilmot developed what he saw as the central theme of the play, that theme cannot be dismissed as easily as O'Connor suggests and it could provide the basis for a play worth seeing. And third, it is likely that, however stung, de Bhilmot took some of O'Connor's criticisms to heart as he continued to evolve as a playwright.

He must have taken comfort from reading the anonymous review in *An Phoblacht*. This critic liked the play, seeing it as 'an effort of expressionism, illustrating the continuity of Irish history … an imaginative fantasy having several strongly dramatic situations' (*Poblacht*, 19 October 1929). 'S.' shared this view in *The Standard*, praising de Bhilmot for his ambitious attempt to break new ground in Irish-language drama (*Standard*, 26 October 1929). The reviewer for the *Irish Independent* also saw some positive features in the work, although he felt that the plot was 'unbelievable' (*do-chreidte*) (*II*, 21 October 1929). Less impressed was the anonymous critic for *The Star / An Reult*, who wrote: 'No industry nor ability on the part of actors and actresses can compensate for a poor play, and it is to be hoped that when next the Comhar come before the public it will bring better dramatic fare' (*Star*, 9 November 1929).

The next time de Bhilmot himself came before the public his play was more traditional in setting and style than was *Casadh an Rotha*. A one-acter, *An Casán* (The Path) was staged by An Comhar Drámaíochta in the Gate theatre under the direction of Micheál Mac Liammóir in December 1931, with both Béaslaí and Ó Lochlainn in the cast. The critic for the *Irish Independent* called *An Casán* 'a poignant tragedy' that 'dealt with elemental things of the Irish countryside', while 'C' in *The Nation* declared: 'The beginning of "An Cosan" [*sic*] contained *vraisemblance* to a degree rare in theatres' (*Nation*, 7 April 1928). The action of the play is set against the background of the Irish civil war in County Kerry, the scene of some of the most brutal events of that conflict, and features predictably enough two brothers fighting on opposite sides. The civil war does not at first seem to play any direct role in the play, which instead focuses on an aged and land-obsessed farmer's determination to keep another family from taking away what he sees as his right to the path he uses to harvest his turf. But what de Bhilmot is suggesting here is that it is just such self-righteous inability to compromise that makes civil war possible if not inevitable. When his wife urges her husband to forego violence, he responds with angry pride:

> Don't blame me. Blame the father and the mother I had. Blame the power that gave me sight to see the cows coming home on a dewy summer morning and the ears to be hearing them and they grazing fine and easy and unhurried in quiet fields on an autumn night. Blame that power. Don't blame me. Leave me on my own road in God's name.[28]

He expects help from his younger son, an anti-treaty rebel on the run, but the young man is disgusted by what he sees as his father's greed and pettiness, expressing this feeling in the key thematic speech in the play: 'Blood, blood again … Bloodshed and blood vengeance. Will we ever have anything different in this country?'[29] His father then hears someone approaching whom he assumes to be his enemy, grabs his gun, and tells his son to stand back, for 'I would kill my own son tonight'.[30] And he does, shooting the man approaching only to discover that his victim is his older son, an officer in the Free State army. As the play ends, the old man is left with no one who even wants the land for which he has so thoroughly debased himself. Here, an individual's unwillingness to consider the practical and ethical consequences of his choices and actions leads to personal tragedy for himself and his family and serves as an example of the kind of moral blindness that makes disasters in the wider world unavoidable.

The move to Galway and his involvement with the Taibhdhearc seem to have inspired de Bhilmot. At any rate, his next play was a considerably more imaginative and ambitious effort.[31] *'San Am Soin* (In That Time) was staged at the Taibhdhearc in April 1936 under the direction of Frank Dermody in a shorter version that de Bhilmot would expand after this initial production and that was used for the play's March 1937 revival at the Taibhdhearc, with Dermody again directing. An Comhar Drámaíochta performed the play at the Peacock theatre in Dublin in April 1938, with Seán Ó Conchubhair directing, and Compántas Amharclainne na Gaeilge mounted a production at the theatre of Dublin's Royal Irish Academy of Music in April 1952. The play was broadcast from the Taibhdhearc on Radio Éireann in October 1937, and the same station presented the play again, obviously as part of its Easter programming in March 1954, April 1976 and April 1981 (*II*, 24 March 1954, 16 April 1976 and 25 April 1981).

The play offers an unapologetically political reading of the events of Holy Week. De Bhilmot's Barabbas, played by Gearóid Ó Lochlainn in the production by An Comhar Drámaíochta, is a Jewish patriot and rebel leader who is disappointed that Jesus does not support military action against the Romans: 'O! Isn't it a bitter grief that he would not give proper guidance to the people! He could bind them together, for there is no doubt that he has an extraordinary grip on them.'[32] Barabbas' ex-lover Rebecca, a spy for the Romans, is contemptuous of both Christ and his followers:

'Jesus of Nazareth, King of the Jews! There's a joke! A fake magician leading the people of this country! What would he have to offer them in place of the Roman Rule? His sweet, elegant words about the lilies that grow in the fields would be little help to them …'[33] Rebecca eventually betrays both Barabbas and Christ, but Barabbas is, of course, released and plans to inflict an exemplary vengeance on Rebecca. In the meantime, however, she has been deeply moved by watching the tortured Christ on his way to Calvary. Having given him a cloth to wipe his bloody face and tried to help him when he falls the third time, she is savagely attacked by the angry mob and left to die, now a Christian, a faith she shares with Barabbas' mother, whose illness Jesus has healed. Barabbas is clearly shaken as the play ends, but we can only surmise what the conversion of Rebecca and his mother will mean for him. It is also worth noting that in the play Pilate's second-in-command states that Jesus is far more dangerous than Barabbas and his fellow conspirators, a belief de Bhilmot may have meant to clarify through the words of his John the Baptist, who defends Christ's fondness for the poor and outcast by asking: 'Doesn't the sun shine on everyone … on pure and impure, on living and dead, on saint and sinner? And is the majesty and glory of the sun any the less for that?' More pointedly, he declares: 'It is the way of the nobles to flee from the sun. They prefer the darkness of the night, because it hides their evil deeds.'[34]

The play was an immediate success, with the anonymous critic for *The Connacht Tribune* calling it 'an excellent play' (*togha dráma*) and noting that, unlike on many evenings in An Taibhdhearc, 'there was a very good crowd present' (*bhí sluaighte an-mhaith i láthair*) (*CT*, 18 April 1936).[35] Anticipating the play's revival in March 1937, another anonymous contributor to *The Connacht Tribune*, wrote: 'This play was the subject of one of the Taibhdhearc Company's greatest successes to date. It is an original piece and moves with power and dignity from the rise to the fall of the curtain' (*CT*, 13 March 1937). The revival lived up to expectations, with the anonymous reviewer for *The Connacht Tribune* (probably the same person who wrote the previous comments) declaring:

> Patrons of Taibhdhearc na Gaillimhe (Galway Irish Theatre) were treated over the week-end to a perfect combination – an outstanding dramatic creation presented with an artistry worthy of the piece

> … 'Ag an Am Sin' [*sic*] has life and vigour from the raising of the curtain and moves with power to a brilliant ring-down. In dialogue and situation the play moves without fetters or any evidence of unnaturalness (*CT*, 20 May 1937).[36]

Of the play's 1938 Dublin production by An Comhar Drámaíochta, the critic for the *Irish Independent* pointed out that 'since life at the time of Christ happened to be the subject, it is a play that wouldn't be difficult to ruin', but continued: 'But last night's cast was very successful' (*II*, 5 April 1938).[37] Less impressed was the critic for *The Irish Times*, who wrote of the play that 'too much preliminary praise was responsible for a certain amount of disappointment over the production, for the first time in Dublin, of de Bhilmot's drama of the first years of the Christian period' (*IT*, 6 April 1938).[38] When the play was revived by An Compántas in Dublin in 1952, the critic for the *Irish Independent* wrote: 'Certain it is that his play is no mere piece of devout pageantry but a gripping drama' (*II*, 2 April 1952). In an insightful review on the play's publication in 1944, An tAthair P. Eric Mac Fhinn wrote: 'It would, I would think, be easier to produce than the usual Passion play since it is not holy characters from the Gospel itself that are to be shown on the stage, but rather ordinary people as there would be in any other play. And at the same time, the story of the Passion is excellently shown, and there is both naturalness and piety in it' (*AA*, August 1944, p. 5).[39]

If *'San Am Soin* was de Bhilmot's best play to date, it did not hold that title for long, as Galway audiences were soon treated to the best play de Bhilmot ever wrote, one that broke new ground for him and suggested bold new directions for drama in Irish. *Grádh níos Mó* (Greater Love) had its premiere at the Taibhdhearc in January 1938, with Frank Dermody directing. The play was performed for a single night only by An Comhar Drámaíochta at the Gate theatre in Dublin in May 1941 with Seán Ó Conchubhair directing and Gearóid Ó Lochlainn again in a leading role. Radio Éireann broadcast the play in October 1937 (*CE*, 9 October 1937).

If the general impression, even at the time, was that writing in Irish was almost of necessity insular, focusing overwhelmingly on just Irish or even just Gaeltacht concerns, de Bhilmot's play engaged in an entirely contemporary, relevant and even prophetic way with pressing issues of European and world significance. Anticipating the opening night of 'a powerful original war play by Séamus Wilmot', an anonymous contributor to *The Connacht Tribune* wrote: 'It is one of the biggest productions undertaken by the company and gives plenty of scope for spectacular staging' (*CT*, 29 January 1938). Given Frank O'Connor's dismissal of *Casadh an Rotha* as a play that would never have been produced had it not been in Irish, de Bhilmot must have been particularly gratified by the praise given his new work in a lengthy review by the same paper's anonymous critic (quite possibly the same person who wrote the advance notice) who declared: 'Had Séamus de Bhilmot chosen the English language as the medium of expression in his new play, "Greater Love", its production would have marked just another notable contribution to the English stage, but because it is an Irish language piece it is hardly inaccurate to describe it as an historic event in the Irish drama movement.' For this critic,

> 'Greater Love' is a very clever study in psychology … The theme is a big one, but it received brilliant treatment by Séamus de Bhilmot. Neither was it too much for that very efficient company of which Proinsias Mac Diarmada is manager and producer. The play was treated with understanding and sympathy by the actors at the premiere production on Sunday night.

Of interest here is that this critic stressed that the intellectual and theatrical sophistication of the play owed a great deal to the Taibhdhearc's often maligned policy of staging translations of modern plays from other languages:

> Although born in the Irish drama movement this new play in conception, scope and treatment has distinctive characteristics. Behind it is the suggestion of wider influence. The staging of such a play in Taibhdhearc na Gaillimhe … does not create any surprise, for here have been produced plays translated from English, French, Spanish, Russian, Dutch and Portuguese, as well as original pieces.[40]

Obviously, the audience shared his or her appreciation of the play: 'That the "full house" which greeted the premiere were unanimous in their appreciation of the play and production was shown in no uncertain way when the curtain down [*sic*] on the last act. The audience rose to their feet in a burst of applause and there were repeated calls for the playwright' (*CT*, 5 February 1938).

The critic for *The Irish Press* was slightly more restrained, noting that the applause on opening night was 'something more than the usual cheers which any new play might provoke'. But he was every bit as impressed by the play, writing of its warm reception: 'It was an appreciation of a significant portent in the life of the modern Gaelic drama.' For this critic, de Bhilmot 'on his sixth successful play in the Irish language, automatically establishes his claim to a high place in the pioneer ranks of the founders of a new native dramatic art', while the play itself was 'the latest and perhaps most important contribution to the real national drama ... an epoch in the Gaelic theatre' (*IP*, 31 January 1938).[41] When An Comhar Drámaíochta revived the play at the Gate theatre in 1941, the anonymous critic for the *Irish Independent* was impressed, writing: 'The movement of the play is fine, and the plot makes a strong case against war. As for the acting, it is enough to say that one would think that every one of the actors was cut out for the part he had to fill' (*II*, 19 May 1941).[42] Reviewing the published text of the play in 1948, 'M.' wrote: 'In this short play Séamus de Bhilmot gives us an imaginative experience that is very significant at the present time ... This little play is propagating a useful message' (*II*, 26 June 1948).[43] 'M. Ó D.' (Máirtín Ó Direáin) in his review of the published text called *Grádh níos Mó* 'a powerfully, truly moving play the author has made of the tense material he has, that is, the conflict between the gentle, humane, chivalrous nature of Jean Moreau and the military mind that would not allow any scruple of the sort to come between it and victory' (*Feasta*, May 1948, p. 14).[44]

Set in the present in the capital city of the fictitious European country of Urania, the play dramatises the events surrounding the invasion of the country by its former imperial overlord, which uses the pretext of a border dispute to reduce Urania to its previous colonial status. When the feckless Uranian government is unable to marshal an effective defence, influential citizens appeal to the great hero of their independence struggle to assume the presidency. Faced with the irresistible military superiority of the enemy, the new president must decide whether to employ his ultimate weapon, a particularly deadly form of poison gas. De Bhilmot tackles several crucial moral questions confronting leaders and citizens of modern states, among them what an emergent post-colonial state can do to assert its place in the world, what constitutes a legitimate target in modern warfare, and what price one should be willing to pay for military victory. His protagonist Jean Moreau is, for example, deeply troubled by the indiscriminate nature of modern total warfare:

> Warfare has changed greatly in the past twenty years ... In comparison with the wars that were fought since, I fear that the war fought between this country and Marsia was an old-fashioned war. That war was a war between soldiers ... but now everyone in the country from the elderly to the children will be part of it. Everyone will be driven into it as a drove of bullocks is driven to the slaughterhouse.[45]

Lamenting that 'the generals and military crowd think there is nothing in this country but soldiers, nothing in the world but soldiers',[46] he states: 'There are other things in this country, and in Marsia, and in the world ... Perhaps they are not as showy, but they exist ... Pierre and his garden ... the young mother looking at her first-born playing on a fine sunny day, the quiet student.'[47] And he insists that the political leader must 'look out over the battlefield and not allow the smoke of the battle to blind him to these things' (*féachaint amach thar pháirc an chatha agus gan leogaint do dheatach an chatha é do dhalladh ar na nidhthe seo*). Moreau is a cultured man of peace – we first see him sitting in his study and listening to a Strauss waltz on the radio – but it is his friend and gardener Pierre who is the real thematic voice of conscience in the play, as when he points out that the army of his own country has become as inhuman and brutal as the forces of the traditional enemy. He blasts the 'professional soldiers who spent their lives with plans of death and blood' (*saighdiúirí gairmiúla a chaith a saoghal le pleananna báis is fola*) and continues: 'But now when their plans are no use, what do they do ... but take the army of Marsia by surprise? They go behind the army and inflict death on the women and children of the soldiers. War! A glorious fight for your country!'[48]

Having bowed to pressure and allowed the use of gas in defence of his people, the president soon realises that he has committed what he sees as 'a sin against the human race' (*peaca in aghaidh an chine daonna*) – what we would now call a war crime – and refuses to allow its use again, even going so far as to destroy the formula for the weapon. Of course, this decision leaves his nation defenceless, and the play ends with him standing in the ruins of his presidential palace as enemy troops advance and enemy bombers fly overhead. Staring at the crucifix on the wall of his office, he recites lines strikingly reminiscent of those at the close of Patrick Pearse's play *The Singer*: 'You stood alone once. You will understand my story. You will understand it.'[49]

After the stirring action and high purpose of *Grádh níos Mó*, de Bhilmot's next play, *Baintighearna an Ghorta*, must be considered a disappointment, despite its sharing an important prize for new work in Irish from the Abbey, which gave the play its first production in November 1938, with Frank Dermody directing. Nevertheless, it received generally positive reviews. For example, the critic for the *Irish Independent* called it 'an auspicious beginning to the policy of the Abbey directorate to stage Gaelic plays from time to time' and wrote that 'the material and presentation of the play showed how flexible Irish can be in the hands of a skilful writer with the Gaelic outlook of Séamus de Bhilmot'. For this critic, de Bhilmot had 'written a very charming play and put it into a beautiful setting. His characters are finely drawn and the interest is well sustained' (*II*, 13 December 1938). More incisive was the critic for *The Irish Press*, who, while he felt the play was 'produced in a superb fashion' and 'unfolds a neat convincing story of a priest's struggle between conflicting forces of loyalty to the patroness of his church … and his duty to his starving people', pointed out that 'any play dealing with the horrors of the Famine of '47 which subdues the grim facts of that period is weakened in proportion to the playing down' (*IP*, 13 December 1938).[50] Much less impressed was the anonymous reviewer for *Ar Aghaidh* (probably An tAthair P. Eric Mac Fhinn), who focused on the Irish in the play: 'As for the Irish in it, it is just weak and thin. It is said that anyone at all could distinguish a translation from an original play on stage, but no one at all could recognise this play from a translation. None of it has a very Gaelic feel to it …' (*AA*, January 1939, p. 6).[51] I have found no record of any other performances of the play.[52]

Baintighearna an Ghorta is indeed set during the Great Famine, but that cataclysmic event merely serves as a backdrop for a play dealing with the fervent faith of a parish priest in County Sligo who has managed at considerable financial expense to return to his church a statue of the Virgin stolen by Protestant yeomen in 1798. He thanks his people for the money they have given him for this purpose and tells them to put their faith in Mary to save them from starvation. The priest is later criticised for misusing the money of the sick and starving by a stranger who offers him a large amount of money for the statue. The priest eventually agrees to sell it to this suave tempter for thirty pieces of silver. Bitterly remorseful, the priest then notices the statue has disappeared. Shortly thereafter a beautiful woman is seen in the vicinity distributing bread, and the statue reappears. Needless to say, we are meant to assume the woman is the Blessed Virgin, come to replace the statue, end the blight and famine, and vindicate the faith of the priest, which has saved his people. As the play ends, the priest stands before those people with the sun forming a halo around his head.

While the religious theme in *Baintighearna an Ghorta* is dealt with much too heavy-handedly, it is worth noting that de Bhilmot again expresses his solidarity with the poor rather than the rich and their lackeys, like the well-fed sacristan or the doctor in the play who tends to the rich at the expense of the poor. Also in keeping with the philosophy expressed in his earlier plays is his emphasis on the value and power of an individual's idealism in face of an obdurate reality. Here, de Bhilmot makes all of the arguments used against the priest seem logically irrefutable, but allows him to triumph through the strength of his unshakeable faith.

De Bhilmot's next play, *Déamar agus a Bhean* (Damer and His Wife), produced by An Comhar Drámaíochta in January 1941 under the direction of Seán Ó Conchubhair, is by far the lightest of his stage plays.[53] Taibhdhearc na Gaillimhe first presented it on a twin bill of de Bhilmot plays in June 1942, performing it with *An Ráidhteas Oifigeamhail*, Walter Macken directing both plays.[54] Two years later, Compántas Amharclainne na Gaeilge produced it in the Gaiety theatre during Oireachtas week in October 1944.[55] Reviews were mixed. The anonymous critic for the *Irish Independent* wrote of the 1941 premiere:

> The audience greatly enjoyed 'Déamar agus a Bhean', the new comedy by Séamus de Bhilmot ... This new one is a play that was written lightheartedly in which there is a great deal for the actors to do, and it is full of down-home fun. The dialogue was excellent

> and the audience kept its full attention on the stage as long as the performance lasted (*II*, 29 January 1941).[56]

Writing in *The Irish Press*, 'A. Ó M.' (Antoine Ó Maolaoidh / Tony Molloy) was less taken with the play. Having begun his review by remarking that 'a new play in Irish is something of an event, and when it is written by a writer like Séamus Wilmot it is doubly so', he continued:

> But 'Déamar agus a Bhean' … which was produced last night … by An Comhar Drámaíochta did not show this playwright at his best. Undoubtedly there were very many funny lines but, on the other hand, there were too many speeches on the flight from the land. They were all a little too solid and a little overdone for real comedy (*IP*, 29 January 1941).

More positive in this regard was 'H. O'D.', who wrote in *The Leader* that the play 'sets a new standard in Irish Plays' and added that there was a serious theme beneath the 'genuine and unforced laughter' (*Leader*, 8 February 1941). Writing of the 1944 production of the play by An Compántas under the title '"Black Night" for Drama in Irish', 'T. W.' (Terence Ward) said almost nothing about the play, instead devoting his review for *The Irish Press* to an attack on the apathy of Irish speakers with regard to the theatre, writing that 'Compántas Amharclainne na Gaedhilge … a competent group of players, some of whom have played professionally, presented Séamus Wilmot's pleasant comedy "Déamar agus a Bhean" to a house filled with the depression of emptiness'.[57] Thus, while the evening's performance 'showed that we have the talent for this type of theatre, it is asking the impossible to expect anything like the best in putting over a comedy to an empty house, but these players did give an indication of what they could do under anything like favourable conditions'. As it was, 'the play did not move fast enough and … there was a little stilted movement, but on the other hand there was clear and vigorous enunciation and a good sense of atmosphere … The play would be excellent if played with a more rollicking style' (*IP*, 27 October 1944).

In *Déamar agus a Bhean* de Bhilmot offers his own comic take on matchmaking, one of the hoariest subjects in Gaelic theatre, indeed in

Gaelic revival literature in general. Here, a young man needs to get his aunt married and out of the house so he himself may wed his fiancée. The problem is that the aunt, a voracious reader of romance novels, insists that she will only marry 'the right man or ... Prince Charming' (*an fear ceart nó ... an Prionsa Álainn*), and she regards arranged marriages with horror:

> What you want for me is to follow the ugly old custom of this area and go into Molly Moran's pub and up to the parlour in the company of a man I know nothing about ... he drinking ugly pints of white-foamed porter and I nibbling currant biscuits. Meanwhile in another room so-called sensible people would be trying to sell us as if they were selling an old ass at the fair.[58]

A local man returned from America and able to talk to her about New York's Great White Way seems a candidate for her Prince Charming, especially when he appears to be about to buy a farm and settle in the area. The returned Yank does indeed proffer the highest bid for the property, but we soon learn that, unlike the fabulously wealthy John Damer of Irish folklore, he lacks the funds to make the purchase, his proxy having been driven to far higher bids than were anticipated by the aggressive representative of an anonymous would-be purchaser. As the play ends, we discover that the aunt was that mysterious bidder and that she had driven the price so high knowing that the Yank could not afford it and that his financial embarrassment would enable her to capture him.[59]

While the play is mostly a send-up of an overworked theme in Irish theatre, de Bhilmot does address the depopulation of rural Ireland, as when the travelling musician (*ceoltóir taistil*) played by Gearóid Ó Lochlainn states: 'A great change has come over this area. There is nothing to be heard now but the barking of the dogs and the lowing of the cattle. The bright laughter of the children coming from the school is no longer to be heard.'[60] Unfortunately, however, his introduction of this important contemporary subject does not work well paired with his comic treatment of arranged marriages. More successful is his take on one of the reasons for this flight from the land. His 1947 English-language novel *The Splendid Pretence* deals with the intolerable pressure put on John Kelly, a young Kerryman from Lislawn (i.e. de Bhilmot's native Listowel) trying to live up to the inflated image of his success – the 'splendid pretence' – his mother has created for the neighbours. Having lost a job he loved teaching classics at St Benin's secondary school in his native town, he is urged by friends to go to Dublin, 'the only place in Ireland where a fellow with ability gets a chance'.[61] It is not, however, the kind of chance he is looking for: 'Success? What was this thing called Success? Your name in the papers, money and the power to command money and power, possession of more goods and chattels than one required for one's legitimate needs.'[62] When he gets a minor post at University College Dublin, his mother immediately inflates its importance. Meanwhile, he feels lost and miserable in the city: 'He had the feeling that he was but one of the great common denomination, that he had been deprived of everything individual to him except his name, and that even that did not matter really, except, possibly, to a policeman, if an accident happened.'[63] In Dublin he 'saw nothing but darkness and dark figures groping – and they were happy or pretended to be'.[64] Yet, his mother's pride, which he shares, compels him to maintain the pretence of a happy and successful life in the capital, for he knows full well the truth of his mentor Father Browne's analysis of the small-town mentality:

> Father Browne knew the code as well as he knew it himself. Father Browne knew that a small town is insatiably curious about any of its children who take up a post, be it in the next town or Dublin, or London or New York. If he be a shining success or a dismal failure, the small town does not need to bother further. The migrant has then made things easy for them … But the small town becomes almost prurient about the man who is far from being a failure but who is equally far from the high peaks of success.[65]

The returned Yank in *Déamar agus a Bhean* is a victim of the same syndrome, confessing to a friend that 'It's little gold I ever got sight of, but I was slaving in the company of Italians, Japanese and Hungarians until I could not stand on my feet for the exhaustion and hardship. I never saw the Great White Way except from the bottom of a trench on the road.'[66] Not surprisingly then, he finally admits:

> I hate the States. When I made a little money, I decided to come home. But a wild horse could not drag me back to Ireland unless I

> had money. I'd rather stay among the black men in Harlem ... Pride was the cause. It seems to us Irish that we are people who went to the States in search of gold ... that it is a kind of adventure ... and we do not like to admit that we failed.[67]

Indeed, he feels that many of the Irish emigrants in America are in a virtual conspiracy to conceal the truth about their lives there: 'The Irish who go to America are a strange lot. A kind of class apart. The one who comes home realises that he must not inform on the others, although it would make your hair stand on end if he told you how bad their lives are.' But now he has learned his lesson: 'Why wouldn't we use the intelligence we have for the benefit of our own country.'[69] The play then closes on a conventionally happy note. Equally conventional, though no doubt heartfelt, is the anti-emigration message in the play, another theme that goes back to the very beginning of the revival.[70] Still, if the play does nothing else, it gives us a more rounded and sympathetic portrait of the returned Yank than is usual in twentieth-century writing in Irish.[71]

The one-act *An Ráidhteas Oifigeamhail* (The Official Statement) was first produced by An Comhar Drámaíochta in January 1942 on a bill of three short plays in the Gate theatre, with Frank Dermody directing. In June 1944, the Taibhdhearc staged the play, directed by Walter Macken.[72] The only other production for which I have found a record was by students at Dublin's Coláiste Mhuire for Feis Átha Cliath in May 1969, with the student Éamonn Ó hUanacháin directing. It was broadcast over Radio Éireann in September 1944 and November 1954 (*IP*, 12 September 1944 and *CE*, 17 November 1954).

In this play, de Bhilmot returned to both contemporary politics and lighthouses. The play is set in wartime on 'the coast of any country on the European seaboard' (*cósta aon tíre do thíorthaibh imeallbhórd na h-Eórpa*).[73] A technician has been sent to a lighthouse to set up a radio link to convey the *ráidhteas oifigeamhail* concerning the beacon's fate. When the message finally arrives, it is incomplete, but not surprisingly given the enemy's air raids, the officer on the spot orders that the light be extinguished to deprive the bombers of its guidance. In this play, the lighthouse keeper is the voice of peace and civilisation, in effect reprising the role of the gardener in *Grádh níos Mó*: 'But there are certain things that have no connection with warfare.

They exist for the benefit of the human race in general.'[74] He later asks the officer why it is necessary 'that this light be drawn into the mad struggle that is going on' (*go dtairrgeóchthaí an solas so isteach ins an gcoimheasgar buile atá ar siubhal*). As in *Grádh níos Mó*, de Bhilmot is too honest a playwright to present just one side of the argument and allows the warriors to make their case as well. Here, the officer briefly describes what modern aerial warfare means:

> There is no horror like it. The slaughter! ... The butchery! ... Little children screaming ... The wild terror in their hearts! ... The wild look in their eyes ... Mothers make a protective shield of their bodies to save their children! The thunder and the screeching of the anti-aircraft guns and the bombs bursting as if the skies themselves would be torn asunder ...[75]

But the lighthouse keeper's logic seems ethically irrefutable if practically unrealistic:

> In the midst of all this butchery, that is the only benevolent light shining ... The people giving those orders, they have no understanding of the sea. They do not understand the benevolence of that light up there that gives help to everyone without distinction. They are gradually extinguishing the old lights of Europe. Leave this light shining.[76]

Still, as in *Grádh níos Mó*, the opposing arguments are rendered moot. The extinguishing of the light leads to a shipwreck that improbably enough involves the vessel on which the keeper's son is sailing. Nor does the resulting blackout save the nearby village from aerial bombardment in which the officer's family is presumably killed.

Reviewing the premiere of the play in *The Irish Press*, 'A. Ó M.' (Antoine Ó Maolaoidh/Tony Molloy) wrote: 'Bhuilmot's [*sic*] "An Ráidhteas Oifigeamhail" was the most exciting piece [of the three performed that evening] and was carried to its greatest heights of tension by Séamus Ó hÉilidhe's powerful acting ably supported by Gearóid Ó Lochlainn.' He found the play's subject and theme 'powerful stuff ... though bordering slightly on the melodramatic' (*IP*, 12 January 1942). Of the school production by Coláiste Mhuire, Earnán P. de Blaghd felt that the students had chosen a 'very difficult' (*rídheacair*) and 'very gloomy' (*rídhuairc*) play, but also wrote of the young director: 'He handled the play well enough for us to expect the best the next time that Éamonn puts a play on stage' (*II*, 7 March 1969).[77] In his review of the published text of the play, 'C.' wrote that while he was 'not particularly taken with this play by Séamus de Bhilmot' (*gan bheith íontach tógtha ag cluiche seo Shéamuis de Bhilmot*), it was 'a piece that moves fairly well' (*píosa a ghluaiseas measardha maith*) and the 'atmosphere was created effectively' (*an t-atmosfaer curtha ar fáil go héifeachtach*). Still, 'there is nothing new in the play and we all know from the time the Keeper's son is first mentioned that he will be drowned at the end because of the extinguishing of the light'. Despite these objections, however, 'C.' concluded that while the play was not 'wonderful' (*go híontach*), 'it is polished and has a modern feel to it that will make it very suitable for the Drama Festivals' (*Comhar*, April 1945, p. 8).[78] Writing of the same published text in a review of several plays for *The Irish Times*, Peter Kavanagh rather confusingly stated that the play was 'indifferently constructed', but that 'the author, unlike the others mentioned, has the right idea of playwriting' (*IT*, 10 February 1945).[79]

De Bhilmot's last full-length play, *Prólóg don Réim Nua* (Prologue to the New Order), directed by Nioclás Ó Cinnéide, was the inaugural production of Compántas Amharclainne na Gaeilge in March 1944. Among those in the audience at the Gate theatre were An Taoiseach Éamon de Valera and his wife, the former Sinéad Ní Fhlannagáin, who had acted regularly in Gaelic League entertainments in the early years of the language revival. The play was obviously influenced by Ibsen's *An Enemy of the People*, a play de Bhilmot must have seen in Gearóid Ó Lochlainn's Gaelic version translated directly from Ibsen's *Riksmål* original.[80] The enemy of the people here is Brian Ó Domhnaill, a shopkeeper in 'Lioslán' and the advocate of the 'new order' in which if producers seek only a reasonable price for their goods, consumers will only have to pay a similarly fair price for goods provided by others. His whole philosophy and programme can be summed up in a few sentences: 'In this New Order that will be established after the war, everyone, rich and poor, should just get what is right and just. Everyone can play his own little part in this effort by not thinking too much about himself, but instead remembering that we can only live by cooperating with each other.'[81] In practical terms, Ó Domhnaill urges local farmers to grow potatoes instead of the wheat the government wants them to cultivate, with the result that while there is a shortage of potatoes in the nation at large, the farmers of Lioslán have a bumper crop.[82]

Initially, the local people are delighted with the implications of the new order, but greed soon makes its appearance, most notably in the machinations of the local gombeen man Liam Ó Ceallacháin, who plots with a Dublin merchant to smuggle potatoes into Northern Ireland and eventually turns the people against Ó Domhnaill and his scheme of social and economic justice. The merchant declares: 'A business must make the greatest profit it can achieve … This reasonable profit is just another name for cutting prices.' And the gombeen man is quick to agree: 'He has ruined me in this town at any rate … himself and his reasonable profit.'[83] Ó Ceallacháin, who is able to use the people's debts to him to manipulate them, quickly manages to convince the local farmers to use their potato monopoly to try to enrich themselves – and, of course, to enrich him in the process. Before long, the locals are boycotting and even attacking Ó Domhnaill's shop, accusing him of communism,[84] although as he points out, his thinking is rooted in papal encyclicals and is entirely consistent with the lessons the people learned in their catechism: 'We think that those truths have nothing to do with us as soon as we put aside the little book. We think that religion and ordinary daily affairs are two things with no connection. We think that religion is something we take out every Sunday … and put back in the coffer as soon as Sunday is over.'[85]

In one of the most important scenes in the play, Ó Domhnaill debates Áine Ni Bheoláin, a university student who sympathises with his goals, but who after living in the community for six months finds his methods unworkable. Recalling that 'before I came here I had nothing but ideas and theories' (*roimh theacht annseo dhom ní raibh agam ach smaointe is teoiricí*), she now argues that 'the individual himself is all that matters and no scheme or system or order will succeed that is not based on his weaknesses as well as his virtues'.[86] For Áine, the people's desire to exploit their monopoly makes perfect sense given the world in which they live: 'They owe money to the bank … debts to the shopkeeper … and the whole point of their labour is to pay some of those bills … Now, for the first time, they have a chance to put an end to that [old] order with one blow … They will be independent. That is the New Order that will come to them.'[87] Ó Domhnaill is, however, insistent that merely palliative changes will not solve the problems these people face: 'But would it not be better to get to the bottom of the situation and make an attempt to settle the whole question instead of, as you might say, mending and patching the old system.'[88]

The local people want no part of this, and soon Ó Domhnaill finds himself boycotted. Now, however, his response seems more pigheaded than principled. As his shop assistant Máire says, 'Brian will do nothing to explain his side to the people. As long as he is doing the right thing, he doesn't care about the opinions of others.'[89] The eyes of the people are finally opened when they learn that Ó Ceallacháin has set up his own potato business and is indeed smuggling potatoes to the North for confiscatory prices far above those the Irish government, in face of the monopoly, has been forced to impose. And worse, a young local man driving a truckload of these potatoes has been killed by the police in the North. One of the men who had acted against Ó Domhnaill pronounces a terse judgement on the gombeen man: 'Oppressive interest paid with blood, Liam Ó Ceallacháin!'[90]

Despite his obvious admiration for his protagonist, de Bhilmot does not deal with the issues in purely black and white terms. Thus, one man insists, as does Áine of course, that the locals in the play are not inherently callous people, but rather often root their desire for greater profits in emotive evocations of past injustices: 'We could never raise our heads in this country, instead being constantly oppressed and destroyed. When the landlord wasn't trampling on us, the gombeen man was crushing us.'[91] More resonant still is their battle cry, 'The land for the people and the road for the bullocks', a slogan used in the 1930s by both Peadar O'Donnell with the Republican Congress and by Máirtín Ó Cadhain with Muinntear na Gaedhealtachta, the group that spearheaded the movement to move Gaeltacht people to rich repossessed lands in County Meath.[92] As the play ends, the implication is that the people of Lioslán have returned to their senses and will once again support Ó Domhnaill and his *Réim Nua*.[93] But will they? In de Bhilmot's other plays about the exercise of individual conscience in the so-called real world, such happy endings are altogether absent, and unless the Ireland of the 1940s was a very different place from de Bhilmot's Urania, war-torn Europe or allegorical Méara, Brian Ó Domhnaill should expect heartbreak ahead.

The anonymous critic for *An Glór* praised de Bhilmot for writing a play of ideas about contemporary Irish life, but felt he could have gone further in his engagement with issues of immediate importance to his audiences: 'We are given something to think about, a rare thing to find on the Gaelic stage. Moreover, the subject deals with contemporary life, something that **could** happen with regard to potatoes but **is** happening with other goods. I'm surprised that since the author took the road he did that he did not draw on things that are **actually** happening today' (*Glór*, 1 April 1944).[94] Writing in *The Irish Press*, Terence Ward found the play a bit on the didactic side, writing that while 'the characters were well drawn … the author seemed at times to speak for them rather than through them'. But he also acknowledged that 'this is almost unavoidable in a play of ideas, but when the author has an interesting thesis, one can sit back and bear with him to the end' (*IP*, 20 March 1944).[95]

An Compántas produced his one-act play *Caithfidh na Táncanna Dul Tríd* (The Tanks Must Go Through) in March 1957 at Dublin's Dagg Hall, on a bill with Irish translations of Eugene O'Neill's *Ile* and Eugène Ionesco's *An cantatrice chauve* (*IP*, 18 March 1957). The play has not been published. Writing in *The Irish Times*, 'P. Mac A.' offered a summary of the plot:

> A victorious general, marching through a half-defeated country, has just captured a town, but cannot move on with his tanks as the roads leading from the town are black with refugees. He gives an order that the refugees are to be machine-gunned from the air. The order is obeyed by all except his own son, who at the last moment decides to put his love of humanity before his blind loyalty to his commander (*IT*, 18 March 1957).

In *The Irish Press*, 'B. Ó hE' (Breandán Ó hEithir?) wrote: 'It deals with a general whose brutality is the cause of his only son's death' (*Baineann sé le ginearál mí-thrócaireach a bhfuil a bhrúidiúlacht ina thrú báis dá aon-mhac*). 'B. Ó hE' found the play 'interesting despite the clumsy title' (*suimiúil in ainneoin an tiodail mhí-stuama*) (*IP*, 18 March 1957).[96] 'P. F. B.' wrote of the plot of the play in the *Evening Herald* that 'Nemesis comes to a General who has hundreds killed in an air attack in order "that the tanks go through"' (*EH*, 18 March 1957). Here, de Bhilmot was clearly re-visiting ideas with which he had already dealt more effectively in earlier plays.[97]

It is, however, worth noting that he did offer what was for him a quite different perspective on the morality of violence in his one-act English-language play *The Curlew Call*, published in *The Shannonside Annual* for 1958.[98] In this short play, 'suggested', he tells us, by 'a similar incident' from Tom Barry's *Guerilla Days in Ireland* (1949),[99] de Bhilmot for the first time since *An Casán* in 1931 addressed the issue of wartime violence in a specifically Irish context. The play opens with the British intelligence officer Captain Bertram Hardy speaking with his fellow spy Mabel Lloyd about how information he has provided has enabled the Auxiliaries to set a trap for IRA men sheltering in a nearby barn. De Bhilmot's global anti-colonialism is evident when he has Hardy boast of his past service in India and a coming assignment to Rhodesia. We also learn in this first scene that Mabel is in love with him, but that he is leaving her for another woman. Two Auxiliary officers arrive with proper credentials and tell him the ambush will take place when the curlew calls. Smug in his sense of superiority over the 'peasants', Hardy tells the Auxiliaries that he has tricked the IRA using 'the typical Englishman stunt', explaining:

> You see, I'm taken for granted by the peasants as Captain Hardy, a fair-minded Englishman, who, of course, believes that we English should remain in Ireland, but as we have to fight to do so, we should fight fair. You see the idea. The peasants appreciate the attitude. The ex-officer, but always the gentleman attitude always does the trick in the local down in the village. I picked up the trick from a hardened service man when I was in India (*SSA*, 1958, pp. 23–4).

This tactic has already allowed him to lure an important IRA leader into a trap that leads to his death while he is supposedly trying to escape. The ambush at the barn apparently goes off without a hitch, and three IRA prisoners are hauled in. Hardy turns his back to pour celebratory drinks, but when he turns around again he finds that the Auxiliary officers are actually IRA men in captured uniforms. The distraught Mabel is told she has twenty-four hours to leave Ireland. Trying to save Hardy, she tells the IRA men that if he is spared, she will name an important local informer. The ranking IRA man replies that that informer has already been executed, whereupon they lead Hardy out, followed by Mabel shouting 'Don't! Don't!' A volley of shots announces his execution, and the play ends with Mabel collapsing into a chair.

Absent from this play is de Bhilmot's usual principled pacificism. We certainly get the sense that he sheds no tears for Hardy or the other spy executed during the course of the action. One wonders whether this apparent acceptance of their punishment reflects de Bhilmot's belief that the IRA guerillas fighting against such formidable odds in a morally justified war of liberation had no choice but to use such tactics. Or did he simply believe that the limited and personal scope of this violence didn't begin to compare with the inhuman horrors of modern total warfare. Still, *The Curlew Call* stands as an anomaly among de Bhilmot's plays. Yet, even if he seems more accepting of wartime violence in this play, we should also remember that through the otherwise unnecessary and rather repellent character of Mabel, he shows the effects of violence on those who lose loved ones, however despicable.

In his review of *Prólog don Réim Nua* above, Terence Ward puts his finger on two of de Bhilmot's weaknesses as a playwright. His plays are obviously didactic, but while the ideas in them are relevant, challenging and intellectually gripping, his inability to create credible human characters considerably lessens their potential emotional impact. Often, the people in his plays seem more like walking and talking ideas than flesh and blood human beings. Given his central interest in how individuals react to the most intense moral challenges, it is unfortunate that he was not able to create relatable characters as complex as the crises in which they find themselves. Both of these shortcomings are compounded by the fact that all of his plays were quite short, some obviously too short. To be fair, plays in Irish at that time were not in general very long, perhaps so as not to task the attention span of audiences who included a good number who had recently and/or inadequately mastered the language. The longest of his plays as published were *Prólog don Réim Nua* (fifty-three pages), *Déamar agus a Bhean* (forty-four pages), *Grádh níos Mó* (thirty-nine pages) and *'San Am Soin* (thirty-five pages). *An Ráidhteas Oifigeamhail* was all of thirteen pages long, *Múchadh an tSolais* ten. De Bhilmot packed a lot into these short plays; one can only wonder whether he could have done more had he been given, or given himself, greater scope.

On the other hand, as noted above, he deserves a great deal of credit for in effect introducing into literature in Irish the serious political play dealing with issues of contemporary concern. Perhaps the best way we can appreciate this contribution is to look at two of the vanishingly few plays from the 1920s, '30s and '40s whose titles and subject matter suggest they would deal with the politics of their day.[100] *An Coimisinéar* (The Commissioner) by UCG professor of chemistry Tomás Ó Diolúin ('Tomás Ó Súilleabháin') had its premiere at Taibhdhearc na Gaillimhe in September 1932, with Frank Dermody directing (*CT*, 16 September 1932), and it was performed by the Abbey for the Oireachtas in October 1942 (*II*, 26 October 1942) and again in April 1943 (*IP*, 31 March 1943), with Frank Dermody directing both productions. The Limerick Drama Society brought the play to that city in a production directed by Seán Mac Cathbhaid in March 1943 (*LL*, 6 March 1943), and it was revived at the Abbey with Tomás Mac Anna directing in March 1955 (*II*, 18 March 1955). Reviews were favourable in both Galway and Dublin.[101]

As the play begins, a young woman informs her would-be fiancé, a teacher, that her father, a hard-headed businessman and chairman of the town council, opposes their engagement because he has no respect for education and less for culture. The council over which he presides is in perpetual discord, agreeing only that they must continue and protect their own corrupt schemes. Those schemes have included a rigged contract for concrete that provided lucrative kickbacks, and, more sinister, a deal with a butcher that allowed the sale of tainted meat in the town with no regulatory consequences. Word has, however, arrived that a civil service commissioner from Dublin will be coming soon to take control of the town's affairs in place of the council. By a coincidence not entirely unpredictable, the commissioner is the father of the young suitor, who decides that given his education and close observation of his father at work, he can assume the role of the commissioner and perform his own investigation of the council. The rest of the play shows him outfoxing the politicians, in particular his girlfriend's hard-headed father. Loosening the father's tongue with drink, he is able to get details of their crimes and uses the information not to reform the town's government, but to unite the council behind a new money-making scheme. The father is duly impressed and accepts the trickster as his future son-in-law. The play ends with their drinking to their future partnership.[102]

Mise an Méire (I Am the Mayor) by Tomás Ó Máille was first produced at the Taibhdhearc in April 1944, with Walter Macken directing and playing the title role. The play seems never to have been revived, although judging from the brief comments in *The Connacht Tribune* and *The Connacht Sentinel*, audiences seem to have enjoyed it (*CT*, 1 April 1944; *CS*, 13 March 1945). Here, the protagonist is an inept mayor who tries to impose some of his own theories on his city and its inhabitants while the city's treasurer (*sparánaidhe*) is away on his holidays. As the play begins, his first cause is the welfare of stray cats, but he soon begins to dream higher. Having discovered – apparently for the first time – how little financial assistance the unemployed receive, he raises the sum considerably, defending the unfunded increase by saying 'I am the Mayor' (*Mise an Méire*). Soon, the citizens realise that they can get more money while unemployed than while working, and the number of unemployed swells. Not surprisingly, the mayor's assistants panic, wondering where all the necessary money will come from. Untroubled, the mayor says that he will borrow it from the banks and sends a young clerk to collect the loan. The city's bankers, afraid to reject the mayor's demand, pool their resources to make up the amount needed. Perhaps astounded that his plan seems to be working, the mayor suspects the money the bankers send is counterfeit, and when the bankers reject this idea, he shows his confidence in his intuition by burning the banknotes. As the mayor and bankers argue the point, the treasurer returns to find the city full of idle citizens, its finances in chaos. The situation is resolved when the young clerk steps forward as the hero of the piece, announcing that he had been worried about what the mayor might do and so had borrowed counterfeit bills from a friend who conveniently kept such things around his house, and then hidden the real banknotes under the fake ones. Thus, it was the counterfeit bills that the mayor burned. The treasurer thereupon deposes the mayor and re-establishes order by lowering the dole payments to their original level and returning the money to the bankers.[103]

As should be obvious, neither of these plays is in any meaningful sense political. Instead, both take subject matter that in real life would have been serious and could have made gripping political theatre and play it as farce, with just a touch of harmless satire. To Gaelic audiences whose expectations of political plays were shaped by works like *An Coimisinéar* and *Mise an Méire*, plays like de Bhilmot's *'San Am Soin*, *Grádh níos Mó*, *An Raidhteas Oifigeamhail* and *Prólog don Réim Nua* must have been a jolt, albeit for many a welcome one, replacing easy laughs with challenging ideas and high ideals at a time in both Irish and world history when both ideas and ideals were more important than ever.

Speaking at Feis Maitiú in 1951, the year before his own final play was produced, de Bhilmot was pessimistic about the genre to which he had devoted his creative efforts in Irish: 'The state of Irish-language drama is bad at present due to a lack of interest. Although we have the actors and the theatres, there are fewer productions now than there were ten years ago' (*IP*, 21 May 1951).[104] What he could not have known was that even then he was living in the twilight of the good old days. He must, however, have been aware that he had done more than his share to combat any lack of interest in Gaelic drama. All of his plays, with the possible exception of the conventionally pious *Baintighearna an Ghorta* and the rather frothy *Déamar agus a Bhean*, dealt in a mature and thoughtful manner with major thematic issues of pressing contemporary relevance in the Ireland of his time. Again and again, he challenged his protagonists to do the right thing in highly ambiguous situations, and then left them, as their only consolation in the ruins, the fact that they had met that challenge. In this honesty he paved the way for the Gaelic playwrights whose later accomplishments helped push his own work into an unmerited obscurity.

CHAPTER FIVE

'That Galwegian of Many Talents': Walter Macken (1915–67)

In 1943, a writer in *The Connacht Tribune* called Walter Macken 'that Galwegian of many talents' (*CT*, 4 September 1943). The description was altogether apt, for Macken (1915–67) was one of twentieth-century Ireland's most versatile, prolific and popular writers, one who worked in both of the nation's official languages. His reputation now rests largely on his fiction in English. Between 1948 and his sudden and premature death in 1967, he published ten novels and five story collections for adults, as well as two novels and another five story collections for young readers. In addition, he left behind two as yet unpublished novels and an autobiography. Virtually all of these published works were popular when they appeared, gaining a considerable audience not only in Ireland, but also elsewhere in the English-speaking world, most notably Great Britain, where they were first published, and North America, where two of the novels were Literary Guild selections.[1] Many of these books remained in print for decades and some are still available today in paperback.

Macken's first love was, however, the theatre, and his success as a prose writer in English represents only the third of three distinct stages into which his career, with a few slight overlaps, so neatly falls: actor, director and playwright in Irish (1932–45), actor and playwright in English (1946–60), and writer of fiction in English (1948–67). Had his father, also Walter, not been killed fighting in the British army in 1917, the very year his son was born, one might have been tempted to see Walter Jr's attraction to the stage as an inheritance from Walter Sr, who had acted in the Father Crotty Hall in Galway's Middle Street, the same street in which stands Taibhdhearc na Gaillimhe, where a teenaged Walter Jr first came as a bit-player in 1932.[2] He then rose rapidly through the ranks to become, as Bháitéar Ó Maicín, not only a leading actor, but also a director of plays, the theatre's manager and, in 1939, what we would now call its artistic director. Of even greater relevance for us, he also began to write plays in Irish. It is, of course, his work at the Taibhdhearc that will be the principal focus of this chapter, and that work will be discussed in detail below. First, however, we should take at least a quick look at the second period of his artistic career, the years he made his mark as a respected actor and significant playwright in English.

Like several of his colleagues – perhaps most notably Proinsias Mac Diarmada (Frank Dermody) and Siobhán Nic Chionnaith (Siobhán McKenna) – Macken left the Taibhdhearc, departing in 1948 for the Abbey theatre in Dublin. Unfortunately, he did not leave the Taibhdhearc on good terms, for he was feeling underpaid and had had disagreements with the theatre's board, of which, surprisingly, he was never a member.[3] The most notable of these disputes concerned his policy of staging translations of foreign plays rather than the purely original work the board wanted. (Where he was to get all that original work does not seem to have troubled the directors.) From 1948 to '51 he was a member of the Abbey's famed repertory company. Macken would return to the Abbey in 1965, first as the Irish government's second representative on the theatre's board, and then as assistant manager and 'artistic adviser' to Ernest Blythe, apparently with the understanding that he would succeed Blythe when the latter retired. This position as 'adviser' would evolve into that of artistic director, although Macken would be gone by then, returning to his home in Oughterard, County Galway, in 1966. His departure after such a brief stay at the Abbey was the subject of considerable interest and some controversy at the time, although there seems to be no reason to doubt his own explanation that he simply wanted to go home and resume his career as a writer of fiction in English.[4]

While a member of the Abbey company between 1948 and 1951, Macken played, as did all Abbey actors, a wide range of roles, major and minor. Moreover, he also acted regularly in the theatre's productions in Irish and continued to act at the Abbey and elsewhere from time to time after 1951. Among his more notable parts in English were those of Quilter the matchmaker in George Fitzmaurice's *The Country Dressmaker* (1949); the title character in George Shiels' *The Jailbird* (1949); Marks in Brinsley

MacNamara's *Marks and Mabel* (1950); Seamus Rua in Yeats' *The Countess Cathleen* (1950); Ructions McGowan in Seamus Byrne's *Design for a Headstone* (1950); Old Mahon in Synge's *The Playboy of the Western World* (1953); and Paddo O'Reilly in his own play *Home is the Hero* on Broadway in New York (1954).

Judging from contemporary reviews, Macken would seem to have been a competent if not entirely consistent actor in English, capable of some memorable performances but by no means consistently brilliant. Of course, that same judgement could probably be made of most professional actors anywhere. A few examples should give some sense of how his acting was judged at the time. In Brinsley MacNamara's *The Grand House in the City*, 'J. J. F.' felt that Macken 'shows high relish for the shades of character in Owen Lynam, the erstwhile cattle-jobber' (*EH*, 1 February 1949). Reviewing Macken's performance as Circus Jack in Bryan MacMahon's *The Bugle in the Blood*, 'K.' declared that his acting 'kindled a new flame of hope for the survival of Abbey acting ...' (*IT*, 15 March 1949). Commenting on the Abbey's revival of George Fitzmaurice's *The Country Dressmaker* two months later, 'K.' wrote in *The Irish Times*: 'Walter Macken as Quilter, the sloothering matchmaker ... rocked the house and dominated the stage while he was on, and carried, with Miss Ní Loinsigh, the weight of the production' (*IT*, 24 May 1949). Reviewing Ralph Kennedy's *Ask for Me Tomorrow*, 'K.' noted that Macken in the unpromising role of 'a not particularly imaginative spectator and commentator on the disruption of the Browne family, gives a richly comic Macken performance' (*IT*, 4 October 1949). Macken's last role in a full-length play as a member of the Abbey company was in Jack P. Cunningham's *Mountain Flood*, and while the play itself was not a success, the critics felt that was no fault of Macken's. Thus, the reviewer for the *Irish Independent* stated that 'Walter Macken, as he always does, brings force and meaning to the stage ...' (*II*, 11 August 1950). And when three years later he played Old Mahon in Jack MacGowran's production of Synge's *The Playboy of the Western World* at Dublin's Gaiety theatre, 'K. M. G.' of *The Irish Times* praised 'Walter Macken's powerful portrait of the "Playboy's" misused father', adding parenthetically that 'apart from his commanding presence he is almost the only actor I know who looks as if he might possibly survive a couple of fearful blows of a loy!' (*II*, 25 July 1953).

It was, however, in the lead role of Bartley Dowd in Molloy's *The King of Friday's Men* that he achieved his greatest success. Of his performance in Ria Mooney's Abbey production of the play in 1948, 'K.' wrote:

> From the acting viewpoint, the play is almost entirely Walter Macken's. To the part of Bartley Dowd, Mr. Macken brings a rich knowledge of the locale of the play, a good physique and, above all, a voice sensitively tuned to bring out every cadence of some of the loveliest lines written in the Irish theatre since the death of Synge. These qualities combine to give Mr. Macken's performance a satisfying wholeness such as has not been seen since Cusack's 'Playboy' in a part of the kind (*IT*, 19 October 1948).

When the Abbey took the play to London later that year, 'Quidnunc' of *The Irish Times* wrote that while Niall McGuinness, who played Bartley Dowd in this production, was 'almost perfectly cast in physique and appearance' and 'gave a performance of high quality by normal standards', nonetheless 'his interpretation suffered badly by comparison with Walter Macken's, one of the best individual combinations of feeling, subtlety, and strength seen on the Abbey stage since [F.J.] McCormick died' (*IT*, 5 September 1949). While the play had a disappointing reception in New York, running a mere four nights on Broadway, Macken's performance as Bartley Dowd was generally praised, with Brooks Atkinson writing in *The New York Times*: 'Walter Macken has come here from Ireland to play the part of the superhuman fighter. When he is on the stage "The King of Friday's Men" has strength, excitement and sincerity. It also has moments of tenderness. For Mr. Macken is a fine figure of a man with girth and muscle, humor and humility; and he can make Mr. Molloy's wildest fancies seem wholly true' (*NYT*, 22 February 1951).[5]

Of course, not all of Macken's reviews were as positive, even glowing, as those above. From time to time there were comments that he seemed 'uncomfortable' in a role or that he overacted – a failing that seems to have been creeping into Abbey acting at this time. It is, however, unfortunate that perhaps his greatest failure as an actor occurred in the 1954 New York production of his own *Home is the Hero* in the full glare of the Broadway publicity machine.[6] Writing from New York in a piece in *The Irish Times* entitled 'From Galway to Broadway/"Home is the Hero"', Vivien Mercier used quotations from New York reviews to explore why a play that was a smash success in Dublin failed on the Great White Way. Mercier began by referring to some of the positive reviews. Thus, he notes that Wolcott Gibbs wrote in *The New Yorker* that 'as his own confused and belligerent hero, Mr. Macken gives an admirable performance, managing to suggest a great deal more than is apparent in the text'. Brooks Atkinson of *The New York Herald Tribune* felt that the play was 'in the final analysis ... a dull play about a disagreeable fellow', but that Macken stood out for playing his role 'with skill and force'. Walter Kerr of *The New York Times* declared that Macken 'has all the roaring authority to make Paddo O'Reilly a convincing tyrant'. Indeed, Kerr believed that the play's shortcomings were due to Macken's writing, not his acting, an idea with which Mercier disagreed sharply, writing that 'the lines were all right; it was Mr. Macken's handling of them that was all wrong ... Mr. Macken seems obsessed with strength in his plays and novels; it is also the one quality that his acting strives for, at the expense of everything else, including, ultimately, strength itself. Looking back on his performance in "The King of Friday's Men", I can see that it, too, suffered from the same monotony and vain pursuit of force'. For Mercier, 'the play was essentially a worthwhile one, but that Mr. Macken botched his own handiwork by a monotonous, unimaginative performance. Many of the other members of an excellent cast extracted far more from the lines Mr. Macken had written than he himself did' (*IT*, 2 November 1954).[7]

Macken also acted in two movies as well as on radio and television. The first film in which he appeared was the cinema version of *Home Is the Hero,* directed by Fielder Cook with screenplay by Henry Keating. It was shot in Ireland at the Ardmore Studios in Bray and released in 1959. The BBC had already broadcast a version of the play for television – in which Macken did not appear – three years earlier in 1956. In 1961, Macken played Warder Regan in the film version of Brendan Behan's 1954 play *The Quare Fellow,* directed by Anthony Havelock-Allan with screenplay by Arthur Dreifuss. This film was also shot in Ireland.[8] Macken recreated his role as Bartley Dowd for Radio Éireann's adaptation of *The King of Friday's Men* in October 1952 (*IP*, 3 November 1952), and played the part of Morgan

Cummiskey in Philip Rooney's adaptation of Macken's *Voices of Doolin* in 1961 (*BH*, 18 March 1961).

If Macken never managed to achieve success as a playwright in New York, the situation was quite different at home, at least at the beginning of his career as an English-language dramatist. Even before he left the Taibhdhearc for the Abbey in 1948, he had already made his mark as a playwright in English with *Mungo's Mansion* (1946), a play about life in the Galway slums that not surprisingly was immediately compared to the plays of Sean O'Casey's great Dublin trilogy, *The Shadow of a Gunman* (1923), *Juno and the Paycock* (1924) and *The Plough and the Stars* (1926). He followed this play with *Home is the Hero* (1952), *Twilight of a Warrior* (1955) and *Look in the Looking Glass* (1957), all at the Abbey, and *Voices of Doolin* (1960) at the Gaiety. His 1948 play *Vacant Possession*, which under the title 'Three Days in the Gantry' had been submitted to and rejected by the Abbey in 1946, has never had a professional production.[9] In fact, despite the success of his first two English plays in particular, Macken was to experience as much rejection as recognition as a playwright in English, with the Abbey turning down *Flat to Let* in 1940, *Rude Forefathers* in 1942, *Vacant Possession* in 1946, *The Boys Come Home* in 1948, and *Merchant's Road* as late as 1963. It is also worth noting that Macken left behind several unperformed and unpublished plays, some of which exist under more than one title.[10]

Of those plays that were performed, by far the most successful were *Mungo's Mansion, Home is the Hero* and *Twilight of a Warrior*, to which we may now turn briefly. *Mungo's Mansion* had its premiere at the Abbey on 11 February 1946, with Macken's old Taibhdhearc colleague Frank Dermody directing, F.J. McCormick in the title role, and the former Taibhdhearc actress Siobhán McKenna as Mungo's daughter Nellie. Among others in the list of characters are 'innumerable children!' Macken himself missed the first night because he was acting in that year's Taibhdhearc pantomime *Cúirt an Ghrádha* (The Court of Love), which he also, as usual, directed. Critical response to the play was mixed, but more positive than otherwise. Particularly impressed was 'T. W.' (Terence Ward), who in *The Irish Press* called Macken 'the O'Casey of the West', writing: 'The author, who was born twenty years after O'Casey, missed the opportunity which the

Dublin dramatist had of integrating the ready-made drama of the fight for freedom, but he was right up to the minute on the social problems of 1946 as they colour life in the West.' Having stated that the playwright belonged to 'the modern realistic Ireland', one whose 'drama is hard' and whose 'mind works within the ambit of a state in which doles are more important than dreams, and where St Vincent de Paul is a greater power than the Dark Rosaleen', 'T. W.' argued that 'consequently, the play makes a big demand on an audience which has been used to the misty sophistries of playwrights reared on the nationalistic catch-cries'. For 'T. W.', 'Walter Macken set a new tradition in Irish drama by connecting the ordinary drama of Irish life with the occasional tragedies which pierce it. He has mixed the tears with the smile in a way that is convincing as life itself' (*IP*, 12 February 1946).[11]

Also impressed, though considerably less effusive, was 'J. F.', who in the *Irish Independent* saw *Mungo's Mansion* as 'first and foremost a comedy' into which 'tragedy comes suddenly and violently like a blow on the face'. Having dismissed Macken's plot as 'a feeble enough basis for a story', 'J. F.' continued, 'but the author carried his comedy along with the wealth of his dialogue and the picturesqueness of his characters' (*II*, 12 April 1946). The anonymous critic for the *Sunday Independent* referred to 'the strange haphazardry of comedy, tragedy and modified knockabout in "Mungo's Mansion"', and stated that while it was 'not what would be called an important play in any sense', it was nonetheless 'a pleasantly varied version of a piece of small-city life unusual in the Abbey repertory' and added that 'Mr. Macken is to be congratulated on his credible illusion of Buttermilk Lane as seen through a vivid, homely, fundamentally refined if too ingenious group of characters ... The author has done something worthwhile anyhow' (*SI*, 17 February 1946). 'K.' was far less enthusiastic in *The Irish Times*, writing rather dismissively that as 'a dramatic essay in the comedy and tragedy of slum life in Galway' *Mungo's Mansion* 'evokes, inevitably, comparison with Sean O'Casey – not entirely to the advantage of Mr. Macken' (*IT*, 12 February 1946).

Under the title *Galway Handicap*, the play was in 1947 produced in Bournemouth, Cambridge, and finally the Lyric theatre in London, where Macken saw it and wrote to its English director Irene Hertschel that 'I did not believe – (having suffered exceedingly at the Abbey last year) –

that it could be done so well and was accordingly shocked with surprise and delight when I saw unfolding in front of my eyes, the play which I had written and not just a bowdlerized version, gelded by half-wits.'[12] *Mungo's Mansion* was also translated into Irish by Seán Ó Cearra as *Árus Mhungo* and produced at Taibhdhearc na Gaillimhe in 1968 and again as recently as 2006. Writing of the 1968 production, an anonymous critic in *The Connacht Tribune* stated that 'it was a triumph for Walter Macken that characters he created in his imagination could be seen as real people', adding that it was 'a play that will definitely give you a really good laugh' (*CT*, 14 June 1968).

Set in 'the second-story room of a house in Galway's Buttermilk Lane', the play deals with the efforts of Mungo's son and daughter to get their widowed and disabled father to leave his 'mansion' in the slums for more spacious and salubrious housing elsewhere in the city. Nellie spells out to her father the threat their current home poses to a family with eleven children: 'It's no place to try and rear children. You know that! Sure they don't see a bit of sunshine from one end a the day to the other. It'll kill them off like flies, eventually, wait'll you see.'[13] Mungo is, however, adamant: 'When I lave Number Thirty-Five Buttermilk Lane, I'll lave it in me coffin and not before.'[14] The kindly doctor treating Mungo's son Tomeen also tries to sway Mungo by stressing the immediate threat the slum environment poses to the sickly boy: 'But I had a hard job bringing that little kid into the world and I'm going to work harder to keep him in it. He's not strong, Mungo. He has a touch of bronchial trouble now, and believe me that the air in Buttermilk Lane won't do him a bit of good.'[15] Mungo's answer is altogether predictable: 'Look, Doctor, I know what I'm doin', none better. And the day I'm carried outa this place it'll be in me coffin.'[16] Even after he wins a £2,000 sweepstake prize and learns his son may have diphtheria, he will not yield, declaring with breathtaking selfishness: 'I had eleven children, hadn't I? And not a brack on one of them since the day they were born. A man has a right to have one sick child out oo eleven, hasn't he? Even a brood a chickens has more sick ones in them than that.'[17]

What finally shocks him out of his blind intransigence is the murder of his neighbour Mrs Manders by her husband, driven mad by his inability to find work. At one point, Mungo himself is threatened by the murderer, only to be saved by his friend, the tramp Mowleogs. Having decided to leave the tenement, he tells Mowleogs he is not going because of his children but because 'somethin' says teh me, the oul' Lane'll never be the same again. I liked that Mrs. Manders, Mowleogs. I'd never feel the same here agin after it.'[18] Yet, to his son Mairteen he hypocritically claims his decision is based on his love for his family: 'I'm a good father that doesn't want his children teh be passin' out wan be wan down here in front of me eyes.'[19] The play ends in unsuccessful anticlimax with Mowleogs walking away despite Mungo's plaintive pleas that he stay to plan future gatherings in his new house. With Mowleogs gone and his old life in Buttermilk Lane over, Mungo snatches up the telegram announcing his sweepstakes winnings, 'throws it violently to the floor', and calls fruitlessly for his daughter Nellie to bring him a cup of tea as the curtain falls.[20]

The influence of O'Casey's *Juno and the Paycock* is obvious throughout this play. We have the pairing of Mungo and Mowleogs, although Mungo is never either as funny or as despicable as Captain Jack Boyle, nor is Mowleogs the entertaining though hypocritical and manipulative parasite O'Casey created in Joxer Daly.[21] We also have the young adult children Mairteen and Nellie, whose future, like that of Johnny and Mary Boyle, depends to a great extent on the vagaries of a wilful and delusional father – though in Macken's play their situation is even worse as there is no Juno to shelter them. Finally, we have the plot twist of unexpected financial windfall and a mixing of comedy with potential and actual tragedy. In Macken's play, the comedy is largely provided by Mungo's neighbours Mowleogs and Winnie the Wild Ducks Gilhealy, who, in a scene reminiscent of the party in the second act of O'Casey's play, attempt to jerry-rig a radio so that they can hear the horse race for which Mungo has his sweeps ticket. *Mungo's Mansion* is no *Juno and the Paycock*, but the play does have its moments of both genuine pathos and raucous laughter.

Vacant Possession, the next play in what would become Macken's Galway trilogy, was published by Macmillan in 1948 but has never been produced professionally.[22] It's not hard to see why. The play attempts to be the same kind of O'Caseyesque tragicomedy as *Mungo's Mansion*, but here the two never mesh together and after a comic opening, the tragic scenes seem out of place in the play. Moreover, six of the people in the play are unappealing, the only sympathetic ones being Chicken Delaney and the two female characters, the long-suffering Mrs Maggie Delaney and the improbably innocent Prissy Hartnet. Even more problematic is the fact that many of what are meant to be dramatic, even tragic, scenes in *Vacant Possession* are more off-putting than either moving or enlightening.[23]

The play opens with two comic bumblers, Fixit Maloney and Gunner Delaney, breaking into a derelict building called 'The Gantry'. Both have been evicted from their homes, and Gunner has brought along his wife Maggie and son Chicken. Clearly, Macken intended Fixit to remind the audiences of Captain Boyle, with his phonograph and his boasts, such as the one about a general praising his voice as 'the sweetest tinor vice oo any man I ever heard'.[24] But Gunner is no Joxer Daly, and while there is some humour in the scene where Fixit repairs Gunner's wooden leg, would-be comic bits like their argument about Parnell and Daniel O'Connell fall flat. Fixit and Gunner both know they are failures and that they have now sunk to a new low squatting in a condemned building. As Fixit says, 'What have I got to boast about after a lifetime? Bounced from pillar to post like an oul' yoke of an ass that has gone long in the tooth.'[25] Gunner's case is more complicated. He does odd jobs with his horse and cart and should be able to support his family on what he makes. However, after an accident that costs him a leg, he has become an alcoholic who drinks the money that should house and feed his family. When Chicken hears him ask Mrs Delaney for money for 'a quick wan', he explodes angrily: 'Lissen, Ma, if yeh give 'm the couple a bobs I gave yeh, I'll lave, d'yer hear? Lookit, Ma, I'm not goin' to wirk any more so that me man can go out swillin' porter and puttin' us in the cart.'[26]

Later in the play Mrs Delaney tries to stop a man from giving Gunner his drinking money, and when Gunner tells her to 'keep outa this' she replies: 'Too long I've kept out oo't when the oul' horse brings you home as drunk as a lord every night near, an' yer own child at home without a drop of milk teh put in his mouth. I've kept out oo it too long, Gunner.' Enraged, 'in a fury of temper, exasperation, the need for a drink and being ashamed of it all', he slaps her across the mouth and, as Macken's stage direction says, 'would immediately have given anything in the world not to have done it'. Maggie then decides she has had enough: 'Well, that's done it, Gunner. That's done it now. Whatever else yeh done all these years, yeh never did that … I'm lavin' yeh, and yeh'll never see Maggie agin. Goobye now, Gunner, and from here on forever yeh can stew in yer own porter juice.'[27]

This is the most important scene in the play, but through the reactions of his other characters Macken pretty much lets Gunner off the hook. Thus, Fixit offers the following defence: 'Lookit, wife-hittin' is a bad business, but he never done it before an' I don't think he meant it. Better min than the Gunner ever was bet their wives. Ye'd be surprised … at the number a sober Christian gintlemin that hammer hell outa the better halves.'[28] Right after Maggie leaves, Fixit tells his friend that 'yeh can fix a lot of things but yeh can't fix this', and suggests that he 'go down an' get a few drinks for yerself and mebbe we'll thinka somethin'.'[29] As we saw above, Gunner immediately feels remorse for his action, but that remorse is mixed with a great deal of self-pity and denial: 'I was a good fella one time too, a long time ago, an' it's hard teh believe, I know. But whin I lost the leg, I lost something inside a meself too, an' it never kem back … Lookit, when you become as used to the booze as I am … you're not in yer right mind when you're without it. Mebbe if I had a couple I'd be able teh think better about what to do. If I'd had a few this'd never have happened.'[30]

In a scene whose interpretation depends entirely on how it is played on stage, Maggie decides to return to Gunner: 'Yes, God forgive me. I've come back. I'm too old, Fixit, teh be runnin' away now. It's a bit late in the day teh be runnin' away now whin I didn't run away tin or fifteen years ago.' To which Fixit responds, 'Look, you never said a truer word than that. What's the use now, an' mebbe yer goin' off like that'll be a lesson to the Gunner an' he'll turn over a new leaf, or a new half leaf anyhow.'[31]

At this point, Maggie is spared having to think about her future life with Gunner when she learns from Chicken that he has – conveniently enough – been fished out of the water at the docks, a victim of accident or possibly suicide. Her conventionally pious response here is as troubling to a modern reader as is her return to Gunner: 'It's all the will a God.'[32] The most realistic response to Gunner's death is that of his son Chicken: 'I say that Gunner is better off out oo it altogether. He was goin' down the drain, the Gunner was, an' he was pullin' us down with 'm … It's the best thing that happened to me mother that he went out like that now … I'll have the oul' horse an' cart now … Now I'll have it, an' she'll be well off agin for the first time in her life. We'll eat agin regular, Fixit, an' we'll be able teh walk up the town an' not be ashamed a the neighbours.'[33] Fixit is unimpressed: 'Ah, go on an' take yer oul' horse an' cart an' become a respectable citizen! ... but I still say yeh'll never be as good a man as yer father ...'[34]

This plot involving Gunner, Maggie and Chicken, the most emotionally engaging in the play, runs alongside two others significantly less interesting. The first involves whether or not Fixer will be able to remain in possession of the Gantry against the combined efforts of the 'Dummy', Mr Kilcullen, who has responsibility for the building, and Jamsey 'Revenge' Horgan, Fixer's landlord, whom Kilcullen has hired. Here, the force of the law is too strong, and Fixer at the end finds himself again on the street. The other plot involves the robbery of a pub by a flashily dressed 'masher' named Wee-Wee Brady. Brady is initially provided an alibi by Gabbler Blake, an elderly, well-spoken and seemingly benevolent man Brady claims to have helped make his way home to his beloved Galway from the poorhouse in Loughrea.[35] A garda sergeant eventually solves the case, revealing that the 'kindly' old man is actually a career criminal and is in cahoots with Wee-Wee, who actually did commit the robbery.

The characters quickly and viciously turn on each other as the garda sergeant presents his case, undercutting the working-class identity and solidarity Fixit, Gunner and Wee-Wee assert at various points in the play, as when Fixer says to Revenge Horgan as he takes a sledgehammer to the Gantry at the end:

> Don't lave a stone on a stone oo it, because yeer pullin' down the freedom a man on top a yeer own dirty heads. Let ye sing at yeer work a pullin' down the oul' Ganthry, because the oul' Ganthry is ended and so is the rights a' the common people ... Let ye give great shout outa ye because yeer knockin' the props from under democracy, and it'll fall like a corpse under the foundations a the Galway Ganthry. Democracy? How are yeh![36]

Then, in a leap for which there has been no preparation, Macken turns the destruction of the Gantry into an indictment of Irish society in general. As a bit of plaster is knocked from the ceiling, the gramophone Fixit has turned on plays, and 'the baritone on the record is singing feelingly, "Sure, a little bit of Heaven fell from out the sky one day"', and as the curtain finally descends he bawls, '"They called it Ire-e-e-e-land."'[37] This is stirring stuff, but the play does not deserve its ending. Knockabout farce, the tragedy of alcoholism and the destruction of a family, whodunnit, or socialist call to action – the problem is that *Vacant Possession* is a bit of all of these and thus none convincingly.

Macken's next play for the Abbey, *Home is the Hero,* directed by Ria Mooney, opened on 28 July 1952 at the Queen's theatre, where the Abbey company had relocated after the 1951 fire. It was to have a record-breaking run of seventeen weeks, three weeks longer than the run of George Shiels' *The Rugged Path,* whose fourteen-week stay on the stage of the old Abbey building in 1940 had previously held the record. Commenting on this lengthy run, the *Nationalist and Leinster Times* called it 'an achievement which by the Abbey's, or any, standards gains in lustre from a comparison between the seating capacity of the old Abbey and that of the Queen's'. This paper also reported that by the end of the run the play 'will have been seen by something over 90,000 people, a very much greater number than have bought tickets for the Abbey during the run of any previous play'. Moreover, 'it has netted its author an estimated £1,300 which, by any standards, is by no means hay' (*NLT,* 22 November 1952).[38] This writer in the *Nationalist* makes an important point here. When the Abbey relocated across the Liffey to the Queen's theatre after the disastrous fire in 1951, the company moved into much larger quarters, creating a new set of challenges, not the least of which were financial. Much smaller audiences could fill the old Abbey, making it possible for relatively few playgoers to keep a play going for several weeks. Filling the Queen's was a different proposition altogether, making Macken's success with *Home is the Hero* even more impressive. Also, the success of a long-running play in the Queen's could help balance losses incurred by plays that lacked such popular appeal, and this kind of financial reasoning dictated that the Abbey management – which at this time pretty much meant Ernest Blythe – would milk a successful play for all it was worth. As a result, runs of successful plays at the Queen's were likely to be longer than those at the old building on Abbey Street. Indeed, Macken's record with *Home is the Hero* only lasted a year before it was broken by Louis d'Alton's *This Other Eden,* which ran for twenty-four weeks and was seen 'by an estimated 115,000 people' in 1953 (*IP,* 1 December 1953).[39]

Although Blythe felt the play was 'no masterpiece', he was delighted with its success and the money it brought to the Abbey's coffers: 'We can now feel more fully satisfied than before that with a little bit of luck and the arrival of two or three new plays as good as *Home is the Hero* ... we can face the future without any excessive financial trepidation.' Over its seventeen-week run, *Home is the Hero* brought in some £2,700.[40] Moreover, as Máire Ní Chatháin pointed out in a piece in the *Evening Herald*, that windfall meant that 'the Abbey directors should again be able to throw their net wide and take a risk with new writers. Therefore, in the long view rising young Irish dramatists may have much to be thankful for to Walter Macken and his Galwegian slum creations' (*EH*, 11 October 1952).

As noted above, *Home is the Hero* was also produced – with little success – in New York. In addition, a production was mounted in Cork in 1952, 'probably the first Irish play to be given a second production in another city while the original production is still running' (*IT*, 27 September 1952). In 1954, the play was staged by the Liverpool Repertory Theatre where, according to *The Irish Times*, it was 'doing record business' and 'the demand for seats has been greater for this show than for any other production since the war' (*IT*, 13 December 1954).[41] By the following year, Michael Monks could report in his 'Limelight' column in *The Irish Times* that *Home is the Hero* 'is proving one of the biggest successes in the provinces: a couple of weeks back it was playing in at least three provincial towns – Dungarvan, Clonmel, and Kilkenny – to crowded houses' (*IT*, 10 July 1953). The play was also translated into Irish by Seán Ó Carra in 1971 as *An Laoch ar Ais* (The Hero is Back), which opened in Gweedore, County Donegal, in April before coming to the Taibhdhearc. Micheál P. Ó Conaola was the director (*CT*, 18 June 1971).[42]

A newspaper strike at the time of the play's opening meant it received no reviews, nor was this situation remedied when the papers resumed publication. On the other hand, there was a one-sided controversy about the play in the letters column of the *Evening Mail* when that paper reappeared.[43] This kerfuffle started when an American tourist from New York named James J. Munro wrote that after seeing *Home is the Hero* his opinion was that 'the play has for its plot a revolting theme in that it presents not the true cultural and religious phase of the Irish people but, on the contrary, portrays the lowest caste of the Irish people, marked by drunkenness and crime …' (*EM*, 7 October 1952). A few days later, 'Playgoer' wrote that he was 'ashamed and disgusted with it, and if this is the sort of thing our National Theatre portrays as being Irish then we cannot complain if visitors to our country go away with wrong impressions …' (*EM*, 10 October 1952). Mrs Marie Behan also agreed with Munro, invoking the patriot dead when she declared: 'It was not for this type of culture that Pearse and the rest of the heroes died' (*EM*, 13 October 1952). Macken was, however, defended by one E. Stapleton, who wrote: 'The language used, the drunkenness and the kind of crime portrayed in the play – the first being very typical, the second quite common, and the third not unduly rare – did not, in my opinion, detract in any way from the more estimable characteristics of the Irish people' (*EM*, 9 October 1952).

In a snide comment in his 'In the Theatre' column in *The Irish Times*, 'K. M. G.' stated of *Home is the Hero*: 'The play has made money for the Abbey – that is the sole justification for allowing it to occupy the theatre for more than four months' (*IT*, 15 November 1952). 'K. M. G.' was, however, more measured in a year's-end round-up of theatre news the following month, writing: 'But despite its mammoth run, opinion is divided upon its merits. However, nobody will be likely to quarrel if it is nominated as the **MOST SUCCESSFUL** play of the year' (*IT*, 27 December 1952). If, however, the Dublin critics never had a chance to review the play, the same was not true of their counterparts in New York when they saw *Home is the Hero* with Macken himself in the lead role. Brooks Atkinson's notice in *The New York Times* pretty much sums up the American response to the play: '"Home is the Hero" seems to be a self-contained and earnestly written play not worth the labor that has gone into it … With one or two exceptions the characters are uninteresting. The writing is pedestrian. There is no vitality under the surface bickering of the story' (*NYT*, 23 September 1954).

Home is the Hero is set in 'the general living-room of a house in a long avenue of houses in the town of Galway'.[44] A mother, son and daughter are waiting in some trepidation for the return of their husband/father Paddo O'Reilly, who has just been released after serving five years in prison for accidentally killing a neighbour during an argument in a pub. The years have been hard ones for the family. Paddo's wife Daylia has begun to drink, his daughter Josie has become embittered because of the ridicule she has suffered as the child of a convict, and his son Willie rejects any notion his father is a hero. Actually, Willie is at first the most sympathetic of the three towards Paddo, even though he owes his own physical handicap to his drunken father's failure to catch him after throwing him in the air as an infant. Unlike the members of his family, some of his old friends plan to welcome him home triumphantly: 'All the oul' butties will be at the station and the kids have been learnin' a song to sing in the street. When the first darkness falls we're goin' to light a bonefire under the lamp. He'll never forget comin' home ... Doesn't everyone love him? Isn't he a proper hayro?'[45]

Not surprisingly, Paddo is not the same man he was, and not just in his more aged physical appearance. Seeing his welcoming committee before they see him, he manages to avoid them and slip home, where he finds everything has changed. Soon he is lashing out at his family, though he also recognises that much of the blame for what has occurred in his absence falls on him: 'Well! And it's my fault, let none of ye think I don't know that. I know that. When I chopped meself down I chopped the three of ye down with me. That's part of the hard things I thought. I had lots of time to think.'[46] Paddo is also weighed down with the guilt of having killed Pat Green, whom he calls 'one of the finest and most kindly men in the whole town ... He had more brains in the tip of his finger than I had in my whole body. And that was why I killed him.' Indeed, he feels that 'they should have hung me. I wasn't punished enough for what I done.'[47] The fact that the man's wife and his daughter Lily forgive him only exacerbates his self-loathing.

Nevertheless, despite his guilt and self-pity, Paddo seems almost eager to impose his will on his family. He is, for example, determined to end Josie's relationship with the callow and foppish Manchester Monaghan. Even more important to him is preventing the marriage of his son Willie and Lily Green: 'Can't ye hear what people will say? Can't ye see the day that ye will have to tell yeer children the story of yeer beginnings?' It is, however, himself he worries about most: 'How much agony can a man stand? Do ye want to pile on more agony into me mind until I go out of my head?'[48]

He is, of course, no longer dealing with the adolescents he left five years earlier, and both Josie and Willie stand up to him, sending him into a rage in which he coarsely insults Josie and then beats her with a strap. Despite his behaviour, neither Josie nor Willie is at this point able to escape Paddo because their mother is still unwilling to leave him and they feel duty-bound to stay with her. Thinking he has solved his family problems with 'a few strokes of the strap', Paddo says all he now wants is 'liberty', a notion that Willie rejects out of hand: 'You're not talking about liberty, Paddo. You're talkin' about licence. You didn't learn much. All you learned was because someone took away your liberty, you'd take away ours.'[49] By now even Paddo's erstwhile admirers like 'Dovetail' are disgusted with him: 'You know what they think about you now, Paddo? Stinking, you are, in the noses of the citizens. No good, Paddo. No bloody good … Have you any friends now, Paddo? No friends. Wouldn't throw you a rope in a swalla hole.'[50] When Paddo threatens Daylia and Dovetail comes to her defence, Paddo strikes his former friend, knocking him down a flight of stairs. Coldly, Willie lets his father think he has killed again, leaving Paddo in terror that he will be sent back to prison. When Paddo sees that Dovetail is still alive and that his own son lied to cause him pain, he realises there is no longer a place for him in the family and he leaves for good, with only Daylia feeling any regret at his departure.

There are obviously some powerful moments in *Home is the Hero,* and its long run proves that it could hold and move audiences. It is, however, a deeply flawed play. In the first place, Paddo is a character inconsistent to the point of incoherence. We are told by Lily Green early in the play that 'he was a nice man', one who handed out sweets to children when he got paid, one of 'the good giants that wouldn't hurt a sinner'.[51] Yet we see virtually nothing of this gentle giant in the bombastic and threatening would-be tyrant of the play itself. There are also plausibility issues, as it seems at the very least difficult to accept that both Mrs Green and Lily would be so willing not only to forgive but also to embrace the man who had so wronged them by killing Pat Green. Furthermore, while Macken had at least tried to emulate O'Casey's tragicomic approach in *Mungo's Mansion,* here what he gives us is too often melodrama pure and simple. There may be a fleeting dash of comedy, but on the whole the mood of the play is relentlessly dark and the register consistently strident. Given the complete change in direction represented by Macken's next play for the Abbey, one wonders if he himself had decided that whatever his understanding of his milieu, he would never match O'Casey with his Galway trilogy.

That next play of Macken's was *Twilight of a Warrior,* which opened at the Queen's theatre on 21 November 1955 with Edward Golden (Éamonn Guaillí) directing the Abbey company. The lead role of the 'warrior', Dacey Adams, was played by a young Ray McAnally. Reviews were once again mixed. Writing in *The Irish Times,* 'K.' felt Abbey audiences should be grateful to Macken because 'he has brought a new, different, and contemporarily credible character on to the Abbey stage' and written 'an Abbey play which has something of interest to say and which says it with immense theatrical effectiveness' (*IT,* 22 November 1955). 'I. M.' in the *Irish Independent* found *Twilight of a Warrior* 'a play of contradictions', its theme 'developed with some of the lushness of a Victorian novelette', while its 'approach to the characters' was 'in the psychological plane of modern intellectual drama'. For 'I. M.', this awkward blending of two such disparate modes of thought did not work, creating a play 'where the mechanics are often cruder than might be expected from an author who knows the theatre as actor, author and producer' (*II,* 22 November 1955). Far more positive was 'J. J. F.' in the *Evening Herald.* Having begun his review by exclaiming, 'At last, after a river of disappointments, a new Abbey play of substance, filled with dialogue that does not insult the intelligence', he went on to praise the play as 'the almost-wholly gripping story of the later life, and death, of an IRA hero, a story told with some of the undertones of Greek drama, suspected close kinship plus a few drumbeats of Eugene O'Neill ... whose *Mourning Becomes Electra* it occasionally brings to mind'. Macken's work seems to have been all too successful at bringing to mind that of better playwrights! 'J. J. F.' did add that 'I cannot say that Macken has adequately resolved all the many interesting points he has raised', but he insisted that 'at least he has written a play tingling with life and one that tries to throw a bridge from the Ireland of the recent past to what in his mind is the disillusioned Ireland of to-day' (*EH,* 22 November 1955). On the other hand, when the play was given an amateur production by the Vocational Players of Scariff, County Clare, at the 1961 Limerick Drama Festival, no less a figure in Irish theatre than Hilton Edwards pronounced it 'a false proposition' and said he did not believe a word of it (*EH,* 1 March 1961).

This performance at the Limerick Drama Festival was one of several such productions *Twilight of a Warrior* would receive, as the play remained fairly popular with local theatre groups for the next two decades. It was also translated into Irish by Tomás Mac Eochaidh as *Bua an Bháis* (The Triumph of Death) and produced at the Taibhdhearc in 1959 with Traolach Ó hAonghusa directing. It has not been revived or retranslated.

Twilight of a Warrior is set in the study of Dacey Adams' lavish home near Dublin. Adams, a legendary IRA hero from the war of independence, is now a wealthy industrialist, a power broker in the state, and an authoritarian head of household. Into his life comes Abel Martin, a young man whom his daughter Josie has brought home to get her father's blessing for their marriage. Martin is only the most recent of a series of unacceptable potential spouses the rather flighty Josie has introduced to her father, and not surprisingly Adams is opposed to the match. Yet, instead of simply sending Martin away, Adams engages him in a strange conversation in which he lays bare the complex workings of his family and reveals secrets of his heroic past he has never spoken of before. Much of this information concerns his relationship with Mary Ann, a young woman who had nursed him after he was badly wounded in a skirmish in County Mayo. One of the questions Macken raises during their conversation is the possibility that Martin is Dacey's son by Mary Ann. When we meet Adams' actual son Ross, a would-be poet and alcoholic in the making, we can see why Dacey might see Martin as a more suitable heir.

Adams' real problem is that he cannot stop seeing himself as a warrior long after the war is over. Indeed, in many ways one gets the impression that since the war ended, he has been at a loss, with leftover life to kill. As he says to Martin, 'Look, the only thing a patriot can do is to die for his ideals in the middle of a revolution. You understand that? It is better for a patriot to die then.'[52] Having survived the war that defined him, he has lived his entire life since as one long war on many fronts, regardless of the cost to others, most notably to his family. He has estranged his wife; turned his bachelor brother – a decorated hero in the British army in the First World War – and his spinster sister into virtual servants in his household; broken the spirit of his adult children; and humiliated an old employee of whom his wife has been fond since her childhood. Martin, however, resists him, in the end stripping him of his idealised image of

Mary Ann, claiming that instead of being a patriotic heroine and his own mother, she was a pragmatic woman who married a former British soldier who had fought against the IRA in Mayo.

When Dacey sends his son Ross to bring the previously noted old employee to him to be insulted and fired, Ross botches the job, drunkenly kills the man in a car crash, and now faces arrest and disgrace. Needless to say, Dacey believes he can take care of the problem, only to be thwarted when Ross surprisingly insists that the truth be told. Finally overwhelmed, Dacey collapses and dies, with Martin the only one present to hear his dying words of baffled regret: 'Want to know – are there marks for loving your country, scorched with love? Is it misapplied? The pain of frustration? Is that purgatory? And does it balance against all the rest? Yes, I know I'm dying. All alone. They don't know. Dead, I want to be a happy warrior. Yes. Oh yes, I am sorry; oh I am heartily sorry – because – and I'm ...'[53]

Twilight of a Warrior is by no means a great play. It may, however, be Macken's best. It is certainly his most interesting, and as a play about fame and power and their tendency to corrupt both individuals and societies, it can be seen as a precursor to later plays like Máiréad Ní Ghráda's *Breithiúnas* (Judgement) (1968), on which it may well have been a significant influence, or Sebastian Barry's *Hinterland* (2002). And contemporary audiences must have been struck by its immediate relevance, with the revolutionary generation holding on to power after three decades of independence – Éamon de Valera still taoiseach, Seán T. O'Kelly in the presidency, and Seán Lemass waiting in the wings to assume control.

Unfortunately, the promise of *Twilight of a Warrior* was not realised. Neither of Macken's last two plays produced in English, *Look in the Mirror* at the Abbey in 1958 and *Voices of Doolin* at the Gaiety in 1960, had anywhere near the success of his first three, nor did they signal any meaningful new direction in his evolution as a playwright. Of *Look in the Mirror* 'M. K.' wrote in *The Irish Times* that while the opening night audience who had braved snow to come to the theatre 'appeared to enjoy it without reservation', he was not impressed and could not 'blame my feelings exclusively on the ambient snow'. He found 'the first act ... short and funny, the second short, skimpy and disjointed', and the third falling back on 'Mr. Macken's old and apparently abandoned resource – physical violence'. Professing himself an 'unreasonable admirer of his [Macken's] talents', 'M. K.' hoped that 'this villainously titled play, whatever its popular success, represents merely an off-moment' (*IT*, 11 March 1958). In the *Irish Independent*, 'I. M.' wrote that Macken seemed unwilling to realise the genuine potential of his own play: 'It brings tragedy in its wake, but Mr. Macken is determined not to be serious, even if he has to wallow through sentiment to reach his happy ending'. For 'I. M.', in the end 'one is left with the feeling that the characters which he has so surely and so realistically created could say so much more if given more plausible situations to cope with' (*II*, 11 March 1958). 'N. C.' of *The Irish Press* felt that the playwright 'has a fine theme, which he handles admirably, although the customary Macken sparkle is often lacking in the writing and there is quite an amount of unnecessary repetition' (*IP*, 11 March 1958). The most negative opinion of the play was, however, the one that counted most. In his manager's report for 19 March 1958, Ernest Blythe stated flatly: 'The Macken play is turning out to be a definite failure. It plays much less well than it reads.' The Abbey's board agreed, pulling the play before the end of its scheduled run and declaring in its meeting of 2 April 1958 that 'the Macken play fulfilled our gloomiest expectation and did worse in its second week than in its first'.[54]

Voices of Doolin seems to have been meant principally as a vehicle for Cyril Cusack, and as such it was a success. Critics were, however, far more impressed by the star than the play itself. Particularly harsh was 'K.' of *The Irish Times*, who wrote: 'The influence of Henrik Ibsen lies heavily on "The Voices of Doolin"; the skill of the old master-builder unfortunately does not.' 'K.' had expected that Macken, 'a journeyman of the theatre with many years' experience behind him', would provide 'at the least a tautly constructed play, and not a rambling tract on the evils of alcoholism with fairly audible echoes more reminiscent of "The Drunkard" than "The Doll's House"' (*IT*, 16 September 1960). Macken continued to believe in the play, writing to his friend Rita Joyce in January 1961: 'The play I wrote in the fall was not successful. Nobody but myself and a wonderful actor [Cusack] seemed to understand what it was about … However, it was a good play and someday its merit might be seen.'[55] So far, he's been wrong. *Merchant's Road*, the last play Macken submitted to the Abbey, was rejected by the theatre in 1963. It should, however, be noted that it was *Recall the Years*, his dramatic review of the theatre's history, that was selected to open the new Abbey building in 1966.

A fair amount of space has been devoted here to Macken's dramatic work in English, but this discussion seems necessary as background to the comparison that will be made below between his plays in English and those in Irish. Now, however, we may turn to our main subject, Macken's contribution to theatre in Irish as actor, director and playwright. That contribution was prodigious, making him arguably the most important figure in Irish-language theatre in the 1930s and '40s. As we have seen, he arrived at the Taibhdhearc as an actor in 1932, and by the following year he was already assisting the manager / artistic director Frank Dermody, doing some translation work, designing and building scenery, and acting. In 1937 he eloped with fellow Taibhdhearc actor Peggy Kenny, a member of the family known for their Galway bookstore, and settled in London. However, when Frank Dermody left the Taibhdhearc for the Abbey, Macken was invited back to replace him.[56] Thus, at twenty-four years of age, Macken was put in charge of the national theatre for the Irish language. The title was a lot more impressive than the job. Macken himself gives us an idea of what that was like in his account of Mahon, the manager of a small English-language theatre in Galway, in his semi-autobiographical novel *Sullivan* (1957): 'He worked an average of twelve to fourteen hours a day holding the small theatre together. He designed and painted the scenery, he made flats and stretched the canvas on them, he kept the accounts, drew up the advertising, learned off long parts, trained new actors to become presentable, making as he thought silk purses out of sow's ears.'[57] He himself was to keep up this kind of workload for nine years, in addition to producing and directing ninety-six shows, seventy-six of them plays, in almost all of which he had a role, often a major one.[58] It should also be noted that as a salaried employee of the theatre, he received no additional compensation for his acting. Somehow, it was also during these years that he began his brief career as a playwright in Irish.

Perhaps the best way to make sense of all he did is to examine his contributions in each area separately. Since he began his work at the Taibhdhearc as an actor, we can begin with his work on stage. Among the parts he played between 1932 and 1948 were Monsieur Jourdain in *Sodar i ndiaidh na nUasal* (Trotting after the Quality), a translation of Molière's *Le bourgeois gentilhomme*, Diarmaid in Micheál Mac Liammóir's *Diarmaid agus Gráinne*, Bernard in *Beatha Iongantach Bhearnáird Óig de Menthon,* a translation of Henri Ghéon's *La merveilleuse histoire de jeune Bernard de Menthon,* Tristan in *Tristan agus Isolde,* a translation of Joseph Bédier and Louis Artus' *Tristan et Iseult,* all in 1936; Domhnall Ó Cearnaigh (Donal Kearney) in *Grádh na Spréidh* (The Love of the Dowry), a translation of T.C. Murray's *Sovereign Love,* in 1937; Captain Stanhope in *Deireadh an Aistir,* a translation of R.C. Sherriff's *Journey's End,* and James Clarence Mangan in *Fear an Clóca,* a translation of Louis d'Alton's *The Man in the Cloak,* both in 1940; Seamus Shields in *Sgáil an Óglaigh,* a translation of Sean O'Casey's *The Shadow of a Gunman,* and the title roles in *An tImpire Mac Seoin,* a translation of Eugene O'Neill's *The Emperor Jones,* and in Shakespeare's *Macbeit* (*Macbeth*), all in 1941;[59] Fluther Good in *An Céachta agus na Réalta,* a translation of O'Casey's *The Plough and the Stars* in 1942; Isaac Butt in *An Choróin v. an Ceallach* (The Crown v. Kelly), a translation of Roger McHugh's *Trial at Green Street Courthouse,* and the director in Labhrás Mac Brádaigh's *An tÚghdar i nGleic* (The Author in a Quandary), both in 1943; Lucifer in Máiréad Ní Ghráda's *Giolla an tSolais* (The Lad of Light) in 1945; Cathal Buidhe Mac Giolla Gunna in Eibhlín Ní Bhaoighill's *Cathal Buidhe* and George in *Cinneamhain* (Fate), an adaptation of John Steinbeck's novel *Of Mice and Men,* both in 1946; and Charles Marlow Jr in *Ísliú chun Buadha,* a translation of Oliver Goldsmith's *She Stoops to Conquer,* in 1947. And there were many more.

What kind of an actor in Irish was Walter Macken? The first thing to remember is that when he came to the Taibhdhearc in 1932 he was an apprentice, with a great deal to learn not only about acting, but also about Irish. Like many working in the Taibhdhearc at the time, Macken was not a native speaker of Irish, and therefore in 1936 the theatre's board of directors sent him to stay with the writer Criostóir Mac Aonghusa in Rosmuc in the Conamara Gaeltacht to improve his command of the language. Judging from a letter Macken wrote from Rosmuc to his wife-to-be Peggy Kenny quoted in his son Ultan's biography, Mac Aonghusa made him work: 'I'd read a bit and then he would correct my pronunciation. He's certainly well up in Irish. There are millions of different words that I was pronouncing incorrectly and he pointed out each and every one to me.'[60] This growing awareness of the challenge facing him (and others at the Taibhdhearc) is clear in other letters to Peggy that he wrote from Rosmuc. At first, he found his Irish 'not so bad as I thought it was', adding

'All it needs is good brushing up.'[61] It did not take long for him to change his mind, however, so that he was soon writing pessimistically: 'The old Irish is improving anyhow but the whole expedition [*sic*] is a fallacy for the simple reason, that none of us – and that includes Dermody and all the directors – save Liam Ó Briain can talk Irish. Our knowledge of the language is only superficial and you would want to spend about 5 years at least in the Gaeltacht before you could acquire even the semblance of a *blas* [proper accent]. And I find out that I am like a German talking bad French to Alexander [*sic*] Dumas. They don't know what the devil I'm talking about and they have nothing on me because I don't either.'[62] In another letter he laments that 'my Irish is terribly poor. I didn't really know how poor and weak it was until I came out here. I'm barely able to put a sentence together and as a matter of fact I don't know whether it is broken Irish or broken English, I am speaking.'[63] He must have been experiencing a natural and temporary frustration, because if he actually believed his own Irish was so bad and the entire Taibhdhearc enterprise a 'fallacy', he would hardly have gone back to work so hard at the theatre for another twelve years. Given all the major roles that he played and the fact that he was to try his hand at writing plays in Irish, we can probably assume that, while never entirely at home in the language, he had achieved enough command of it to take the stage with confidence.[64]

What we know about his acting in Irish comes almost exclusively from anonymous reviews in *The Connacht Tribune*, and here another caveat is in order. Unlike the modern, sophisticated and highly cultured city that is Galway today, Galway town in the 1930s and '40s was a provincial backwater. What was available to Galwegians with an interest in the theatre was the work of local amateurs and occasional visits by Irish or British touring companies. Needless to say, as a result, theatre critics in the town were amateurs who probably had little personal experience of fine acting and based their reviews on standards of the art they had developed on their own. That said, they approached their job seriously and with enthusiasm, and for the most part they enjoyed the performances of Walter Macken. Thus, the critic in *The Connacht Sentinel* wrote of his performance as the male lead in Micheál Mac Liammóir's *Diarmaid agus Gráinne*: 'Bhaitéar Ó Maicín (Diarmuid) and Máire Nic Giolla Mháirtín (Gráinne) gave delightful touches of artistry in their portrayals. The scene between these two in the last act, prior to Diarmuid's exit to the fatal hunt, was a wonderful piece of acting' (*CS*, 13 October 1936).[65] The following year the reviewer for *The Connacht Tribune* declared: 'Uaitéir Ó Maicín carried the honours of the Taibhdhearc production. The young actor who has had innumerable successes to his name gave a delightful reading of Domhnall Ó Cearnaigh' in the Irish version of T.C. Murray's *Sovereign Gold* (*CT*, 16 January 1937). Macken's 'vivid portrayal' of the British officer Captain Stanhope in *Deireadh an Aistir* (R.C. Sherriff's First World War play *Journey's End*) was lauded in October 1940.

Macken also seems to have shone in the challenging role of Fluther Good in the Taibhdhearc's 1942 translation of O'Casey's *The Plough and the Stars*: 'Walter Macken's versatile genius had full scope in the part of "Fluther" Good and he made the most of it, especially in the drunken scene and the looting episode' (*CT*, 7 November 1942). In *Sonas gan Saidhbhreas* (Happiness without Wealth), the Irish version of Louis d'Alton's *The Money Doesn't Matter*, 'Bhaitéar Ó Maicín gave a forceful portrayal of the father ... so much so that the action of the play was inclined to fall flat when he was not on the stage' (*CT*, 9 November 1946). He could also apparently shine in a minor role. Thus, we read that in *Ag Seasamh an Fhóid* (Standing One's Ground), the Irish version of J.H. Darley's *Facing the Music*, 'in his role of clergyman he was not very much before the audience, but his interpretation was a grand piece of work' (*CT*, 9 March 1940). He was apparently also a fine verse speaker, as reported in a brief anonymous piece about *Meascán* (Miscellany), the Taibhdhearc's St Patrick's Day show in 1947: 'A feature of the show was the verse-speaking of the producer, whose spirited interpretation brought new life and vigour to a number of well-known Irish poems' (*IT*, 19 March 1947).[66]

The presumably more cosmopolitan Dublin critics also enjoyed his acting. For example, having seen the Irish translation of Molière's *Le bourgeois gentilhomme* at the Taibhdhearc, the anonymous critic for the *Sunday Independent* praised Macken for 'a wonderful portrayal in the title role' (*SI*, 3 May 1936). And when the Taibhdhearc company visited Dublin the following month with a translation of Louis d'Alton's *The Man in the Cloak*, 'M. Ó M.' of the *Evening Herald* praised Macken for 'a faithful rendering of the author's fine interpretation of Clarence Mangan's gentle character' (*EH*, 14 November 1940).

Macken not only directed all of the plays he appeared in between June 1939 and January 1948, he directed all of the plays anyone appeared in during that period. He faced a real challenge when he took this job as Frank Dermody, the man he replaced, would go on to become one of the country's best-known directors at the Abbey and later at Dublin's Irish-language theatre An Damer. According to Ultan Macken, his father was not intimidated by his predecessor's growing reputation as he had a very different philosophy as a director: 'Although he learned a lot from Dermody, I do not think he agreed with his style of directing. My father felt that each actor must make a part his own, whereas Dermody wanted each actor to play the part strictly as he told them, without giving them the freedom to find their own interpretation.'[67] We will see below that one of the things actors at the Taibhdhearc remembered about him was his commitment to teamwork in the theatre.

Keeping in mind the previously noted caveat about the quality of criticism in Galway at that time, we can still use reviews to get an idea of his abilities as a director at the Taibhdhearc. Of his production of *Ag Seasamh an Fhóid* in 1940, *The Connacht Tribune* reported that Macken 'had the movement at its proper tempo and swinging along in delightful style' (*CT*, 9 March 1940). The following year the *Tribune* had high praise for his work with the pageant play *Caithréim an Sclábhaidhe* (The Triumphant Career of the Slave [i.e. St Patrick]): 'Beauty of grouping, richness of colour and consummate skill in lighting, the seven scenes from the life of St. Patrick presented by Mr. Walter Macken at Taibhdhearc na Gaillimhe on Sunday and last night ... combined to provide one of the most artistic successes yet scored by the Taibhdhearc. This remarkably beautiful production afforded yet another illustration of the artistic genius of the producer ...' (*CT*, 18 March 1941). Reviewing a twin bill of plays by Séamus de Bhilmot, *The Connacht Tribune* again had high praise for Macken as director: 'The cottage scenes in the comedy, "Déamar agus a Bhean", were treated with remarkable skill by Mr. Macken, while in the war play, "An Ráidhteas Oifigeamhail" ... he showed his ability in the production of spectacular work.' This critic also stressed that 'Mr. Macken couples his ability in production work with an enthusiasm that has established a fine team spirit among the members of his company' (*CT*, 13 June 1942). In the Taibhdhearc's production of an Irish translation of J.M. Barrie's *Mary Rose* the same year, the *Tribune*'s critic wrote that 'the production work of Mr. Walter Macken captured all the homeliness, the eeriness and the charm of the play …' (*CT*, 19 September 1942).[68] Of the Irish version of Robert Brennan's *Good Night, Mr. O'Donnell* in 1945, we are told that 'Mr. Walter Macken's production gets the best out of the play …' (*CT*, 29 December 1945);[69] while in Eibhlín Ní Bhaoighill's *Cathal Buidhe* the following year 'the production work by Mr. Macken was very good' (*CT*, 22 June 1946).[70] When the Taibhdhearc performed *Cinneamhain*, an Irish adaptation of John Steinbeck's novel *Of Mice and Men*, the same year, the *Tribune* reported that apart from playing George, one of the two lead roles, 'Mr. Walter Macken gave the play a memorable production' (*CT*, 7 December 1946).[71]

That Macken was willing to play a hunch and take a calculated risk is evident from the 'rare, if not unique' decision he made when he announced the coming production of Tomás Ó Máille's three-act farce *Mise an Méara* [I Am the Mayor], 'for when it was first advertised Mr. Macken had in his hands only the first act and the playwright had not completed the play'. The critic for *The Connacht Tribune* went on to say that 'Mr. Macken's decision … was justified by the result' and to make a broader and far more important point: 'One very important function of the Taibhdhearc is the fact that it has provided the inspiration for many of the best plays written in the Irish language in recent years and is thereby paving the way for a new Irish literature in drama' (*CT*, 1 April 1944). He might have added that it was also inspiring a new generation of actors in the language. Macken was deeply committed to this inspirational and educational aspect of the Taibhdhearc's mission, and he put that commitment into practice by actively seeking out those new actors and playwrights, particularly young ones. Thus, a 1942 editorial in *The Connacht Sentinel* entitled 'Advance Galway!' stated: 'Possibly the best amateur dramatic talent has been seen in the Taibhdhearc where the gifted actor-manager-producer, Mr. Walter Macken, seems to possess a genius for discovering young Irish speakers who possess distinct acting ability which is brought to full fruition under his skilled guidance' (*CS*, 28 April 1942).

To provide new plays for these new actors, Macken in 1942 had the Taibhdhearc offer two prizes for playwriting to all secondary schools in Galway. The prizes – £1/10s and 10s – were for the best one-act plays by students. Speaking to a reporter for *The Connacht Sentinel,* Macken stated that 'the Gaelic playwright of to-morrow is among the young people of to-day'. He also said that he hoped budding playwrights would write about modern life, though 'if any pupils prefer to write a historical play there is nothing to stop them'. Still, 'a play written about modern life would be much better'. Stressing the educational aspect of the contest, Macken continued: 'It is to be hoped to give every pupil who writes a play a reader's opinion – whether the play is accepted or not – pointing out the defects.' He also explained his focus on the schools, stating that 'I believe that you always get a more original thought from a young person' and that he was convinced that 'this scheme will lead to the development of a later [latent?] talent in Galway and that it will be the means of producing competent playwrights'. Winners would be able to draw on the resources of the Taibhdhearc in staging their plays at the theatre. Moreover, he planned to extend the competition the following year to students at University College Galway, with 'much higher prizes' (*CS,* 27 October 1942). Commenting on this scheme, *The Connacht Sentinel* reported that 'the results of the competition, which was confined to St. Ignatius School, have obviously abundantly justified Mr. Macken's enterprise'. Seven one-act plays had been submitted, of which the *Sentinel* stated hyperbolically: 'They are trifles, perhaps, and err on the side of brevity, but they show an astonishing grasp of theatre technique and compare favourably with the work of many more mature Gaelic playwrights.' That comment probably says more about the work of those 'more mature Gaelic playwrights' than it does about that of younger aspirants to the craft. The *Sentinel* then went on in another flight of wishful thinking to praise Macken for having 'launched an enterprise which should do more for Gaelic drama than anything which has been attempted since the Gaelic League was founded' (*CS,* 10 November 1942). The winning play, *An Triúr Neacht* (The Three Nieces) by Pádraic Mac Donnchadha, was performed at a special celebratory concert at the Taibhdhearc and then again on 29 November 1942 at the Taibhdhearc with five other plays entered in the competition (*CS,* 24 November 1942).[72]

Despite all of his responsibilities at the Taibhdhearc, Macken also from time to time promoted theatre in Irish by acting as an adjudicator at amateur drama festivals where plays in Irish were produced. Among the festivals at which he served in this capacity were Feis Luimnigh at Castleconnell, County Limerick (*LL*, 20 July 1940); Feis Shligigh (*IT*, 7 April 1945); Feis Luimnigh in Limerick (*CE*, 15 April 1946); the Ballina Drama Festival (*BH*, 20 July 1946); the County Louth Drama Festival (*ME*, 11 April 1947); the Dundalk Drama Festival (*DD*, 26 April 1947); the Oireachtas Drama Festival in Dublin (*DD*, 2 August 1947; *EH*, 27 April 1966); Feis Carman in New Ross, County Wexford (*ME*, 7 November 1947); and the Meath Drama Festival (*DI*, 3 April 1948).

It should, however, be noted that Macken didn't like the competitive nature of these festivals at which he was deciding winners and losers. Reporting on comments he made at the 1947 County Louth Drama Festival, the *Munster Express* wrote approvingly that he had said 'he would like to see the competitive element taken out of drama festivals, but the question was what they could substitute for it' (*ME*, 11 April 1947). His own preferred method of adjudication seems to have been what we would today call tough love. Thus, looking back over years of amateur drama festivals, Tomás Mac Anna, who had adjudicated more than a few himself, recalled: 'For the record and as far as I can gather, the lowest marks ever awarded at a drama festival were five, out of a possible hundred; the adjudicator was the late Walter Macken, the venue was the Sligo Feis in the late forties, the play was in Irish, and the breakdown of the marks was: one mark for knowing which end of the hall was the stage, one mark for getting the curtain up, and three marks for mercifully getting it down again' (*IT*, 25 April 1983). A contemporary report on that *feis* stated that 'strong criticism of the lamentably low standard displayed in the majority of Irish plays presented at Feis Shligigh was made by Mr. Walter Macken ... Of the eleven plays staged, he said, only five had approached even a fairly high standard, while none of the remaining six should ever have been presented at a festival with the standing of Feis Shligigh' (*IT*, 7 April 1945). In *The Irish Press*, 'T. W.' also reported on this *feis*, calling Macken's remarks as adjudicator among 'the most forthright criticisms of drama groups I ever heard'. According to 'T. W.', Macken 'told the literary competitors that most of them had no errand on any stage, and that they had done harm to the Irish language and Irish drama movements'. He also felt that some of the plays performed should never have been written, much less published (*IP*, 9 April 1945). Lest it seem that Macken was just having a bad day in

Sligo in 1945, we should note that at Feis Luimnigh in Limerick in 1946, he was reported to have begun his remarks as adjudicator by lulling his listeners into a false sense of security, stating that 'the standard of plays he had seen throughout the week was as good if not better than any he had seen before.' Then he let the hammer fall: 'That, however, was not praise, since the standard generally throughout the country was very low, and to make Gaelic drama a force the level would have to be increased.' Therefore, while 'the productions were better than most he had seen with a general high standard of setting and movement', he said 'he was appalled ... by the tendency to overlook the actor. The acting in every case completely lacked sincerity, and since the theatre was primarily devoted to acting, this aspect would have to get far more attention.' It is, however, worth noting that having acknowledged that he 'had marked very low', he added 'in the hope that it would help to increase the standard next year' (*CE*, 15 April 1946). Clearly, Macken believed that if theatre in Irish was to survive, much less thrive, critical standards would have to be raised and that that meant damning what was bad and slipshod as well as praising what was good and polished.[73]

We can now ask whether his own plays lived up to such elevated standards. In *Walter Macken (1915–1967): Playwright, actor and theatre manager*, James E. Reid provides a complete list of Macken's plays in Irish and in English, listing first 'Sceir Criobhéil' [*sic*], which he assumes to be Macken's work and dates to the mid-1930s. He also notes that there exists a handwritten English version of this play titled 'The Coral Reef', as well as a typewritten Irish version, perhaps suggesting that the Irish text is a translation of the English one. At any rate, whether in Irish or English the play is clearly an apprentice effort. Reid calls the plot 'thin and unbelievable' and dismisses the play as 'a naive piece of writing.'[74] Macken certainly never made any attempt to resurrect it in either language, much less to have it produced, and we may safely ignore it here.[75]

It was only after joining the Taibhdhearc that he began to think seriously about writing plays in Irish that would actually be produced. His first effort was a collaboration with the UCG professor of English and Taibhdhearc board member Jeremiah Murphy on a translation into Irish of Murphy's play *Mayor Lynch of Galway* as *Ceart agus Cúiteamh* (Justice and Retribution). It is difficult to imagine what the young Macken's role in the collaboration was. *Ceart agus Cúiteamh* was the first of thirteen plays or *geamaireachtaí* that Murphy provided for the theatre over the next fifteen years, virtually all of which he wrote in English for translation into Irish. In all probability, Murphy knew a great deal more about playwriting than did the nineteen-year-old Macken, and, as we know from Macken himself, his own Irish at this time was not all it could be, making him an unlikely translator. It seems safe, then, to say that whatever he contributed to this play was fairly minor.

His next collaboration was with the UCG professor of Irish and native speaker Tomás Ó Máille. *Caithréim an Sclábhaidhe* was a pageant play on the life of St Patrick first performed at the Taibhdhearc on 16 March 1941 with Macken directing and playing the title role. The show is made up of seven scenes: 'the Escape from Slieve Mish', 'the Monastery of Lérins in Gaul and the Call of the Irish to Patrick', 'the Return of Patrick to Ireland and the First Conversions', 'the Paschal Fire and Patrick's Triumph over the Druids', 'the Well of Cruachu and the Conversion and Death of the High King's Daughters', 'Patrick's Sufferings, Temptations and Triumphs on Croagh Patrick', and finally, 'the Death of Patrick'.[76] The subtitle of the review in *The Connacht Sentinel*, 'Beautiful Series of Tableaux', gives the doubtless correct impression that this was more of a spectacle than a play. Given what we saw above in the glowing review of Macken's work as set designer and director it seems possible his main contribution to *Caithréim an Sclábhaidhe* was visual. He next wrote the variety show *Rúille Búille,* which was produced at the Taibhdhearc in March 1942 and included the skit 'Esmerelda Wynne nó an Croidhe Seasmhach' (Esmerelda Wynne or the Steadfast Heart) with himself in the role of 'An Bhillan' (The Villain), Sir Valentine Ramsbottom.[77]

The following year playgoers at the Taibhdhearc were offered his first serious theatrical work and what would turn out to be his most popular play in Irish. *An Cailín Aimsire Abú* (Salute the Servant Girl) had its premiere on 16 September 1943, with Macken directing and playing the role of Seoirse Mac Donnchadha. In his study of Macken, James Reid states that 'the published version of the play' is in all probability 'a translation of an earlier work, *Lucy Callaghan's Father*', which had been rejected by the Abbey 'about 1941'.[78] The play in Irish has been revived four times at the Taibhdhearc and also produced elsewhere in Ireland, invariably to favourable reviews. Thus, the anonymous critic for *The Connacht Tribune* wrote of the play after seeing its original production that 'it ranks among the most entertaining plays ever put on the Taibhdhearc stage – and among the productions in that theatre were translations of some well-known English farcical comedies'. This reviewer praised 'the cleverly constructed plot', the 'many good scenes which hold the audience until the final surprise', and 'the grand teamwork' of the cast (*CT*, 18 September 1943). When the drama club at University College Dublin gave the play its first Dublin production in March 1945 with Siobhán McKenna in the title role, 'A. Ó M.' compared it in *The Irish Press* to 'the modern American fast-moving comedy', declaring: 'In this gay piece of nonsense the author has brought all his stagecraft experience, creating motion in one mad gush from guffaw to guffaw. His characters are not the sort to leave the man in the parterre time to relax and smile. They are a crazy crew. Each one is an individualist and paddles his own curragh' (*IP*, 6 March 1945).

The first revival at the Taibhdhearc in October 1945 was welcomed by an anonymous reviewer for *The Irish Press* who pronounced the play a success and noted that 'a bigger than usual first-night audience gave his play a hearty greeting' and that 'Macken gave a good performance in one of the main roles' (*IP*, 5 October 1946). The Taibhdhearc brought the play back again in June 1958, when the critic for *The Connacht Sentinel* had some problems with the production but still wrote that while '"An Cailín Aimsire Abú" is not a great play … it is well worth a visit' (*CS*, 3 June 1958). Of the July 1966 revival at the Taibhdhearc, the critic for *The Connacht Tribune* referred to the play as a 'rollicking comedy', adding that 'the characterization is excellent and the situations and dialogue are extremely funny' (*CT*, 23 July 1966). The most recent revival at the Taibhdhearc was in April 1982.

Among other productions of *An Cailín Aimsire Abú* over the years were those by Aisteoirí na Ceathrúin Ruaidhe in March 1959 (*CT*, 28 February 1959); by Dublin's Keating branch of the Gaelic League at the Oireachtas in the capital in 1963, a production that had already won first prize at that year's Leinster Drama Festival (*IP*, 8 April 1963); and by the Carratigue Drama Group of Carratigue, County Mayo, in April 1978 (*WP*, 29 April 1978). In May 2009, John E. Reid directed the Holding Court Theatre Group in the first production of *Salute the Servant*, Macken's translation of *An Cailín Aimsire Abú*, in the Axis theatre in Ballymun, Dublin.[79] I have found no references to other productions, but it is difficult to believe that no Gaelic League or other amateur group was not attracted to the play over the years. Indeed, although it has certainly become dated with time, there seems no reason why *An Cailín Aimsire Abú* could not still amuse an audience as light entertainment in the *Arsenic and Old Lace* mode.

In a February 1947 letter to the English producer of his play *Galway Handicap* (i.e. *Mungo's Mansion*), Macken said that he wrote *An Cailín Aimsire Abú* 'with the idea of taking the Irish Play out of the kitchen, where it seems to be getting bogged down'.[80] The play is set in a middle-class household in Dublin, where a wife, frustrated in her marriage to the ever-distracted would-be novelist Seoirse Mac Donnchadha, has taken in lodgers for company and something to do. Among the play's cast of eccentrics are the two lodgers, Mac Uí Shleabhcháin, a flippant fop who works at the stock exchange, loves the movies, favours American slang, and likes to tell stale, slightly risqué jokes. As the stage direction says: 'He's a proper "Sheik". Around twenty-five years of age, with his hair as slick and shiny as the floor of a dance hall.'[81] The other lodger, Mac Crubóige, is a dyspeptic seventy-year-old miser who is, in the words of Cáit the cook, 'always laying his hands on people' (*i gcomhnuidhe ag leagan a lámha ar dhaoine*).[82] Three plots intertwine in the play. In the first, the man of the house and aspiring novelist Seoirse Mac Donnchadha is often in trouble as a result of his search for 'atmosphere' for his books, believing he should write only of what he has personally experienced. While his literary efforts exasperate his wife, it turns out in the end that he is the pseudonymous author of Dublin's latest literary sensation, *Cabáiste Shráid Uí Mhórdha* (The Moore Street Cabbage). The second plotline deals with the estrangement of Seoirse and his wife Nóra and their ultimate loving reconciliation. The most important storyline, however, involves the eponymous servant girl Sorcha, apparently an innocent from Conamara, who is told by a Dublin solicitor that she has inherited £20,000 from a recently deceased uncle in Los Angeles. It turns out that Sorcha is actually a criminal from Cork named Lú-lú and that she and her 'solicitor' are in cahoots and use the promise of future fortune to extract money from Nóra by playing on her sympathy for Sorcha's 'ailing' mother, who needs an operation she cannot afford. Adding to the comic confusion is the fact that both lodgers have overheard the news of Sorcha's inheritance and have developed an immediate romantic interest in her. At this point Mac Crubóige's life savings are stolen from his room during a farcical blackout scene. We quickly learn, however, that the 'thief' is none other than Seoirse, seeking atmosphere for his fiction and abetted by Cáit's suitor, the ever-hungry and thirsty policeman Timín, who seems a virtual resident of the house. The grifters, claiming to be armed, get away with what they presume to be Mac Crubóige's money, but Seoirse tells everyone that he had substituted a wad of paper for the banknotes and that the robbers have therefore escaped with nothing of value. As the play ends, Seoirse has proven that he is not the fool all have taken him for, whereupon he clears the house of the unwelcome lodgers, and wins back the love and admiration of his wife.

In the same 1947 letter to the English producer of *Home is the Hero* quoted earlier, Macken described *An Cailín Aimsire Abú*, which he had translated into English, as 'not drama with a capital D ... a mixture of an English farce, broad Irish comedy and a sprinkling of satire ... pure box-office'.[83] While the brief summary above may well – and not unfairly – suggest that he was right about the play, it should be noted that *An Cailín Aimsire Abú* was far more competently constructed than most plays in Irish at that time, and unlike many of the Gaelic comedies was actually on occasion funny. Moreover, Macken's choice of an urban middle-class setting shows that he was willing to take on that ongoing challenge of the Gaelic stage – how to write in Irish about people unlikely to use the language in their daily lives. Here, it is of real interest that while Seoirse jokes about Sherlock Holmes and refers to writers of English well-known at the time – Edgar Wallace, Ruby M. Ayres and Maxwell Anderson – his own novel is in Irish and has nonetheless attracted significant notice and a wide readership.[84] And surely it was Macken's intention to create an urban space for Irish that led him to write at the end of his 'Fuireann an Dráma' (*Dramatis Personae*) page, 'the most important thing in the drama is to get Cáit's accent right' (*an rud is tábhachtaighe sa dráma: blas ceart ag Cáit*). That accent is meant to be pure Dublin, but Cáit speaks Irish throughout, an indication that the 'Dublin Irish' (*Gaeilge Bhaile Átha Cliath*) so loathed by many Gaelic purists at the time – and since – was no problem at all for Macken.

Just a month after the production of *An Cailín Aimsire Abú*, the Taibhdhearc performed his short play *Bhí Mac agam Tráth* for a variety show at the Taibhdhearc to celebrate the fiftieth anniversary of the Gaelic League.[85] This play, which he also directed, was either intended as a parody of moralistic melodramas – something along the lines of W.C. Fields' classic short film *The Fatal Glass of Beer* (1933) – or a front-runner in the highly competitive contest for worst play ever written in Irish. To be fair, since we know Macken had already worked with parody in 'Esmerelda Wynne' and also been involved with the Taibhdhearc's annual *geamaireachtaí* or pantomimes, we can probably give him the benefit of the doubt here.

Bhí Mac agam Tráth introduces us to the upper-middle-class Ó Caoilte family, whose only son Seán, played by Macken, is a (very) part-time journalist and a full-time rotter. The stage directions for his first entrance read in part: 'He is dressed very stylishly. To look at him you would say to yourself that he had spent twenty pounds for the clothes he is wearing … He has a hard expression on his face, and the signs of dissipation can be seen in his eyes.'[86] His parents have spoiled Seán, but even with the generous support he wheedles from them he is unable to support his lavish lifestyle. As a result, he has turned to crime, joining accomplices to rob post offices in his native town. After a botched attempt at another robbery in which two of his accomplices die and he kills a man, he returns home wounded and terrified: 'He is not wearing a hat, his coat is torn, his clothes damaged, wet, and dirty. He has a pistol in his right hand, and it can be seen that he has a wound that is still bleeding in his left arm.'[87] The gardaí are hot on his trail, but even in this dire situation he finds time to blame his parents for making him the criminal he has become, telling his father: 'You gave me money when I was young. You gave me money when I was grown, but you gave me nothing else … And then the time came when you didn't give me enough money and I had to go out and get it for myself.'[88] When he asks his mother to shelter him from the police, she answers: 'I'd rather my son was dead than as he is now.'[89] She gets her wish as the play ends noisily with a shootout between Seán and the gardaí, with Seán yelling, 'Damn you, mother. Damn you …'[90] Startlingly, *Bhí Mac agam Tráth* was translated into English as *I Had a Son* and performed by the UCG Dramatic Society in Athlone (*CT*, 13 January 1945). That

Macken himself had a proper sense of the play's value is clear from the fact that he left it unpublished in either Irish or English.

His next play, the full-length *Oighreacht na Mara* (The Heritage of the Sea), was a far more serious and impressive piece, closer to the plays he would write in English about the lives of Galway's poor. In addition, there is nothing at all escapist in this play, which instead, like the plays of Séamus de Bhilmot, confronts head-on major economic, social and political issues in the Ireland of its time. *Oighreacht na Mara* had its premiere in the Taibhdhearc on 22 June 1944. Once again Macken directed the play himself and also took the major role of Seán Breathnach. The critic for *The Connacht Tribune* was impressed, writing: 'The play moves to stark tragedy early in the third act and the intense note, aided by some clever symbolic touches, is well maintained until the end' (*CT*, 24 June 1944). A brief note in the same paper the following month reported that on a one-night revival the play had drawn a full house and that 'the players had to respond to several "curtain" calls, and Mr. Macken went out in response to calls for "An t-Ughdar" [Author]' (*CT*, 15 July 1944). When the Taibhdhearc brought the production to the Abbey for two performances in June 1945, the critic for *The Irish Press*, having called *Oighreacht na Mara* 'something taken out of the heart of Galway', declared: 'Bhaitéar Ó Maicín ... knows his native town and his play comes with the freshness of an Atlantic breeze ... The action keeps on an even keel throughout and achieves good, sound dialogue and theatre' (*IP*, 28 May 1945). The *Irish Independent* stated: 'If the first and third acts were as good as the second act, this play would be one of the best in Irish. Still, it is better than many of the plays seen in Dublin' (*II*, 28 May 1945).[91] *The Irish Times* praised Macken's 'fine acting ability' and added that 'the production by the author was unusually interesting' (*IT*, 28 May 1945).

The central thematic focus in the play is on the clash between the future and the past, one of the most common themes in all of modern literature in Irish up to that time. Right at the outset we are told that the setting is 'one of the new houses that were put up in the Claddagh in place of the wretched huts that had been there' (*ceann de na tighthe nua a cuireadh suas sa gCladach i n-áit na mbothán suarach a bhí ann cheana*). But in this play Macken is interested in issues that, while painfully relevant to Irish fishermen in the 1940s, transcend the merely local context, showing a traditional society confronting the challenges of inexorable technological change and globalisation through the tragedy of one family. Máirtín Breathnach is a Claddagh fisherman saddened by his son Seán's refusal to join him on the sea. Seán has instead taken a job in a Galway shop, seeing that as the first step to a successful career in business. All Máirtín wants from life is a simple sufficiency and the knowledge that 'when I die, I will be satisfied that I did my share and never in my life hurt anyone'.[92] Seán, however, is much more conventionally ambitious, telling his father: 'I'm making money where I am now. In a few years I will be a big man in this city. Even now people respect me. I have a place in the city. But you want me to spend my life out on the sea ... And how would I benefit from that?'[93] Unfortunately, Seán's legitimate desire for what he sees as a better life is corrupted when he feels the need to satisfy the demands of his insufferably snobbish and materialistic girlfriend Sorcha, whose favourite word for life in the Claddagh is 'wretched' (*suarach*). Speaking to Seán's sister Nóra, she makes clear her own vision of a satisfying life: 'When Seán and I are married, you will come to see us. We will, I expect, be living on the Crescent, where the doctors and the bigshots live, you know.'[94] Her immediate need is, however, for flashy clothes, expensive gifts and constant excitement, all at Seán's expense. Before long he is keeping late nights and drinking too much. Short of funds to finance his new lifestyle, he embezzles money from his employer. Like much in this play, his crime would have an immediate contemporary relevance in the Ireland of the Second World War – he has sold goods from the shop at black market prices but only put the legal value of those goods in the till.

Meanwhile, Máirtín and some of the other fishermen have decided that they must take action against one of the large and powerfully motorised English trawlers threatening their livelihood by illegally fishing in Irish waters. It is Máirtín who speaks for the group: 'God helps the strong man ... I have had a plan in my head for a long time to play a trick on them so that the foreigners will regret that they ever came into Galway Bay.'[95] Macken makes clear here that they take this risky decision as a last resort due to the failure of the Irish government to protect their interests. Thus, Máirtín responds ironically to a policeman inquiring into their preparations: 'We trust the Government! We know that they will do something. They won't let any foreign trawler come into Galway Bay and steal the fishermen's earnings without anyone stopping them.'[96]

As Máirtín and his comrades are ready to set sail, Seán and Sorcha appear on the quay. A bitter quarrel ensues, and in a fit of rage Máirtín strikes Seán and says: 'I regret the day you were born, Seán. You were never any good! … Perhaps someday you will find out that money isn't as mighty as you think! That it's better to be poor and healthy than rich with a twisted soul!'[97] Shortly thereafter Máirtín is accidentally killed in the clash with the trawler, and his death, along with the revelation of his own crime, causes Seán some serious soul-searching. With Seán no longer under her spell, Sorcha drops him at once: 'I should have had sense from the first day. They all told me to have nothing to do with anything from the Claddagh! … I lowered myself down to your level and I hope that none of the dirt has been left on me!'[98] Disgusted by Sorcha's selfishness and hypocrisy and having learned from his mother how much his father had loved him, he becomes a different person, eager to pay his employer back and proud at having a new mission in life that will reconcile his ambition with his father's desire for continuity. Pulling on his father's old gansey, he declares he will take over Máirtín's boat and build up a fleet of independent fishermen able to compete with the foreign trawlers and restore the local fishery: 'A competent man can bring all the fishermen together so that there will be a big fleet of fishing boats afloat out there! … so that every man in the Claddagh will be a fisherman!'[99] The arrival of a ship from the Irish naval service and its seizure of the trawler suggest that Seán's initiative, with appropriate support from the state, might just succeed.

This ending is, of course, in the final analysis unconvincing. However stirring his commitment to reviving the Galway fishery on a wide-scale modern basis, Seán was probably more realistic in an earlier comment to his mother: 'The fisherman is dying in the Claddagh. Before the last war there were around a hundred fishing boats in Galway Bay, and now not even a score of them are left. Money can't be made from it with the number of trawlers and companies sweeping fish from the sea. It's foolish to hope that I would follow that trade …'[100]

Yet, despite this forced optimistic conclusion, *Oighreacht na Mara* is an important play in the history of drama in Irish. First of all, after setting up a stereotypical and loaded confrontation between rooted traditional values and the ambitions and at times often materialistic ethics of modern life, Macken tries, albeit unsuccessfully, to work out a viable synthesis of these worldviews. Moreover, by focusing on mechanised foreign interference in an important native industry, the play would have an immediate contemporary relevance, a point underscored in a piece in *The Connacht Sentinel* the week before the play opened: 'The play is particularly topical just now in view of the controversy and the recent Departmental Inquiry regarding seine net fishing in the bay and the efforts of the Galway City Vocational Education Committee to arouse an interest among the youth of Galway in the sea as a career' (*CS*, 13 June 1944). Macken was here joining Séamus de Bhilmot in exploring theatrical territory otherwise virtually ignored in Gaelic theatre at the time. It is, then, particularly unfortunate that he did not write more plays of this kind in Irish, plays that might attract an audience that had as much – if not more – interest in the ideas as the language in which they were expressed.

As noted above, in its setting among Galway's poor and working-class people, *Oighreacht na Mara* is also the only one of Macken's plays in Irish that deals with the kind of material he so often worked with in English. Regrettably, he was not to continue in this vein in his writing for the Gaelic stage. For this reason alone, his next play, *An Fear ón Spidéal* (The Man from Spiddal), subtitled *Geandráma Áilteóireachta* (A Farcical Comedy), represents a step backwards for him as a playwright in Irish.[101] On the other hand, we should note that in his review of the published text of the play in 1952, his fellow playwright Gearóid Ó Lochlainn was taken with the work, praising Macken for creating an entertaining farce with a cast of zany characters, adding: 'And there is plenty happening in it – complicated love affairs, deception, robbery, trick against trick, strange occurrences, peculiarity, and an unexpected ending, and through all the ructions, plenty of fun.'[102] Ó Lochlainn was particularly impressed with how Macken handled the challenge of providing a satisfactory conclusion to all the chaos: 'But the author's resourcefulness did not fail here, and it seems to me that he rose above any loss of interest there is in the resolution with the effective ending he gave it.' Ó Lochlainn was convinced 'that the performance of this play would make for an excellent night full of fun' (*go ndéanfadh teasbántas den dráma so oíche ghrinn thar barr*) (*Feasta*, July 1952, p. 20).[103]

An Fear ón Spidéal had its premiere at the Taibhdhearc on 26 July 1945. Once again, Macken was the director and played one of the lead roles as Persí Ó Conchubhair. James E. Reid informs us that *An Fear ón Spidéal* seems actually to have been based on two earlier, unpublished and unproduced works in English. The first of these was 'Ring for Langford (or Longford)', the second 'Rude Forefathers', which the Abbey rejected in 1942. Macken apparently also wrote another unpublished and unproduced play in English called 'The Man from Spiddal', that also seems likely to have provided a basis for *An Fear ón Spidéal*. In addition, he wrote a three-act play in Irish titled 'Páirt Thaidhg', again never published or produced. Reid says that the manuscript of this play in Macken's archive at the University of Wuppertal is 'almost identical to *The Man from Spiddal*'.[104]

Reviewing the play for *The Connacht Tribune*, the critic might as well have dusted off an old review of *An Cailín Aimsire Abú* for all the detail he provided: 'As for Mr. Macken's play itself, it contains good dialogue, and many amusing situations, building up to a cleverly conceived climax. Altogether it makes good entertainment' (*CT*, 28 July 1945). The play was revived at the Taibhdhearc in October 1960, directed by Traolach Ó hAonghusa. Apparently, the second production was an improvement on the original, at least if one can trust the judgement of the again anonymous critic for *The Connacht Tribune*: 'This may not be Macken's greatest play, but judging from the gusts of laughter which swept the auditorium at the preview on Wednesday night, it must be one of his funniest ... The play is well worth a visit' (*CT*, 29 October 1960). A second Taibhdhearc revival was staged in December 1966, again directed by Traolach Ó hAonghusa. In a brief review in *The Connacht Tribune* 'Ronnoc' wrote: 'Don't miss this comedy – if you don't guffaw at least you will certainly giggle and, thanks be, it's good clean fun' (*CT*, 2 December 1966).

Like *An Cailín Aimsire Abú*, *An Fear ón Spidéal* does not seem to have been as popular with amateur groups as might have been expected. Among other productions were those by actors from the Gaelic League's Craobh Sheáin Uí Dhubhláin in Derry at Féile Náisiúnta na Drámaíochta in Dublin's Damer theatre in April 1966 (*IP*, 27 April 1966); by the students of Belmullet, County Mayo's Convent of Mercy in March 1967 (*WP*, 18 March 1967); and by Cumann Drámaíochta Chlár Clainne Mhuiris from Claremorris, County Mayo, at Féile Náisiúnta na Drámaíochta in the Damer in May 1973 (*IT*, 9 May 1973).

Again, like *An Cailín Aimsire Abú, An Fear ón Spidéal* is set outside the Gaeltacht, near Dún Laoghaire in County Dublin. Now, however, we are among the *nouveau riche* as represented by Séamus Ó Máille, once a butcher in Cork but now 'the Sausage King of Ireland' (*Rí Isbíneach na hÉireann*), his ignorant and snobbish wife Áine (who has a Cork accent she tries to conceal),[105] his daughter Máire and his down-to-earth mother-in-law Bean Uí Néill. Obvious symbols of their lifestyle are a newly acquired butler, whom Áine boasts once worked for 'Lady Winding Stairs over in London' (*An Bhaintiarna Staighre-Chasta thall in Londuin*),[106] Áine's retinue of self-proclaimed artists (painter, writer, actor) and Séamus' hobby of collecting valuable gold figurines. The plot revolves around Bean Uí Néill's determination to marry Máire to the man she actually loves, the hapless Persí Ó Conchubhair, who also loves her, rather than to Tadhg Ó Tuathail, the eponymous Conamara farmer with whom she has become infatuated and brought back from a trip she took to the Gaeltacht to improve her Irish. For once, Bean Uí Néill and her daughter in agreement, although Áine objects to Tadhg because of his rough rural background. Meanwhile, Tadhg is in love with the Ó Máilles' servant Nóra, whom he has come to Dublin to woo but who has decided he is a two-timing 'Casanova'.[107] Frustrated by the timid Persí's inability to stand up to Tadhg, Bean Uí Néill gets him drunk, hoping that will make him more manly: 'I'm not a man, but God of Glory, if I were a man no Romeo wearing a bawneen would steal my girl from me.'[108] Soon, the drunken Persí is attacking first the bandleader at a party in the Ó Máilles' house, and then gardaí in the street.

Meanwhile, one of Áine's necklaces is stolen. At first it seems that the butler did indeed do it, but we soon learn that he did so at the request of Bean Uí Néill, who wants to shock everyone into thinking about all their own fixations and subterfuges. Unfortunately, once in possession of the jewellery the 'butler', who is not an Englishman but rather plain old Micín Ó Floinn from the Aran Islands, decides he might as well keep it and add to the take a golden miniature for which Ó Máille had paid £5,000. Ó Floinn and an accomplice make off with the loot, but predictably enough for anyone who has seen or read *An Cailín Aimsire Abú,* the stolen miniature is actually a fake – apparently Macken allows foolish Áine to lose her necklace – and thus the thief has got away with much less than he expected. Thereupon the play ends happily with two marriages, a chastened Áine and a triumphant Bean Uí Néill, who explains how she manipulated all of the other characters. In response, a friend of the family who is present can only say: 'Well, compared to you, madame, Machiavelli was only a child.'[109]

Despite its similarities to *An Cailín Aimsire Abú* – the assumed identities, the confused love affairs, the thwarted robbery – *An Fear ón Spidéal* is not without interest of its own. For example, it satirises, albeit in a pretty toothless way, the social and Anglophile pretensions of the *arriviste* Áine. Less successful is Macken's attempt to poke fun at the play's pseudo-intellectual 'artists'. Much more could have been done with this trio, perhaps along the lines of what Denis Johnston did with his thinly disguised Irish writers in *The Old Lady Says 'No!'* (1929). While Doiminic O'Riordain was too harsh in dismissing the entire work as 'Walter Macken's tedious satire on artistic pretensions' (*IT*, 9 May 1973), it is certainly true that given the time they spend on stage these characters contribute little to either the plot or the humour of the play.[110]

More interesting and effective is how Macken goes out of his way to establish why people of this sort would be speaking Irish. Áine tells us early in the play that the language has become 'very fashionable' (*an-fhaisiúnta*) and 'it is being used by many big shots' (*tá sí 'á húsáid ag a lán boc mór*). She herself has become a collector of idioms (*cora cainte*) and keeps a notebook for them. And, of course, it was to improve her Irish that Máire went to Spiddal in the first place.[111] Macken is having fun here with the belief in some circles that a knowledge of Irish would help the upwardly mobile secure desirable government appointments. More intriguing is the implication that the members of the Ó Máille family and their circle speak decent Irish. At one point, Micilín, the native speaker who is Tadhg's friend and Nóra's father, says of those in the house that he can no more understand them than he could Russian, but he also makes clear that the problem is not that they use bad Dublin Irish, but that they use acceptable Irish to discuss abstruse subjects: 'There is one lad in there and he spent the whole night describing the beauty of the onion.'[112]

Walter Macken was obviously a far better playwright in English than he was in Irish. This should, of course, come as no surprise, as he was a native speaker of English who hadn't really felt comfortable with his Irish until several years after he first entered Taibhdhearc na Gaillimhe. Moreover, besides being a native speaker of English, he was also a native thinker of English, and therefore troubled about whether he could ever deal with the subjects most important to him adequately in Irish. Could he ever get inside the heads of his characters, capture and convey their ideas, moods and emotions in a language he had learned? Certainly his plays in English are much more thematically and psychologically ambitious and complex than are his plays in Irish. Part of the problem here is, of course, that he knew so well from his own upbringing the exact kind of English spoken by his favourite kind of character, the poor and working-class people of Anglophone Galway, people whom in his unpublished novel 'Cockles and Mustard' he called 'the Urbans' and whom he described at length:

> You will find the Urbans at the end of the procession, the ragtag and bobtail, but you could swear your oath that there will be laughter down there and many a coarse jest with a terrific point in it, and there will be jostling and pinching, and scuffling and jeering, and in fact a great time will be had by all, because they have nothing to lose, neither dignity nor coppers. They don't know it themselves but they are the salt of the earth … So there are our Urbans, scavengers who prefer to be called dustmen, and timber workers, and flour workers and barbers and boot-repairers and saw-sharpeners, and plasterers and carpenters and coachbuilders and dock-labourers, and ordinary labourers, and road menders and corporation workers, not to mention those who didn't work at all but who managed to kick out a time for themselves by sending their wives to wash here and scrub there for two and a tanner a day …[113]

These were the people of his plays in English, and nothing could have been more natural for him than to write dialogue for such characters in the language that they spoke and that he clearly relished. In his comedies in Irish he felt the need and had the nerve to bring that language into settings, particularly middle-class and urban settings, alien to it, even if just in the highly artificial world of farce.[114] Only in *Oighreacht na Mara*, set in the Claddagh, where there was still some Irish spoken at this time, did he attempt to write of the life he knew best in his acquired second language. His decision to return to comic fantasy in Irish and then full-time to English after that was probably due to his sense that while that play was the best he could do on the subject in Irish, it would have been a far more authentic and personally satisfying work if written in his own Galway English. When he returned to the Claddagh and much of the same material he had used in *Oighreacht na Mara* in his third novel, he chose to write that book, *Rain on the Wind*, in English,[115] in all probability convinced that it simply made more sense to have the people of the Claddagh (as well as the tenement dwellers of Galway in *Mungo's Mansion*) speak English.[116]

Again, it should be remembered that in his Galway plays, novels and stories in English, the 'Urbans' do not speak standard English, but rather the English he had heard growing up in the city. A brief piece of dialogue from his unpublished novel 'Cockles and Mustard' gives the flavour of this dialect: 'Ah, jay, Bitt! … Look I got money so I have that I whipped from the oul wan this mornin'. Listen, Bitt, I shagged this off the plate at the chapel; when me man wasn't lookin!'[117] This is also the language of the tenement characters in *Mungo's Mansion* and *Home is the Hero*: 'Have yeh ever suspicioned Mungo King, Mister Skerret, of bein' capable of jiltin' on the rent? Have yeh ever been afraid for a minnit that Mungo'd do the moonlight flit?'[118] There is nothing like this in Macken's plays in Irish, where all of the characters speak the standard Conamara Irish he himself had learned. On the *Dramatis Personae* page of the published text of *Mungo's Mansion*, the author informs us that 'the mis-spelling of certain words in the dialogue is an attempt at the phonetic interpretation of the Galway accent'.[119] No such attempt to capture the nuances of dialect is found in any of his plays in Irish. Indeed, the only note at all similar to the one in *Mungo's Mansion* is found in *An Cailín Aimsire Abú* where, as we have seen, we are told that getting Cáit's accent right is 'the most important thing in the play' (*an rud is tábhachtaighe sa dráma*). Unfortunately, he makes no attempt to provide eye dialect in Irish to capture that Dublin accent.

None of this is to say that his plays in Irish have no value. If far from a great playwright in Irish, he was in his own time one of the more competent ones, and he did write three full-length plays that helped meet the hard-pressed Taibhdhearc's need for new original work and, as we know from the reviews, that work impressed and/or amused both contemporary critics and audiences for whom theatre-going in the first official language was as often a penitential duty as a source of pleasure. Also, as we have seen, in these plays he addressed what is still an insistent challenge for writers of Irish – how to use the language when dealing with life in the Anglophone Ireland in which most Irish people make their lives. At this point in time, none of these plays is likely to be revived often, if at all. It would, however, be a real injustice to write them off, assuming that they did not make a very real contribution to the survival and development of theatre in Irish at a time of challenging transition.

That said, Macken's place in the history of theatre in Irish owes at least as much to his work as manager, producer, director, actor and mentor as to his contributions as a playwright. As he wrote in a 1948 article in *The Irish Press*, theatre for him was 'a job of work, where people have to work very hard for long hours, just as they would if they were dock-labourers or turf-cutters or insurance collectors' (*IP*, 6 March 1948). In his years at Taibhdhearc na Gaillimhe, and particularly the years between 1939 and 1948, he worked very hard indeed, as Siobhán McKenna stressed in 1954 when she spoke of 'the heartbreaking efforts of Walter Macken, during his period as producer there, to hold a team together' (*DP*, 4 December 1954).[120] For a decade he staged and acted in an impressive range of plays both original and translated, thus building on the achievements of his predecessors Micheál Mac Liammóir and Proinsias Mac Diarmada (Frank Dermody). In the process, he left his own unmistakable stamp on the theatre's repertoire and style, and in the face of often daunting obstacles, established the Taibhdhearc as a significant institution in the cultural life of his nation.[121]

Of course, he was always quick to point out that residents of Galway itself did not always appreciate that institution in their own town. Indeed, even at a dinner honouring him as he left for Dublin and the Abbey in 1948, he could call Galway 'one of the most anti-Irish towns in Ireland' and declare that 'the Taibhdhearc is a terrific success in spite of, rather than because of, Galway' (*CT*, 8 January 1948). This was, however, just the frustration of a man about to depart a town he felt had not always treated him and his theatre well. More typical of Macken was the idealism and vision in his 1943 interview with *Comhar*: 'Remember that drama in Irish is still just a child. It must be nourished. Let us give young people a chance to see the best dramatic work from Europe, well-produced, and it is certain that the great native writer will come yet to establish the new school' (*Comhar*, May 1943, p. 9).[122] Whether or not Macken will ever come to be seen as prophetic with regard to the bright future of Gaelic drama, in the difficult circumstances of his own time and place he did play a major role in laying and securing the foundations that would make such a future possible.

Transition and Tradition

As we saw in the introduction to this study, the playwright Labhrás Mac Brádaigh believed that despite all the challenges facing the Gaelic theatre movement in 1945, there was real hope for the future, for far better days ahead, and that 'this golden age will evolve from the hearts and minds of our playwrights if they set to work with loyalty to their ideals' (*Glór*, 1 December 1945). He was right, for the 1950s and '60s were to be the closest thing to a golden age that theatre in Irish has ever experienced. The Taibhdhearc continued to offer Galwegians full schedules of original and translated plays every year. Compántas Chorcaí, founded in 1953, was performing in Cork. Aisteoirí Ghaoth Dobhair and Aisteoirí an Spidéil were making a name for themselves in the Donegal and Conamara Gaeltachtaí respectively.[1] In Dublin, the Abbey, while its commitment to full-length plays in Irish was certainly open to question,[2] was performing short plays in the language in imaginative productions by Tomás Mac Anna both on the main stage at the Abbey and in exile from 1951 to '66 at the Queen's theatre.[3] Unfortunately, Compántas Amharclainne na Gaeilge ceased operation in 1958, although earlier in the decade they had continued to offer their popular variety shows in Irish as well as a few original plays and interesting translations.

At any rate, the loss of An Compántas was more than balanced in the capital by the opening in 1955 of An Damer, a small theatre in St Stephen's Green that, under the auspices of An Club Drámaíochta, and with the sponsorship of Gael Linn, was to become for nearly two decades the most important proving ground for the work of Gaelic playwrights, producing plays by Máiréad Ní Ghráda, Séamus Ó Néill, Eoghan Ó Tuairisc, Seán Ó Tuama (more usually associated with Compántas Chorcaí), Críostóir Ó Floinn and Breandán Ó Beacháin (Brendan Behan), as well as other new works, revivals and translations. The theatre also attracted some of the finest directors in the Gaelic theatre movement, among them Frank

Dermody and Tomás Mac Anna.[4] Meanwhile, while scholars may debate their value, the Abbey's *geamaireachtaí* or Gaelic pantomimes that had begun in 1945 continued to attract the largest audiences ever seen at entertainments in Irish before or since. And, of course, plays in Irish were still being performed at Gaelic League *feiseanna* and local drama festivals. Moreover, in this 'golden age', the Taibhdhearc, Compántas Chorcaí, Aisteoirí Ghaoth Dobhair, the Damer actors and, of course, the Abbey had their own theatres, a luxury denied to An Comhar Drámaíochta throughout the 1920s and '30s as well as to other companies since. Mac Brádaigh would surely have been gratified had he in 1945 been granted a vision of the state of Gaelic theatre over the quarter century that followed his prediction.

The obvious question here, of course, involves whether the playwrights in this study had any role in bringing about this golden age. Did they, in effect, assist in any meaningful way in the transition from the apparently distressing state of play in the 1920s, '30s and '40s to the more vibrant Gaelic theatre scene of the 1950s and '60s? First of all, it should be noted that none of them got to share in the benefits of the promised land. With the exception of the Abbey's productions of de Bhilmot's *Baintighearna an Ghorta* in 1938 and Ó Lochlainn's *Ag an Ladhrán* in 1941, neither the Abbey nor An Damer staged a play by any of our playwrights in the 1950s and '60s – or after, for that matter. Indeed, of the five, only de Bhilmot had a new play in Irish produced after 1950, and that play, the one-act *Caithfidh na Tancanna Dul Tríd* (1957) was pretty much a rehash of familiar subject matter and themes.[5] Béaslaí's last play in Irish, *Blúire Páipéir*, was first produced in 1936; Ó Lochlainn's *Ag an Ladhrán* in 1941; and Macken's *An Fear ón Spidéal* in 1945.

The five playwrights' reasons for turning away from the Gaelic stage were, predictably enough, varied. By the 1940s, Béaslaí had every reason to be disillusioned by how little progress Gaelic theatre had made over the four decades he had been actively involved with it. Indeed, as is clear from Pádraig Ó Siadhail's biography, he was bitterly discouraged by what he saw as the Irish state's abandonment of its commitment to the Gaelic vision of those who had created it. As a result, he could write in his diary as early as 1942: 'The main point that has been annoying me has been the realisation of all my errors and failures, since the time I was foolish enough to waste my energies producing literature in Irish.'[6] It is certainly clear that playwriting was no longer among his main concerns. As he aged, he seems to have felt an ever-greater responsibility to leave behind an accurate, often first-hand, account of many of the events and personalities of the Irish struggle for independence from the Easter rising to the end of the civil war. In the process, he produced a good amount of historical writing in journals and particularly newspapers, an invaluable record that should by now have been collected, edited and published.[7] Gearóid Ó Lochlainn, on the other hand, continued to appear on occasion in plays in Irish, but as he was a professional actor who needed to make a living, the overwhelming majority of his work on stage from the 1950s on was in English. His very personal and pragmatic experience of the realities of Irish theatre at the time may have led him to question the point of writing plays in Irish, although it seems more probable that his demanding performance schedule in English left him little time to write such plays.

Leon Ó Broin found his true calling as a historian, and once he added researching and writing about the past to the responsibilities he bore as a senior civil servant, he would have had little time left for the theatre. The pressures of his day job as registrar of the National University of Ireland may have similarly contributed to ending Séamus de Bhilmot's career as a Gaelic playwright, although, as we have seen, he continued to take an active interest in theatre in general through his membership of the Abbey's board of directors, and in theatre in Irish in particular through his service as an adjudicator at various *feiseanna,* and his willingness to challenge the Abbey's policy (or lack thereof) towards plays in the language. For Macken, the evidence is clearer. As a native speaker of English, and in particular the English of Galway city, he was far more comfortable, and obviously more accomplished, writing for the stage in that language rather than in his acquired Irish. And, of course, he went on not only to write plays in English for the Abbey, but also to become a prolific and popular novelist and story writer in that language. However, the fact that all our playwrights ceased to write plays in Irish raises a larger question – one that could be asked of many Gaelic dramatists from the start of the revival into the 1950s and beyond: when they started writing plays in Irish, was their primary motive to advance the language or to contribute to the theatre? Or, to be blunt, were their plays at least as much linguistic exercises as they were creative works for the stage? In the absence of first-hand evidence, this question obviously cannot be answered with any certainty, but it should be asked.

Yet, even if language was more important to some of them than dramatic art, all five of our playwrights were genuinely interested in the theatre. Indeed, it is that interest and involvement that most distinguishes them from their predecessors and so many of their contemporaries in the Gaelic theatre movement, for whom the question of the competing claims of language and art seems never to have been a problem. Béaslaí was fascinated by the theatre as a teenager in Liverpool before he ever came to Ireland.[8] Ó Lochlainn's dedication to his craft as an actor led him all the way to Copenhagen and back and kept him on stage in Dublin for more than four decades after his return. Ó Broin threw himself into the work of An Comhar Drámaíochta from the start, first as an actor and then as a playwright, though he never seems to have directed plays. De Bhilmot was neither a director nor an actor, but he not only wrote plays, but also devoted time and effort to administrative work for the Taibhdhearc, Compántas Amharclainne na Gaeilge and the Abbey. Macken was following in his father's footsteps when he became an actor, and he soon thereafter threw himself into all aspects of the Taibhdhearc's operation. And he was also to put in time at the Abbey. Whatever else they did – and they all did a great deal – these were theatre people.

As a result of all their experiences, they, unlike so many of the playwrights from the beginning of the Gaelic theatre movement on, had some idea of how a play should actually work on stage in front of an audience. Thus, they paid attention to how a plot could be credibly developed; they eliminated unnecessary scenes and the equally unnecessary additional set changes such scenes required; and, aware of the headaches large casts of amateur actors created for producers and directors, they kept the number of characters in their own plays within reasonable limits. And once they had those casts on stage, they knew how to move them around effectively as well as how to get them on and off logically and gracefully. Moreover, they for the most part avoided long, static speeches and cut the bombast and fustian from their dialogue in historical plays and/or tragedies. Certainly, none of them would ever, even in the rowdiest farce, have thought of bringing a cow on stage!

Above all, however, no matter what their reasons for beginning (and ceasing) to write plays in Irish, write plays in Irish they did, answering Mac Brádaigh's 1943 challenge to Gaelic dramatists to provide 'worthwhile new plays … something new, something to think about in Irish'. Béaslaí's historical plays *An Danar* and *An Bhean Chródha* addressed concerns immediately relevant to audiences in post-independence Ireland, while his short comedies with urban and town settings reflected a life most Irish-speakers at the time outside the Gaeltacht knew far better than they did that of Tomás Ó Criomhthain's islanders or Conamara and Donegal native speakers. Audiences could engage with Ó Lochlainn's questioning of national identities and loyalties in *Na Fearachoin,* enjoy his fast-moving comic thriller *Na Gadaithe,* and appreciate the stylistic innovation in *Ag an Ladhrán*. Confronted by a rapidly changing and frightening world, Irish speakers could be challenged by de Bhilmot's powerful and prophetic depictions of modern total warfare and the ethical questions he raises in *Grádh níos Mó* and *An Ráidhteas Oifigeamhail,* or inspired to ponder the consequences of the kind of changes he saw necessary to create a more rational, equitable and ethical economic and social order in *Prólóg don Réim Nua*. Macken both amused playgoers with his cleverly plotted and zany urban comedies, and made them think about the problems Ireland faced in a more globalised and competitive future in *Oighreacht na Mara*. These plays and a small number of other innovative efforts in the period may well have been swamped by the time-worn rural comedies, predictably patriotic historical melodramas and the copious translations, but they established that in the right hands the Irish language had the capacity, the vitality and the flexibility to be the medium for a thematically and aesthetically mature dramatic art worthy of comparison with that in any other language.

Needless to say, it is impossible at this time to really know how Gaelic audiences reacted to the plays of Béaslaí, Ó Lochlainn, Ó Broin, de Bhilmot and Macken. It does not, however, seem at all far-fetched to think that those plays could have contributed to the development – often the creation – of a Gaelic audience more open to experiment, more willing to take the language for granted and value a play on its own terms as a work of theatrical art, rather than seeing playgoing as a means of improving linguistic skills or asserting allegiance to the cause. As we have seen, this issue of audience was central in de Bhilmot's thinking, as is obvious from comments he made in a 1942 interview with Kitty Clive. He first noted that 'many' Gaelic playwrights had stopped writing in the past few years. Then, having identified the playwright and the audience as 'the two principal parties' in the creation of a theatre movement, he said that 'the latter is the most [*sic*] fluid in so far as it can be created. The dramatist cannot ... The dramatist is either there or he is not. In order that he might go on and produce, he must be encouraged, and the audience is his chief inspiration' (*Leader*, 9 May 1942).[9] As he would have been well aware, the Irish state's policy of Gaelicising the population through the schools, however controversial, had produced a not insignificant number of potential playgoers with enough Irish to at least consider attending a play in the language. Plays like the best of those of our playwrights – and in his interview with Clive, de Bhilmot himself stressed that 'the audience is not created unless the plays are good' – could have given them a reason to take a chance. In addition, while blanket assertions are impossible in the absence of the kind of direct evidence we now lack, such plays could also have galvanised actors and directors tired of the potatoes and *poitín*, the matchmaking, mawkishness and militarism that had long been staples on the Gaelic stage, in the process challenging them to hone their skills and live up to their own ambitions and ideals as performers and artists. Of course, none of this is to say that any of our five playwrights were major dramatists in their own right. That does not, however, mean that they should be forgotten or ignored. The work of Béaslaí, Ó Lochlainn, Ó Broin, de Bhilmot and Macken showed what could be done at a time when there were vanishingly few such models in Irish. It broadened the horizons and suggested future possibilities for the Gaelic stage. It challenged Gaelic actors, directors and other theatre personnel to a greater level of professionalism and sophistication, and showed audiences, particularly those in Irish cities, that plays in Irish could engage as well as amuse. Had these playwrights not written, the appearance of their more gifted immediate successors – dramatists like Ó Tuairisc, Ó Tuama and Ó Floinn – would have seemed – like that of Shakespeare soon after *Ralph Royster Doyster* – a bolt from the blue, a development without any clear source in what had gone before.

In 1943, Walter Macken was asked whether he and his colleagues at the Taibhdhearc were 'doing anything for the development of the Drama, apart from producing and acting in plays' (*ag déanamh aon rud do fhorfhás an Dráma, seachas drámaí do léiriú agus a aithris*)? Politely ignoring the lack of reference to the writing of plays, Macken responded: 'Yes. We are making a machine for the time to come, for the great writer who is to come' (*Comhar*, May 1943, p. 1).[10] But now that a fair number of significant Gaelic playwrights have appeared, not only those discussed in *An Underground Theatre* but also those working in what could be thought of as a second golden age for Gaelic drama if not theatre – writers like Antaine Ó Flatharta, Seán Mac Mathúna, Eilís Ní Dhuibhne, Micheál Ó Conghaile, Celia de Fréine, Alan Titley, Gearóid Mac Unfraidh, Joe Steve Ó Neachtain and Darach Ó Scolaí – it may be time to start thinking seriously about a tradition and a canon of theatre in Irish. In a 1957 piece in *Comhar*, Frank Dermody wrote that Séamus de Bhilmot once asked, 'Is it true to say that there is any such thing as Irish-language drama?' adding, 'Isn't it more accurate to say that there is a certain number of plays in Irish ...?' (*Comhar*, February 1957, p. 10).[11] Perhaps Macken was merely building a machine and de Bhilmot was just writing 'a certain number of plays', but their modesty should not conceal the fact that by doing such things they and their comrades Béaslaí, Ó Lochlainn and Ó Broin were hastening the transition from the 'Ralph Royster Doyster' stage to an era of sophisticated and accomplished drama in the Irish language.[12]

Endnotes

INTRODUCTION. *The Ralph Royster Doyster* Stage and Beyond

1 *Ralph Royter Doyster* (*c.*1553) by Nicholas Udall is a rollicking farce dealing with middle-class life in London. It is commonly linked with William Stevenson's rural farce *Gammer Gurton's Needle* (also *c.*1553) and the earliest English tragedy, *The Tragedy of Gorbuduc* (*c.*1570), of which Thomas Norton is said to have written the first three acts and Thomas Sackville the second two, to illustrate the astoundingly rapid evolution of a native English drama in the second half of the sixteenth century. See Albert C. Baugh (ed.), *A Literary History of England*, 2nd edn (Englewood Cliffs: Prentice-Hall, 1967), pp. 448–9, 452. The development of theatre in Irish in the first half of the twentieth century was to be as rapid if not as magnificent.

2 *Tabhairfimid an chéad leabhar de* Bhanba *arís do'n té 'neosfaidh dúinn cionnus a chuirfidhe tonn ar bogadh ar an árdán, cionnus a chruinneochadh móir-sheisear fear timcheall puill phludaigh ann, agus bó do tharrac amach as le téadaibh agus le málaibh, cionnus dfhéadfaidhe an bhó a choimeád 'na leidhpín ar an árdán agus uisce is pluda ag scéitheadh ó na slineánaibh, cionnus thiomáinfidhe as san go dtí an cró í, cionnus, – cionnus, – cionnus a chuirfear an dráma ar an árdán, sin é atá uainn.*

3 Labhrás Mac Brádaigh would joke about the tendency of Gaelic playwrights to create unnecessary scene changes in his 1943 play *An tÚghdar i nGleic* (The Author in a Quandary). The play has never been published, but the script is available in the Taibhdhearc na Gaillimhe papers at the National University of Ireland, Galway.

4 Amazingly, the play was also produced in Cork (*Leader*, 7 December 1907).

5 It is worth noting that in 1895 Eoghan Ó Neachtain published a translation of Boucicault's *The Colleen Bawn* for the *Galway Pilot*. It was never produced.

6 The text of this scene can be found in Robert Hogan and James Kilroy, *The Irish Literary Theatre 1899–1901* (Dublin: Dolmen Press, 1975), pp. 137–44. The first true play in Irish was *An Bárd 'gus an Fó* (The Poet and the Prince), translated by Pádraig Ó Beirn from the English of Paul McSwiney, who also wrote the music for the piece. It was produced in the Steinway Hall in New York City in November 1884. The first play in Irish performed in Ireland may have been the one-act farce *An Fiaclóir*, Micheál Mhag Ruaidhrí's translation of John Cannon's *The Dentist*, performed by the Blackrock branch of the Gaelic League in April 1900.

7 In an note to their edition of plays based on monologues recited by Conchubhar Ó Deasmhumhna (1871–1928), Áine Uí Chuill and Seán Ó Morónaigh state that little needed to be done to turn Ó Deasmhumhna's narratives into simple little plays for Aisteoirí Chúil Aodha: 'Since he was only thinking about narration by one person in the original writings, Conchubhar Ó Deasmhumhna only gave one side of the dialogue – most of the dialogue from one person and the speech of the

other character conveyed in the second person. The only way Aisteoirí Chúil Aodha "adapted" these episodes for the stage was by putting that bit of the speech in the second person into the first person' (*Agus aithriseoireacht aonair in aigne aige sna bunscríbhinní, níor thug Conchubhar Ó Deasmhumhna ach aon taobh amháin den chomhrá – an chuid is mó den chaint ag carachtar amháin agus caint an charachtair eile curtha in iúl sa dara phearsa. Ní deineadh de 'chóiriú drámaíochta' ar na heachtraí úd ag Aisteoirí Chúil Aodha ach an beagán cainte sin sa dara phearsa a chur sa chéad phearsa*). See Áine Uí Chuill and Seán Ó Morónaigh (eds), *Drámaí ó Thobar Mhúscraí le Conchubhar Ó Deasmhumhna* (Plays from the Well of Muskerry by Conchubhar Ó Deasmhumhna) (Camas: An Comhlachas Náisiúnta Drámaíochta, 2013), p. 12. It should, however, be noted here that not all of these adaptations were limited to two characters. Uí Chuill and Ó Morónaigh refer to Ó Deasmhumhna as 'narrator/actor' (*aistritheoir/aisteoir*) (p. 13). All of the plays in this volume have been performed in Ballyvourney, County Cork, some elsewhere in the Gaeltacht, as well as in the National Library of Ireland.

8 Pádraig Ó Siochfhradha ('An Seabhac') published three short 'plays' (*drámaí*) collected by Fionán Mac Coluim from Tadhg Ó Conchubhair of Lispole, County Kerry, in *An Lóchrann* in 1909–10 and 1918. Ó Conchubhair said that he had got them from Muiris Ó Gríofa. These are curious hybrid constructions, complete with rudimentary stage directions, the source of which is unclear. They have been edited by Seán Ó Morónaigh in *Drámaíocht ó Dhúchas ó Bhéalaithris Thaidhg Uí Chonchubhair* (Drama from the Native Tradition from the Narration of Tadhg Ó Conchubhair) (Camas: An Comhlachas Náisiúnta Drámaíochta, 2005). In May 1915, students from Patrick Pearse's Scoil Éanna (St Enda's School) performed a piece called 'Dúnlaing Óg agus a Leannán Sidhe' (Young Dúnlaing and His Otherworld Lover). This little skit, published in *Irisleabhar na Gaedhilge* in 1899, had been collected by Séamus Ó Fiannachta from Seán Chrocháin Ó Beirn of Sneem, County Kerry, in 1898. Writing of the piece in *An Claidheamh Soluis*, Tadhg Ó Donnchadha ('Torna') stated that it was thought to be 'at least three hundred years old' (*trí chéad bliadhain ar a laighead*), to which *An Claidheamh Soluis* added that its existence 'disproved ... the accepted statement that native Irish literature had never evolved a drama (*ACS*, 22 May 1915).

9 Several of these are among the plays collected in *Drámaí ó Thús na hAthbheochana* (Plays from the Beginning of the Revival), ed. Éadaoin Ní Mhuircheartaigh and Nollaig Mac Congáil (Galway: Arlen House, 2008).

10 Doyle suggested that audience members should be provided with a translation so that they might 'wag their heads, as well as their tails, wisely, if not intelligently'. It is worth noting that from its earliest years to the present, Taibhdhearc na Gaillimhe has included in its programmes for playgoers a summary in English of the evening's play(s) 'for those with little Irish' (*dóibh siúd ar bheagán Gaeilge*).

11 *Do b'fhearr labhairt ró-righin ná ró-thapaidh an fhaid a's bhímid ag braith ar lucht foghlumtha na teangain – nó d'iarraidh iad do thabhairt isteach agus misneach do chur ortha ba chirte a rádh.*

12 *Ní h-ionann eólas ar an nGaedhilge agus suim i ndrámaidheacht sa Ghaedhilge. Ní ceart a bheith ag súil le Gaedhilgeoir do dhul go dtí léiriú drámaí ach an oiread a raghadh sé go dtí aon chaitheamh-aimsire Gaedhealach eile. See also de Bhilmot, 'An Pobal agus Drámaí Gaedhilge'* (The Public and Plays in Irish), *Éire: Bliainiris Ghaedheal*, 1942, pp. 75–9.

Writing in *An Stoc* just as the Taibhdhearc was mounting its first ever production, Micheál Mac Liammóir had high hopes for the future of Gaelic drama: 'We hope that they will come to us, not only out of great respect for the language of St Patrick and St Brigid but because they want to go to the theatre, and because it is a natural thing, in Galway, to go to the theatre in Irish, just as it is natural, in Seville, to go in Spanish …' (*Tá súil againn go dtiocfa siad chugainn, ní hé amháin i ngeall ar an meas mór atá acu ar theangain Naoimh Pádraic is Naoimh Brighid acht i ngeall gur nádúrtha an rud é, in Gaillimh, bheith ag dul chuig an amharclainn sa Ghaedhilg, díreach mar is nádúrtha, i Sébhilla, dhul chuice sa Spáinnis …*) (*Stoc*, August–September 1928, p. 4). León Ó Broin, perhaps with tongue in cheek, suggested a radical solution to the problem: 'And above all there must be an immediate divorce between the people who believe in the drama for the drama's sake and the people who are interested in the drama because it is Gaelic drama or because the Irish language is the medium of expression' (*Star*, 20 July 1929).

13 He also told Clive that 'a Gaelic audience is a most intelligent audience'.

14 *Is mór an díobháil i n-aghaidh dráma na Gaedhilge, daoine do chur ar an árdán agus ná feadair siad ó thalamh an domhain cad é an bhrigh atá leis an méid cainte adeirid. Is deacair daoine oireamhnacha d'fhagháil ins gach aon áit, agus is dócha go gcaithfimíd cur suas leis an earra atá againn go dtí go bhfuighmíd ceann níos fearr.*

15 *Níl éinní is mó in ao' chor a chuireann déistean ar lucht éisteachta ná Gaedhilg lag-bhriste. Má ghlacann aisteoir air féin páirt do ghabháil ba cheart an pháirt sin do bheith i gceart aige agus munar cainnteoir ó dhúthchas é bheadh sé ceart aige ana-thaithí a dhéanamh ar na fuaimeanna.*

16 *Níor mhór an Ghaedhilg a bheith go blasta aca mar níl éinní is mó a ghoilleann ar an lucht éisteachta ná bheith ag iarraidh droch-Ghaedhilg a thuisgint agus tá sé fíor-dheacair ar fad í thuisgint.*

17 *Is minic a bhí masmas orm féin agus mé im' shníomhadh féin sa suidheachán toisc teanga chomh hálainn léithi nuair a labhartar i gceart í a bheith dá loit agus dá milleadh ar árdán. Níor cheart do dhream ar bith a mbeadh meas aca ar a dteangaidh cur suas leis.*

18 *Caithfidh an drámaidheacht a theacht as an áit a bhfuil an Ghaedhilg dá labhairt go nádúrtha ag na daoiní. Déarfaí liom ar ndóighe nach bhfuil eolas na ceirde sin ag muintir na Gaedhealtachta. Aidhmhighim. acht dá olcas iad tá siad chomh maith leis an dream a bhí i n-Amharclainn na Mainistreach le cúig bhliadhna. Ins an chéad chás níl siad i muinghin Ghaedhilg Liverpool.* This reference to Liverpool was a dig at Piaras Béaslaí, who was born in that city, as was Gearóid Ó Lochlainn.

19 Comments about An Comhar's reliance on prompters were not uncommon in reviews at the time. For example, in 1929 'An Scrúdóir' wrote of An Comhar's production of Béaslaí's *An Bhean Chródha*: 'No doubt the slip-shod memorising of their parts by the players accentuated this defect [occasional unintelligibility and incoherence] and more than once "position" on stage was sacrificed in order to keep in ear-shot of an over-worked prompter' (*Star*, 13 April 1929).

20 It is safe to say that no actor ever expected to get rich by performing in plays in Irish.

21 *Cén fáth nach sgríobhann léirightheóirí agus aisteóirí na Gaedhilge na drámaí iad féin, gan duadh a chur ar an úghdar bocht ar chor ar bith? Cuirim i gcás, má thagann tú go dtí an léiriú is cinnte nách n-aithneóchaidh tú do dhráma féin, mar beidh sé chomh h-athruighthe*

sin againne … Cuirfe sinn daoine ar an ardán freisin nách bhfuil féith an aisteóra ionnta, nách raibh ariamh agus nách mbeidh go deó, agus nách bhfuil guth aisteóra aca, acht tá sin ar fad, dar ndóigh, de réir an nósa Ghaedhealaigh, agus tá drámaidheacht na Gaedhilge mar atá sí. In all fairness, it should be said that throughout the '20s, '30s and '40s there were also favourable reviews of both the linguistic competence and the acting ability of Gaelic actors, especially those at the Taibhdhearc. See Philip O'Leary, *Gaelic Prose in the Irish Free State 1922–1939* (Dublin: UCD Press, 2004), pp. 472–3; and Philip O'Leary, *Writing Beyond the Revival: Facing the future in Gaelic prose 1940–1951* (Dublin: UCD Press, 2011), pp. 294–8. It is, however, clear that attending plays in Irish at this time was a hit or miss proposition at best, and many audience members must have felt they had lost the bet, along with the price of admission and a few hours of their time. By the way, there were also frequent (and justified) complaints about the quality of theatre criticism in this period.

22 It should be noted that not all of the plays translated were either minor or insipid.

23 The Taibhdhearc still regularly performs translations from a wide variety of sources, and many of them have been popular with audiences.

24 He was, of course, thinking of translations here, particularly translations from English.

25 *Ní fhuil muinntear na tíre seo comh giallmhar sin ar an nGaedhilg. Tá drámaí de dhíth ortha a b'fhiú a léiriughadh i dteanga ar bith agus i dtír ar bith agus is mithid dúinn anois a leithéid seo a chur ar fagháil i n-ionad drámaí beaga, lochtacha gan bhrigh, gan chéill.*

26 *Tá rud de dhíth air, adhbhar machtnaimh tré mheadhon na Gaedhilge – rud éigin ná faca sé léirighthe ar stáitse cheana sa Bhéarla. Go dtí go mbeidh ré'n* [recte *rud*?] *de'n tsaghas seo ar fagháil fanfaidh cúrsaí drámaidheachta Gaedhilge ins an iomaire ina bhfuil sí* [*sic*] *i láthair na h-uaire.*

27 *Fásfaidh an ré órdha seo as croidhe agus aigne ár ndrámadóirí má chromaid ar obair le dílseacht dá bhforshamhail.* Needless to say, not everyone with an interest in Gaelic drama shared his optimism. Thus, in 1946, 'Mac Alla' wrote: 'It is strange that we have not found a single good playwright among Irish speakers so far … Perhaps we are not fated to create great drama in Irish' (*Is iontach an rud é nár éirigh linn drámadóir maith amháin a fháil ameasg lucht na Gaeilge go dtí seo … B'fhéidir nach bhfuil sé i ndán dúinn drámuíocht mhór a chumadh sa Ghaeilg*) (*Comhar*, July 1946, p. 7).

28 See Liam Ó Flaithearta, *Dorchadas: Tragóid trí ghníomh*, ed. Brian Ó Conchubhair (Dublin: Arlen House, 2011). O'Flaherty himself translated the play into English. See Liam O'Flaherty, *Darkness: A tragedy in three acts*, ed. Brian Ó Conchubhair (Dublin: Arlen House, 2014).

29 The play has never been published but the script is available in the Taibhdhearc na Gaillimhe papers at the National University of Ireland, Galway.

30 The play has never been published but the script is available in the Taibhdhearc na Gaillimhe papers at the National University of Ireland, Galway.

31 See Labhrás Mac Brádaigh, *Céad Feadha Síos: Dráma aoin-ghnímh* (Baile Átha Cliath: Oifig an tSoláthair, 1953). The play was performed by An Comhar Drámaíochta as *Cá bhFios Dúinn?* (How Do We Know?) at the Peacock in February 1942.

32 And, of course, as with much of Pearse's literary output, these plays were overshadowed by his political and military activities and the mythology they created. See Patrick Pearse, *Collected Plays/Drámaí an Phiarsaigh*, ed. Róisín Ní Ghairbhí and Eugene

McNulty (Sallins: Irish Academic Press, 2013); and Eugene McNulty and Róisín Ní Ghairbhí (eds), *Patrick Pearse and the Theatre/Mac Piarais agus an Téatar* (Dublin: Four Courts Press, 2016).

33 See Pádraic Ó Conaire, *Bairbre Rua agus Drámaí Eile*, ed. Pádraig Ó Siadhail (Béal an Daingin: Cló Iar-Chonnachta, 1989). Ó Siadhail's introduction and notes are a valuable source of information on Ó Conaire as playwright. Two of his plays – *An Uacht* (The Will) and *Na Gaisgidhigh* (The Heroes) – share the same title and general plot with two of his short stories. Another, *Caitlín na Clúide* (Kathleen of the Chimney-Corner), is a version of the Cinderella story.

34 Leon Ó Broin, *Just Like Yesterday: An autobiography* (Dublin: Gill & Macmillan, n.d.), p. 144. The other two plays he mentions – not by name – are 'an adaptation of a French farce' (*Labhartar Béarla Anseo*) and 'a nativity play' (*An Oíche Úd i mBeithil*).

35 *Is beag an gaol – más gaol i bhfad amach é – a shamhlaítear a bheith idir an bhilleog breactha d'fhocail fhuara thirime agus an leagan stáitse de dhráma mar a bhfeictear pearsana samhlaíocht an údair á dtabhairt chun beochta maraon le friotal is fealsúnacht an údair á méadú agus á saibhriú de dhroim guthanna, gluaiseachtaí is geáitsí na n-aisteoirí. Níl sa scríbhinn ar shlí ach an iarlais a bhí nó a bheidh ag brúchtaíl le beocht is beatha ar an stáitse. Is léir, mar sin, nach aon dóithín fiúntas dráma i scríbhinn, cibé acu i lámhscríbhinn nó i leabhar priontáilte é, a mheas. D'fhéadfadh breall a bheith ar an léitheoir is oilte.*

CHAPTER 1. The Indispensable Man: Piaras Béaslaí (1881–1965)

1 The play was published with the title *Coramac na Cuile* in the so-called 'Litriú Simplí' (Simple Spelling), a phonetically based orthography that Béaslaí took an early interest in. The system never caught on, and Béaslaí himself was never really committed to it. See Pádraig Ó Siadhail, *An Béaslaíoch: Beatha agus saothar Phiarais Béaslaí (1881–1965)* (Béaslaí: The life and work of Piaras Béaslaí) (Baile Átha Cliath: Coiscéim, 2007), p. 186. I will use the modern standard spelling of the title throughout this book except in direct reference to the published text. Quotes from the play will be as spelled in the text.

2 While he never denied having been born in Liverpool, he was more than willing to obfuscate this fact. See Ó Siadhail, *An Béaslaíoch*, pp. xxiii and xxviii.

3 See ibid., p. xx.

4 See ibid., p. 435.

5 Ó Siadhail sees Béaslaí's life as starkly divided between the time up to 1924 when he was centrally involved in the great events of his time, and the period after 1924 in which he was on the margins of such events. See Ó Siadhail, *An Béaslaíoch*, p. xxxii.

6 Almost all of its members had ties to Munster.

7 This group was eventually absorbed by Cumann na Scríbhneoirí.

8 Ó Siadhail and I read this novel somewhat differently. See Ó Siadhail, *Béaslaíoch*, pp. 535–58; and O'Leary, *The Prose Literature of the Gaelic Revival*, pp. 444–8.

9 See Ó Siadhail, *An Béaslaíoch*, p. 475. He was not, of course, entirely alone. Both Patrick Pearse and Pádraic Ó Conaire were early advocates of a more sophisticated approach to literature in Gaelic circles.

10 *Cionnus fhéadfadh éinteanga a dul chun cinn agus a leithéid de thuairim ag furmhór na scríbhneoirí?*

11 *Ach an mhistéir thar mistéirí dob í an 'aigne Ghaedhlach' í. Tá an aigne sin chomh diamhair, chomh deacair sin a thuigsint nach féidir ach do bheagán de dhaoine tógtha dul amach uirthe ná í léigheamh.*

12 He had spent a bit of time in the Kerry Gaeltacht as a young man and also spent several summers at Coláiste na Mumhan in Ballyvourney in the west Cork Gaeltacht.

13 *Is í an cheist í ná cé'ca saol den dá shaol atá i nÉirinn is mó tábhacht, cé'ca is treise agus is mó is fiú cuimhneamh air in obair na teangan. Tá dhá shaol i nÉireann i láthair na huaire, an seana-shaol agus an saol nua, saol na Gaeltachta agus an saol atá sa chuid eile d-Éirinn … Is í an cheist í, mar sin, an ceart dúinn seana-shaol na Gaeltachta agus a mbaineann leis a shábháil, má's féidir é, agus a thabhairt thar n-ais sa chuid eile den tír, nú an saol nua atá ann a thógaint mar atá sé agus bheith ad iaraidh é ghaedhlú … Pé'ca olc maith an ní é, is é art an lae inniu an t-aon art amháin a bhfaghan muintir an lae inniu blas air.*

14 Ó Siadhail argues convincingly that his turn to English was the result of disillusionment with the language movement and the need to earn a living by writing in a language that offered more opportunities and paid better than did writing in Irish. See Ó Siadhail, *Béaslaíoch*, p. 47.

15 Piaras Béaslaí, quoted by Ó Siadhail, *Béaslaíoch*, p. 47.

16 See ibid., p. 122; and James Kilroy (ed.), *The 'Playboy' Riots* (Dublin: The Dolmen Press, 1975), p. 89. Later in her life she was to call him 'General Béaslaí'. See Ó Siadhail, *Béaslaíoch*, pp. 648–9.

17 *'Saoirse cluichí' an eadh? Tá go breágh, a tháilliúir. Beidh rud éigin le rádh agam i dtaobh 'saoirse cluichí' i nÉirinn sar a fada. Tá eolas agus taithighe agam ar an gceist. Ba cheart go mbéadh trá's gur mhúin Liam féin dom cad is saoirse ann. Tuigim an scéal anois tharla gur bh'éigean dom dhá phunt airgid do dhíol as an teagasc. Sin 'saoirse cluichí' i nÉirinn agaibh!*

18 Béaslaí, quoted in *'Playboy' Riots*, p. 85. He never changed his mind, writing in 1938: 'I repeat my opinion that the *Playboy* is a poor thing, hardly worth making a fuss about one way or another. Synge does not seem to have known clearly what he was about when he wrote it.' See Ó Siadhail, *Béaslaíoch*, p. 118.

19 *Tá sé buailte isteach im aigneadh gur mithid dúinn féin claoi le chéile chun Amharcla a chur ar bun dúinn féin … B'fhiú dúinn iostadh a cheannach nó do thógáil i mBaile Átha Cliath i gcomhar úr-chluichidheachta.*

20 Perhaps the next line explains his motive here. He continued: 'The Gaelic League would be well advised to subsidise the work of the Aisteoirí.'

21 See 'Na hAisdeoirí', *FJ*, 2 December 1912.

22 Ó Siadhail, *Béaslaíoch*, pp. 211–12. He is called 'the energetic manager' in a brief note in *II*, 2 May 1913.

23 See 'The Drama in Dublin/A Gaelic Repertoire Theatre/Important Enterprise', *FJ*, 11 April 1913.

24 See the picture of Béaslaí and some of his fellow Aisteoirí, *II*, 23 January 1914.

25 *Nuair a chuir Piaras Béaslaí na hAisteoirí ar bun roinnt bhlianta ó shoin chun drámaí a léiriú sa chathair agus sa Ghaeltacht d'éirigh go hana-mhaith leis. Is mór an truagh gan cumann den tsórd san bheith ann anois. Is fearr go mór d'éireochadh leo ná mar éirigh leis*

na sean Aisteoirí … B'fhéidir go bhféadfadh Piaras iad a mhealladh isteach sa chumann airís dá gcuirfadh [sic] *sé ar bun é. An dtabharfaidh sé faoi?*

26 See 'Gaelic Dramatic League', *IT*, 21 November 1925; and 'Gaelic Dramatic Society / Big Programme Discussed at Annual Meeting', *IT*, 7 December 1927.

27 See Ó Siadhail, *Béaslaíoch*, p. 686.

28 See ibid., p. 788. See the picture of Béaslaí and his colleagues in *II*, 12 November 1923.

29 See ibid., pp. 757–8.

30 *D'fhéadfaidhe 'Amharclann Ghaedhealach' do chur ar siubhal (cuir i gcás) agus sgoil drámaidheachta agus aistigheachta do bhunughadh i gceart, ní i gcóir Bhaile Átha Cliath fé leith ach i gcóir mhuinntir na hÉireann.* See also Ó Siadhail, *Béaslaíoch*, p. 392.

31 Piaras Béaslaí, Letter to Ernest Blythe, 8 August 1928, Ernest Blythe papers, National Library of Ireland Ms. 20,708. *Is é ár dtuairim láidir nach féidir dúinn, an fhaid is bheimíd i dtaobh le seacht léirithe in aghaidh na bliana, iarracht níos fearr … a dhéanamh, agus ná beidh a thuille fáis ná dul chun cinn san obair.*

32 Piaras Béaslaí, quoted by Ó Siadhail, *Béaslaíoch*, p. 728. See also pp. 733, 753, 778–80, 801–2, 829.

33 The production was staged in May 1947.

34 Piaras Béaslaí, quoted by Ó Siadhail, *Béaslaíoch*, p. 788. See also pp. 801–2.

35 Ó Briain's piece appeared in *The Star* on 15 June 1929.

36 He was also reported as suggesting that 'the ancient history of lreland would provide plenty of material for some of the best Gaelic dramas'.

37 This was in all probability translated from an English version of the play.

38 In the Béaslaí papers in the National Library, there is a translation of another Bendix play as 'Cúrsaí Fiaigh' (Hunting Matters), in which he retains the German names of the characters.

39 There is a picture of a scene from the production in *II*, 30 November 1929.

40 Piaras Béaslaí, 'Don Léiritheoir' (To the Director), in Oliver Goldsmith, *Isliú chun Buadha*, tr. Béaslaí (Baile Átha Cliath: Oifig an tSoláthair, n.d.), pp. 5, 9–12. *Isé bhí uaim ná go dtuigfadh lucht éisteachta na Gaedhilge gach abairt agus gach puinte san dráma, go raghadh éifeacht an sgéil i bhfeidhm ortha i gceart, agus rud eile, go mbeadh suidheamh na bhfuaimeanna agus rith cainte oireamhnach d'aisteoirí ar an stáitse – rud a dhearmhadann a lán scríbhneoirí go bhfuil togha Gaedhilge aca, de cheal taithighe ar an aisteoireacht.*

41 In his review for *The Standard*, 'N. Ó D.' also noted the poor attendance, but attributed it at least in part to playgoers' preference for original work over translations (*Standard*, 14 December 1929).

42 *Ach a bhfeileann a leithéid do'n tsaoghal Ghaedhealach? Rinne Piaras a chuid oibre go maith, acht is deacair cuma agus craiceann an tsaoghail Ghaedhealaigh a chur ar dhráma de'n tsórt seo. Ach is cosamhail go gcaithfidhear an saigheas sin a bheith againn go mbeidh ar ndíol drámaí Gaedhilge againn.*

43 *Más é seo an meas atá aca* [An Comhar] *ar an bpobal is beag an t-iongnadh go dtugann Gaedhilgeoirí a n-aghaidh ar an antlás ghallda nó go mbíonn suidheacháin fholmha in Amharclainn na nGaedheal.*

44 Piaras Béaslaí, quoted by Ó Siadhail, *Béaslaíoch*, pp. 787–8. *Isé mo thuairim gur ceart dúinn an rud atá uatha a thabhairt do phobal na Gaedhilge. Isé atá uatha ná greann,*

caint shimplí agus smaointe a thuigfadh leanbh. Tá go maith – tugtar an méid sin dóibh. Pobal atá uainn – agus má's gádh dúinn an pobal a mhealladh chughainn le drámaí simplí grinn, fé mar a mheallfá leanbh le milseáin, deinimís é i n-ainm Dé.

45 *Acht ní hé sin an ceann is measa dhen scéal. Dá mba rud é ná raibh ag Gaedhilgeóiribh Bhaile Átha Cliath acht togha na Gaedhilge, ba chuma soin. Is é an Béarla an teanga a bhaineann le saoghal na cathrach so. Teanga ná baineann le gnáth-shaoghal na cathrach, ní chumfar litridheacht na cathrach aisti. Ní fhásfaidh éin-litridheacht as leacachaibh Bhaile Átha Cliath go dtí go mbeidh an Ghaedhilg i n-a gnátheangain age muinntir Bhaile Átha Cliath.* See also Béaslaí, 'Literature and the Gaedhealtacht', *SF*, 16 March 1912.

46 He wrote '*ná fásfaidh éin-litridheacht Ghaedhilge as clochaibh Bhaile Átha Cliath go ceann i bhfad. Is baoghalach gur beag duine a thuigeann an méid sin. Ní thuigeann Eoghan Mac Néill é. Ní thuigeann Colm Ó Conaire* [Pádraig Mac Piarais] *é.*'

47 The title obviously echoes Patrick Pearse's reply to Richard Henebry's attack on his narrative methods in his short stories. See O'Leary, *Prose Literature*, pp. 91–2.

48 The play deals, of course, with Michael Collins' legendary escapes from British patrols in Dublin. Most of the characters are, like Collins, real historical figures. Béaslaí's two protagonists are, however, fictional, with, as Ó Siadhail points out, Muiris Mac Aodha based on the author himself – 'except he is made a man of action rather than an uninteresting publicist' (*ach amháin go ndéantar fear aicsin de seachas fear leamh poiblíochta*) and Eibhlín Ní Lórdáin based on Béaslaí's lover Lily Mernin, who in real life smuggled secret information out of Dublin Castle where she worked. See Ó Siadhail, *Béaslaíoch*, p. 765. A typescript of the play can be found in the Béaslaí papers in the National Library of Ireland.

49 See ibid., pp. 747–8.

50 See ibid., pp. 776–7. In the Béaslaí papers in the National Library there are also pages of what is called 'First Draft of Pe in Eirinn I.' [*sic*]. What exists of this undated handwritten play is set in 'Tigh Ósta Sheáin Uí Thuama' (Seán Ó Tuama's pub) and features the eighteenth-century 'Poets of the Maigue' ('*Filí na Mágha*'). Despite the title and the subject matter of the manuscript, it is in English, although the many songs listed for it were apparently to be in Irish.

51 See ibid., p. 108. See also p. 138.

52 Of Béaslaí's acting in the lead role, this critic wrote: 'His impersonation was thoroughly meritorious. His study of the impetuous young warrior was manly and straightforward, and his declamation left nothing to be desired. His mannerisms are by no mean unattractive.'

53 Piaras Béaslaí, *Coramac na Cuile: Cluihe trí vír* (Dublin: James Duffy & Co., 1909), p. 6. *Ní eacuís én teó ryav ach an cahav atá aguing le diàny inieg uesleachda na Ngoul. Tà gleoguire desviàlach ó Chorcuig na Lúnng ansò inis – Donacha Mac Heig as ainim dó – agus as dialha an fear é chun Galaviàrla do sdeala chúing-na.*

54 Ibid., p. 29. *A vearta, a chôrli gliucuis, a lúba as a chamsdyl! A vlayman as a vusdar nuer a hílean sé go leogfar les é! Agus an brasuire úd láiv les ig ésdeacht ling agus a leavgháirí! Go roud fé vráca an vróin go deo má sguilím les a hile.*

55 See Ó Siadhail, *Béaslaíoch*, p. 682.

56 Jules Moinaux, *Les deux sourds*, ed. I.H.B. Spiers (Boston: D.C. Heath & Co., 1906), p. 1; and Piaras Béaslaí, *Beirt na Bodhaire Bréige*, in *An Sgaothaire agus Cúig Drámaí*

Eile (Baile Átha Cliath: Muinntir C.S. Ó Fallamhain i gcomhar le hOifig an tSoláthair, 1929), p. 127. *Sasanach iseadh é, is dócha. Bíonn ainmneacha grána greannmhara ar na Sasanaigh i gcónaí.*

57 No first prize was awarded.

58 Their production won first prize in that year's Oireachtas drama competition for Irish-language intermediate schools (*IP*, 26 February 1935).

59 There is a picture of Béaslaí and the cast in *II*, 23 January 1914.

60 *Is cuma nó dráma nódh é. Ní hiad na daoine céadna atá san dá dráma. Ní hé an sgéal céadna atá ionnta ná na scenes céadna. Níl de chosmhúileacht eatartha ach go bhfuil bruighean ag lánamhain nódhphósta um chluiche cártaí san dá dhráma.*

61 Piaras Béaslaí, 'Rémh-Rádh', in *An Sgaothaire*, p. v. *Fuaireas an bun-smaoineamh ó dhráma Beurla do cheap Art Ó Murchadha san bhliadhain 1764* – 'What We Must All Come To, or Three Weeks After Marriage', *ach dheineas dráma nua dhe. Sgéal nua agus daoine nua ar fad atá im dhráma-se. Níl de chosmhúileacht ag an dá dhráma le chéile ach go mbíonn lánamha nua-phósta ag troid i dtaobh cluiche cártaí i ngach ceann díobh.*

62 Arthur Murphy, *Three Weeks After Marriage*, in Murphy, *The Way to Keep Him and Five Other Plays*, ed. John Pike Emery (New York: New York University Press, 1956), p. 321.

63 Piaras Béaslaí, *Cluiche Cártaí*, in *An Sgaothaire agus Cúig Drámaí Eile*, p. 57. *Chuirfeadh sé seirbhthean ar éinne! Is féidir liom gach cárta dá raibh san imirt d'aimsiú arís. Sin iad iad. Mar sin a bhí sé – ní headh – mar sin – ach mo dhearmhad! – Seadh, táid siad agam anois. Mar sin a bhí sé. Bhíodar a chúig ar fhichid agus ní rabhamair ach a chúig déag … Tá an sgeul ag dul amú orm. Do chuir an bhean mhí-ádhbharach úd measgán mearaí orm.*

64 Ó Siadhail, *Béaslaíoch*, p. 235. *Áit a bhfuil an aoir nimhneach is an tsaol-thaithí nimhneach chiniciúil fite fuaite trí fhronsa Murphy, níl againn i ndráma Bhéaslaí ach an choiméide éadrom. Áit a bhfuil plé lárnach ar bhréagluachanna na huasaicme is sodar na meánaicme i ndiaidh na mbréagluachanna céanna sa fhronsa Béarla, níl aon tráchtaireacht shóisialta d'aon chineál in Cluiche Cártaí Bhéaslaí a thugann áit lárnach do rómánsaíocht bhaoth na leannán óg.*

65 *Is trua nach dtugann Piaras Béaslaí a thuilleadh drámaí mar seo dúinn – tá féith na ceapadóireachta ann gan bhréig gan mhagadh. Cineál de 'Taming of the Shrew' atá ann, ach má seadh féin, tá greann agus scléip Ghaelach ann – greann a bhaineas le hÉirinn agus le Gaedhil fé leith.* He added: 'This is a good example of how much can be done with comic plays in Irish' (*Sompla maith é seo ar an méid is féidir a dhéanamh le drámaí grinn sa Ghaelig*). He also stressed that Irish writers in search of plays to translate should go to 'the great masters who have fame and reputation in foreign languages' (*na h-árd-mháistrí a bhfuil clú is cáil ortha in sna teangacha iasachta*) and ignore 'the mediocre things we have in English – even in the English used in Ireland' (*na rudaí lag-mheasardha atá againn i mBéarla – fiú amháin i mBéarla na hÉireann*).

66 *Ní fada go mbéidh an oiread aithne againn ar fhuirinn an drama so is bhíodh againn ar an 'Eloquent Dempsey'.* William Boyle's comedy *The Eloquent Dempsey* (1906) was a popular play in the repertoire of the early Abbey.

67 There is a picture of a scene from this production in *IT*, 21 November 1934.

68 Donncha Ó Súilleabháin, *Scéal an Oireachtais 1897–1924* (Baile Átha Cliath: An Clóchomhar, 1984), p. 83.

69 Ó Siadhail, *Béaslaíoch*, p. 266.

70 Samuel Foote, *The Lyar: A comedy in three acts* (London: G. Kearsly, 1764), p. 13.

71 Piaras Béaslaí, *An Sgaothaire*, in *An Sgaothaire agus Cúig Drámaí Eile*, p. 83. *Tá an chainnt go líomhtha agat agus an intinn go haibidh agus taoi ar fheabhas chun grinn; ... Ach ní shásóchadh an saoghal tú gan sgéalta iongantacha d'innsint d'fhonn is go leathfadh na súile ar an lucht éisteachta.*

72 Ibid., p. 91. *Féach air sin anois! Bhí na smaointe céadna ag Eoghan Ruadh agus agamsa. Tuiteann a leithéid amach uaireannta.*

73 Ó Súilleabháin, *Scéal an Oireachtais*, p. 183.

74 *Tá céard an drámadóra á foghluim ag Piaras Béaslaí ... Is ait an smuta grinn an dráma beag so* [ach] *níl aon chontabhairt sa sgéal agus laghdú ar an ngreann 'seadh é sin. Dá mhéid é an chontabhairt 'seadh is mó an greann.*

75 *Maidir leis an gcéad phíosa 'Fear na Milliún Púnt' níl mórán agam le rá. Ní raibh sé leath chomh maith leis an tarna dréacht.*

76 Piaras Béaslaí, *Fear na Milliún Púnt*, in *An Sgaothaire agus Cúig Drámaí Eile*, p. 151. *Má thárlaigheann Liam Ó Súilleabháin an treó so, ní misde dhúinn súil i n-áirde bheith aguinn. Má chuireann sé fé i nInse Geimhleach, bainfam ceól as an million punt, geallaim dhuit é! Cadé an mhaitheas do dhuine bheith na 'Phúncánach agus million púint aige, agus gan an t-airgead do sgaipeadh go rabairneach.*

77 They make use of most of the American stereotypes found in Irish-language writing at the time. See Philip O'Leary, 'Yank Outsiders: Irish Americans in Gaelic fiction and drama of the Irish Free State, 1922–39', in Charles Fanning (ed.), *New Perspectives on the Irish Diaspora* (Carbondale: Southern Illinois University Press, 2000), pp. 263–5.

78 Béaslaí, *Fear na Milliún Púnt*, p. 169. *Nár cheart dúinn tabhairt amach a bheith againn. Sgaipfidh sé an t-airgead – chun a shláinte d'ól!*

79 Ó Siadhail, *Béaslaíoch*, p. 673. *Is ar éigin is féidir amharc ar Cúigeachas mar chéim chun tosaigh i scríbhneoireacht Bhéaslaí ... Níorbh ionann is na coiméidí luatha, bhí teachtaireacht le cur abhaile ag an Bhéaslaíoch agus níorbh fhéidir leis gan ì a chraobhscaoileadh go lom díreach – 'Is fearr liom éan sort Gaedhilge ná an Béarla. Ní Gaedhilg ná Gaedhilge ná Gaoluinn an namhaid – ach Béarla.'*

80 There is a picture of cast members in *FH*, 7 March 1959.

81 The director of the play was either Béaslaí himself, Gearóid Ó Lochlainn or Pól Ó Fearghail. See Ó Siadhail, *Béaslaíoch*, pp. 685–6.

82 A brief review in the same paper stated of the 1933 revival of the play: '*An Danar* is one of the nicest and most poetic plays yet written in Irish, although it is not the best with regard to action and movement. And the production staged last night was the best yet' (*Tá 'An Danar' ar na drámaí is deise agus is milse cainnt dár sgríobhadh sa nGaedhilg fós, cé nach é is fearr gníomh is gluaiseacht. Agus ba é an léiriú a rinneadh aréir an léiriú ab fhearr fós*) (*II*, 2 May 1933).

83 *Siar agus aniar ag lucht an dráma: gach duine ar a thoil féin agus é le feiscint go glé againn gur daoine ionnta féin, gach neach aca. A gcomhrádh is mó a léirigh a dtréithre dhúinn agus, dar ndóigh, d'fhág san an dráma ar chaol-chuid gnímh ó am go h-am. Acht ar a shon san is uile b'í an chainnt bhreágh snasta fhileata í nár lag léi cruaidh-cheisteanna na feallsamhnachta do chur tré chéile go mion.* Writing in 1951 to challenge Tomás Mac Anna's opinion that Béaslaí lacked courage as a dramatist, his fellow playwright

Gearóid Ó Lochlainn praised Béaslaí for his essential work with An Comhar and noted that despite his awareness that short comedies were what his audiences wanted, he had challenged them with 'a couple of serious full-length plays' dealing with subjects 'far more difficult than he treated in his comedies and far more difficult than those in the work of Irish-language playwrights who preceded him' (*i bhfad níos deacra ná mar a bhíodh aige insna drámaí grinn agus níos deacra ná a bhíodh ag na drámathóirí a tháinig roimhe*) (*Comhar*, May 1951, p. 22). For Mac Anna's comments on Béaslaí, see *Comhar*, February 1951, p. 4.

84 Piaras Béaslaí, quoted in Ó Siadhail, *Béaslaíoch*, pp. 699–700.

85 Piaras Béaslaí, *An Danar: Dráma trí mír* (Baile Átha Cliath: Muinntir C.S. Ó Fallamhain i gcomhar le hOifig an tSoláthair, 1929), p. 5. *Ní stair ná seanchaidheachta* [*sic*] *ba mhó a bhí ag cur cúraim orm, áfach. Ní raibh uaim ach saoghal, am agus ionad a bheadh oireamhnach do sgéal Olaf agus Inga.*

86 See also ibid., p. 21.

87 Ibid., p. 14. *Ní foláir do gach duine a chion féin d'aoibhneas agus do shuaimhneas aigne a bhaint amach ar a shlighe féin. Maidir liomsa, is bárr sógha agus sástachta liom mo shaoghal a chaitheamh annso im biadhtach, ag tabhairt éistis d'óglaigh agus d'éigsibh, do mhairnéalaigh agus do lucht taistil ó thíorthaibh tar lear. Is breágh liom bheith im shuidhe annso, ag éisteacht le na laoithe agus sgeulta.*

88 Ibid., pp. 14–15. *Tá rud éigin ionnam ná leigfadh dom mo shuaimhneas do cheapadh.*

89 Ibid., p. 20. *Maidir leis an tsíothcháin – níl éin tsíothcháin ar an bhfarraige. Sin buaidh atá aice. Ní imthigheann éan chalcadh ná truailliú uirthi, fé mar imthigheann ar shaoghal na talmhan.*

90 Ibid. *Is iomdha duine a ghrádhann an mhuir. Feuch ormsa, ná deaghaidh amach ar an bhfarraige móir ariamh, ach níorbh fholáir liom m'árus do thógáil le hais na farraige. Is binn liom torann na dtonn i n-aice liom.*

91 Ibid. *Níl éan chion agam ar an bhfarraige ... Máthair dom is eadh an chré. Ach cuireann sgréach amplach na mara uamhan orm. Namhaid don chine dhaonna seadh í – níl neart aige uirthi – ní truagh ná taise aici dhó.*

92 Ibid., p. 24. She speaks of '*daoine ... a chloiseann mar a bheadh glór ag glaodhach ortha – glór ná tugann suidhe suaimnhnis dóibh ach dá síor-bhrostú ar lorg lúthghára níos doimhne, níos díochra, níos breághtha, ná mar atá le faghháil ar an saoghal so.*'

93 Ibid. *Is áluinn 's is iongantach an t-athasc é sin agat, a Inghean an Rí. Is iomdha rúndiamhair a thuigeann tú.*

94 Ibid., p. 31. *Bhí saoghal ciúin cneasta againn go dtí go dtáinig seisean nár measg. Bhí ár slighte féin againn chun ár ngnóthaí a dheunamh ach tá atharrach saoghail ... ann feasta.*

95 Ibid., p. 32. *Níl éan dúil aca san tsuathadh ná ins na hiarrachtaí nuadha so. Saoghal socair sásta atá uatha. Níl aon ionntaoibh aca as Olaf. Braithid siad gur fear dásachtach mí-chuibheasach é, a threóróchaidh i n-iomar na haimiléise iad.*

96 Ibid., p. 33.

97 Ibid., p. 35. *Cad a bhí ionnam an tráth úd do bhuail sí umam i dtigh Thorolf ach fear gan áird, gan toradh ag éinne orm, gan chabhair, gan mhaoin, gan treó ná cuspóir san tsaoghal, go searbh díom féin. Seo anois mé ar an bhfear is tréine 's is mó comhacht is réim i nDúibhlinn ... Isí Inga fé ndeara san; isí do chuir an misneach agus an éirim ionnam.*

98 Ibid. *Níor labhras. Is amhlaidh sheachnas í. Is fearr liom fanamhaint chun go mbeidh sé ar mo chumas labhairt léi go neamhbalbh.*
99 Ibid., p. 36. *Tá breith ag duine ar aon ní ach a chreideamhaint go bhfuil. Cúrsaí creidimh iseadh é.*
100 Ibid., p. 41. *Tá slighe ann chun tú féin d'árdú chun bheith i n-ionnanas le héin Chríostaidhe beó … Is féidir liom fuadar níos aoirde, níos uaisle a theasbáint duit ná éin ní a bheartuighis féin.*
101 Ibid. *Is fíor dhuit. Is tusa mo threoruidhe ar bhealach na glóire. Radharc do shúil agus an beagán briathar a chanais liom anuiridh do dhein taoiseach mór den fhánuidhe bocht searbh.*
102 Ibid., pp. 44–5.
103 Ibid., p. 46. *Isiad leithéidí Olaf, agus a n-árdmhianta agus a mbaoth-thaidhreamh is mó fé ndeara buairt agus anró an tsaoghail. Péaca éirigheann leó nó teipeann ortha, ní thagann as a n-árd-fhuadar ach ár is éirleach, léirsgrios is bochtaineacht.*
104 Ibid., p. 48. *Is feárrde duine creideamh éigin a bheith aige a sháróchaidh eagla an bháis … Thugas tréan iarracht chun an chumhacht ab aoirde, an sgiamh ba bhreághtha, an maitheas ba mhó a bhaint amach dom féin. Isé gnó gach duine cuspóir éigin a chur roimis agus a dhícheall a dheunamh ar a shon. Níor éirigh liom, ach is cuma son. Ní san bhuaidh atá an tairbhe ach san troid.*
105 Ibid., p. 49. *Isí an mheasardhacht an buaidh is feárr do dhuine – bheith sásta leis an maitheas go bhfuil breith aige air.*
106 Ibid., p. 55. *An chuid díom ná faighidh bás, sroisfidh sé thú. Is leatsa m'anam. Ní haithrighe liom éin ní. Nílmid sgartha ó chéile go deo.*
107 Ibid., p. 56. *Is feárrde duine rud éigin nó duine éigin gur fiú leis bás d'fhagháil ar a shon.*
108 Ibid. *Maith an sgeul sinn a bheith réidh leis an dtionnsgalóir buile sin. Beidh an seana-shaoghal socair againn feasta, fé mar bhíodh sul ar chuir Olaf isteach orainn.*
109 Ó Siadhail, *Béaslaíoch*, p. 705. As Ó Siadhail makes abundantly clear throughout his biography, Béaslaí despised de Valera for his opposition to Collins and the treaty and for his role in hastening the civil war.
110 It is worth noting that Seán Ó Tuama made similar use of a historical play about the more distant past to examine the attitudes that led to the Irish civil war in his 1955 play *Gunna Cam agus Slabhra Óir* (A Pistol and a Golden Chain), first performed in 1956. See Philip O'Leary, *An Underground Theatre: Major playwrights in the Irish language 1930–1980* (Dublin: UCD Press, 2017), pp. 191–7.
111 Piaras Béaslaí, quoted by Ó Siadhail, *Béaslaíoch*, pp. 707–8. He continued: 'Also the ideal, the prize of Cormac & Astronár finds its expression through patriotism – the Dane has no such clear light but he has gleams of a bigger reality behind the controversies of life.'
112 Ibid., p. 734.
113 There is a picture of a scene from the play in *II*, 2 April 1929.
114 Piaras Béaslaí, 'Réamh-Rádh', in *An Bhean Chródha: Dráma cheithre mír* (Oifig Díolta Foilseacháin Rialtais, 1931), p. 5. This preface is dated 21 August 1930. *Do rug an smaoineamh son greim orm agus do chlaoidh liom leis na bliadhanta fada. D'fhás agus d'aibidh an dráma im aigne. Chonnacthas dom Máiréad agus Domhnall agus an Coronal, chuireadar a dtréithe is a gcáiliochtaí i n-umhail dom, i ndiaidh ar ndiaidh. Tá*

aithne agam ortha chó fada son gur deacair dom a chreideamhaint gur mé féin do cheap iad.

115 *Níl an dráma i ngiorracht bheith chó maith leis 'An Danar'.* He felt there was far too much talk in the play.

116 Béaslaí, 'Réamh-Rádh', in *An Bhean Chródha*, p. 5. *Isé bun-chúis an truagh-dhráma so, mianta ná faghann a sásamh nádúrtha, mianta ná tuigfear do dhuine féin, a mheallann é ar bhealach a bhasgtha. Baineann sé leis an 'sub-conscious' … Béidir ná fuil san dráma so go léir ach saobh-aisling. Béidir go raibh Máiréad – agus Domhnall – beagán as a meabhair.* He then added: 'But I have no remedy for or control over them. Let them speak for themselves' (*Ach níl leigheas ná neart agamsa ortha. Labhraidís ar a son féin*).

117 Ibid., p 8.

118 Ibid., p. 12. *Ó fhágas tigh m'aintín táim ar buile chun an sealad beag saoirse do chur chun críche. Tuirseach atáim de bheith ag féachaint amach an fhuinneóg. A Agata, is dóich liom ná fuil im shaoghal ar fad ach – féachaint amach an fhuinneóg.*

119 Ibid., p. 15. *Nárbh fhiú dul i gcontabhairt an bháis chun gníomh mór uasal mar sin a dhéanamh?*

120 Ibid., p. 16. *Isé an brí a bhainimse as, ná – nach mar a chéile an saoghal míorbhúilteach do cheap Dia agus an saoghal leamh meata so fé riar na bhfear – go bhfuil éachta is iongantaisí ar an dtaobh thall den chloidhe teórann do chuir nósa agus riaghalacha timcheall orainn – gur féidir gabháil thar an gcloidhe – gníomh éachtach, glórmhar a dhéanamh – gníomh a líonfadh an croidhe de lúthgháir agus d'uathbhás –*

121 Ibid., p. 18.

122 Ibid., p. 19. His wife, on the other hand, is an outright snob. *Bhí sé i gcúirt Shasana (an dara Seárlas) ar feadh i bhfad agus do chaith sé tamall i gcúirt le Grand Monarque. Tá meón díchreidmheach aige, gan éan tuairimí láidre i dtaobh creidimh ná polaitíochta, gan ionntaoibh as dúthracht ná díoghrais, ach bíonn sé foidhneach, fulangach le tuairimí daoine eile. Tarcaisnigheann sé cumhangas aigne agus neamh-fhulaingeacht na ndaoine go mbíonn sé ag plé leo; ach leagann sé air bheith ar éin intinn leo, ach is follus gur cuma leis ciaca creidid siad é nó ná creidid. Sásuigheann sé a mheón le fonóid futha – fonóid nach léir dóibh.*

123 Ibid., p. 27. *Is fíor gurb eol dom an dúthaigh seo. Is ann do rugadh is do tógadh mé, agus tá mo shliocht préamhuighthe go daingean i dtalamh na tíre. Do chaitheas na bliadhanta thar lear, agus níl éan chion ag na Gaedhalaibh orm toisg gur ghabhas páirt le na namhdaibh – le cúis Dé, a mheasas a rádh – ach is feárr a thuigimse iad ná éan chaptaen Gallda, nó éan bhúistéir ó Lúndain …*

124 Ibid., p. 24.

125 Ibid., p. 72. *Tá truagh agam dó. Ba mhaith liom greim fhagháil air, ach níl éan droch-chroidhe agam dó. Tá uaisleacht ann – agus misneach dá réir – ach tá an fear bocht as a mheabhair. Tá sé ag déanamh ana-cheataighe dhúinn. Ní foláir é a ghabháil.*

126 Ibid., p. 77. *Ní mian liom géirleanamhaint d'imirt ar mo chó-dhaonnaidhthibh de ghrádh Dé. Ní dheinim ach an saoghal do ghlacadh mar atá sé, agus géilleadh don fhírinne. Níl uaimse ach mo leas féin gan dochar d'éinne eile, san chíorthuathaill mhí-adhbharaigh seo i nÉirinn idir aicmí buile baoth-chreidmheacha.*

127 Ibid. *Ar an dtaobh so tá Bateman agus Beastún agus a leithéidí eile, agus ar an dtaobh eile tá Tadhg Taodach agus Diarmuid na Buile. B'éigean domhsa páirt do ghabháil le*

taobh den dá thaobh – agus ghabhas leis an dtaobh go raibh deallramh gnótha ortha. Tá Tadhg agus Diarmuid curtha fé chois. Tá síothcháin san tír arís. Is feárrde cách an sgéal d'fhágaint mar sin, gan a thuilleadh coimheasgair do spreagadh. See also p. 23.

128 Ibid., p. 35. *Brughann sé fé an mhórdháil, an fíoch agus an teasuíocht atá istigh ina chroidhe. Is annamh a sgaoileann sé leo, ach ar uairibh tagann ráig bhuile air de gheit. Fear gur deacair é thuigsint, mar ní thuigeann sé a mheón féin, ná ní nochtann sé an méid a thuigeann sé dhe.*

129 Ibid., p. 41.

130 Ibid., p. 47.

131 Ibid., pp. 38–9. *Thar éin ní eile, bé b'fhearra liom, ná na Gallaphuic ramhra, grána do dhíbirt as talamh mo shinnsear le torann claidimh. Ach tá fhios agam nach féidir liom son a dhéanamh. Níl im chumas ach staincín a dhéanamh ortha – agus deinim é. Bím dá gcrádh is dá gcreachadh, agus annson mar chaitheamh amsire, seinnim an fheadóg, nó cuirim síos ar an bhfilíocht leis an sagart, nó – deinim mion-chomhrádh leis na béithibh.*

132 Ibid., pp. 64–5. *Do samhluigheadh dom, tráth, mé bheith im thaoiseach mór i gcogadh Gaedhal le Gallaibh, ag cur áir is léirsgrios ar na cóbaigh – nó ag fagháil buadha is caithréime thar lear, thall san bhFrainnc nó san Spáinn … Maidir liomsa, bhí breall ar mo shaoghal. Dheineas roinnt troda le Gallaibh, ach ní raibh ann ach spairinn gan éifeacht. Níor rugas éan bhuadh ná bladh liom. Chuadhas thar lear im mhac léighinn, ach níor leanas dó. Cheapas roinnt filíochta ná raibh ach cuibheasach.*

133 It is interesting that he does not translate the term 'republic' here. Of course, had he done so using his own preferred translation, *saorstát*, he would have only introduced a confusing political note for audiences in his own time.

134 Béaslaí, *An Bhean Chródha*, p. 73. *Creideamh agus dísle? Gan amhras, a chroidhe, rud an-úsáideach, ana-thairbheach seadh an creideamh – agus is áiseach an ní an dísle – dísle chun rí éigin nó fiú republic – cúis éigin. Muna mbeadh an creideamh agus an dísle bheadh an saoghal na chíorthuathail; ní fhéadfaí smacht ná eagar do chur i bhfeidhm. Muna mbeadh éin chreideamh ann, níorbh fholáir ceann a cheapadh.*

135 Ibid., p. 89. *Is mór an truagh son! Bhí súil agam le héachta uaidh.*

136 Ibid., p. 64. *D'fhéachais ins na súilibh orm agus chuiris dubhshlán fúm. An spréach a bhí it chléibh a d'adhain an splannc ionnam.*

137 Ibid., p. 67. *Braithim go bhfuil ionnam gníomhartha níos fearr a dhéanamh, gur dual dom saoghal níos breátha, níos glórmhaire, do bhaint amach dom féin. Tá an lasair im chléibh fós … Creidim gur tusa an bhanfhlaith do chonnacthas dom tré aislingí m'óige, an spéirbhean do sháruigh cách le breághthacht, le maordhacht, le cródhacht.*

138 Ibid., p. 68. *Caidé an brí atá leis na mianta gan sásamh a bhíonn dár gcrádh? Ca' na thaobh ná faghaimíd blas ar an ngnáth-shaoghal slán, socair, is eol dúinn? Cad do spriocann sinn chun é d'atharú? Is baoghalach ná fuil de bhun leis ach saobh-aislingí agus ná tiocfaidh as ach – brón agus géar-chrádh agus bás.*

139 Ibid. *Claoidhimís le n-ár n-aisling. Leanaimís dár ndúchas, gan beann ar chomhairle na sean. Gabhaimís ár mbóthar féin, bíodh an bás ar an dtaobh thiar den chloidhe.*

140 Ibid., p. 60. *Ní thuigimíd go ró-chruinn cad is fíor-bhun le n-ár ngníomharthaibh. Deinimíd an gníomh agus annson ceapaimíd leathsgéal chun é mhíniú dhúinn féin.*

141 Ibid., p. 65. *Ní thuigeann éan duine fíor-bhunchúis a ghníomhartha. Is féidir leis cúiseanna luadh – ach ní ionnta ach an croiceann a chuireann a réasún ar an sgéal. Is treise an dúchas ná an réasún.*

142 See Ó Siadhail's comments on the play's shortcomings in *An Béaslaíoch*, pp. 721–3.

143 It is, however, interesting to note that in a piece on 'Seán an Díomais mar Ábhar Dráma' (Shane the Proud as a Subject for a Play), Séamus Ó Néill recalled Béaslaí expressing his surprise that no one had ever written a play about this sixteenth-century Ó Néill chieftain (*Indiu*, 4 April 1947).

144 *Tá caint bhreágh scríbhte ag an ughdar tríd a lán den dráma ach cad é an mhaitheas san nuair ná bíonn tabhairt amach na cainnte sna hAisteoirí.*

145 The anonymous critic for the *Cork Examiner* called the production a success, but also described *An Bhean Chródha* as 'an exceptionally difficult play' (*CE*, 29 November 1937).

146 Piaras Béaslaí, quoted by Ó Siadhail, op cit., p. 787. *Bhrathas gur fearr le pobal na Gaedhilge cainnt shimplí, gnáth-chainnt comhrádh (ní mór ná go ndéarfainn cainnt chomónta) ná cainnt liteardha nó cainnt shamhluítheach ... Ní maith le pobal Gaedhilge an lae cainnt chasta agus ní maith leó aon doimhneas ná neamh-choitcheantacht smaointe.* In the unpublished 'Proem' from 1936, he stated that when he wrote *An Danar* and *An Bhean Chródha* – 'my last spells of inspiration' – he had risen to his 'full stature'. See Ó Siadhail, op. cit., p. 754.

147 An unsigned note on 'An Comhar' in *An t-Éireannach* stated that the play showed 'some of the characteristics of the comedies of the Abbey Theatre' (*cuid de thréithe drámaí grinn Amharclainn na Mainistreach*) (*Éireannach*, 20 October 1934). The play was broadcast over Radio Éireann in 1946 and 1947 (*CE*, 14 January 1946; *IT*, 16 June 1947). I have found no revivals, although it seems improbable that there were none.

148 Piaras Béaslaí, 'Fógra don Léiritheor', in *An Fear Fógraidheachta: Fársa trí mír* (Baile Átha Cliath: Oifig an tSoláthair, 1938), p. 3. *Fársa is eadh an dráma grinn seo agus ní foláir é léiriú dá réir, go mear, gníomhach.*

149 An anonymous critic for *The Irish Press* wrote: 'The play would, perhaps, be better if the pace were sped up a bit' (*Do b'fhearr-de an dráma b'fhéidir géarú leis an imtheacht bhí fé beagán*) (*IP*, 16 October 1934).

150 Béaslaí, *An Fear Fógraidheachta*, p. 10. *Tá a lán cleasaidheachta agus diabhlaidheachta ag baint le gnóthaí fógraidheachta.*

151 Ibid., p. 29.

152 *Sé Piaras Béaslaí an Gaedhilgeoir is fearr – murab é an t-aon Ghaedhilgeoir amháin é – a bhfuil céard na drámaidheachta aige. Tá sé i ndon na píosaí a chur le chéile go cliste ealadhanta i gcaoi go mbeidh dráma suimheamhail so-léirighthe aige.*

153 I have not found any revivals, but again it seems likely that the play would have appealed to amateur groups. *Dráma grinn trí mír 'Blúire Páipéir'. Cúrsaí grádha, coimplicéala is intrígeanna, réiteach, gach éinne sásta sa deireadh ... É chó maith le h-aon dráma dá shórt dár scríobh Piaras Béaslaí. An-oiriúnach d'aisteoirí Gaedhilge. An plota ar fheabhas.*

154 See Ó Siadhail, op. cit., p. 748.

155 See Ó Siadhail, op. cit., pp. 776–7.

156 Indeed, in 'An Appreciation' of Béaslaí written just after his death, Liam Ó Briain stated that he was 'the very first in the language movement to know anything about stage production' (*IT*, 24 June 1965).

157 I am quoting here from the section of Ó Cuív's little book published in *SI*, 18 February 1934. *Dá bhfiafruightí dhíom cé hé an túghdar, ach An tAthair Peadar Ua*

Laoghaire, is mó tábhacht i saothrú na Gaedhilge, déarfainn gan aon mhearthall gurab'é Piaras Béaslaí é … Níl a sárú le fáil ach oiread.

158 Of course, he felt that his work had been unfairly ignored by An Taibhdhearc. As yet no one has sorted out who was responsible for a regrettable situation that prevented potentially fruitful co-operation between a leading Gaelic playwright and one of only two major theatre companies working in Irish at the time.

159 *Thig linn an méid atá déanta aige ar son drámuidheachta na Gaedhilge a chur i gcomparáid leis an méid atá déanta ag Lady Gregory ar son drámuidheachta an Sacs-Bhéarla* [sic].

CHAPTER 2. Pragmatic Idealist: Gearóid Ó Lochlainn (1884–1970)

1 He sent articles to Gaelic journals in both Dublin and London. See, for example, 'Seanscéalta Lochlannacha' (Scandinavian Folktales), *SF*, 30 July to 1 October 1910; 'Ó'n Mór Roinn Thoir-Thuaidh' (From the Northeast of the Continent), *ACS*, 28 September 1912; 'Aisteoireacht 'san Íslinn' (Acting in Iceland), *ACS*, 5 October 1912; 'Beo-Phictiúirí' (Moving Pictures), *Éireannach* (London), May 1912, pp. 1–2; and 'Éire agus an Saoghal Eorpach' (Ireland and the European World), *Éireannach*, January 1912, p. 3.

2 Muiris Ó Droighneáin, *Taighde i gComhair Stair Litridheachta na Nua-Ghaedhilge ó 1882 Anuas* (Research for a History of Literature in Modern Irish since 1882) (Baile Átha Cliath: Oifig Díolta Foilseacháin Rialtais, 1936), p. 219.

3 He did not like Synge's play, writing decades later: 'I felt that there was something ugly and bitter about it. It was unnatural. I liked the first couple he wrote a good deal – I still hadn't seen *The Tinker's Wedding* or *The Well of the Saints* – but I could not make out what the devil was driving him to write this strange, unbelievable play' (*Bhraitheas go raibh rud éigin gránna searbhasach ag baint leis. Bhí sé mínádúrtha. Thaitin an cúpla ceann tosaigh a scríobh sé go mór liom – ní raibh* The Tinker's Wedding *nó* The Well of the Saints *feicthe agam fós – ach chuaigh sé díom a dhéanamh amach cad é an riach a bhí á phriocadh nuair a cheap sé an dráma aduain dochreidte seo*). See Ó Lochlainn, *Ealaín na hAmharclainne* (The Art of the Theatre) (Baile Átha Cliath: Clódhanna Teoranta, 1966), p. 40. On the other hand, he did defend Synge – in particular *In the Shadow of the Glen* – from the puritanical attacks of Máighréad Ní Annagáin (*Leader*, 8 November 1924). More will be said about his debate with Ní Annagáin later in this chapter.

4 Diarmuid Breathnach and Máire Ní Mhurchú, *1882–1982: Beathaisnéis a Trí* (Biography 3) (Baile Átha Cliath: An Clóchomhar, 1992), p. 116.

5 Ibid.

6 Ibid.

7 *Trí aithne a chur ar lucht nuachtán d'fhéadfhainn an fhírinne a chraobhscaoileadh faoi ghluaiseacht náisiúnta Shinn Féin, mar bhí páipéirí Shasana le seal anuas ag forleathadh tuairiscí bréagacha ina taobh ag iarraidh dallamullóg a chur ar mhuintir na gcoigríoch.*

8 For this biographical sketch I have drawn on Ó Droighneáin, op. cit., pp. 219–20 (Ó Droighneáin based his biographical accounts in this book on material provided by the writers themselves); Breathnach and Ní Mhurchú, *Beathaisnéis a Trí*, pp. 115–17;

and on the three sets of articles Ó Lochlainn published in *Comhar* and *Feasta* under the titles 'Aisteoir Fáin' (A Wandering Actor) (*Comhar*, March to August 1945); 'Ag Amharc Siar Dom' (As I Look Back) (*Feasta*, February to May 1962); and 'I dTír na nDanar Dom' (When I Was in the Land of the Danes) (*Feasta*, August 1968 to January 1969). In addition, Professor Pádraig Ó Siadhail generously allowed me to read his essay 'Gearóid Ó Lochlainn: The Gate theatre's other Irish-speaking founder', forthcoming in *The Gate Theatre: Cultural convergences*, ed. Pilney, Van den Beuken and Walsh.

9 He lectured on his experiences in the Danish theatre to An Comhar Drámaíochta in 1926 (*Leader*, 10 July 1926) and to Cumann na Scríbhneoirí in 1948 (*Indiu*, 1 October 1948).

10 See Carolyn Swift, *Stage by Stage* (Swords: Poolbeg, 1985), p. 266. See also the picture of Ó Lochlainn in his *Rose Tattoo* role as Father de Leo in the book's photo section. It is interesting to note that the Taibhdhearc performed Peadar Ó Cualáin's translation of this play without incident in February 1992. The script is in the Taibhdhearc papers at the National University of Ireland, Galway.

11 There is a picture of him in costume with Behan and the other cast members in Máiréad Ní Chinnéide, *An Damer: Stair amharclainne* (The Damer: History of a theatre) (Baile Átha Cliath: Gael Linn, 2008), p. 54.

12 *Thug sé gach gníomh agus gach geáitse leis chomh healadhanta is dá mba Scapin féin ó thús a shaoghail é. Ní bréag a rádh gur fada ó chonnacthas a leithéid d'aisteoireacht ar aon stáitse.*

13 There is a picture of him with other members of An Comhar in *II*, 15 November 1924.

14 *Ní raibh aonghnó ag an 'Mhainistir' den Chomhair, dar ndóigh, is den deontas a bhí dá fháil ag an gComhar a bhí gnó acu – ar mhaithe le drámaíocht na Gaeilge, ní gá a rá … Níl suim ag lucht éisteachta na Mainistreach i ndrámaíocht Ghaeilge, ní theastaíonn sí uathu agus is fánach mar ghnó é bheith ag cur drámaí Gaeilge ar an chlár i dteannta na ndrámaí Béarla ad iarraidh iad a bhrú orthu.* See also Ó Lochlainn, *Ealaín na hAmharclainne*, p. 67.

15 The only other shows in Irish that drew similar or even larger crowds were the Abbey's *geamaireachtaí*. For the *geamaireachtaí*, see O'Leary, *Writing Beyond the Revival*, pp. 339–48.

16 See 'Thoughts and Tidings / Theatre Club', *DP*, 20 November 1954.

17 In *Ealaín na hAmharclainne*, he wrote: 'In that period at the Gate, drama in Irish blossomed as it never had before or has since' (*Sa tréimhse sin sa Gate, bhláthaigh an drámaíocht Ghaeilge thar ma bhláthaigh sí riamh roimis ná ó shin*) (p. 37).

18 See Alan Simpson, *Beckett and Behan and a Theatre in Dublin* (London: Routledge & Kegan Paul, 1962).

19 See, for example, 'Gaelic Drama Course at Ros Goill', *DP*, 18 July 1953; 'In Gweedore', *DP*, 25 July 1953; and 'Closing Night of Derrybeg Drama Course', *DP*, 6 August 1955.

20 A columnist for the *Derry People* claimed in 1938 that among the plays the group had performed was 'one written specially by Gearóid Ó Lochlainn, the famous Gate actor' (*DP*, 7 May 1938). I have found no record of such a play written specially for Aisteoirí Ghaoth Dobhair.

21 See Proinnsias E. Ó Súilleabháin, *Láimh-leabhar Drámaidheachta* (Baile Átha Cliath: Brún & Ó Nualláin, n.d.), pp. 19–23. The booklet includes material from the 1938 Féile Drámaidheachta na Scol.

22 For example, he lectured to An Comhar Drámaíochta on 'Guthaidheacht Stáitse' (Stage Vocalisation) and 'Drámaí Lochlainn' (Scandinavian Plays) in 1926 (*Leader*, 3 and 10 July 1926); on 'The Development of Irish Drama' at the Glenfinn Aeridheacht in 1940 (*IP*, 9 August 1940); and on Danish theatre to Cumann na Scríbhneoirí in 1948 (*Indiu*, 1 October 1948).

23 See, for example, 'Seanscéalta Lochlannacha' (Scandinavian Folktales), *SF*, 30 July–1 October 1910; 'The Danish Theatre', *Banba*, November 1921, pp. 16–21; 'Ludwig Holberg', *Branar*, April 1925, pp. 77–85; 'Staid na hAmharclainne i nÉireann', in *Aistí Gaedhilge (Irish Essays for Examination)* (Baile Átha Cliath: M.H. Mac Ghoill & a Mhac, 1935), p. 50; 'Drámaíocht an Oireachtais/Léiritheoireacht Bhocht' (Drama at the Oireachtas/Poor Production), *Comhar*, November 1951, pp. 8 and 24; 'Drámaíocht na Danmhairge' (The Drama of Denmark), *Feasta*, October and November 1957; and 'An Drámathóir a Tharrthaigh Teanga: An Danar Ludwig Holberg' (The Dramatist who Saved a Language: The Dane Ludwig Holberg), *Feasta*, June 1960, p. 5.

24 For example, he directed the students of Dublin's Scoil Mhuire in the Olympia theatre in productions of *Cailín na Boihéime*, a Gaelic version of Balfe's *The Bohemian Girl*, and of Romberg and Donnelly's *An Prionnsa Mac-Léinn*, a Gaelic version of *The Student Prince*, the former in 1946 (*IP*, 4 March 1946), the latter the following year (IP, 27 January 1947).

25 See 'Theatre for Drama in Irish Is Planned', *IP*, 18 December 1954.

26 See 'Actors Want More State Interest in Stage Abroad', *IP*, 8–9 April 1955.

27 See, for example, 'Dublin Broadcasting Station – 2RN/Programme for Next Week', *IT*, 2 February 1928. He was a baritone. It should also be noted that he did not limit himself to Scandinavian songs. For example, he performed a programme of 'sea chanties [*sic*] with guitar' on 2RN in February 1926 (*CE*, 25 February 1926).

28 *Idir an dá linn má's féidir fuireann d'aisteoirí lán-aimsearacha do chur ar fágháil dosna drámaí Gaedhilge tré leigint dóibh bheith páirteach i ndrámaí Béarla chomh maith sin í an tslí is praiticeálta chun bun ceart do chur fé'n obair.*

29 *Nárbh'fearr amharclanna seasta lán-aimsearacha a d'fhéadfadh drámaí do léiriú ins an dá theangain na h-amharclanna agus an cheárdacht go léir bheith ar thaobh an Bhéarla agus an drámaidheacht Ghaedhilge ag seasamh ar iarrachtaí aisteoirí báidhe ná bíonn aon chaoi acu ar a gcuid oibre do thabhairt chun foirbhtheachta.* He was even willing to see plays in English at Taibhdhearc na Gaillimhe, which at that time would not rent the theatre to groups playing in English.

30 *Dá gcuireadh na foirne go léir sa tír le chéile, ní déarfainn ná go bhféadfaí plean éigin a cheapadh chun cúrsa a chur ar bun uair nó dhó i gcaitheamh na bliana le haghaidh léiritheoirí. Ba cheart go gcabhródh a leithéid go mór chun caighdeán na hoibre d'ardú.* Reviewing the published text of Walter Macken's comedy *An Fear ón Spidéal* (The Man from Spiddal) in 1952, Ó Lochlainn wrote: 'Another thing, he has put down every direction with regard to the action so that it can be said that the full directorial plan is available in the book, something that will help whatever groups will undertake to put it on stage' (*Rud eile, tá gach treoir maidir leis an ngníomhaíocht curtha síos aige*

ionas gur féidir a rá go bhfuil plean iomlán na léiritheoireachta ar fáil sa leabhar, rud a chabhróidh go mór le pé foirne drámaíochta a thabharfaidh féna chur ar an stáitse) (*Feasta*, July 1952, p. 20).

31 *Is é bun agus bárr an scéil ná sroisfear an caighdeán san [.i. an caighdeán árd a bhí d'aidhm againn nuair a bunuigheadh an Comhar] go dtí go mbeidh buan-amharclann Ghaedhilge ann ina mbeidh fuireann d'aisteoirí oilte gan gnó ar bith eile acu ach an aisteoireacht.*

32 *Amharclann Ghaeilge i bpríomh-chathair na tire. B'in é príomhsprioc an Chomhair Drámaíochta. Deallraíonn sé anois go bhfuilimid níos faide uaithi ná riamh, agus muna ndéantar beart taobh istigh de bheagán blian eile is baolach go mbeidh sé ró-dhéanach.* See his more optimistic view from 1945 in 'An Amharclann agus an Ghaedhilg', *Éire*, 1945, p. 82.

33 *Is mairg an té a bhíonn chó lag-mhuinghíneach as féin nach fuláir leis fanamhaint i n-aineolas ar smaointe agus thuairimí a chó-dhaonnaithe ar eagla go raghaidís go ró-láidir i bhfeidhm air. Is éigcéillí an rud é, leis, gan suim a chur i gclisteacht do chomharsan agus rud d'fhoghluim uaidh, má's féidir.*

34 *Admháil isea é sin go bhfuil spéis éigin againn i saothar inntleachtach agus i gclisteacht ealadhannach ár gcó-náisiún – rud a raghadh i dtairbhe dhúinn, b'fhéidir.*

35 *Agus go dtí go mbéidh go leor bundrámaí dá scríobhadh i nGaedhilg ní misde dhúinn aistriúcháin ar dhrámaí foghanta a léiriú.*

36 This translation was fairly popular, being revived by An Comhar in the Abbey the following year. One critic who was considerably less than impressed was Frank O'Connor, who wrote of *Heirciléas* and another one of An Comhar's plays: 'I will do anything to prevent the performance of *An t-Athrú Mór* or *Heirciléas*, short of blowing up the theatre in which they are performed' (*IS*, 12 December 1925). The play was published by An Comhar in 1926.

37 In 2009 Galway's Moonfish Theatre Company joined with An Taibhdhearc to produce Ó Lochlainn's translation in Galway and Dublin. The text was published by An Gúm in 1947.

38 *An Craipí Óg: Ceol dráma gearr*, trans. Muiris Ó Catháin, and arranged as a musical play by Gearóid Ó Lochlainn (Baile Átha Cliath: n.p., n.d.). This four-page pamphlet has only two pages of text. Ó Lochlainn also revised An tAthair Tomás Ó Ceallaigh's 1908 play *An Foghmhar* (The Harvest) for production by An Comhar Drámaíochta in 1932. The critic for *The Irish Times* wrote of this work: 'For last night's production Gearóid Ó Lochlainn had altered his [Ó Ceallaigh's] rather simple pioneer drama, and the alterations had improved it considerably' (*IT*, 13 December 1932).

39 *Agus ní dócha go bhfuil éinne againn gur mian leis an púicín tragóideach, an púicín tromsmaointeach, ar an drámaíocht i gcónaí, is maith linn an geann eile, aghaidh-fidil an ghrinn, anois agus arís.*

40 *Níor ghabhas le haisteoireacht chun a fhoghluim conus drámaí do scríobhadh, do ghabhas léi toisc gurbh é ba mhian liom agus ba dhual dom. Níor chuireas romham riamh bheith im' dhrámathóir, ach taréis roinnt bhlian tháinig fonn orm dráma do scríobh agus dheineas é. D'éirigh go maith leis, agus scríobhas ceann eile ó am go ham ina dhiaidh sin … Ní raibh de bhaoth-thuairim im cheann gur sár-dhrámaí a bhí á gceapadh agam, mar chun sár-dhráma do scríobhadh teastaíonn buanna aigne ná bíonn ag coitiantacht na ndrámathóirí.* On the other hand, writing in 1951, Tomás Mac Anna, who was in

charge of plays in Irish at the Abbey, could praise Ó Lochlainn as a playwright in Irish 'because he knows his craft; he is a man of the stage, a craftsman' (*toisc go raibh eolas a cheirde aige; is fear stáitse é, is ceardaí é*). Moreover, Ó Lochlainn himself specifically mentioned that it was only after learning to act and spending time in the theatre that he tried his hand at playwrighting. In other words, he had been 'willing to spend the exhausting years learning the dramatic craft' (*sásta na blianta tuirsiúla a chaitheamh ag foghlaim céirde na drámaíochta*) (*Comhar*, February 1951, p. 4).

41 Indeed, this was at least in some sense true of all of the playwrights discussed in this book.

42 If this is, as it must be, the play by 'An Lochlannach' submitted in the Oireachtas competitions in 1922, it actually received a positive response from one of the judges, the other disliking it and claiming it showed the influence of the cinema (*FL*, 4 February 1922).

43 *Ní fheadar an amhlaidh go raibh an iomarca de'n 'Mhúineadh' ann, agus d'anáil an Abbey uaidh, acht, ar aon chuma, níor thaithnigh sé liom.*

44 Gearóid Ó Lochlainn, *Bean an Mhilliúnaí: Dráma i n-éan gníomh amháin* (Baile Átha Cliath: Clódhanna Gaedhealacha, 1923), p. 23. *Coga is ea an gnó … agus isiad gliocas agus airgead na h-airm troda a mbaintear úsáid asta sa gcoga san. An té ná tuigeann i gceart conus feidhm a bhaint as an dá ghleus san, buailtear ar lár é gan trua gan trócaire. An duine do leigfeadh don charthannacht nó don trua é chur óna ghnó a chur chun cinn, bhéadh sé chó maith aige cur suas don chluiche ar fad!*

45 Ibid., p. 27. *Nuair adubhairt an fear so liom ó chianaibh gurbh' fhear gan croí gan coinsias thú, gurbh' fhear neamh-scrupallach, sanntach thú, níor chreideas é, ach – Och, is baol liom ná raibh eolas ceart agam riamh ort go dtí anocht.*

46 Ibid. *Dar ndóigh, ní'l éan rud le maitheamh duit agam, a chailín ó! Eadrainn féin, an dtuigeann tú, ní deurfainn ná go raibh cuid mhaith den cheart agat!*

47 He did like Ó Lochlainn's acting in the play. *Maidir le 'Cótaí Móra', bhí coinne agam le h-iarracht níos fearr ó-n ughdar. Tá sé ró-ghairid agus ró-chaol ar fad. Má b'fhiú le Gearóid Ó Lochlainn é sgrí, níor bhfhiú dhó é chur ar árdán. Truagh gur dhein.*

48 *Ní fheadar féin cadé tuairim an Chomhair ar dhrámaí beaga mar é seo, ach im thuairim féin ba cheart níos mó measa bheith aca ar Ghaedhil na cathrach so go bhfuil seans aca drámaí d'fheiscint i mBéarla. Tar éis an tsaoghail daoine iseadh iad a thuigeann cad is ann do dhráma agus cad is ann do ghreann freisin.* 'Teachtaire' called the play 'an unfinished effort' (*iarracht nár críochnuíodh*), but wrote of Ó Lochlainn's performance: 'One would think when listening to Gearóid that this clever actor spent his life in the Gaeltacht' (*Ba dhóigh le duine is é ag éisteacht le Gearóid gur sa Ghaedhealtacht a chaith an t-aisteoir cliste seo a shaoghal*).

49 *Ní miste a rádh gur bhain an lucht éisteachta taithneamh a gcroidhe as an gcluiche … Rud nua sa Ghaedhilg dráma lorgaireachta agus ní mhiste a ghaisce a thraoslú le Gearóid Ó Lochlainn.*

50 *Molaim é do gach Gaedheal, do mhúinteoirí agus do mhacaibh léighinn, óg nó sean.*

51 Gearóid Ó Lochlainn, *Na Gaduithe: Dráma grinn i dtrí gníomha* (Baile Átha Cliath: Oifig Díolta Foillseacháin Rialtais, 1935), p. 8.

52 Ibid., p. 101. *Caith uait na gunnáin sin, adeirim, agus tóg do dhá láimh! Beidh tú agam beo nó marbh! Déanfad cóimhreamh go dtí n-a 'trí' agus ar an trí tollfad le piléaraibh thú! A haon! A dó –*

53 Ibid., p. 12. *Ja, Ja; Deutschland über alles – nicht wahr? Ach ní gábha dhuit Gearmáinis liom-sa do labhairt. Tá an Ghaedhilg maith* [*sic*] *agam-sa – das heizst, ziemlich – cuibhseach maith? Verstehen sie?*

54 Ibid., p. 99. See also pp. 40–3.

55 Gearóid Ó Lochlainn, *Ealaín na hAmharclainne*, p. 53. *Sa dráma seo thug O'Casey pictiúr fírinneach réalaíoch de shaol agus de smaointe na ndaoine comónta, áithritheoirí na dtionóntán, lena linn sin. Thuig sé go bun iad, agus bhí a bhá riamh leo.*

56 His brother did, however, see action during Easter week in precisely the neighbourhood in which the play is set. See Ó Lochlainn, *Ealaín na hAmharclainne*, p. 50.

57 'Sinéad' did add that the play needed a bigger stage to be fully effective. See also the positive comments on the play from the anonymous reviewer in *Ar Aghaidh* (probably by An tAthair P. Eric Mac Fhinn), *AA*, May 1937, pp. 4–5; and 'Plays and Films', *DO*, May 1937, p. 96.

58 Gearóid Ó Lochlainn, *An t-Éirighe Amach: Dráma éin-ghnímh* (Baile Átha Cliath: Oifig an tSoláthair, 1944), p. 14. *Go bhfóire Dia ar na buachaillí bochta san. Agus go maithidh Dia é do sna daoine thiomáin isteach 'sa chogadh so iad – ar a nglúnaibh ba chóir dóibh a bheith anocht ag iarraidh párdúin Air i dtaobh an droch-ghnímh atá déanta acu agus an t-éirleach is an scilimis seo a tharrac anuas 'sa mhullach orainn.*

59 Ibid., p. 10. *Agus mura n-éirighidh féin ní cúis bhróin ná náire d'Éirinn é, ach a mhalairt ar fad … Sean-fhear iseadh mé anois … ach ina dhiaidh sin féin is thíos ar an dtaobh thall den tsráid ba cheart dom a bheith imeasc na mbuachaillí breághtha dílse sin agus mo ghunna im' láimh agam chómh maith le cách.*

60 Ibid., p. 17. *Tá áthas ar mo chroidhe go bhfuil mac liom imeasc na bhfear dílse cródha san a raibh sé de mhisneach ionnta dubhshlán na nGall a thabhairt d'aindeoin na bhfealltóirí is na meatachán a dhíolfadh Éire le n-a náimhde.*

61 Ibid., p. 27. *An mar sin é? Tusa an chéad duine dár sliocht a theip nuair a tháinig an t-am agus an chaoi chun buille a bhualadh ar son na tire mí-ádhmharaighe seo.*

62 Ibid., pp. 27–8. *Marbhuigheadh beirt taobh liom … Fuair duine acu cúpla piléar tríd an scórnaigh. Thuit sé agus é 'á thachtadh leis an bhfuil. Bhí sé ag ionnfairt ar an urlár mar a bhéadh ainmhidhe ann agus an fhuil ag brúchtghail as, ar feadh deich neomant sar a bhfuair sé bás.*

63 Ibid., p. 34. *Sílim go bhfuair Pádraig bocht an bás do b'fheárr leis féin. Solas na bhFlaitheas dá anam, agus d'anam gach fir dílis dá short …*

64 *Tá scéal an dráma curtha le chéile go h-ealanta* [*sic*] *agus b'éifeachtach an léiriú agus an chainnt a chonnacthas agus a chualathas.*

65 Of course, Ó Lochlainn was original in his willingness to engage with painful and controversial issues from the more recent past in this play.

66 *I gceapadh na bpearsan bhí sé ró-thógtha le nochtadh tuairimí d'fhonn an tréimhse a mhíniú chun bacaint mórán le foillsiú buintréithíochta. D'fhág san gur mó atá an phearsanrádh samhaltasach ná bunadhsach.* Reviewing the text of the play published by An Gúm in 1946, the critic for *Indiu* commented that there was 'a great deal going on in it – some of it fairly melodramatic' (*neart gluaiseachta ann – cuid di … measartha melodramatic* [*sic*]), but that those in charge of the upcoming Oireachtas would be well advised to remember that most Gaels would prefer to see again an original play like this than a revival of one of the usual translations (*Indiu*, 1 November 1946).

67 Gearóid Ó Lochlainn, *Na Fearachoin ('Fearachoin Groidhe ná Claoidhfeadh Céadta'): Dráma trí gníomh* (Baile Átha Cliath: Oifig an tSoláthair, 1946), p. 22. *'Seadh, an dtuigeann tú, a Mhéidhsir, tá difríocht bheag 'sa chás so. Ní Gearmánaigh iad na Sinn Féinnithe ach Éireannaigh – agus is Éireannaigh sinn-ne, leis, bíodh ná fuilimíd ar aon aigne leo maidir le leas na tíre seo.*

68 Ibid.

69 Ibid., p. 23. *Is fearr dúinn-ne bheith neodrach 'sa chogadh so.*

70 Ibid., p. 14. *Á, dá leanadh muinntir na hÉireann Seán Réamonn bocht bhéadh a mhalairt de scéal ann.*

71 Ibid., p. 29. *Sibh-se, Gall-Ghaedhil, ar a shon go bhfuil sibh préamhuithe i nÉirinn lesna céadta blian níl tuiscint dá laghad agaibh don tír i n-a gcomhnuigheann sibh. Tá sibh fós mar a bhéadh treabh iasachta i n-ár measc agus lagmheas agaibh ar gach rud Gaedhealach … Ina dhiaidh sin a's uile ní Sasanaigh sibh ach Éireannaigh.*

72 Ó Siochfhradha's play was first produced under the title *Dia 'Á Réidhteach* (God Settling It) by An Comhar Drámaíochta at the Gate, with Micheál Mac Liammóir directing.

73 He has also come to accept the IRA as worthy military opponents rather than outlaws or terrorists. See Ó Lochlainn, *Na Fearachoin*, pp. 86–9.

74 Ibid., p. 30. *Ní fios dúinn deireadh an scéil ag an gcine daonna. B'fhéidir gur ag útamáil romhainn mar chréatúirí bochta baotha dalla a bhéimíd go deo. Ach an lá ná béidh fir ann a sheasóchaidh agus a dhéanfaidh troid i gcoinne an uilc agus na h-éagcóra tá an cine daonna damnuithe go bráth.*

75 There is a picture of Ó Lochlainn in character in *Ealaín na hAmharclainne* between pages 28 and 29.

76 *Ní heol dúinn gur léiriodh ceachtar de na drámaí ar aon ardán riamh.* He was correct about Ó hAodha's play, which was, however, broadcast over Radio Éireann twice in 1953 (*DP*, 17 January 1953; *IP*, 4 November 1953) and once in 1966 (*IP*, 24 March 1966). *An Réalt* (The Star), a one-act version of Ó hAodha's play, won a prize at the 1939 Oireachtas, but also does not seem to have been produced.

77 *Dráma éifeachtach é, ach dráma atá ann nach dtiocfadh ach le h-aisteoirí oilte a cheart a thabhairt dó. Ní fhuil mórán ar bith gluaiseacht ann, agus bhéadh ar na h-aisteoirí iomlán bhrígh an dráma a bhaint amach le n-a gcuid guth – rud nach dtiocfadh le h-aisteoirí báighe a dhéanamh.*

78 *Cogadh de shaghas eile atá sa dara dráma – cogadh idir an fear a chuaigh chun cinn sa saol agus a choinsias, a óige nó an Doppel-Ganger* [*sic*]. *Bíodh a bhreithiúnas féin ag gach éinne. Is éifeachtach mar léiríonn an t-údar teannas thar meán an dráma seo trí choigilt focal agus abairt. Tá sé lom rite mar oireann dá chineál.*

79 Gearóid Ó Lochlainn, *Ag an Ladhrán: Dráma éin ghnímh* (Baile Átha Cliath: Oifig an tSoláthair, 1946), p. 7. *Ag teacht a's ag imtheacht a bhíonn siad. Gach duine agus a scéal féin leis. Gach duine agus a rúin féin ina chroidhe … Agus 'bhfuil fhios agat rud eile a ritheann isteach im' aigne? Cuid acu, 'sí an traein deiridh dóibh í – dá mbéadh fhios acu é.*

80 Ibid., p. 11. *D'imrigheas an cluiche do réir na riaghalacha. Gach duine ar a shon féin.*

81 Ibid., p. 17. *Éist liom, a Philib. Táimíd ag an ladhrán, ag an áit 'na scarann na bealaighe taistil ó chéile. Leig dom an turas so a dhéanamh i n-éinfheacht leat. Dá mb'é an turas deiridh é.*

82 Ibid., p. 21. *An turas deiridh! Mo thruagh thú ... Mo thruagh go deo thú!*

83 Ibid., p. 22. *Do b'ait an chuma a bhí ar an duine uasal san. Mar a's go mbéadh rud éigin ag goilleamhaint air.*

84 *B'fhiú do léirightheóir cliste a bhfuil dhá aisteóirí maithe san bhuidhin aige, triall a bhaint as.* Actually, such a director would need three good actors.

85 In their entry for Ó Lochlainn in *Beathaisnéis a Trí*, Breathnach and Ní Mhurchú attribute to him a play entitled *Éamonn an Chnuic* (Éamonn of the Hill) (p. 117). I have found no record of this play, but Pádraig Ó Siadhail suggests it may be an Irish-language version of his English-language play *The Rapparee*.

86 While acting in Copenhagen, Ó Lochlainn had appeared in a movie dealing with a group of young painters (*Comhar*, April 1945, p. 3).

87 Gearóid Ó Lochlainn, *An Balbhán Bréige* (Baile Átha Cliath: Oifig an tSoláthair, 1954), pp. 22–3. The joking reference here is, of course, to the prices charged for goods on the Irish black market during the war.

88 Ibid., p. 28. *De réir na bhfuaimeanna tá's agat. Tá fuaimeanna an-dheacra sa chanúint sin leis. Agus chun an scéal a dhéanamh níos measa déanann siad na comharthaí sa litriú nua.*

89 Actually, despite their superficial sophistication the friends turn out to be pretty conventional and down-to-earth people.

90 *An duine a rachadh go dtí Féile Drámaíochta an Oireachtais agus súil aige le h-ard-chaighdeán – ní áirmhím caighdeán na gairmiúlachta, ach abraimís an caighdeán is airde a sroistear i ndrámaíocht amaitéarach sa Bhéarla – cuirfí díomá air ... Go cinnte, bhí furmhór na hoibre lochtach, agus cuid di analochtach, ach má bhí, taispeánadh anso agus ansúd tuiscint agus clisteacht go leor chun an faobhar a bhaint de dhíomá na coda eile.*

91 Ó Lochlainn, *Ealaín na hAmharclainne*, p. 47.

CHAPTER 3. Accidental Playwright: Leon Ó Broin (1902–90)

1 Leon Ó Broin, *Just Like Yesterday*, p. 144. The other two plays he mentions – not by name – are 'an adaptation of a French farce' (*Labhartar Béarla Anseo*) and 'a nativity play' (*An Oíche úd i mBeithil*).

2 His obituary in *The Irish Times* also makes little reference to his work for the theatre, stating simply that he 'wrote a number of plays in Irish' (*IT*, 27 February 1990).

3 Ó Broin, *Just Like Yesterday*, pp. 22–3.

4 Máire Ní Mhurchú and Diarmuid Breathnach, *1983–2002: Beathaisnéis* (Baile Átha Cliath: An Clóchomhar, 2003), p. 95.

5 Ó Broin, *Just Like Yesterday*, p. 50.

6 Ibid., p. 137.

7 Quoted in Ní Mhurchú and Breathnach, op. cit., p. 98.

8 Ó Broin, *Just Like Yesterday*, p. 175. See also Ray Cleere, 'Ringing in a Holy Year with "Live" Angelus', *SI*, 1 August 2010 and 'Craig Royal Academy Member', *II*, 18 March 1971.

9 Ó Broin, quoted by Robert J. Savage in *Irish Television: The political and social origins* (Cork: Cork University Press, 1996), p. 196. Savage provides an excellent account of Ó Broin's role in bringing television to Ireland. See also John Horgan, *Irish Media: A critical history since 1922* (London: Routledge, 2001).

10 Ó Broin, quoted by Savage, op. cit., *Irish Television*, p. 98.

11 Ó Broin, *Just Like Yesterday*, pp. 209–10. See also Ó Broin, 'Teacht na Teilifíse' (The Coming of Television), *IT*, 14 August 1986.
12 See 'Beul-Oideas Náisiúnta (National Folk-Lore)/New Society Formed', *MC*, 5 February 1927; and 'Members Appointed by Government', *CE*, 9 March 1935.
13 See 'Day to Day/Club Leabhar Annual Dinner', *IP*, 21 November 1951; 'Irish Books Club Is Going Ahead', *IP*, 28 October 1954; and 'Welcome Revival of Cumann na Scríbhneoirí/Gaelic Book Club', *II*, 6 November 1963.
14 Ní Mhurchú and Breathnach, op. cit., p. 98.
15 See Ó Broin, *Just Like Yesterday*, pp. 128–30, 147–56. For a dissenting view on his religious activism, see 'Converting Jews', Letter, *SI*, 17 July 1911.
16 Ó Broin felt that someone should write 'something sound' (*rud fónta éigin*) about Ó Rinn (*IP*, 27 June 1978).
17 Ó Broin, *Just Like Yesterday*, p. 20.
18 Ibid., p. 25.
19 Ibid.
20 Ibid.
21 Ibid., p. 57.
22 See 'Seán Sabháiste', *Cois Life* (By the Liffey) (Baile Átha Cliath: Oifig Díolta Foillseacháin Rialtais, 1936).
23 Muiris Ó Droighneáin, *Taighde*, p. 107. *Baineann furmhór mo shaothair liteardha le saoghal Bhaile Átha Cliath ... Tuige nach mbainfeadh? Tuigim muinntir na cathrach agus ní thuigim muinntir na Gaeltachta acht an oiread agus a thuigeann lucht na Galldachta iad. Creidim, ámh, go bhfuil sgéal le hinnsint ag an gcathair don tuaith agus ní misde Gaedhilg úsáid chun a innste.*
24 Aisling Ni Dhonnchadha, *An Gearrscéal sa Ghaeilge 1898–1940* (The Short Story in Irish 1898–1940) (Baile Átha Cliath: An Clóchomhar, 1981), pp. 265–6. *Ilghnéitheacht an ábhair, úire na cumadóireachta, tagracht na tráchtaireachta – táid seo ar roinnt de phríomhthréithe shaothair Uí Bhroin. D'fhóin a chur amach agus a chleachtadh ar chúrsaí drámaíochta dá cheárdaíocht sna gearrscéalta. Thuig sé teorainneacha a chumais féin i réimse na gearrscéalaíochta ionas nár thug sé faoi mhórlitríocht dhomhain fhuaimintiúil a chur de riamh. Agus an méid sin ráite, is cinnte gurb ábhar misnigh agus spreagadh croíúil é a shaothar.*
25 Ó Broin, *Just Like Yesterday*, p. 67. See also Piaras Béaslaí, 'Moods and Memories / The Dictionary that Was Never Published', *II*, 30 September 1964.
26 *Cúis áthais agus adhbhar misnigh 'seadh é a leithéid seo de leabhar Gaedhilge a bheith ar fáil. Tá taighde agus staidéar déanta ag an údar i dtreo is gur fearr atá fios fátha an scéil aige ná mar bhí ag aoinne dár chuir síos ar bheatha Pharnell as Béarla agus tá a rian san ar a shaothar ó thús deire.* For Blythe, *Parnell* was 'a big, important book ... an accurate, fair and objective book that will help to dissipate confusion and misunderstanding' (*leabhar mór táchtach ... leabhar cruinn féaráilte réidh-chúiseach a chabhróchaidh le scaipeadh do chur ar mhearbhall agus ar mhí-thuiscint*) (*II*, 8 June 1937). Ó Broin discusses the book's reception in *Just Like Yesterday*, p. 111.
27 Ó Broin, ibid., p. 113.
28 See also 'Captain Mac', 'History Helps Us Know Ourselves', *IP*, 26 August 1964. 'Captain Mac' had a regular column for young readers in *IP*.

29 The anonymous reviewer for *The Connacht Tribune* wrote: 'Leon Ó Broin has succeeded in piercing the romantic haze that has always surrounded the great patriot and presenting us with Emmet the man – with his faults and virtues' (*CT*, 4 June 1955).
30 His interest had been piqued when he learned that he was living in the house in Booterstown in which Madden had died in 1886. See Leon Ó Broin, *An Maidíneach: Staraí na nÉireannach Aontaithe* (Madden: The Historian of the United Irishmen) (Baile Átha Cliath: Sáirséal & Dill, 1971), p. 9. Madden was also, of course, a vigorous opponent of slavery.
31 Ó Broin, *Just Like Yesterday*, p. 113.
32 He relates a comic incident that occurred while he was on stage in Furbo, County Galway, in *Just Like Yesterday*, pp. 74–5.
33 Pádraig Ó Siadhail, *Stair Dhrámaíocht na Gaeilge*, p. 58.
34 Ó Broin, *Just Like Yesterday*, p. 70.
35 Quoted in Ó Siadhail, op. cit., pp. 91–2. He moved '*gur mheas sé go mba chóir, nuair a bheadh an foirgneamh nua ar fáil, go gcuirfí deireadh leis an Comhar* [sic] *Drámaíochta agus go gcuirfí oibliogáid dleathach ar an Mainistir freastal ar dhrámaíocht na Gaeilge*'.
36 Ó Siadhail, op. cit., p. 93. Mac Anna told me this same story in conversation in the mid-1990s.
37 Speaking about the 1938 Feis Átha Cliath, Ó Broin and his fellow adjudicator were reported as having said that they 'thought it a pity that some of the groups had not chosen plays more in keeping with their capabilities as actors' (*IP*, 28 March 1938).
38 In the end he did not award either a first or a second prize, feeling the best entrant in the competition deserved no better than third place.
39 He did have reservations about the actors' Irish.
40 Ó Broin, *Just Like Yesterday*, pp. 94–5.
41 Examples he cites include Ibsen and Pirandello.
42 *Céard 'tá i ndán do dhrámuíocht na Gaedhilge? Fás! Fásfaidh sí, chomh cinnte agus fásann an leanbh, agus ní gádh chuig an bhfás ach duine nó beirt nó mion-dosgán daoine. Is maith an sgéalaí an aimsir.*
43 *An stráinnséara nach mbéadh aon aithne aige orainn, dá léigheadh sé furmhór na sgéalta do scríobhadh i dtaoibh na h-Éireann le n-a seacht nó a h-ocht de bhlianta, dá dtéigheadh sé ag breathnú ar chuid mhór de na drámaí a léirigheadh i gcaitheamh an achair sin, céard adéarfadh sé fúinn?*
44 *Tá rian na tréithe sin go láidir ar dhrámaí na Mainistreach agus ar dhrámaí na Gaedhilge … Is é dualgas ár scríobhnóirí an nádúr d'aithint; gur i nÉirinn agus i ngach aon tír eile, níl sa nádúr ach an gáire is an gol dá gcoimheasgadh.*
45 See O'Leary, *Gaelic Prose*, pp. 462–3; and *Writing Beyond the Revival*, pp. 303–7.
46 In *The Capuchin Annual* for 1935, Ó Broin was much more positive about An Gúm than were many, perhaps most, writers of Irish. See especially pp. 128–9. Nowhere is his attitude towards the linguistic potential of translation more evident than in his praise of the translation staff of Dáil Éireann, of whom he wrote in *Just Like Yesterday*: 'I saw at close quarters the work of the translation staff and frequently turned to them for guidance in the matter of terminology' (p. 90).
47 In *Just Like Yesterday*, he tells of how he translated stories by Alphonse Daudet from French to Irish while briefly imprisoned in Dublin after the 1916 rising (p. 35).

48 *Ní féidir an rud seo do rádh ró-mhinic: drámaí, drámaí agus tuille drámaí an rosg catha is fearr agus is feileamhnaighe don dine* [sic] *atá suas faoi láthair. Drámaí, idir aistriúcháin agus bun-drámaí, a theastuigheas.*

49 *Chomhairleóchainn dóibh, áfach, gan bun-dráma do chur le chéile go dtí go mbeidh roinnt mhaith drámaí iasachta aistrithe aca nó léighte go cúramach is go staidéartha aca.*

50 *Rachaidh an ghluaiseacht nua drámaíochta chun cinn i bhfad níos mire má bhíonn gasra líonmhar de dhrámathóirí oilte a' cabhrú linn. Ní fiú tadaí é daoine gan aon eolas aca ar riaghalacha an árdáin ná ar phrionsapail ceapadóireachta is comhráidh a bheith a' sgríobhadh drámaí.*

51 *Nil in aistriúchán, d'á fheabhas, ach scéal scéil ... Is fearr d'iarracht féin d'á dhonacht, ná aithris a dhéanamh ar shaothar an duine thall d'á fheabhas dá mbeadh sé.* He was open to translation as a means for Gaelic playwrights to learn their craft.

52 He continued: 'If at the commencement of the race we worry ourselves with questions of language limitation then we might as well get out and not disgrace the track with our fifth-rate performances.'

53 He had actually had four original plays produced by 1930.

54 Nor does his unproduced and unpublished play in English 'James Carey Has a Visitor', the manuscript of which is in the National Library of Ireland. The NLI catalogue gives the date as 195? (*sic*).

55 'D. Ó D.' also noted that the prompter was kept busy during the production.

56 Leon Ó Broin, *Rogha an Dá Dhíogh: Dráma trí mír*, in Ó Broin, *An Mhallacht agus Trí Drámaí Eile* (Baile Átha Cliath: Oifig Díolta Foillseacháin Rialtais, 1931), p. 69. *B'é Cathal de Fréinne ... a rug slán ó na Dubhchrónaigh sinn. B'é siúd an duine a leag an plíoma mór gránna úd a bhí ag iarraidh mé a phógadh ... Níorbh ionann é is an chuid eile aca. Bhí féith na huaisleachta ann ar chaoi éigin.*

57 Ibid., p. 78. *Chuas ins na Dubhchrónaigh, an dtuigeann sibh, ní le grádh do Shasana nó le teann fuatha d'Éirinn, ach go mb'éigean dom é dhéanamh ar mhaithe leis na hÓglaigh.*

58 The fatuous poet seems to simply disappear about halfway through the play.

59 *Is i Warsaw i dtír na Pólainne a fuair an t-údar an t-ionad, agus dar leis do bhain an scéal le h-éirghe-amach an Taoisigh Pylowski sa bhliain 1925.*

60 Micheál Breathnach, *Cuimhne an tSeanpháiste* (The Old Child's Memories) (Baile Átha Cliath: Oifig an tSoláthair, 1966), p. 216. *Níl ar intinn agam cur síos a dhéanamh ar an dochar a rinne an Cogadh Cathartha ná ar na drochiarsmaí a d'fhág sé ina dhiaidh. B'fhearr liom brat mór dubh a ligean anuas ar an tréimhse sin agus é a chur as mo chuimhne ar fad dá bhféadfainn é.*

61 Ó Broin, *Just Like Yesterday*, p. 49.

62 See Frank O'Connor, 'Guests of the Nation', in O'Connor, *Guests of the Nation* (New York: Macmillan, 1931), pp. 1–19; Ernie O'Malley, *On Another Man's Wound* (Dublin: Anvil, 1979), pp. 333–8. See also Micheál Breathnach's one-act play *Deire an Chunntais* (The End of the Account), which was first produced by An Comhar Drámaíochta in 1931 at the Gate with the title *Dia 'á Réidhteach* (God Settling It). Micheál Mac Liammóir was the director.

63 Ó Broin, *An Mhallacht*, p. 7. *Do chaith Séamus a phost breágh uaidh chun imtheachta leis in Arm an tSaorstáit – ag troid má's é do thoil é.*

64 Ibid., p. 10. *Aréir agus sinn annseo ag trácht ar an aighneas seo eadrainn féin, idir lucht cosanta an tSaorstáit agus na Poblachtóirí mheasas go bhfaca an tseansgáil úd ar a cheannaighteacha – an sgáil úd do bhíodh air aimsir na teangmhála faoi mar do bhéadh misneach a aigne ag iarraidh buachtaint ar laige a chuirp ... Troid na gcarad ní bhíonn sí buan.*

65 Ibid., p. 11. *An sean-ghrádh teasmhar do bhí agam d'Éirinn, d'imthigh sé ar fad amach as mo chroidhe. Ní raibh feasta agam ach grádh buan-tseasamach do Cholm. An sean-dúthchas sin atá ins na mnáibh go léir dubhairt sé liom go raibh Éire ag iarraidh na cosa do ghearradh fúm amhail do ghníodh an Chailleach Bhéara leis na spealadóirí – má's fíor do na sean-daoine – ag baint na sál díom in aghaidh mo tholach.*

66 Ibid., p. 12. *Tuige an bhfuil Éire chomh craosach sin, chomh mí-fhoighneach sin go gcaithfidh sí plúr na bhfear d'alpadh, nach féidir léi an ghlún seo do leigean thairsti.*

67 Ibid., pp. 14–5. *Is amhlaidh do bhíomar ag gáirí agus ag maoidheamh as a ndearnadh de dhíoghbháil don arm Gallda ... Dhearmadamar go raibh mná na beirte sin ann, go raibh máithreacha agus clann aca a' déanamh truaighe dhóibh agus ag tabhairt a míle mallacht ag an dream d'fhuadaigh uatha go deo iad. Tá an mhallacht san fós orainn. Mallacht fola na bhfear agus mallacht caointe na mban.*

68 Ibid., p. 17.

69 The other plays on the bill were *Cliamhain Isteach* (A Man Married into the Farm) by Diarmuid Ó Súilleabháin ('Diarmuid Ó Duibhne') and *An Casán* (The Path) by Séamus de Bhilmot.

70 Ó Broin, *Rogha an Dá Dhíogh*, in *An Mhallacht*, pp. 28–9. *Taobh istigh de cheathramha uaire chluig bhíomar amuigh ar an staighre sa doircheacht ag suirghe le n-a chéile – ní h-eol dom anois cé againn ba mheasa. Faoi cheann na leath-uaire bhíos tar éis í phógadh thar cuimse.*

71 *Léirigheadh an dá dráma so ag an gComhar roinnt bhlian ó shoin ach tá a lán Gaedhilgeóirí sa chathair ná faca riamh iad agus na daoine a chonnaic bhaineadar an oiread san suilt asta an uair sin gur cinnte go dtiocfaidh siad airís.*

72 *Bhí na daoine a chonnaic iad aréir lán tsásta leo.* See also 'M. MacD.', 'Drámaí Grinn' (Comic Plays), *IP*, 20 November 1934.

73 *Tá tuigbheál mhaith ag an ughdar do'n drámaidheacht. Is cliste mar bhain sé úsáid as an ghuthán i n-áit muid a thuirsiughdh le 'soliloquy' fhada. Tá a cheard 'suas chun dáta' aige ins an mhéid sin. Is mór an truagh gan fairsingeacht drámaí de'n chineál seo againn i nGaedhilg mhaith.* He published the same review in the *Dundalk Examiner*, 5 December 1936.

74 It was produced by students from the Trim Technical School at the County Meath Drama Festival in 1959 (*MC*, 28 February 1959). In a 1970 letter to *The Irish Press*, S. Ua hÉigeartaigh of Cobh, County Cork, suggested that *An Clósgríobhaí* would make a good television play (*IP*, 17 October 1970).

75 Ó Broin, *An Sgríbhinn ar an mBalla*, in *An Mhallacht*, p. 93. *Níl ann ach slíomodóir. Tá súil aige leat-sa i gcleamhnas, dar liom, ach ní ar do shon féin a phósfadh sé thú dá mbeitheá toilteannach cleamhans do dhéanamh leis, ach ar son an tighe tábhairne.*

76 Ibid., p. 94. *Seachain é, a mháistreás, mar i gcomórtas leis an bhfear a bhí agat is é an diabhal buidhe é.*

77 Ibid., p. 104. *Admhuighim go bhfuil sé an-dian ort ach ba chóir go mbeadh a fhios agat nach raibh aon tseans agat nuair a bhí Seán Mac Maolagáin, Comhairleoir Conndae, dá hiarraidh.*

78 Ibid., p. 105. *Seo chugat ar ais mé, ar mo charn aoiligh féin agus a oiread tharta orm go nólfainn Loch Oirb Éireann dá mbeadh gob caol orm.*

79 Ibid., p. 106. *Agus ní dheachaidh tú go dti an cogadh tar éis an tsaoil, a Sheáin. Acht ar ndó, beatha duine a thoil, agus bás i n-Éirinn. Is dócha gur Sinn Féinnidhe tusa um an dtaca seo. Seo, cá bhfuil do lámh ar chaoi ar bith. Craith lámh liom.*

80 Ibid., p. 107. *Bhí sí dílis duit go nuige seo, acht ní fada eile a bheadh sí dílis meireach go dtáinic tú abhaile i n-am tráth.*

81 Ibid., p. 109. *Déanaimís margadh. Troidimís! An té a bheas beo tar éis an chomhraic bíodh an bhean aige agus an tigh tábhairne. Beidh a phictiúr ar an mballa.*

82 Ibid., p. 110. *Ní theastuigheann … ní theastuigheann an bhean uaim. Níl aon ghrádh agam di … Níl … níl.*

83 Ibid. *Is mairg a bheadh ina theetotaller agus tigh tábhairne láimh leis.*

84 There is a picture of a scene from the play in *IP*, 20 December 1939.

85 Leon Ó Broin, *An Oíche úd i mBeithil: Dráma aoin-mhíre* (Baile Átha Cliath: Oifig an tSoláthair, 1949), p. 7. *Céard a dhéanfadh tír seo Iúda, mara mbeadh muidne ann thar ceann Róimhe chun iad a choinneáil ó scornaigh a chéile?*

86 Ibid., pp. 7–8. *Ní bheadh sí pioc níos measa ná mar atá sí i láthair na huaire. Ní heol dúinne aon tslí chun síocháin a bhunú ach saoirse a bhaint de dhuine nuair a nochas sé a mhí-shástacht le rud éigin, le hocras, cuir i gcás, nó le cánacha troma, nó le hiarracht ar an ngrá atá aige dá dhéithe féinig a mhúchadh ina chroí. Ní hiad na hairm amháin atáim-se a cháineadh; tá gléasanna eile ann seachas airm agus póilíní Stáit chun saoirse an duine a chur ar ceal … Cén fáth a bhfuil an Róimh ag iarraidh an domhan uilig do thabhairt faoi smacht?*

87 Ibid., p. 8. *B'fhearr liom-sa go mbeadh daoine níos sonasaighe, go mbeadh caoi aca ar a saol do chaitheamh gan beann ar airm agus ar Impireachtaí, ar chomhacht agus ar shaidhbhreas. Dá mbeadh siad mar sin thiocfadh leo deagh-thréithe a gcroidhe is a n-aigne d'fhorbairt. Bheadh áit ann don áilneacht agus don fhírinne.*

88 Ibid., pp. 9–10. *Agus féach ar an Róimh … An bhfuil aoinní ar domhan is leimhe ná an Róimh? Tá buaidhte glan aici ar náisiúin na cruinne. Shílfeá le féachaint uirri ar an uachtar nach bhfuil aoinní a chroigfeadh í, ach tá a fhios againne a tóigeadh i gCathair na Róimhe féin nach bhfuil an chathair mar a tuairisg. Go bhfuil na clocha buinn ag meath agus ag lobhadh in aghaidh an lae faoi'n Impireacht agus nach fuláir go dtitfidh an t-árus breágh as a chéile luath nó mall.*

89 Ibid., pp. 10–11. *Nuair a bhrúchtfaidh sé amach … go mbeidh ár ndóthain le déanamh againn chun iad do chur faoi chois. An tráth deireannach a thárla sé … ní rabhas anseo … ach d'airigheas gurbh éigin trí mhíle dhíobh do chrochadh mar shampla don chuid eile.*

90 Ibid., p. 16. *Sé m'eolas-sa ariamh gurab é sin díreach an cineál duine a mbuailtear cos air. An Stát atá dhá cosaint againn-ne anseo in Iúda, níl truagh ar bith aige dá bhfuil umhal agus mín ina gcroidhe.*

91 Ibid., p. 25. *Laghdaíonn solus na lampaí diaidh ar ndiaidh go mbíonn an stáitse ar fad faoi dhorchadas. Sos beag … Tosuigheann ceol mistéireach neamh-shaolta dá sheinnm agus, do réir a chéile, lonnuíonn an spota-sholus ar éadan an Árd-Aingil, Gaibrial, atá ina sheasamh i gceart-lár an ardáin.*

92 Ibid., p. 35. *Má's é an leanbh an Messias, tuige nach bhfuil comhartha eicínt le feiceál againn annseo gurab é? Níl ann ach lánúin choitchianta agus páiste coitchianta.*

93 Ibid., pp. 37–8. *Téirigh ar ais* [go Nasaireit] *chó tapaidh agus fhéadfas tú. Lean ort ag obair leat mar is gnáthach agus ná leig d'aoinne malairt córtais a chur ort. Síocháin a theastugheas ó'n Róimh agus ní miste léi corr-dhuine do thárnáil don chrois anois agus arís ar a son. Ba mhór an truagh dá dtárluigheadh aoinní den tsórt sin d'aoinne agaibh.*

94 Ibid., p. 42. *Is annseo amháin a gheobhair mian do chroidhe, an t-é go rabhais ghá lorg. Dia na Síochána a rugadh i gcolainn daonna chun an domhan do shábháil ... Creidim agus ní chreidim. Ó, a Dhia na Glóire, cuidigh lem' dhí-chreideamh.*

95 Ibid. *Árduíonn Muire an leanbh agus beannuíonn an Captaen leis.*

96 Ibid. p. 42. *Tosuíonn an curfá agus na soillse a' dul i ndísg i leaba a chéile go mbíonn an lán-dorchadas ann. Airítear an ceol mistéireach neamh-shaolta arís.*

97 Ibid., p. 46. *Nach é seo an rud go bhfuil tú ag súil leis le fada an lá?*

98 Ibid. *Braithim gur mhaith liom féin an ... naoidheanán seo fheiceál ... Rachamuid ann in éindigh. Tara uait. Go beo!*

99 For An tAthair Piondargás (Preandargás), see Seán Mac Giollarnáth, *Annála Beaga ó Iorrus Aithneach* (Little Annals from Iorrus Aithneach) (Baile Átha Cliath: Oifig an tSoláthair, 1941), pp. 64–81.

100 Leon Ó Broin, *Slán le Muirisg: Dráma aon-mhíre* (Baile Átha Cliath: Oifig an tSoláthair, 1944), p. 7. *Bhí buachaillí na mbailteacha uilig ag corrruighe amach an mhaidin sin a bhailigh muid faoi'n gCruaich. Bhí an lá le Gaedhil, shíl siad. Shíl mé féin sin.*

101 Ibid., p. 12. *Níl ceachtar agaibh crochta fós, agus má dhéanann ár ndaoine féin amuigh an rud a gheall siad, ní crochfar duine ar bith againn.*

102 Ibid. *Má thagann an eochair, beidh an imeacht éasgaidh. Mara dtagaidh, caithfimíd an lámh láidir a fhéachaint.*

103 Ibid., p. 18. *Is í obair shagairt anamacha a shlánú agus gan iad a dhamnú.*

104 According to the account in *Annála Beaga ó Iorrus Aithneach*, he did not mean to kill the man but only render him unconscious.

105 Ó Broin, *Just Like Yesterday*, p. 144. Ó Broin writes: 'I don't know if the score has survived.'

106 Leon Ó Broin, *An Boisgín Ceoil: Saoilneas aon-mhíre* (Baile Átha Cliath: Oifig an tSoláthair, 1945), p 4. *Moltar do dhream ar bith a bhéas ag léiriú na dráimín seo srian a ligean leo féin agus an oiread áibhéile agus is mian leo a dhéanamh maidir leis an bhfeistiú agus leis an aisteoireacht.*

107 Ibid., pp. 10–11.

CHAPTER 4. Questions of Conscience: Séamus de Bhilmot (1902–77)

1 He wrote this in a review of several plays, among them plays by some of those accomplished later playwrights – Ó Floinn, Ó Néill and Ó Tuama – for whom he had been a trailblazer. *Níl na húdair sin i dtaobh leis an scéal amháin. Úsáideann siad é chun a ndearcadh is a bhfealsúnacht féin a léiriú chun sinn a chur ag machnamh ar chúrsaí nach raibh ár mbuaireamh cheana, b'fhéidir.*

2 'Aisteoir ar Stáitse an tSaoil: Ronan Wilmot faoi agallamh ag Máire Ní Néill', *Comhar*, July 2010, p. 26.

3 Séamus Wilmot, *Mise Méara* (Corcaigh: Cló Ollscoile Chorcaighe, 1946) and Séamus Wilmot, *And So Began …* (Cork: Mercier Press, 1972). *Mise Méara* received very positive reviews on its publication, with both Micheál Ó Siochfhradha and An tAthair Eric Mac Fhinn stating that they preferred it to Myles na gCopaleen's *An Béal Bocht* (The Poor Mouth). See Ó Siochfhradha's review in *Circle*, Easter 1947, p. 7; and Mac Fhinn's in *AA*, October 1947, p. 1.

4 Obviously de Bhilmot himself was considerably more ambitious than his protagonist, who wants nothing more than to spend his life in Lislawn

5 Some members of the Galway Urban Council felt the job should have gone to the acting city clerk. See 'Appointments Crux/Galway Council's New Move/Town Clerkship', *II*, 30 August 1935; 'Town Clerkship of Galway/Council's Protest', *II*, 6 September 1935; and 'A Grave Injustice', *CS*, 6 August 1935.

6 Rather curiously, the doctorate was LL.D. rather than D.Litt.

7 See also 'Obituary/Dr. Seamus Wilmot', *IT*, 29 January 1977; and Seamus McConville, 'Comment', *K*, 4 February 1977.

8 In 1978, the year after de Bhilmot's death, Liam Ó Murchú recalled discussing with him whether a writer might also make a good businessman and how de Bhilmot 'became very testy about it and said he had no time for the whiz kids of business who thought they had the tablets of stone when they were telling you about a balance sheet!' (*IP*, 6 September 1978). Speaking at Lismore Writers' Week in 1973, de Bhilmot declared that 'the aim of the Writers' Week is to correct the balance and to keep the writer before the public: to show that he is important – more important, possibly, than the man of industry – to a community' (*II*, 14 April 1973).

9 In his 1943 article 'Do Cheapamar Drámaidheacht Nua' (We Created a New Drama), his fellow playwright Gearóid Ó Lochlainn called attention to the 'useful original plays' (*bundrámaí foghanta*) de Bhilmot contributed to the Taibhdhearc during the 1930s (*Éire*, 1943, p. 31).

10 A little over a year later, Ward wrote: 'Seamus Wilmot learned his theatrical lore at the Taibh [*sic*]. Later in Dublin he became one of the doughtiest workers for Gaelic drama in the Capital. But it was when he applied the Taibhdhearc lessons of variety in Irish, through the [*sic*] Compántas Amharclainne na Gaedhilge, that the theatre in Irish began to be noticed' (*IP*, 21 January 1946). The Taibhdhearc produced Gaelic *geamaireachtaí* (pantomimes) before the Abbey did. See O'Leary, *Gaelic Prose*, pp. 491–2.

11 An Compántas also produced the premiere of his *Prólóg don Réim Nua* in 1944, and revived his full-length plays *Déamar agus a Bhean* in 1944 and *'San Am Soin* in 1952.

12 See 'Appointed Abbey Theatre Director', *II*, 24 July 1958; 'Abbey Theatre to Have New Shareholders', *II*, 13 January 1965; and '25 Agree to Be "Abbey" Shareholders', *IP*, 17 February 1965.

13 See 'Simple Ceremony Re-establishes the National Theatre', *IP*, 19 July 1966; 'But Old Hands Raise the Curtain', *IP*, 19 July 1966; 'Hopes Reputation Will Be Enhanced', *II*, 19 July 1966; and 'New Abbey "Recalls the Years"', *IT*, 19 July 1966. He also welcomed de Valera when he came to the theatre to lay the foundation stone for the new building. See 'To Lay Abbey Theatre Stone Today', *IP*, 3 September 1963. The only major Gaelic theatres with which de Bhilmot did not have an official connection were

Dublin's An Damer, Cork's Compántas Chorcaí and Aisteoirí Ghaoth Dobhair in the Donegal Gaeltacht, none of which ever produced one of his plays.

14 See, for example, 'Theatrical Seminar for Listowel', *K*, 28 November 1970; 'People and Places', *IP*, 2 June 1971; 'N. Kerry Talks About Its Own Writers', *IT*, 7 June 1971; 'Many Attractions for Writers' Week', *II*, 14 April 1973; 'Five Literary Wins', *II*, 29 May 1974; and 'Usual Bunch of Playwrights, Poets, Publicans, Odd-Balls at Listowel', *IT*, 29 May 1974. After his death the organisers of Listowel Writers' Week inaugurated an annual Séamus Wilmot Memorial Lecture in his honour.

15 Tomás Mac Anna, who was brought into the Abbey by Ernest Blythe in 1947 to direct plays in Irish, wrote of his work with 'short plays in Irish' (*cluichí gearra Gaeilge*) that he decided 'to turn away from realism, the common style of the plays in English [at the Abbey] and make use of every device of stagecraft that was in my power, and one or two that weren't yet' (*cúl a thabhairt leis an réadaíocht, stíl choitianta na ndrámaí i mBéarla, agus úsáid a bhaint as gach uile ghléas stáitsíochta a bhí ar mo chumas, agus ceannn nó dhó nach raibh go fóill*). He adopted this strategy because 'I often thought that drama in Irish was too much under the influence of that realistic style of the Abbey' (*Ba mhinic mé ag ceapadh go raibh an drámaíocht Ghaeilge rómhór faoi stíl réadúil sin an Abbey*). See Mac Anna, *Fallaing Aonghusa: Saol amharclainne* (The Cloak of Aonghus: A life in the theatre) (Baile Átha Cliath: An Clóchomhar, 2000), p. 126.

16 He wrote '*go bhfuil cuid den fhírinne ag an té a dubhairt go bhfuil gluaiseacht na drámaidheacht sa Ghaedhilge beagáinín beag airtifiseálta toisg nach Gaedhilgeoirí ó dhúthchas furmhór na ndaoine go bhfuil baint aca leis an drámaidheacht*'.

17 He was at one time the president of this organisation.

18 He was aware that not all local drama societies might even know what was available to them and for this reason in this same speech he urged county librarians to stock 'every play in Irish that had been published' (*gach dráma Gaedhilge atá follsighthe*) and to send out 'at certain times … a brief note with the titles of the new plays and a brief account of each of them' (*meabhrachán gairid le h-ainmneacha na drámaí nua agus cuntas gairid ar gach dráma aca*) (*II*, 27 May 1940). He stated '*gurab'é an gearán is mó a bhíonn ag dreamanna a bhíonn ag léiriú drámaí ag feiseanna ná bíonn aon drámaí nua le fagháil aca agus gura lughaide a suim ina an obair é*'. See also 'Keeping Thought Alive in the Age of Machines/Drámaidheacht', *II*, 27 May 1940.

19 His radio plays include *An Fear a Cheannaigh Móin i Londain* (The Man who Bought Turf in London), which won second prize in a Radio Éireann competition for plays in Irish and was broadcast over the station on 18 November 1939; *An Ghlóir d'Imthigh ag Cionn tSáile* (The Glory that Died at Kinsale), broadcast over Radio Éireann on 3 January 1941; *Máthair Shagairt* (A Priest's Mother), broadcast over Radio Éireann on 6 May 1941, 2 December 1978 and 16 May 1981; and in 1940 and 1941 a series of short historical sketches in a series entitled 'An Gaedheal i gCathracha na hEorpa: Tuairisc drámathach ar imtheachta deoraidhthe suaithinseacha' (The Gael in the Cities of Europe: A dramatic account of the doings of remarkable exiles), which included works on, among others, L'Abbé Edgeworth (15 January 1941), The O'Gorman Mahon (22 January 1941) and Myles Byrne (2 April 1941). All information from the radio listings in *II* and *IP*.

20 Short pieces he wrote for shows by An Compántas include *Children Not Wanted*, a bilingual modern nativity play in *Pléaráca na Nollag* (1945); *Oddest Man Out* in *Nú-Seadh* (1947); *Under Two Flags* in *Hot-Seadh* (1948); *Resistance* in *More-Seadh* (1949); *An Bosca Dubh* (The Black Box) in *Úr-Seadh* (1952).

21 *Thaitin an léiriú go mór leis an lucht éisteachta. B'fhiú do gach Gaedheal sa chathair na drámaí seo a fheiceáil. Múchadh an tSolais* was on a bill with *Gruagach Dúr an Deagh-Chroidhe*, Maghnus Ó Domhnaill's translation of Carlo Goldoni's comedy *Le Burbero Benefico*.

22 Séamus de Bhilmot, *Múchadh an tSolais* in *An Casán agus Múchadh an tSolais: Dhá dhráma aon-mhíre* (Baile Átha Cliath: Oifig Díolta Foillseacháin Rialtais, n.d.), p. 22. *Féach ar an riaradh atá ar an saoghal so. Níl aon árd-aigne 'á stiúradh. Dá mbeadh, ní bheadh daoine bochta ag iomrascáil leis an mbás ar an bhfairrge agus daoine saidhbhre 'na 'smístibh saille go breágh compórdach cois teine – agus an Dia céadna ag féachaint anuas ortha go léir – ach níl aon Dia ann …*

23 Ibid., p. 24. *A Dhia! … a Dhia! Bhís ann … bhís 'á gcosaint. Mise bháidh iad … le daille – tré mhúchadh an tsolais.*

24 Gearóid Ó Lochlainn played two of them. O'Connor wrote sarcastically in his review that he and Tadhg Mac Firbisigh 'deserve censure for introducing an alien atmosphere of dramatic intelligence' (*IS*, 26 October 1929).

25 In his review O'Connor wrote that in the play the Battle of Kinsale had been lost 'we are led to understand, through the treachery of a returned Yank' (*IS*, 26 October 1929). De Bhilmot was correcting O'Connor's misinterpretation (*IS*, 9 November 1929).

26 The plot summary here is based on O'Connor's review. The descendant is trying to tamper with the lighthouse, but this behaviour is not explained in the review. O'Connor wrote that he was 'foiled by a wireless operator', but in his letter to *IS* responding to O'Connor, de Bhilmot asked 'Was he?' (*IS*, 9 November 1920).

27 It is worth noting that de Bhilmot would later write a radio play entitled *An Ghlóir a d'Imthigh ag Cionn tSáile*, broadcast over Radio Éireann in January 1941 (*IP*, 3 January 1941).

28 Séamus de Bhilmot, *An Casán* in *An Casán agus Múchadh an tSolais*, p. 7. *Ná cáin mise. Cáin an t-athair agus an mháthair a bhí agam. Cáin an chómhacht a thug an radharc dom chun na ba d'fheiscint ag teacht abhaile maidin drúchtmhar shamhraidh, agus na cluasa dhom bheith ag éisteacht leo agus iad ag inbhear go breágh, bog, réidh, oidhche fhóghmhair i bpáirceannaibh ciúine. Cáin an chómhacht san. Ná cáin mise. Fág im aonar ar mo bhóthar féin mé i n-ainm Dé.*

29 Ibid., p. 10. *Fuil, fuil arís … Dortadh agus díoghaltas fola. A' mbeidh a mhalairt choidhche againn sa tír seo?* In his story 'An Fear Ciúin' (The Quiet Man), one of the characters is a veteran of the war of independence who cannot stomach the civil war and takes no part in it. See Séamus de Bhilmot, 'An Fear Ciúin' (The Quiet Man), in *Eochair na Sráide: Cnuasach gearrscéalta* (The Street Key: A collection of short stories) (Baile Átha Cliath: Oifig an tSoláthair, 1967), p. 32. De Bhilmot did not, however, think that tragedies like the one in this play were limited to civil wars. In 'Grá Triúir' (Three People's Love), two friends take different paths in the war of independence. One joins the British army, believing it is his duty as an Irishman to fight German aggression and that through doing this duty he and his compatriots in the army will

advance the cause of home rule. The other becomes a leader in the IRA. When the two meet on a street in their Kerry town in Easter week 1916, the IRA man, without realising the identity of his target, shoots and kills his friend, after which he soon goes mad. See de Bhilmot, 'Grá Triúir', in *Eochair Sráide*, pp. 1–12.

30 Ibid., p. 13. *Mharbhóchainn mo mhac féin anois.*

31 That de Bhilmot was open to different and less commercial kinds of plays is evident from his remarks at a 1957 debate at University College Dublin on verse drama, where he is reported to have stated that 'verse drama was an attempt to preserve the identity of the theatre against not only the cinema, but television, radio and all the other attacks on it' (*IP*, 16 March 1957).

32 Séamus de Bhilmot, *'San Am Soin, Dráma Ceithre Mír* (Baile Átha Cliath: Oifig an tSoláthair, 1944), p. 8. *Ó! Nach é an léan géar ná tabharfadh sé an treóir cheart dos na daoine! D'fhéadfadh sé iad do shnaidhmeadh le chéile, mar níl aon amhras ná gur iongantach an greim atá aige ortha.*

33 Ibid. *Íosa Nasaret, Rí na nIúdach! Cúis gháire chughainn! Draoi bréagach, bog-bhriatharach ag treorú muinntir na tíre seo! Cad a bheadh aige le tairisgint dóibh i n-ionad an Riaghaltais Rómhánaigh? Ba bheag cabhair dóibh a bhriathra binne blasta i dtaobh na lilí a fhásann 'sna páirceannaibh …*

34 Ibid., p. 27. *Ná taithneann an ghrian ar gach aoinne … ar ghlan agus ar neamh-ghlan, ar an bheó agus ar an mharbh, ar naomh agus ar pheacach? Agus an lughade sin mórdhacht agus glóir na gréine? … Sé nós na n-uasal teicheadh ó'n ngréin. Is feárr leo dorchadas na hoidhche, óir clúduigheann sé sin a gcuid droch-ghníomh.* De Bhilmot's concern for the poor and the anonymous, evident in *Múchadh an tSolais* and his later plays, was given explicit expression in an appreciation of Maurice Walsh he wrote in 1965. After asking 'What do we look for in the history of past ages?' and mentioning 'kings, potentates, emperors … politicians with their manoeuvring and trimming, generals and their appalling, bloody, buried mistakes', he asked: 'Is it these or the faceless, nameless people, who labour, strive, play, scheme, laugh and die, the small people who, Abraham Lincoln remarked, must be very dear to God, He made so many of them [?]' (*K*, 20 February 1965). See also 'Croke Park, Reflex of Ireland/On "Final" Day the Triumph', *II*, 22 September 1938.

35 This critic did, however, devote more attention to a play produced the following month, *Fear na nAmhrán*, Liam Ó Briain's translation of Patrick Pearse's *The Singer*.

36 Among members of the cast was Gearóid Ó Lochlainn.

37 *Ó tharla gurb'é an saoghal i n-aimsir Chríost atá i gceist ann is dráma nach deacair a mhilleadh … D'éirigh go breágh le fuirinn na h-oidhche aréir.*

38 He said that the play was saved by good acting, including that of Gearóid Ó Lochlainn as Barabbas.

39 *B'fhurastaí, cheapfainn, é a léiriú ná gnáth-dhráma Páise, ó tharla nach iad na caraictéirí beannuighthe as an Soisgéal fhéin atá le teasbáint ar an árdán, ach gnáth-dhaoine, mar a bhéadh i ndráma ar bith eile. Agus san am chéadna léirightear sgéal na Páise ar fheabhas, agus tá idir nádúrthacht agus cráibhtheacht ann.*

40 One does, of course, have the right to wonder how many of these plays were translated from the original languages.

41 De Bhilmot must have been delighted by the critic's pronouncement that 'the Gaelic dramatist is not bounded by the barriers of the English-speaking world, as most Abbey writers seem to be, but turns his mind naturally to the vast field of European culture and thought'. The critic did feel that de Bhilmot was not always successful at 'maintaining a balanced, correct atmosphere', particularly in the last act, but stressed that 'the psychology of the play is amazingly good' and that 'there are many profound passages where the ethics of modern engines of war are put under the searchlight of pitiless analysis'.

42 He also pointed out that the theatre was 'full to the door' (*lán go doras*) for the play. *Tá gluaiseacht an dráma go breágh, agus nochtuigheann an scéal cúis an-láidir in aghaidh cogaidh. Maidir leis an aisteoireacht, is leór a rádh go measfadh aoinne go raibh gach duine des na h-aisteoirí gearrtha amach don pháirt a bhí le líonadh aige.*

43 *Sa dráma goirid seo tugann Séamus de Bhilmot samhlughadh dhúinn atá go han-éifeachtamhail san am atá i láthair … Tá soisgéal fóghanta ghá chraobhscaoileadh ag an ndráma beag seo.* Rather surprisingly he added: 'The play is also appropriate for schoolchildren' (*Oireann an dráma, fresin, do pháistí scoile*).

44 *Dráma cumasach, fíor-chorraitheach atá déanta ag an údar as an damhna teannais a bhí aige, sé sin an choinbhliocht idir aigne shéimh, dhaonna, niadhcha Jean Moreau agus an aigne mhíleata nách leomhfadh aon scrupal den t-sórt a theacht idir iad agus an buaidh.*

45 Séamus de Bhilmot, '*Grádh níos Mó*' (Baile Átha Cliath: Oifig an tSoláthair, 1947), p. 15. *Is mór an t-atharú atá tagaithe ar chúrsaí cogaidh le fiche bliadhain … I gcomparáid leis na cogaithe a troideadh ó shoin i leith, sé is eagal liom gur cogadh sean-aimseardha a bhí sa chogadh a troideadh idir an tír seo agus Marsia. Cogadh idir saighdiúirí a bhí sa chogadh san … ach anois beidh gach duine sa tír ó liath go leanbh páirteach ann. Tiomáinfear gach aoinne isteach ann mar tiomáinfí sgata mart go tigh an bhúistéara.*

46 Ibid., p. 28. *Ceapann na generáil agus an aicme mhíleata ná fuil sa tír seo ach saighdiúirí, ná fuil sa domhan ach saighdiúirí.*

47 Ibid. *Tá nidhthe eile sa tír seo, agus i Marsia agus sa domhan. B'fhéidir nach bhfuil siad chomh taidhbhseach ach táid ann … Pierre agus a ghairdín, cuir i gcás, an mháthair óg ag féachaint ar a céad-ghein ag súgradh lá breágh gréine, an mac léighinn ciúin.*

48 Ibid., p. 35. *Ach anois nuair ná fuil aon mhaith le n-a bpleananna cad a dheinid … ach teacht aniar adtuaidh ar arm Mharsia? Téigheann siad taobh thiar den arm agus imreann siad bás ar bhantracht is ar chlann na saighdiúirí. Cogadh! Troid ghlórmhar ar son do thíre!*

49 Ibid., p. 43. *Do sheas Tusa it' aonar tráth. Tuigfidh Tusa mo sgéal. Tuigfidh Tusa é.* It is instructive here to compare de Bhilmot's war plays with Labhrás Mac Brádaigh's one-act *Céad Feadha Síos* (A Hundred Fathoms Down), performed by An Comhar Drámaíochta as *Cá bhFios Dúinn?* (How Do We Know?) at the Peacock in February 1942. Mac Brádaigh's play is striking for its setting aboard a disabled submarine in the Second World War and its cast of German sailors. However, despite its wartime setting, the play has little to say about war itself. The sailors are trapped and rapidly running out of oxygen, unable to reach the escape hatch because a pump has broken down and the chamber where the hatch is located has flooded. The play then focuses on the decent and humane captain's decision to surreptitiously drug the crew to spare them from awaiting the inexorable approach of death. However, just after the men

lose consciousness the pump almost miraculously begins to work again. The subject of the play is thus the random and often tragic role of chance in human life, and this point could have been made as effectively in a peacetime setting, in a pit in which miners have been trapped, for example. For Mac Brádaigh in this play, war was a background; for de Bhilmot it was always a central concern.

50 It is, however, difficult to see how this critic could say that 'the author's new play ... shows, I imagine, considerable improvement in technical skill over most of his other works'.

51 *Maidir leis an nGaedhilge atá ann, níl sí ach lag tanaidhe. Tá sé ráidhte go n-aithneochadh duine ar bith aistriúchán thar bun-dhráma ar an árdán, ach ní aithneochadh duine ar bith an dráma seo thar aistriúchán. Níl dul ró-Ghaedhealach ar aon chuid de ...* He did add, 'we would not, however, say the Irish in it was bad' (*ní abróchaimís, ámh, gur droch-Ghaedhilge atá ann*).

52 The play was broadcast over Radio Éireann on 3 January, 1942. See 'Radio Programmes', *IP*, 3 January 1942.

53 Once again Gearóid Ó Lochlainn had a major role in the cast. After the first night's performance, the audience called for de Bhilmot, who came on stage to thank both An Comhar and the audience (*II*, 29 January 1941).

54 The review in *The Connacht Tribune* said virtually nothing about the play, focusing instead on 'Mr. Macken's brilliant work' (*CT*, 13 June 1942).

55 I do not know who directed this production.

56 *Bhain an lucht éisteachta spórt mór as* 'Déamar agus a Bhean', *gean-dráma nua le Séamus de Bhilmot ... Dráma a scríobhadh go h-aerach ina bhfuil neart le déanamh ag na h-aisteoirí, agus é lán de ghreann tíoramhail an ceann nua seo. Bhí an chainnt ar fheabhas agus chimeád an lucht éisteachta a aire iomlán ar an stáitse fhaid is a bhí sé dá léiriú.*

57 Ward called the opening night 'a black night for the ideal of drama in Irish' as the actors played 'to a house filled with the depression of emptiness': 'The gallery was empty; the upper circle and stalls almost so, and in the dress circle, including critics, there were 14 persons.'

58 Séamus de Bhilmot, *Déamar agus a Bhean: Dráma aon-mhire* (Baile Átha Cliath: Oifig an tSoláthair, 1952), p. 8. *Sé ba mhaith leat go ndéanfainn-se aithris ar an nós ghránna na dúthaighe seo agus go raghainn isteach go tigh tábhairne Mhallaí Ní Mhóráin agus suas go dtí an párlús i gcuideachtain fir ná fuil aithne ná eolas agam air ... é ag ól piúntaí salach pórtair cubhar-bháin agus mise ag cogaint brioscaí cuirríní. I rith an ama san bheadh daoine ciallmhara fadaradharcacha, mar dheadh, i seomra eile ag iarraidh sinn a dhíol fé mar a bheidís ag díol sean-asail ar an aonach.*

59 De Bhilmot indicates in his opening stage direction that the play is set in the year 1929, 'the time that businesses were failing in the United States' (*an tráth a raibh meath ar chúrsaí gnótha sna Stáit Aontuighthe*). See Séamus de Bhilmot, ibid., p. 5.

60 Ibid., p. 16. *Tá athrú mór ag teacht ar an dúthaigh seo. Níl le cloisint anois ar fuaid an cheanntair ach tafann na madraí is géimneach na mbeithidheach. Geal-gháire na bpáistí ag teacht ón sgoil, níl sé sin le clos a thuilleadh.*

61 Seamus Wilmot, *The Splendid Pretence* (Dublin: Clonmore & Reynolds, 1947), p. 18. It is clear that while there are strong autobiographical elements in the novel, de Bhilmot himself was far more adventurous and ambitious than his protagonist.

62 Ibid., pp. 18–19.

63 Ibid., p. 49.

64 Ibid., p. 145. See also pp. 53–4, 72–3, 160–1.

65 Ibid., pp. 65–6. In some way the novel offers a rather pallid reworking of the theme of Brinsley MacNamara's 1918 novel *The Valley of the Squinting Windows*. The novel goes on to recount Kelly's ever-growing problems in the big city – debt, alcohol, failure to attend to his religious obligations, and involvement in a law case that shatters the image he has created for the people back home, where 'for the first time Mrs. Kelly's pride had suffered a fall, and some in Lislawn were only too glad to rub salt into the wound' (p. 213). As the novel ends, he marries his landlady in Dublin and runs a boarding house and cramming school, but he can never forget Lislawn.

66 de Bhilmot, *Déamar agus a Bhean*, p. 39. *Ach ba bheag radharc a fuaireas riamh ar an ór, ach mé ag sglábhuidheacht i gcuideachtain Iodálach, Seapánach agus Ungárach go dtí nár fhéadas seasamh ar mo chosaibh uaireannta tré chorp laige is cruadhtain. Ní fheaca riamh An Bealach Mór Bán ach ó bhun trínse ar an mbóthar.*

67 Ibid. *Is gráin liom na Stáit. Nuair a shaothruigheas beagán shocruigheas ar theacht abhaile. Ach ní thairrgeochadh capall buile thar n-ais go hÉirinn mé mara mbeadh an t-airgead agam. B'fhearr liom fanamhaint imeasc na bhfear ndubh i Harlem … Uabhar fé ndeara é. Samluightear dúinne Éireannaigh gur daoine sinn a chuaidh go dtí na Stáit ag lorg óir … gur saghas eachtra é … agus ní maith linn admháil nár éirigh linn.*

68 Ibid., p. 40. *Is ait an dream na hÉireannaigh a théigheann go hAmeiriocá. Saghas aicme fé leith iad. Tuigtear don duine a thagann abhaile go gcaithfidh sé gan sgéith ar na daoine eile, cé go dtógfadh sé gruaig do chinn dá neosfadh sé dhuit a dhonacht is a bhíonn an saoghal aca.*

69 Ibid., p. 43. *Cad ina thaobh ná cuirfimís a bhfuil d'éirim aigne againn chun tairbhe ár dtíre féin?*

70 See O'Leary, *The Prose Literature of the Gaelic Revival*, pp. 141–54; O'Leary, *Gaelic Prose*, pp. 124–7, 129, 154–5, 299–300; and O'Leary, *Irish Interior*, pp. 143–9, 416.

71 See O'Leary, 'Yank Outsiders: Irish-Americans in Gaelic fiction and drama of the Irish Free State, 1922–1939', in *New Perspectives on the Irish Diaspora*, pp. 253–65; and O'Leary, 'Castles of Gold: America and Americans in the fiction of Séamus Ó Grianna', *Éire/Ireland*, vol. 21, no. 2, 1986, pp. 70–84.

72 Writing in *Comhar*, 'T. de Bh.' (Tomás de Bhaldraithe) commented on the dreadful attendance in Galway, saying there were only nine people in the audience on opening night and that only 100 in total attended the five nights of the play's run (*Comhar*, July 1942, p. 9). The play was broadcast over Radio Éireann on 12 September 1944 and again on 17 November 1954. See 'Radio', *IP*, 12 September 1944, and 'Radio Éireann', *IP*, 17 November 1954.

73 Séamus de Bhilmot, *An Ráidhteas Oifigeamhail: Dráma aoin-mhire* (Baile Átha Cliath: Oifig an tSoláthair, 1944), p. 3.

74 Ibid., p. 33. *Ach tá rudaí áirithe ann ná fuil baint aca le cúrsaí cogaidh. Táid ann chun leasa an chine daonna i gcoitchinne.*

75 Ibid., p. 8. *Ní uathbhás go dtí é. An t-éirleach! … An bhúistéireacht! … An sgannradh! … Páistí beaga ag sgreadaigh! … An sgeimhle 'n-a gcroidhthe! … An sgeon fiadhain 'n-a súile! Máithreacha ag déanamh sgiath chosanta dá gcuirp chun a bpáistí féin do*

shábháil. Toirneach is sgréacháil na spéir-ghunnaí agus na bombaí ag pléasgadh amhail is dá réabfaí na spéarthaí féin ...

76 Ibid., p. 13. *I lár na búistéireachta seo go léir sin é an t-aon solas carthannachta amháin atá ar lasadh ... Na daoine atá ag tabhairt na n-órduighthe sin, níl aon tuisgint aca don bhfairrge. Ní thuigeann siad carthannacht an tsolais sin thuas a thugann cabhair do gach aon fré chéile. Táid ag múchadh sean-shoillsí na h-Eórpa do réir a chéile. Fág an solas so ar lasadh.*

77 *Rinne sé lámh sách cumasach den dráma le go mbeadh súil leis an scoth againn an dara huair a chuirfidh Éamonn dráma ar ardán.*

78 *Níl aon nuaíocht sa dráma, agus tá's againn go léir ón uair a gcéad-luaitear Mac an Choimeádaí go mbáthfar ag an deire é i ngeall ar mhúchadh an tsolais ... Tá slacht agus cuma nua-aoiseach air a dhéanfas feiliúnach go maith do na Féiltí Drámaíochta é.* At the beginning of the review he did say that he was getting sick of lighthouses in one-act plays in Irish!

79 Among those others was Gearóid Ó Lochlainn, with the text of whose *An t-Éirighe Amach* Kavanagh also dealt in this review.

80 The play was performed by An Comhar Drámaíochta in the Peacock in April 1939.

81 Séamus de Bhilmot, *Prólóg don Réim Nua: Dráma trí mír* (Baile Átha Cliath: Oifig an tSoláthair, 1954), p. 7. Seán Mac Saoirse, de Bhilmot's protagonist in his language parable *Mise Méara* (I Am Méara), is also a pragmatic idealist with a radical and very simple plan to which he is entirely committed. A fluent speaker of Méarachas (Irish) from the Maoltacht (Gaeltacht), he comes to his newly independent nation's capital with a plan to revive the dying native language: 'If you have Méarachas, speak it ... That's my plan. That's all there is' (*Má tá Méarachas agat, labhair é. Sin é mo phlean. Níl ann acht an méid sin*). See Séamus Wilmot, *Mise Méara*, p. 65. His plan eventually involves him in the kind of institutional bureaucracy he hates, and before long he finds himself opposed by a new organisation founded to protect the status of *Galldas* (English) in the country. The novel ends with two armed linguistic camps facing off against each other.

82 For Fianna Fáil's moves to encourage the production of wheat, beginning in the 1930s and made compulsory during the Emergency, see Joe Lee, *Ireland 1912–1985: Politics and society* (Cambridge: Cambridge University Press, 1989), pp. 184–5, 233.

83 de Bhilmot, *Prólóg don Réim Nua*, p. 6. *Ní gnó go dtí an phraifíd is mó is féidir a bhaint amach ... Níl in san bpraifíd réasúnta so ach ainm eile ar ghearradh praghasanna ... Tá scrios déanta aige orm-sa sa bhaile seo pé scéal é ... é féin agus a phraifíd réasúnta.*

84 At another point they accuse him of being a Jew. See de Bhilmot, ibid., p. 51.

85 Ibid., p. 42. *Ceapaimíd ná fuil aon bhaint ag na fírinní sinn linn chomh luath a chuirimíd i leathtaoibh an leabhairín. Ceapaimíd gur dhá nídh scartha ó chéile iad an creideamh agus gnáth-chúrsaí an lae. Ceapaimíd gur rud an creideamh a thógaimíd amach gach Domhnach ... agus a chuirimíd thar n-ais sa chófra chómh luath agus a bhíonn an Domhnach thart.* With regard to the encyclicals, he doubtless had in mind Leo XIII's *Rerum Novarum* (1891) and Pius XI's *Quadragesimo Anno* (1931), and perhaps even Benedict XIV's *Vix Pervenit* (1745).

86 Ibid., p. 31. *Is é an duine féin bun is barr an scéil agus ní éireochaidh le haon scéim ná córas ná réim ná bunóchtar ar a laigí chomh maith le n-a subháilcí.*

87 Ibid., pp. 32–3. *Bíonn billí ag an mbanc ortha … fiacha ag an siopadóir ortha … agus is é aidhm iomlán a saothair ná cuid de sna billí sin d'íoc … Anois don chéad uair tá seans deireadh a chur leis an ré sin d'aon bhuille amháin.*

88 Ibid., p. 33. *Ach nár bh'fhearr an scéal do scrúdú go bun agus iarrracht do dhéanamh ar an gceist go léir a shocrú in ionad a bheith ag cur deisiúcháin is paistí, mar a déarfá ar an sean-chóras?*

89 Ibid., p. 46. She also acknowledges that those others wouldn't listen anyways. *Pioc ní dhéanfaidh Brian chun a thaobh féin do mhíniú dos na daoine. An fhaid is atá an ceart á dhéanamh aige, is cuma leis fé thuairimí daoine eile.*

90 Ibid., p. 57. *Gaimbín fola … a Liam Uí Ceallacháin!*

91 Ibid., p. 41. *Níor fhéadamar ár gceann do thógaint riamh sa tír seo ach cos ar bholg agus éirleach dá dhéanamh orainn i gcómhnaidhe. Nuair ná raibh an tighearna talmhan ag satailt orainn, bhí an fear gaimbín ag brúghadh síos orainn.*

92 Ibid., p. 10. *An talamh do sna daoine agus an bóthar do sna buláin.*

93 In a 1938 essay on 'Croke Park, Reflex of Irish Ireland', de Bhilmot wrote with what Myles na gCopaleen would call 'the plain people of Ireland' in mind: 'Croke Park, as it is to-day, is a result of the long years of struggle against heavy handicaps, of apathy, the chilling of the nation's inner life, flying to the fleshpots, selling of the nation's birthright for a mess of pottage' (*II*, 22 September 1938).

94 This critic also felt that de Bhilmot's characterisation was weak in the play. *Tugadh adhbhar machtnaimh dúinn, nidh gur annamh fhagháil ar an stáitse Gaedhilge. Rud eile, do bhain an t-adhbhar le saoghal an lae indiu, ach b'é rud a d'fhéadfadh a thuitim amach maidir le prátaí ach atá ag tuitim amach maidir le h-earraí eile. Is iongnadh linn é, ó thárla gur ghaibh an t-údar an bealach do ghaibh sé, nár dhein sé tarraingt as chúrsaí an lae go fíor.*

95 The paper's regular theatre correspondent (and perhaps the author of this review) had written in anticipation of the production that the play's subject matter was 'not alone … an interesting proposition but it is one that lends itself to some very good situations of which the author takes full advantage' (*IP*, 18 March 1944).

96 'P. Mac A.' felt that 'the theme was rather hackneyed, and the surprise ending failed to be a surprise'.

97 An army officer is more personally vicious in de Bhilmot's story 'An Laoch Anaithnid' (The Unknown Soldier), in which a high-ranking officer in an Eastern European army eliminates a rival in love by assigning him and all his men to a particularly dangerous post in battle. See de Bhilmot, 'An Laoch Anaithnid', in *Eochair Sráide*, pp. 103–4.

98 I have found no evidence that this play was ever produced.

99 The play actually draws from more than one incident in Barry's book. See the chapter 'Execution of Spies' in Commandant General Tom Barry, *Guerilla Days in Ireland* (Tralee: Anvil Books, 1962 [1949]), pp. 99–107.

100 I omit here plays that deal with the kind of constitutional issues that led to the civil war and were still the subject of intense debate in the years of the Irish Free State and after. Most such debates had by this time calcified into standoffs between unyielding ideologies and were thus almost more theological than political. De Bhilmot's *An Casán* offers a more interesting perspective on the roots of the civil war than most of them.

101 I could find no review of the Limerick production.
102 The play has not been published. The summary here is based on the typescript of the play in the Taibhdhearc papers at NUIG.
103 The play has not been published. The summary here is based on the typescript of the play in the Taibhdhearc papers at NUIG.
104 In 1955, de Bhilmot was reported as telling his audience at the Sligo Feis that 'the production of Irish plays in Dublin has fallen considerably, with ruinous reaction on the rural areas ... As far as Irish drama was concerned, Dublin had not been giving a lead and, in the whole Irish language revival movement, Irish drama had become a Cinderella' (*IT*, 18 April 1955).

CHAPTER 5. 'That Galwegian of Many Talents': Walter Macken (1915–67)

1 The two were *Rain on the Wind* (1950) and *Seek the Fair Land* (1959). Three of his novels, *Quench the Moon* (1948), *I Am Alone* (1950) and *The Bogman* (1952) also had the distinction of being banned by the Irish state censorship board. See Michael Adams, *Censorship: The Irish experience* (Tuscaloosa, AL: University of Alabama Press, 1968), p. 248.
2 See the account of how he came to the Taibhdhearc in his son Ultan's book *Walter Macken: Dreams on paper* (Cork: Mercier Press, 2009), pp. 70–1.
3 James E. Reid, *Walter Macken (1915–1967): Playwright, actor and theatre manager* (Dublin: Carysfort Press, 2012), Kindle e-book, loc. 445. The Taibhdhearc board had its grievances as well. It was from reading *The Connacht Tribune* and/or *The Connacht Sentinel*, rather than from direct communication, that board members learned of Macken's resignation from the theatre. Macken did apologise to the board for this mix-up. See Reid, loc. 671.
4 See the Irish national dailies at the time for running reports of what was believed to be happening at the Abbey. For a succinct account with the benefit of historical hindsight, see Reid, *Walter Macken*, Chapter 5: 'The Abbey Board Member, Assistant Manager and Artistic Adviser'. Reid also mentions poor health as a plausible contributing cause for Macken's resignation in the year before his sudden death.
5 Reid quotes Tomás Mac Anna as saying that Macken brought 'to every performance that personality of his which fills the stage'. See Reid, op. cit., loc. 3902.
6 The play ran for thirty performances. See Reid, op. cit., loc. 1514 ff.
7 Mercier felt that Macken's failings as an actor were the result of his lack of professional training.
8 Four years after Macken's death, Ralph Nelson directed his own adaptation of Macken's *The Flight of the Doves* (1968), a novel for young readers.
9 Reid, op. cit., loc. 788 ff.
10 See Reid, op. cit., loc. 3667 ff. One of the most interesting is 'Erse in Éire', a brief sketch satirising how the Irish civil service struggled first to deal with the mandated use of Irish after independence, and then, in the 1940s, with the switch from the 'Gaelic' font to the Roman and to the new standard orthography for Irish.
11 The following week he called the play 'a comedy with a tragic undertone'. Since he also stated that the 'second-week packed audience laugh continuously at "Mungo's

Mansion"', it seems that the audience was more aware of the comedy than the 'tragic undertone' (*IP*, 19 February 1946).

12 Macken, quoted by Ultan Macken, op. cit., p. 190.
13 Walter Macken, *Mungo's Mansion: A play of Galway life in three acts* (London: Macmillan & Co., 1950), p. 7.
14 Ibid., p. 6.
15 Ibid., p. 14.
16 Ibid., p. 16.
17 Ibid., p. 79.
18 Ibid., p. 100.
19 Ibid., p. 101.
20 Ibid., pp. 103–4.
21 In *The Irish Times*, 'K.' wrote that 'Mungo King (F.J. MacCormick) and his satellite Mowleogs Canavan (Harry Brogan) are, at best, pale shadows of Captain Boyle and the immortal Joxer Daly, and, while they are at all times first-rate comedy puppets, good for a stock laugh, at no time do they arrest us with the thought, "Here is the body and soul of life", as O'Casey's characters do' (*IT*, 12 February 1946).
22 I have not found mention of any amateur productions either, at least in Ireland. Reid notes that there are two other versions in the Wuppertal archive, the other two being entitled 'Three Days in the Gantry' and 'Gaels in the Gantry', and writes that 'the three titles are the same play effectively finished and in different editorial versions'. See Reid, op. cit., loc. 2974 ff.
23 Obviously, I disagree with Reid's view that *Vacant Possession* is 'a gripping and entertaining piece of work', whose failure to find a producer is 'surprising'. See Reid, op. cit., loc. 2985.
24 Walter Macken, *Vacant Possession: A play in three acts* (London: Macmillan, 1948), p. 11.
25 Ibid.
26 Ibid., p. 23.
27 Ibid., p. 70.
28 Ibid., p. 73. After Gunner's death he calls him 'one a the finest min underneath all the boozin' that I ever met in me life'. See Macken, *Vacant Possession*, p. 69.
29 Ibid., p. 72.
30 Ibid., p. 71.
31 Ibid., p. 83.
32 Ibid., p. 103.
33 Ibid., p. 87.
34 Ibid., p. 88.
35 See his paean to the city in ibid., pp. 51–2.
36 Ibid., p. 106. Actually, the real ethical voice in the play is that of Prissy Hartnet, a startlingly naive and hardly credible minor character who first appears as the companion of Wee Wee Brady. She is able to see right through Brady's use of socialism to excuse his thievery: 'A fella shouldn't judge himself by what another fella has. I think that if a man isn't big enough on his own to go out and make money he

deserves to be poor.' See ibid., p. 53. She does not, however, address the question of how he will find a job to make that money.

37 Ibid.

38 The *Irish Independent* gives the number who saw the play as 92,000 (*II*, 24 November 1952); *The Irish Press* as 85,000 (*IP*, 1 December 1953). Another piece in *II* said 82,000 saw the play (*II*, 24 November 1952). The piece in *IP* also stated that 'in a run like this an author's royalties would bring in roughly £100 a week', a substantial sum in those days.

39 Ultan Macken is thus incorrect when he states of *Home is the Hero* that 'up to the 1960s and the arrival of Brian Friel's plays, it held the record for the longest running play in the Abbey'. See Ultan Macken, op. cit., p. 307.

40 See Reid, op. cit., loc. 1373.

41 Oddly enough, despite this success it does not seem to have had a London production.

42 See also Ciarán de hÓra, *Na Drámaí a Léiríodh i dTaibhdhearc na Gaillimhe 1928–2003* (The Plays that Were Produced at Taibhdhearc na Gaillimhe 1928–2003) (Gaillimh: Ollscoil na hÉireann, Gaillimh, n.d.), n.p.

43 Reid, op. cit., loc. 1398 ff.

44 Walter Macken, *Home is the Hero: A play* (London: Macmillan & Co., 1953), p. viii.

45 Ibid., p. 8.

46 Ibid., p. 43.

47 Ibid., p. 55.

48 Ibid., p. 65.

49 Ibid., pp. 100–1.

50 Ibid., p. 102.

51 Ibid., p. 15.

52 Walter Macken, *Twilight of a Warrior: A play* (London: Macmillan & Co., 1956), p. 57.

53 Ibid., p. 90.

54 Reid, op. cit., loc. 1729.

55 Ultan Macken, op. cit., p. 376.

56 Dermody provided Macken a glowing reference, which Ultan Macken reproduces in op. cit., pp. 122–3.

57 Walter Macken, *Sullivan* (London: Pan Books, 1976), p. 65. A writer in *The Connacht Sentinel* in 1944 paid tribute to Macken's work as 'actor-manager-producer-author', adding 'to mention only a few facets of that gentleman's many-sided genius'. This writer also praised 'the hard work, remarkable ingenuity, and craftsmanship of which "Wally" and his henchman Tommy King are capable on behalf of their beloved edifice' (*CS*, 12 December 1944). Another anonymous journalist provided an example of that ingenuity and craftsmanship, recalling in 1953 that 'when Walter Macken came as producer he and Tom King built the dressing room accommodation and a store for costumes now known as the "tunnel"' (*CT*, 8 August 1953). See also Michael Monks, 'Galway Gaelic Theatre's Jubilee', *IT*, 10 July 1953.

58 'Producer' was the term then in use for what we would today call the director. In effect, to use the terms as we do now, Macken was both the producer and the director of these plays.

59 *Macbeit* was a significantly abridged version of Shakespeare's play.
60 Walter Macken, Letter to Peggy Kenny, quoted by Ultan Macken, op. cit., p. 113.
61 Walter Macken, Letter to Peggy Kenny, quoted by Ultan Macken, op. cit., p. 100.
62 Walter Macken, Letter to Peggy Kenny, quoted by Ultan Macken, op. cit., p. 108. One actor who certainly had Irish while Macken was at the Taibhdhearc was the poet Máirtín Ó Direáin.
63 Walter Macken, Letter to Peggy Kenny, quoted by Ultan Macken, op. cit., p. 112. It should be noted that he also spent time studying Irish in the Gaeltacht (Na Forbacha) in the summer of 1939. See Ultan Macken, op. cit., p. 131.
64 On the other hand, in a 2008 interview with James Reid, Éamonn Mac Donnchadha, who joined the Taibhdhearc company in 1946, claimed that in 'every single part he had he seemed to have me behind him all the time ... The reason for that in my opinion, I dare not say that was because he did not always have his words good, off by heart, or rehearsed better. He always leaned on me because I always had my words and I have plenty of free Irish and I could tip off the words like that and switch them around. He relied on me mostly to give him his answer at times.' See Reid, op. cit., loc. 853.
65 Mac Liammóir's own performance of the role in 1928 would, of course, have still been in the minds of many in the audience.
66 According to this reporter, the 'most interesting' of these works was 'Speal an Ghorta, 1845' (The Famine Scythe, 1845), Séamas Ó hAodha's poem on the Great Famine of the 1840s that had won a major prize at the 1945 Oireachtas. It can be found in *Nuabhéarsaíocht 1939–1949* (New Poetry), ed. Seán Ó Tuama (Baile Átha Cliath: Sáirséal & Dill, 1950), pp. 20–6.
67 Ultan Macken, op. cit., p. 72. He continued: 'Frank Dermody acted out the part of the character as he believed the actor should play it and demanded that the actor do what he wanted him to do. He was not able to do this with my father, who was very much his own man and who liked to delve deep into the character he was playing, much like the method actors of later years.' In a 1943 letter to his wife Peggy quoted by his son Ultan in his biography, Macken recalled 'the bad old days in the Taibhdhearc na Gaillimhe when Dermody and intrigues were rampant.' See Ultan Macken, op. cit., p. 146.
68 As was frequently the case, Macken took a lead role here, and, as *The Connacht Tribune* reviewer pointed out, 'by his acting he shared with Siobhán Nic Chionnaith [Siobhán McKenna] the honours of the evening. Their performances together in the Hebridean scene was [*sic*] remarkable for its delicate artistry.'
69 This critic also praised Macken for 'a fine performance in the central role.'
70 This critic also noted that 'Mr. Macken, in the title role, captured the acting honours.'
71 This critic also praised Macken for the 'excellently drawn sets painted by him.'
72 Speaking of this competition the following May, Macken said that of the average of eight plays received from each competing school, 'six out of the eight in each case were well worth publishing' (*bhí sé cinn as an ocht i ngach chás go mb'fhiú go maith a bhfoillsiú*). Moreover, 'We got two plays – they were short, of course – that were better than the original dramatic work of any adults that I myself have yet seen, with a couple of exceptions, of course' (*Fuaireamar dhá dhráma – bhí siad gairid ar ndóigh*

– *a bhí níos fearr ná rud ar bith a chonnacas féin fós de shaothar bundrámuíochta daoine fásta, le cupla eisceacht, ar ndóigh*). It is not, then, surprising that he stated: 'Drama in Irish is in the hands of the young' (*Tá an dráma Gaedhilge i lámha an aosa óig*). (*Comhar*, May 1943, p. 9).

73 On the other hand, in a letter to the editor of *The Western People* in 1946, D. Hughes, the president of the Ballina Drama Festival, expressed his anger at what he felt was Macken's own slipshod behaviour as an adjudicator at that competition. He was incensed that Macken had awarded the festival's cup before he had added up the marks for each entrant, and that his refusal to give marks on the spot for a play he did not know meant that the company producing that play was automatically eliminated from consideration for the award: 'If Walter Macken felt that he could not make up his mind on Saturday night could he not have withheld his decision for a few days; then we might all have gotten a fair crack of the whip' (*WP*, 27 July 1946). Ultan Macken wrote of his father that 'what annoyed him was if he gave an adjudication on a particular group and advised them how they could improve, when they came back in front of him the following year in another play, they would make the same mistakes. He found that very frustrating.' See Ultan Macken, op. cit., p. 130.

74 Reid, op. cit., loc. 2689.

75 Ultan Macken writes: 'Later on, while working in the Taibhdhearc, he decided to burn all his early manuscripts. He described them as part of his apprenticeship and did not see any reason to keep them.' See Ultan Macken, op. cit., p. 84. The existence of such apprentice writings in the Macken papers at the University of Wuppertal shows that he did not burn all such work.

76 This information is from the Taibhdhearc's programme for the show in the Taibhdhearc papers at NUIG and the review published in *The Connacht Sentinel* (18 March 1941).

77 This information is from the Taibhdhearc's programme for the show in the Taibhdhearc papers at NUIG.

78 See Reid, op. cit., loc. 2731.

79 Reid, op. cit., loc. 4938.

80 Walter Macken, Letter to Irene Hentschel, quoted by Ultan Macken, op. cit., p. 191.

81 Bháitéar Ó Maicín, *An Cailín Aimsire Abú: Dráma grinn* (Baile Átha Cliath: Oifig an tSoláthair, 1953), p. 15. *'Sheik' ceart atá ann. É timcheall 25 bliana d'aois, agus a chuid gruaige chomh sleamhain lonnrach le urlár seómra rinnce.*

82 Ibid., p. 14.

83 Walter Macken, Letter to Irene Hentschel, quoted by Ultan Macken, op. cit., p. 191.

84 Sorcha at one point refers to Einstein, Shaw and the philosopher C.E.M. Joad. See Ó Maicín, *An Cailín Aimsire Abú*, p. 23.

85 In his biography of his father, Ultan Macken writes that the play was written to celebrate his own birth. See Ultan Macken, op. cit., p. 149.

86 Bháitéar Ó Maicín, *Bhí Mac agam Tráth*, p. 4. Quotations from this play are from a digital copy of the typescript made available to me from the Macken papers at the University of Wuppertal. *Tá sé gléasta go han-ghalánta ar fad. Ag féachaint air déarfá leat fhéin gur íoc sé fiche punt ar na héadaigh atá dá gcaitheamh aige … Tá féachaint chruaidh ar a éadan aige, agus rian ragairne le feiceál ar a shúílí.*

87 Ibid., p. 15. *Tá sé gan hata. Tá a cóta* [sic] *stróichthe* [sic], *a chuid éadaighe loitithe, fliuch agus salach. Tá piostal ina láimh dheas aige agus feictear go bhfuil créacht ina láimh chlé mar tá fuil air* [sic], *atá ag síleadh go fóill.*

88 Ibid., p. 17. He also tells her he was never loved. *Thug tú airgead dom nuair a bhí mé óg. Thug tú airgead dom nuair a bhí mé mór, ach níor thug tú tada eile dom … Agus annsin tháinic an t-am agus níor thug tú mo dhóthán* [sic] *airgid dhom agus b'éigin dom dul amach agus é fhághail dom fhéin.*

89 Ibid., p. 20. *B'fhearr liom mo mhac marbh, ná mar atá sé anois agam.*

90 Ibid., p. 21. *Damnú ort, a mháthair … damnú ort, a mháthair …*

91 *Dá mbeadh an chéad gníomh agus an tríomhadh gníomh chomh maith leis an dara ceann, bheadh an dráma seo ar na cinn is fearr sa nGaedhilge. Mar sin féin is fearr é ná a lán de na drámaí a feictear i mBleá Cliath.*

92 Bháitéar Ó Maicín, *Oighreacht na Mara* (Gaillimh: D.W. Kenny, n.d.), p. 21. *Nuair a gheobhfas bás, beidh mé sásta go bhfuil mo chion féin déanta agam agus nach ndearna mé dochar d'aoinne i rith mo shaoghail.*

93 Ibid., p. 20. *An áit a bhfuilim anois, táim a' saothrú airgid. I gceann cúpla bliain béidh mé in mo dhuine mhór sa gcathair seo. Anois féin tá meas ag na daoine orm. Is duine ar foghnamh mé sa gcathair. Ach ba mhaith leat-sa go gcaithfinn mo shaoghal amuigh ar an bhfarraige … Agus cén brabach a bheadh as?*

94 Ibid., p. 18. *Nuair a bhéas mé agus Seán pósta, caithfidh sibh teacht agus sinn a fheiceáil. Beidh muid 'n-ar gcomhnuidhe ar an gCorrán tá súil agam, an áit a gcomhnuigheann na dochtúirí agus na buic mhóra, tá's agad.*

95 Ibid., p. 5. *Cabhruigheann Dia leis an bhfear láidir … Tá plean in mo cheann le fada an lá le bob a bhualadh orthu i gcaoi is go mbeidh aithmhéal ar na foreigners sin gur tháinigeadar isteach i gCuan na Gaillimhe ariamh.*

96 Ibid., p. 30. *Tá iontaoibh againn as an Riaghaltas! Tá's againn go ndéanfaidh siad rud eicín! Ní leigfidh siad d'aon tráiléara Gallda teacht isteach i gCuan na Gaillimhe agus saothrú na n-iasgairí a ghoid, gan aoinne a' cur bac orthú.*

97 Ibid., p. 36. *Is truaighe liom an lá a rugadh thú, a Sheáin. Ní raibh aon mhaith ionnad ariamh! … B'fhéidir go bhfuighfidh tú amach lá eicín nach bhfuil an t-airgead chomh comhachtach agus a cheapas tú! Gur fearr a bheith bocht sláinteamhail, ná saidhbhir agus anam cam agad!*

98 Ibid., p. 55. *Ba cheart dom ciall a bheith agam ón gcéad lá! Dubhairt siad go léir liom gan a bheith a' déileáil le tada ón gCladach seo! … D'ísligh mé féin síos chugad agus tá súil agam nach bhfuil aon chuid den tsalachar fágtha orm!*

99 Ibid., p. 59. *Is féidir le fear rianamhail na hiasgairí go léir a thabhairt le chéile go mbeidh cabhlach mór bád iasgaireachta a' snámh amuigh annsin! … go mbeidh gach fear san gCladach ina iasgaire!*

100 Ibid., p. 40. *Tá an t-iasgaire a' fághail bháis sa gCladach. Roimh an gcogadh deiridh bhí timcheall 's céad bád iasgaireachta i gCuan na Gaillimhe agus anois níl scór acu fágtha … Ní féidir airgead a dhéanamh as leis an méid tráiléaraí agus comhluchta atá a' sguabadh breac as an bhfairrge. Tá sé seafóideach a bheith a' súil go leanfainn leis an gceird sin.*

101 Comparing *An Cailín Aimsire Abú* and *An Fear ón Spidéal*, James E. Reid writes: 'The former is a credible farce, slowed by repetitious dialogue and a poor ending, while

the latter is just an overdone comedy that does not work.' See Reid, op. cit., loc. 3923. This judgement seems unduly harsh.

102 *Agus ní beag a bhfuil d'imeachtaí ann – cúrsaí achrannacha grá, caimiléaracht, gadaíocht, cleas in agaidh clis, teagmhaisí aisteacha, aduaine, críoch gan coinne léi, agus tríd an rúille búille go léir, raidhse grinn.*

103 *Ach níor theip ar sheiftiúlacht an údair anso agus chítear dhom gur ghaibh sé leastuas de pé leadrán beag atá sa míniú leis an gcrích éifeachtúil do chuir sé leis.*

104 For a perceptive attempt to sort out all of these potential sources, see Reid, op. cit., loc. 2815 ff.

105 Bháitéar Ó Maicín, *An Fear ón Spidéal (Geandráma Áilteóireachta)* (Baile Átha Cliath: Oifig Díolta Foilseacháin Rialtais, 1952), p. 2. At one point she hears the name Cú Chulainn and mistakes it for 'Confucious' (*sic*) (p. 24).

106 Ibid., p. 4.

107 Ibid., p. 30.

108 Ibid., p. 38. *Ní fear mise, ach, a Dhia na Glóire, dá mba fear mé ní ghoidfeadh aon Romeo a mbeadh báinín air, mo chailín uaim.*

109 Ibid., p. 80. *Bhuel, i gcomparáid leatsa, a bhean uasal, ní raibh i Machievelli* [sic] *ach páiste.*

110 The sculptor does at one point make a fake miniature that plays an important role later in the play.

111 Áine is aware that Irish is 'very fashionable now' (*an-fhaisiúnta anois*) and is being used by 'many of the bigwigs' (*a lán boc mór*). Indeed, she has even (mis)learned a few phrases herself, but she is obviously sceptical about her daughter's interest in the language. See Ó Maicín, *An Fear ón Spidéal*, p. 7.

112 Ibid., p. 40. *Tá leaid amháin istigh annsin agus chaith sé an oidhche go léir ag cur síos ar áilneacht an inniúin.*

113 Walter Macken, 'Cockles and Mustard', p. 24. I am working here from a copy of the typescript in the Macken papers at the University of Wuppertal provided to me by librarians there.

114 Of course, he had made an attempt to do just that with considerably less success in *Bhí Mac agam Tráth.*

115 While the play and the novel share the same basic plot, there are significant differences between the two works.

116 Ultan Macken gives another important reason for his father's switch from Irish to English: 'Although he was writing in Irish both for the Taibhdhearc and with a view to publishing, eventually my father came to realise that there was no future in writing in Irish in terms of earning a living from it. He hoped his Irish language writing could help him establish himself as a writer, but on the other hand, he realised quite soon that publishing plays in Irish would earn him very little money.' See Ultan Macken, op. cit., p. 154.

117 Walter Macken, 'Cockles and Mustard', p. 112.

118 Macken, *Mungo's Mansion*, pp. 19–20.

119 Ibid., p. viii.

120 See also 'The Taibhdhearc', Editorial, *CS*, 23 November 1943; and 'Our Only Gaelic Theatre', Editorial, *CS*, 11 January 1944. In this context it is worth noting Reid's

comment that 'Walter Macken was not a manager. The position with Taibhdhearc na Gaillimhe was more of a "missionary" nature'. See Reid, op. cit., loc. 4181.

121 The town's failure to support the Taibhdhearc was a sore point for Macken and many other Galwegians with an interest in theatre, Irish, or both. See, for example, 'Taibhdhearc a Credit to Galway/Chamber of Commerce Urges More Support', *CT*, 6 September 1947.

122 He felt that such a major writer should be a native speaker of Irish. *Cuimhnigh nach bhfuil an Dráma Gaedhilge ach 'na pháiste fós. Caithfear é a chothú. Tugaimís seans do na daoine óga rogha saothar drámuíochta na hEorpa a fheiceáil, é léirighthe go slachtmhar, agus is cinnte go dtiocfaidh an mór-scríbhneoir dúthchasach go fóill chun an scoil nua a thionnscnamh.*

CONCLUSION. Transition and Tradition

1 For Aisteoirí an Spidéil, see Máirín Breathnach Uí Choileáin, *Aisteoirí an Spidéil* (Indreabhán: Cló Iar-Chonnacht, 2015).

2 For example, while the Abbey did offer several full-length plays in Irish in the 1940s, in the following decades, with only one exception, the only full-length works in Irish the Abbey produced were its *geamaireachtaí* or Gaelic pantomimes. That single exception was the premiere of Seán Ó Tuama's *Gunna Cam agus Slabhra Óir*, of which there was only one performance, at the 1956 Oireachtas.

3 See Michael J. O'Neill, *The Abbey at the Queen's: The interregnum years 1951–1966* (Nepean, ON: Borealis, 1999). During the fifteen years after the 1951 fire that destroyed their theatre, the Abbey performed in the much larger Queen's theatre, where it was felt that full-length plays in Irish would not attract adequate audiences to cover expenses. As a result, the company limited its offerings to one-act plays mounted before or after the main show in English.

4 Financial problems led to the theatre's decline and eventual demise in 1976. There was an attempt to reopen it with a professional company during the 1979–80 season, and the company, no longer having its Dublin base, toured during 1980–1 after which the project came to an end. See Máiréad Ní Chinnéide, *An Damer: Stair amharclainne*, pp. 71–87.

5 This play is likely to have been inspired by the Soviet invasion of Hungary in 1956.

6 See Ó Siadhail, *An Béaslaíoch*, pp. 801–2. In another diary entry the same year, he called the Taibhdhearc 'the ridiculous & worthless, if not positively evil thing'.

7 See the list of articles that comprise his memoirs in Ó Siadhail, op. cit., pp. 1043–50.

8 See ibid., pp. 30–1.

9 As we have seen, he developed these ideas at greater length the same year in 'An Pobal agus an Ghaeilge', *Éire*, 1942, pp. 74–9. He felt that An Cumann Scoildrámaíochta (The Schools Drama Association) had also played a role in helping build an audience. For this organisation, see Donncha Ó Súilleabháin, *An Cumann Scoildrámaíochta 1934–1984* (Baile Átha Cliath: An Clóchomhar, 1986).

10 *Tá. Támuid ag déanamh maisín don am atá le teacht, don scríbhneoir mór atá le teacht.*

11 *An fíor a rá go bhfuil a leithéid de rud agus drámaíocht Ghaeilge in aon chor? ... Nach cirte a rá go bhfuil méid airithe drámaí i nGaeilge ... ?*

12 An unintended consequence of their achievement and influence was that they undoubtedly helped maintain the dominance within the movement of playwrights who were not native speakers of Irish. All five of these writers were learners of the language (as indeed were all of those in *An Underground Theatre* with the exception of Seán Ó Tuama, who was raised in an Irish-speaking family in Cork city). Perhaps the major difference between the Gaelic drama of the present and that of earlier times is the prominence of native speakers like Ó Flatharta, Ó Conghaile, Ó Neachtain, Ó Scolaí and Cathal Ó Searcaigh among contemporary playwrights.

Bibliography

MANUSCRIPTS AND UNPUBLISHED TYPESCRIPTS

From the National Library of Ireland:

Béaslaí, Piaras, *Ar Thóir Mhíchíl Uí Choileáin* (Ms. 33,939 {1})
—, 'Ceanndánacht' (Ms. 33,939 {6 and 7})
—, 'Cúrsaí Fiaigh' (Ms. 33,939 {12})
—, 'First Draft of Pe i nEirinn I' (*sic*) (Ms. 33,939 {21})
—, Letter to Ernest Blythe, 8 August 1928 (Ernest Blythe papers, Ms. 20,708).

From Taibhdhearc na Gaillimhe papers, James Hardiman Library, National University of Ireland, Galway (Special Collections at NUIG has renumbered some of these scripts so some numbers here may no longer be accurate):

Mac Brádaigh, Labhrás, *An tUghdar i nGleic* (T1/H/325)
Mac Liammóir, Micheál, *Lúlú* (T1/H/302)
Ó Diolúin, Tomás, *An Coimisinéar* (T1/H/177)
Ó Máille, Tomás, *Mise an Méire* (T1/H/106)

From the Walter Macken papers at the University of Wuppertal:

Bhí Mac agam Tráth (Folder 105)
'Cockles and Mustard' (Folder 98)

NEWSPAPERS AND JOURNALS

Ar Aghaidh
Ballina Herald
An Claidheamh Soluis
Clare Champion
Comhar
The Connacht Sentinel
The Connacht Tribune
Cork Examiner
Cork Weekly Examiner
Derry People and Donegal News
The Drogheda Independent
The Dublin Magazine
Dublin Opinion
Dundalk Democrat
Éire: Bliainiris Ghaedheal: Rogha Saothair Ghaedheal mBeo
Evening Herald
Evening Mail
Fáinne an Lae
Feasta

Freeman's Journal
The Garda Review
An Glór
Iodh Morainn
An Iris
Irish Independent
Irish Library Bulletin
The Irish Press
The Irish Statesman
The Irish Times
Irisleabhar Mhuighe Nuadhat
Irisleabhar na Gaedhilge / The Gaelic Journal
The Kerryman
Kerry Weekly Reporter
Limerick Leader
The Mayo News
Meath Chronicle
Misneach
An Muimhneach Óg
The Munster Express
The Nenagh Guardian
The New York Times
An Sguab
The Shannonside Annual
Sinn Féin
An Stoc
Sunday Independent
An tUltach
Weekly Freeman
The Western People

PUBLISHED PRIMARY TEXTS

Aistí Gaedhilge (Irish Essays for Examination) (Baile Átha Cliath: M.H. Mac Ghoill & a Mhac, 1935)

Barry, Kevin, *Hinterland* (London: Faber & Faber, 2002)

Barry, Commandant General Tom, *Guerilla Days in Ireland* (Tralee: Anvil Books, 1962)

Béaslaí, Piaras, *Astronár* (Baile Átha Cliath: Muinntir C.S. Ó Fallamhain i gcomhar le hOifig an tSoláthair, 1928)

—, *Bealtaine 1916 agus Dánta Eile*, ed. Pádraig Ó Siadhail (Baile Átha Cliath: Coiscéim, 1991)

—, *Beirt na Bodhaire Bréige*, in *An Sgaothaire agus Cúig Drámaí Eile* (Baile Átha Cliath: Muinntir C.S. Ó Fallamhain i gcomhar le hOifig an tSoláthair, 1929)

—, *An Bhean Chródha: Dráma cheithre mír* (Baile Átha Cliath: Oifig Díolta Foillseacháin Rialtais, 1931)

—, *Blúire Páipéir* (Baile Átha Cliath: Oifig Díolta Foillseacháin Rialtais, 1938)

—, *Coramac na Cuile: Cluihe trí vír* (Dublin: James Duffy & Co., 1909)

—, *Cúigeachas*, in Béaslaí, *An Sgaothaire agus Cúig Drámaí Eile*, pp. 62–80.

—, *An Danar: Dráma trí mír* (Baile Átha Cliath: Muinntir C.S. Ó Fallamhain i gcomhar le hOifig an tSoláthair, 1929)

—, 'Don Léiritheoir', in Oliver Goldsmith, *Ísliú chun Buadha*, trans. Béaslaí (Baile Átha Cliath: Oifig an tSoláthair, n.d.)

—, *Earc agus Áine agus Scéalta Eile* (Baile Átha Cliath: Oifig an tSoláthair, 1946)

—, *Éigse Nua-Ghaedhilge I: Tráchtas ar Fhilíbh agus ar Fhilidheacht na Gaedhilge ó 1600 go dtí 1850* (Baile Átha Cliath: Comhlucht Oideachais na hÉireann, n.d.)

—, *Éigse Nua-Ghaedhilge II: Tráchtas ar Fhilíbh agus ar Fhilidheacht na Gaedhilge ó 1600 go dtí 1850* (Baile Átha Cliath: Comhlucht Oideachais na hÉireann, n.d.)

—, *Fear an Sgéilín Grinn* (Áth Cliath: An Comhar Drámaíochta, n.d.)

—, *An Fear as Buenos Aires,* in Béaslaí, *An Sgaothaire agus Cúig Drámaí Eile,* pp. 81–116.

—, *An Fear Fógraidheachta: Fársa trí mír* (Baile Átha Cliath: Oifig an tSoláthair, 1938)

—, *Fear na Milliún Púnt,* in Béaslaí, *An Sgaothaire agus Cúig Drámaí Eile,* pp. 147–71.

—, *Michael Collins and the Making of a New Ireland,* 2 vols (Dublin: Phoenix Publishing Co., n.d.)

—, *Michael Collins: Soldier and statesman* (Dublin: Talbot, n.d.)

—, *An Sgaothaire agus Cúig Drámaí Eile* (Baile Átha Cliath: Muinntir C.S. Ó Fallamhain i gcomhar le hOifig an tSoláthair, 1929)

'Beirt Mhac Léighinn', *Eoghan Ruadh Ua Néill, nó Ar Son Tíre agus Creidimh: Dráma stardha ag baint le cogadh 1641* (Baile Átha Cliath: M.H. Gill & a Mhac, 1907)

Breathnach, Micheál, *Cuimhne an tSeanpháiste* (Baile Átha Cliath: Oifig an tSoláthair, 1966)

Cannon, John, *An Fiaclóir,* trans. Micheál Mhag Ruaidhrí (Dublin: Patrick O'Brien, n.d.)

De Bhilmot, Séamus (see also Wilmot, Séamus), *Baintighearna an Ghorta: Dráma aoin-mhíre* (Baile Átha Cliath: Oifig an tSoláthair, 1944)

—, *Déamar agus a Bhean* (Baile Átha Cliath: Oifig an tSoláthair, 1952)

—, *Eochair na Sráide: Cnuasach gearrscéalta* (Baile Átha Cliath: Oifig an tSoláthair, 1967)

—, *'Grádh níos Mó'* (Baile Átha Cliath: Oifig an tSoláthair, 1947)

—, *Múchadh an tSolais,* in *An Casán agus Múchadh an tSolais: Dhá dhráma aon-mhíre* (Baile Átha Cliath: Oifig Díolta Foillseacháin Rialtais, n.d.)

—, *Prólóg don Réim Nua: Dráma trí mír* (Baile Átha Cliath: Oifig an tSoláthair, 1954)

—, *An Ráidhteas Oifigeamhail: Dráma aoin-mhire* (Baile Átha Cliath: Oifig an tSoláthair, 1944)

—, *'San Am Soin: Dráma ceithre mír* (Baile Átha Cliath: Oifig an tSoláthair, 1944)

Foote, Samuel, *The Lyar: A comedy in three acts* (London: G. Kearsly, 1764)

Gregory, Lady Augusta, *The Gaol Gate,* in Gregory, *Selected Plays,* ed. Elizabeth Coxhead (Gerrards Cross: Colin Smythe, 1975), pp. 97–106

Johnston, Denis, *The Old Lady Says 'No!' A romantic play in two parts with choral interludes*, in *The Dramatic Works of Denis Johnston*, vol. 1 (Gerrards Cross: Colin Smythe, 1977), pp. 13–82

Mac Brádaigh, Labhrás, *Céad Feadha Síos* (Baile Átha Cliath: Oifig an tSoláthair, 1943)

Macken, Walter (see also Ó Maicín, Bháitéar), *Home is the Hero: A play* (London: Macmillan, 1953)

—, *Mungo's Mansion: A play of Galway life in three acts* (London: Macmillan, 1950)

—, *Sullivan* (London: Pan Books, 1976)

—, *Twilight of a Warrior: A play* (London: Macmillan, 1956)

—, *Vacant Possession: A play in three acts* (London: Macmillan, 1948)

Mac Giollarnáth, Seán, *Annála Beaga ó Iorrus Aithneach* (Baile Átha Cliath: Oifig an tSoláthair, 1941)

Mac Liammóir, *Diarmuid agus Gráinne: Dráma trí ngníomh* (Baile Átha Cliath: Oifig Díolta Foillseacháin Rialtais, 1935)

MacNamara, Brinsley, *The Valley of the Squinting Windows* (Dublin: Anvil, 1964 [1918])

MacSwiney, Paul, *An Bárd 'gus an Fó: A Gaelic idyll* (New York: Society for the Preservation of the Irish Language, 1884)

Moinaux, Jules, *Les deux sourds*, ed. I.H.B. Spiers (Boston: D.C. Heath, 1906)

Molloy. M.J., *The King of Friday's Men in Three Acts*, in M.J. Molloy, *Three Plays* (Newark, DE: Proscenium Press, 1975), pp. 7–96

Murphy, Arthur, *Three Weeks After Marriage*, in Murphy, *The Way to Keep Him and Five Other Plays*, ed. John Pike Emery (New York: New York University Press, 1956), pp. 283–330

Ní Ghráda, Máiréad, *An Triail/Breithiúnas: Dhá dhráma* (Baile Átha Cliath: Oifig an tSoláthair, 1978)

Ní Mhuircheartaigh, Éadaoin, and Nollaig Mac Congáil (eds), *Drámaí Thús na hAthbheochana* (Gaillimh: Arlen House, 2008)

Ó Broin, Leon, *An Boisgín Ceoil: Saoilneas aon-mhíre* (Baile Átha Cliath: Oifig an tSoláthair, 1945)

—, *An Clósgríobhaí: Dráma grinn* (Baile Átha Cliath: Oifig Díolta Foillseacháin Rialtais, 1936)

—, *Just Like Yesterday: An autobiography* (Dublin: Gill & Macmillan, n.d.)

—, *An Maidíneach: Staraí na nÉireannach aontaithe* (Baile Átha Cliath: Sáirséal & Dill, 1971)

—, *An Mhallacht*, in *An Mhallacht agus Drámaí Eile* (Baile Átha Cliath: Oifig Díolta Foillseacháin Rialtais, 1931), pp. 5–17

—, *An Oíche Úd i mBeithil: Dráma aoin-mhíre* (Baile Átha Cliath: Oifig an tSoláthair, 1949)

—, *Parnell: Beathaisnéis* (Baile Átha Cliath: Oifig an tSoláthair, 1937)
—, *Rogha an Dá Dhíogh*, in *An Mhallacht agus Drámaí Eile*, pp. 37–84
—, *An Sgríbhinn ar an mBalla*, in *An Mhallacht agus Drámaí Eile*, pp. 85–111
—, *Siamsa Gaedheal*, in *An Mhallacht agus Drámaí Eile*, pp. 18–36
—, *Slán le Muirisg: Dráma aon-mhíre* (Baile Átha Cliath: Oifig an tSoláthair, 1944)
O'Casey, Sean, *Three Plays* (London: Macmillan, 1966)
O'Connor, Frank, 'Guests of the Nation', in O'Connor, *Guests of the Nation* (New York: Macmillan, 1931), pp. 1–19
O'Flaherty, *Darkness: A tragedy in three acts*, trans. O'Flaherty, ed. Brian Ó Conchubhair (Dublin: Arlen House, 2014)
Ó Flaithearta, Liam, *Dorchadas: Tragóid trí ghníomh*, ed. Brian Ó Conchubhair (Dublin: Arlen House, 2011)
Ó Lochlainn, Gearóid, 'Ag Amharc Siar Dom', *Feasta*, February to May 1962
—, *Ag an Ladhrán: Dráma éin ghnímh* (Baile Átha Cliath: Oifig an tSoláthair, 1946)
—, 'Aisteoir Fáin', *Comhar*, March to August 1945
—, *An Balbhán Bréige* (Baile Átha Cliath: Oifig an tSoláthair, 1954)
—, *Bean an Mhilliúnaí: Dráma i n-éan gníomh amháin* (Baile Átha Cliath: Clódhanna Gaedhealacha, 1923)
—, *An Craipí Óg: Ceol dráma gearr*, trans. Muiris Ó Catháin, arranged as a musical play by Gearóid Ó Lochlainn (Baile Átha Cliath: n.p., n.d.)
—, *Ealaín na hAmharclainne* (Baile Átha Cliath: Clódhanna Teoranta, 1966)
—, *An t-Éirighe Amach: Dráma éin-ghnímh* (Baile Átha Cliath: Oifig an Soláthair, 1944)
—, *Na Fearachoin ('Fearachoin Groidhe ná Claoidhfeadh Céadta'): Dráma trí gníomh* (Baile Átha Cliath: Oifig an tSoláthair, 1946)
—, *Na Gaduithe: Dráma grinn i dtrí gníomha* (Baile Átha Cliath: Oifig Díolta Foillseacháin Rialtais, 1935)
—, 'I dTír na nDanar Dom', *Feasta*, August 1968 to January 1969
Ó Maicín, Bháitéar (see also Macken, Walter), *An Cailín Aimsire Abú: Dráma grinn* (Baile Átha Cliath: Oifig an tSoláthair, 1953)
—, *An Fear ón Spidéal (Geandráma Áilteóireachta)* (Baile Átha Cliath: Oifig Díolta Foilseacháin Rialtais, 1952)
—, *Oighreacht na Mara* (Gaillimh: D.W. Kenny, n.d.)
O'Malley, Ernie, *On Another Man's Wound* (Dublin: Anvil, 1979)
Ó Morónaigh, Seán (ed.), *Drámaíocht ó Dhúchas ó Bhéalaithris Thaidhg Uí Chonchubhair* (Camas: An Comhlachas Náisiúnta Drámaíochta, 2005)
Ó Siochfhradha, Micheál, *Deire an Chuntais: Dráma aon-mhíre* (Baile Átha Cliath: Oifig Díolta Foillseacháin Rialtais, 1939)
Ó Súilleabháin, Proinnsias E., *Láimh-leabhar Drámaidheachta* (Baile Átha Cliath: Brún agus Ó Nualláin, n.d.)

Ó Tuama, Seán, *Gunna Cam agus Slabhra Óir: Dráma véarsaíochta thrí ghníomh* (Baile Átha Cliath: Sáirséal & Dill, 1964)
Pearse, Patrick, *Collected Plays / Drámaí an Phiarsaigh*, ed. Róisín Ní Ghairbhí and Eugene McNulty (Sallins: Irish Academic Press, 2013)
Robinson, Lennox, *The Big House*, in Robinson, *Selected Plays*, ed. Christopher Murray (Gerrards Cross: Colin Smythe, 1982), pp. 137–98
Saothar Suadha a Dó (Baile Átha Cliath: Muinntir an Ghoill, 1912)
Wilmot, Séamus (see also de Bhilmot, Séamus), *And So Began ...* (Cork: Mercier Press, 1972)
—, *The Curlew Call*, in *The Shannonside Annual*, 1958, pp. 21–6.
—, *Mise Méara* (Corcaigh: Cló Ollscoile Chorcaighe, 1946)
—, *The Splendid Pretence* (Dublin: Clonmore & Reynolds, 1947)
Yeats, William Butler, *On Baile's Strand*, in Yeats, *Collected Plays* (Dublin: Gill & Macmillan, 1992), pp. 245–78

SECONDARY SOURCES

Adams, Michael, *Censorship: The Irish experience* (Tuscaloosa, AL: University of Alabama Press, 1968)
Baugh, Albert C. (ed.), *A Literary History of England*, 2nd edn (Englewood Cliffs: Prentice-Hall, 1967)
Breathnach, Diarmuid, and Máire Ní Mhurchú, *1882–1982: Beathaisnéis*, vols 1–5 (Baile Átha Cliath: An Clóchomhar, 1986–2002)
—, *1983–2002: Beathaisnéis* (Baile Átha Cliath: An Clóchomhar, 2003)
de hÓra, Ciarán, *Na Drámaí a Léiríodh i dTaibhdhearc na Gaillimhe 1928–2003* (Gaillimh: Ollscoil na hÉireann, Gaillimh, n.d.)
Hogan, Robert, *After the Irish Renaissance: A critical history of Irish drama since 'The Plough and the Stars'* (London: Macmillan, 1968)
Hogan, Robert, and James Kilroy, *The Irish Literary Theatre 1899–1901* (Dublin: Dolmen Press, 1975)
Hunt, Hugh, *The Abbey: Ireland's national theatre 1904–1979* (New York: Columbia University Press, 1979)
Kilroy, James (ed.), *The 'Playboy' Riots* (Dublin: The Dolmen Press, 1975)
Lee, Joe, *Ireland 1912–1985: Politics and society* (Cambridge: Cambridge University Press, 1989)
Luke, Peter, *Enter Certain Players: Edwards, Mac Liammóir and the Gate 1928–1978* (Dublin: Dolmen Press, 1978)
Mac Anna, Tomás, *Fallaing Aonghusa: Saol amharclainne* (Baile Átha Cliath: An Clóchomhar, 2000)
Macken, Ultan, *Walter Macken: Dreams on paper* (Cork: Mercier Press, 2009)

Mac Liammóir, Micheál, *Theatre in Ireland* (Dublin: The Cultural Relations Committee of Ireland, 1964)

McNulty, Eugene, and Róisín Ní Ghairbhí (eds), *Patrick Pearse and the Theatre/ Mac Piarais agus an Téatar* (Dublin: Four Courts Press, 2016)

Nic Eoin, Máirín, 'Contemporary Prose and Drama in Irish 1940–2000', in *The Cambridge History of Irish Literature*, vol. 2, ed. Margaret Kelleher and Philip O'Leary (Cambridge: Cambridge University Press, 2006), pp. 270–316

Ní Chinnéide, Máiréad, *An Damer: Stair amharclainne* (Baile Átha Cliath: Gael Linn, 2008)

Ní Dhonnchadha, Aisling, *An Gearrscéal sa Ghaeilge 1898–1940* (Baile Átha Cliath: An Clóchomhar, 1981)

Ó Cuív, Shán, *Prós na hAoise Seo* (Bleathcliath (*sic*): Brún & Ó Nóláin, n.d.)

Ó Droighneáin, Muiris, *Taighde i gComhair Stair Litridheachta na Nua-Ghaedhilge ó 1882 Anuas* (Baile Átha Cliath: Oifig Díolta Foillseacháin Rialtais, 1936)

Ó Glaisne, Risteárd, *Ceannródaithe: Tuairisc Iriseora (Scríbhneoirí na Nua-Ré)* (Baile Átha Cliath: Foilseacháin Náisiúnta Tta., 1974)

O'Leary, Philip, *Gaelic Prose in the Irish Free State 1922–1939* (Dublin: UCD Press, 2004)

—, 'The Irish Renaissance, 1880–1940: Literature in Irish', in *The Cambridge History of Irish Literature*, vol. 2, ed. Margaret Kelleher and Philip O'Leary (Cambridge: Cambridge University Press, 2006), pp. 226–69

—, *The Prose Literature of the Gaelic Revival 1881–1921: Ideology and innovation* (University Park, PA: Penn State University Press, 1994)

—, *An Underground Theatre: Major playwrights in the Irish language 1930–1980* (Dublin: UCD Press, 2017)

—, *Writing Beyond the Revival: Facing the future in Gaelic prose 1940–1951* (Dublin: UCD Press, 2011)

—, 'Yank Outsiders: Irish-Americans in Gaelic fiction and drama of the Irish Free State, 1922–1939', in *New Perspectives on the Irish Diaspora*, ed. Charles Fanning (Carbondale, IL: Southern Illinois University Press, 2000), pp. 253–65

O'Neill, Michael, *The Abbey at the Queen's: The interregnum years 1951–1966* (Nepean, ON: Borealis, 1999)

Ó Siadhail, Pádraig, *An Béaslaíoch: Beatha agus saothar Phiarais Béaslaí (1881–1965)* (Baile Átha Cliath: Coiscéim, 2007)

—, *Stair Dhrámaíocht na Gaeilge 1900–1970* (Indreabhán: Cló Iar-Chonnachta, 1993)

Ó Súilleabháin, Donncha, *An Cumann Scoildrámaíochta 1934–1984* (Baile Átha Cliath: An Clóchomhar, 1986)

—, *Scéal an Oireachtais 1897–1924* (Baile Átha Cliath: An Clóchomhar, 1984)

Reid, James E., *Walter Macken (1915–1967): Playwright, actor and theatre manager* (Dublin: Carysfort Press, 2012), Kindle e-book

Robinson, Lennox, *The Big House: Four scenes in its life*, in Lennox Robinson, *Selected Plays*, ed. Christopher Murray (Gerrards Cross: Colin Smythe, 1982), pp. 137–98

—, *Ireland's Abbey Theatre: A history, 1899–1951* (London: Sidgwick & Jackson, 1951)

Savage, Robert J., *Irish Television: The political and social origins* (Cork: Cork University Press, 1996)

Simpson, Alan, *Beckett and Behan and a Theatre in Dublin* (London: Routledge & Kegan Paul, 1962)

Swift, Carolyn, *Stage by Stage* (Swords: Poolbeg, 1985)

Uí Choileáin, Máirín Breathnach, *Aisteoirí an Spidéil* (Indreabhán: Cló Iar-Chonnacht, 2015)

Uí Chuill, Áine, and Seán Ó Morónaigh (eds), *Drámaí ó Thobar Mhúscraí le Conchubhar Ó Deasmhumhna* (Camas: An Comhlacht Náisiúnta Drámaíochta, 2013)

Welch, Robert, *The Abbey Theatre 1899–1999: Form and pressure* (Oxford: Oxford University Press, 1999)

Index

Note: Plays listed with an English language version indicate that the play was translated into Irish.

Naas Library